A BOOK-OF-THE-MONTH-CLUB
Alternate Selection
Benjamin Franklin Awards Nominee
"Best Career Title" 1996 & 2001

The Book of U.S. Government Jobs
— REVIEWS —

"About 2.5 percent of the work force is employed by the federal government, with a high percentage of the new employees hired each year being professional and technical workers. In 'The Book of U.S. Government Jobs,' Damp, the author of numerous books on government careers, walks job seekers through the federal hiring process. This revision includes updated statistics, added electronic tools, a discussion of new application forms, a revised picture of the federal job outlook, and some expanded sections. Chapters provide a good overview of qualifications, pay, and benefits; requirements for civil service exams; veteran preference considerations; opportunities for the disabled; and interviewing tips. The text is visually enhanced with a good use of bold topic headings, boxes, margin comments, and tables. Bookhaven Press extends and updates information for this title and other career books by hot-linking to federal agency employment web sites from its own site (http://federaljobs.net). Recommended for academic and public library career collections." [BOMC alternate.]*   **— LIBRARY JOURNAL** *(April 2000 - 7th ed.)*

"Damp's book on federal employment is recognized as one of the more practical guides for finding work with the government... Damp shows how the federal hiring process works. He explains how to find out about vacancies and openings, notes which agencies in which locations have the most positions, shows how to fill out applications, and reassures those concerned about civil service exams..."   **— BOOKLIST**

"Presents realistic job search strategies and viable options to landing a job with the U.S. government and guides job seekers through the maze of the federal hiring process. Revised and updated to reflect the most current requirements and procedures..."
— JOURNAL OF ECONOMIC LITERATURE *(June 2000 - 7th ed.)*

"This is the "bible" of understanding the federal job application process: plenty of examples lend to quick and easy understanding of the facts."   **— BOOKWATCH**

*" **The Book of U.S. Government Jobs** is an easy to read book with plenty of graphics and well-written text. It clearly introduces students to Uncle Sam's world."*
— CAREER OPPORTUNITIES NEWS

Books by Dennis V. Damp
The Book Of U.S. Government Jobs (first through eighth editions)
Health Care Job Explosion! (2001) 3rd ed.
Post Office Jobs: How To Get A Job With The U.S. Postal Service (2nd edition 2000)
Take Charge of Your Federal Career (1998)
Dollars & Sense

What they are saying about *Post Office Jobs*.

"*...This book aims to help applicants identify job openings, match their skills to job classifications, provide information on when and where to take qualifying exams, and deal with applications, resumes, and interviews. Following an overview of the USPS and its hiring process, types of jobs, and benefits, a large portion of the book is devoted to how to take qualifying exams, with sample questions and answers. Bookhaven Press updates this title by hot-linking to federal agency employment web sites from (http://federaljobs.net). Recommended for public libraries.*" — **LIBRARY JOURNAL** (April 2000 - 2nd ed.)

"*Competition for postal jobs is keen, and this well-written book describes the hiring process, provides samples of the examinations used to screen candidates, and tells how to prepare for them. Anyone applying for a postal service job could use this book to good advantage.*"   — **Career Opportunity News**

"*How to Get a Job with the U.S. Postal Service*" *is a great way for a newcomer to learn the ropes quickly. It gets you up to speed on the many different kinds of postal jobs and preps you for the exams you may encounter. From where to look and how to apply, it gives you what you need to know!*"
                          — **Judelle A. McArdle, President Federal Research Services**

What they are saying about *Health Care Job Explosion*!

"*With the growth of the health care industry,* **Health Care Job Explosion** *will be a boon to those seeking jobs... well rounded and special. Recommended for general collections;* **this book will be in demand.**"   — **LIBRARY JOURNAL**

"*The information is extremely well-organized, accurate, and up-to-date. The* **Health Care Job Explosion** *will be enormously useful to individuals seeking employment opportunities or information about particular jobs in the health care field. It should be available in every academic and public library as a resource.*"
                          — **Robert C. Aber, M.D., Associate Dean of Medical Education**
                                  Penn State University, College of Medicine

"*...An ambitious round-up of advice and resources to help health field job seekers make a good connection. Unless you're a research professional, you'd probably not uncover a number of the resources mentioned. A real time saver!*"
                          — **Joyce Lain Kennedy, Nationally Syndicated Careers Columnist**

The Book of
U.S. GOVERNMENT JOBS
Where They Are, What's Available, and How to Get One

Dennis V. Damp

Eighth Edition, Completely Revised

BOOKHAVEN PRESS LLC
Mckees Rocks, PA

The Book of
U.S. GOVERNMENT JOBS
Where They Are, What's Available, and How to Get One
By Dennis V. Damp

Published by: **BOOKHAVEN PRESS LLC**
249 Field Club Circle
Mckees Rocks, PA 15136

Copyright © 1986, 1987, 1989, 1991, 1994, 1995, 1996, 2000, 2002 by Dennis V. Damp

First Printing 1986
Second Printing 1987, completely revised
Third Printing 1989, revised
Fourth Printing 1991, revised
Fifth Printing 1994, completely revised
Sixth Printing 1995, completely revised

Seventh Printing 1996, revised
Eighth Printing 1997
Ninth Printing 1998
10th Printing 2000, completely revised
11th through 13th Printing 2000 & 2001
14th Printing 2002, completely revised

Printed in the United States of America   Cover Design by Salvatore Concialdi

Disclaimer of All Warranties and Liabilities

The author and publisher make no warranties, either expressed or implied, with respect to the information contained herein. The information about periodicals and job services reported in this book is based on facts conveyed by their publishers and operators either in writing or by telephone interview. The author and publisher shall not be liable for any incidental or consequential damages in connection with, or arising out of, the use of material in this book or the software packaged with it.

Library of Congress Catalog-in Publication Data

Damp, Dennis V.
    The book of U.S. Government jobs: where they are, what's available, and how to get one / by Dennis V. Damp. - - 8th ed.,
Completely rev.
        p.   cm.
    Includes bibliographical references and index.
    ISBN 0-943641-21-7 (pbk. :   alk. paper)
    1. Civil service positions--United States.   I. Title. II. Title:
U.S. Government Jobs.
JK716.D36   2002
331. 12' 4125173--dc21   2002022905
                                                                   CIP

For information on distribution or quantity discount rates, Telephone 412/464-6926 or write to: Sales Department, Bookhaven Press LLC, P.O. Box 1243, Moon Township, PA 15108. Distributed to the trade by Midpoint Trade Books, 27 West 20th Street, Suite 1102, New York, NY 10011, Tel: 212-727-0190. Individuals can order this title with credit card toll free (ORDERS ONLY) at 1-800-782-7424.

Table of Contents

Preface

The federal sector has embraced the Internet and the Office of Personnel Management (OPM) and individual agencies have developed new tools for the job seeker. The Internet now offers access to most job vacancy announcements, general employment information, pay scales, and special recruitment programs. Both public and private Internet service providers such as **federaljobs.net** provide visitors instant access to employment information and steer visitors to hundreds of federal agency employment web sites. Most libraries now have Internet access available and many Federal buildings offer online job access through computers located in their lobbies.

The impact of the recent and tragic September 11th attacks have increased the size of a number of agencies that are involved with the war on terror. New law enforcement positions were advertised within a broad spectrum of agencies to keep America safe and 28,000 new federal airport security screener jobs were recently created.

Applicants can now use the simplified OF-612 Form, Optional Application for Federal Employment, or the Federal style resume. Some agencies accept telephone or on-line applications for specific jobs which you complete while visiting that agency's web site. However, the process is still considerably different from the private sector. A federal style resume is nothing like a private sector resume and you must understand the process and the system to land a job.

One significant change that has evolved over the past five to 10 years is decentralization within the federal sector. In the past, the Office of Personnel Management (OPM) was the central human resource department for those seeking employment. Today, many agencies have their own personnel offices that are responsible for recruiting and advertising jobs. Decentralization has created new challenges to those seeking federal employment. Now job seekers must visit specific agency sites to locate current job vacancies. In the past you could apply for most federal jobs directly through OPM. OPM does advertise many jobs on their web site at http://www.usajobs.gov, however, many agencies have their own web sites and you must check those as well to locate all job vacancies. Sites such as federaljobs.net offer hot links to hundreds of federal recruitment sites.

The federal government currently has a total civilian workforce of approximately 2,704,000, a slight decrease since the last edition. However, with the new hiring initiatives in many agencies and new federal organizations that were recently legislated, federal employment appears to be on the rise. Over the last ten years Uncle Sam hired an average of 305,452 new hires each year to replace employees that transferred to other jobs, retired, or stopped working for other reasons.[1] **Considerable job opportunities are available for those willing to seek them out.**

Significant changes have taken place that are favorable to federal employees. Several unions negotiated salary with agencies for the first time and this has opened up the door for other agencies to do the same. New pay plans are in place that are based on what is called "Core Compensation" and it places workers in expanded pay bands out of the General Schedule. Employees in those groups, generally those in the Excepted Service, often compete for annual Superior Achievement pay awards. Recently, Thrift Savings Plan (401K) contributions were expanded.

The completely updated 8th edition of *The Book of U.S. Government Jobs* explains these changes and their impact to help you land the job you want in government. You'll learn about application methods and options, new Internet connections, agency personnel office phone numbers, job listing services, forms and procedures, viable networking techniques, and much more. A new section was added to describe the Knowledge, Skills & Abilities (KSAs) process that is often required with job applications and a new chapter was added on Law Enforcement careers. The new 8th edition provides abundant resources for you to locate government jobs including the latest telephone job hot lines and federal and private sector Internet resources for job listings and information.

You will find succinct updates posted on-line to complement the new 8th edition including new web sites, job hot lines, resources, and program changes at http://federaljobs.net. If you're looking for good pay with excellent benefits, pursue the federal job market. The average annual salary for all full time employees now exceeds $50,000 and you can work at thousands of stateside locations and overseas. Use this book's resources, including the Job Hunter's Checklist in Appendix A, to begin your personal job search.

Dennis V. Damp

---

[1] The Fact Book, 2001, Federal Civilian Workforce Statistics, OWI-07-01

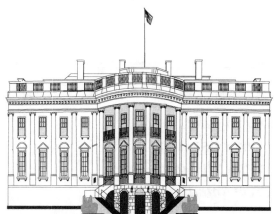

Chapter One
Introduction To
Government Employment

Consider the numbers. Uncle Sam employs over **2,704,000** workers and hires an average of **305,452** new employees each year to replace workers that transfer to other federal or private jobs, retire, or stop working for other reasons.[1] Average annual salary of all full-time employees exceeded $51,000 as of January 2002. The U.S Government is the largest employer in the United States, hiring two percent of the nation's civilian work force.

The average salary now exceeds $51,000 a year

Job hunters will find it easier today to locate job vacancies and to apply for federal jobs. Significant changes were implemented over the past 5 years to streamline the hiring process, including:

- Resumes and simplified optional forms are now used to apply for federal jobs. The Department of Defense has an extensive online resume submission system for most jobs.

- Job seekers can now apply direct to many agencies for job openings.

- Civil service tests are now used for less than 20% of all non-postal service jobs.

- Uncle Sam launched USAJOBS, an interactive career and employment web site, touch screen computers at many federal buildings, electronic bulletin boards, and 24 hour-a-day telephone job vacancy request lines.

- Student employment was consolidated and streamlined into two programs: the *Student Temporary Employment Program* and the *Student Career Experience Program*.

---

[1] The Fact Book, Federal Civilian Workforce Statistics, July 2001, OWI-01-05

You need to know how to take advantage of the federal hiring system and recent changes to successfully land the job you want in government.

Excellent job opportunities are available for those who know how to tap this lucrative job market. All government hiring is based on performance and qualifications regardless of your sex, race, color, creed, religion, disability, or national origin. Where else can you apply for a high paying entry-level job that offers employment at thousands of locations internationally, excellent career advancement opportunities, plus careers in hundreds of occupations?

Uncle Sam hires an average of 305,452 (non-Postal) workers yearly to replace employees that transfer to other jobs, retire, or stop working for other reasons. Add another 40,000 Postal Service vacancies to that figure to see the total picture. Over the past ten years the federal government has hired as many as 351,112 in 1991 to as few as 199,463 in 1996 nationwide.[1] Other vacancies exist in the Legislative and Judicial Branches. **Considerable job opportunities are available for those willing to seek them out.**

> Many additional opportunities will be created as those who are at or beyond retirement age opt to retire. Approximately 28% of the total workforce is now eligible for retirement, that's over 757,000 employees. When current federal employees bid on retirement vacancies, entry level jobs are created.

The following statistical analysis will help you focus on just where the opportunities are. The largest agencies are featured and their employment trends analyzed. Large agencies hire a broad spectrum of workers in hundreds of occupations. It's best to expand your search to as many agencies as possible to improve your chances.

Six agencies including the USPS employ 80 percent of the work force, or 2,136,324 employees. Of the 89,431 federal employees stationed abroad, 71% or 63,248 are U.S. Citizens. The remaining overseas employees are foreign nationals.

---

[1] The Fact Book - Federal Civilian Workforce 2001 Edition, PSO-OWI-01-05, July 2001.

TABLE 1-1
THE FIVE LARGEST FEDERAL AGENCIES

TOTAL WORKERS	2,704,015	100.00 %
Legislative Branch	30,199	1.10 %
Judicial Branch	32,957	1.20 %
USPS & PRC *	856,550	31.70 %
Executive Branch	2,640,859	66.00 %
DEFENSE	670,568	
VA	223,137	
TREASURY	159,274	
JUSTICE	126,711	
AGRICULTURE	100,084	
ALL OTHERS	504,535	

* USPS & PRC is the United States Postal Service and Postal Rate Commission.
Source: Federal Civilian Workforce Statistics - May 2001

The changes in Table 1-1 from the previous 7th edition reveal that two agencies increased in size, two decreased and HHS was bumped off the list by the Department of Agriculture. Overall the total employment decreased by 3.4% while the Judicial Branch increased by 9.6% and the Legislative Branch decreased by a very small .01%. The largest change was in the Department of Defense (DOD); from 723,084 workers in August of 1998 to 670,568 in July of 2001 for a loss of 52,516 jobs. The Defense Department lost a total of 295,518 jobs since January 1993. This trend was projected to continue in the Defense Department until recently. The Department of Defense has downsized considerably over he past decade due to the ending of the cold war, contracting out, and military base closings.

Postal Service employment decreased by 8,624 workers from August 1998 to July 2001. The Postal service gross revenue has increased from 25 Billion a year in 1995 to over 64 Billion in 2000. The U.S. Postal Service continues to hire an average of 40,000 new workers each year to replace those who have retired, quit, transferred to other federal jobs, or left for other reasons.

NATURE OF FEDERAL EMPLOYMENT

The Federal Government affects the lives of Americans in countless ways.[1] It defends Americans from foreign aggressors, represents American interests abroad, provides important public services, creates and enforces laws, and administers social programs. Americans are aware of the Federal Government when they pay their income taxes each year, but they are often unaware of government's influence when they watch a daily weather forecast, purchase fresh and uncontaminated groceries, travel on highways or by aircraft, or make a deposit in a bank. Workers employed by the Federal Government play a vital role in these and many other facets of American life.

This book describes Federal Government civilian career opportunities including jobs with the U.S. Postal Service (an independent agency of the Federal Government). Armed Forces career opportunities are described in the 2000-2001 edition of the Occupational Outlook Handbook.

The Constitution of the United States divides the Federal Government into the legislative, judicial, and executive branches. The executive is by far the largest of the branches, but each is equally vital in running the country. Appendix C provides detailed information for all of the branches of government.

The legislative branch is primarily responsible for forming and amending the legal structure of the Nation. Its largest component is Congress, the primary U.S. legislative body, which is made up of the Senate and the House of Representatives. This body includes senators, representatives, and their staff members. The offices and employees of the legislative branch are concentrated in the Washington, D.C. area.

---

[1] Career Guide to Industries April 2000, U.S. Department of Labor

The judicial branch is responsible for interpreting the laws the legislative branch enacts. It employs the smallest number of people of the three branches, and, unlike the legislative branch, its offices and employees are dispersed throughout the country. The highest rulings are made by the Supreme Court, the Nation's definitive judicial body. Its decisions generally follow an appeal of a decision made by the one of the regional Courts of Appeal, which hear cases appealed from U. S. District Courts. District Courts are located in each State and are the first to hear cases under Federal jurisdiction.

Because of the scope of executive branch responsibility, it employs the vast, majority of Federal workers. In 2001, it employed about 97 percent of all Federal civilian employees (excluding postal workers). The legislative branch and the judicial branch each employed about one and a half percent.

The executive branch is composed of the Executive Office of the President, the 14 executive cabinet departments, and over 90 independent agencies, each of which has clearly defined duties. The Executive Office of the President is composed of several offices and councils that aid the President in policy decisions. These include the Office of Management and Budget, which oversees the administration of the Federal budget; the National Security Council, which advises the President on matters of national defense; and the Council of Economic Advisers, which makes economic policy recommendations.

Each of the 14 executive cabinet departments oversees a vital element of American life. They are referred to as cabinet departments because the highest departmental official of each, the Secretary, is a member of the President's cabinet. The Department of Defense is by far the largest, employing roughly 1.5 million military personnel on active duty in addition to 670,568 civilian workers in 2001. It is responsible for providing the military forces that protect the country and contains the Departments of the Army, the Navy, the Air Force, and a number of smaller agencies.

The other executive departments are not nearly as large as Defense, primarily because their duties do not usually require as many workers. Each, listed by employment size, is described below.

Veterans Affairs (223,137 employees). Administers programs to aid U.S. veterans and their families, runs the veterans' hospital system, and operates our national cemeteries.

Treasury (159,274 employees). Regulates banks and other financial institutions, administers the public debt, prints currency, and performs law enforcement in a wide range including counterfeiting, tax, and customs.

Agriculture (100,084 employees). Promotes U.S. agriculture domestically and internationally and sets standards governing quality, quantity, and labeling of food sold in the U.S.

Justice (126,711 employees. Enforces Federal law, prosecutes cases in Federal courts, and runs Federal prisons.

Interior (72,982 employees). Manages Federal lands including the national parks and forests, runs hydroelectric power systems, and promotes conservation of natural resources.

Transportation (64,131 employees). Sets national transportation policy, runs the Coast Guard, plans and funds the construction of highways and mass transit systems, and regulates railroad, aviation, and maritime operations.

Health and Human Services including SSA (63,323 employees). Sponsors medical research, approves use of new drugs and medical devices, runs the Public Health Service, and administers the Social Security and Medicaid programs.

Commerce (39,151 employees). Forecasts the weather, charts the oceans, regulates patents and trademarks, conducts the census and compiles statistics, and promotes U.S. economic growth by encouraging international trade.

State (28,054 employees). Runs the Nation's embassies and consulates, issues passports, monitors U.S. interests abroad, and represents the U.S. before international organizations.

Energy (15,689 employees). Coordinates the national use and provision of energy, oversees the production and disposal of nuclear weapons, and plans for future energy needs.

Labor (16,016 employees). Enforces laws guaranteeing fair pay, workplace safety, equal job opportunity; administers unemployment insurance; regulates pension funds; and collects economic data.

Housing and Urban Development (10,154 employees). Funds public housing projects, enforces equal housing laws, and insures and finances mortgages.

Education (4,581 employees). Provides scholarships, student loans, and aid to schools.

Numerous independent agencies often perform tasks that fall between the jurisdictions of the executive departments, or that would be more efficiently executed by an autonomous agency. Although the majority of them are fairly small, employing fewer than 1,000 workers (many employ fewer than 100 workers), some are quite large.

National Aeronautics and Space Administration (18,850 employees). Oversees aviation research and exploration and research beyond the Earth's atmosphere.

Environmental Protection Agency (17,968 employees). Runs programs to control and reduce pollution of the Nation's water, air, and lands.

General Services Administration (13,921 employees). Manages Federal Government property and records.

Tennessee Valley Authority (13,230 employees). Operates the hydro-electric power system in the Tennessee river valley.

Some smaller, but well known independent agencies include the *Peace Corps*, the *Securities and Exchange Commission*, and the *Federal Communications Commission*.

WORKING CONDITIONS

Due to the broad scope of Federal employment, almost every working condition found in the private sector can also be found in the Federal Government.[1] Most white-collar employees work in office buildings, hospitals, or laboratories, and most of the blue-collar workforce can be found in factories, warehouses, shipyards, military bases, construction sites, or national parks and forests. Work environments vary from the comfortable and relaxed to the hazardous and stressful, such as those experienced by law enforcement officers, astronauts, or air traffic controllers.

The vast majority of Federal employees work full time, often on flexible "flexitime" schedules, which allow workers to tailor their own work week, within certain constraints. Some agencies also have "flexiplace" programs, which allow selected workers to perform some job duties at home or from regional centers.

The duties of some Federal workers require they spend much of their time away from the offices in which they are based. Inspectors and compliance officers, for example, often visit businesses and work sites to ensure laws and regulations are obeyed. Few travel so far that they are unable to return home each night. Some Federal workers, however, frequently travel long distances, spending days or weeks away from home. Auditors, for example, may spend weeks in distant locations.

---

[1] Career Guide to Industries, U.S. Department of Labor, April, 2000

EMPLOYMENT

In 2001, the Federal Government employed 2,704,015 workers, or about 2 percent of the Nation's workforce. Because of the scope of Government work, it employs workers in every major occupational group. Workers are not employed in the same proportions in which they are employed throughout the rest of the economy, however (table 1-2). Because of the analytical and sometimes highly technical nature of many Government duties, a much higher proportion of professionals and technicians are employed in the Federal Government compared with most industries. Conversely, the Government sells very little, so it employs rela-tively few sales workers.

Table 1-2
Percent distribution of employment in the Federal Government and the private Sector by major occupational group

Occupational Group	Federal Government	Private Sector
Total	*100*	*100*
Executive, administrative, and managerial	17.6	13.9
Professional speciality	30.8	13.7
Technicians and related support	8.3	3.8
Marketing and sales	0.7	10.4
Administrative support, including clerical	22.5	18.7
Service	6.8	16.5
Agriculture, forestry, fishing, and related	0.7	2.1
Precision production, craft, and repair	9.2	10.7
Operators, fabricators, and laborers	3.2	14.0

Although most Federal departments and agencies are based in the Washington, D.C. area, only 16 percent of all Federal employees worked in the vicinity of the Nation's Capital. In addition to Federal employees working throughout the United States, a small number are assigned overseas in embassies or defense installations.

OCCUPATIONS

The Federal Government employed workers in almost every occupation in 2001, including those found only in Government, such as legislators or judges. About 71 percent of all Federal workers were employed in professional specialty, administrative support, or executive, administrative, and managerial occupations.

Approximately 41 percent of all federal workers have a Bachelor's Degree or higher degree. For many jobs, any 4-year bachelor's degree will suffice, but some positions require a specific degree. A graduate or professional degree is necessary to enter some professional jobs.

Professional specialty and executive, administrative, and managerial occupations

Together, professional specialty and executive, administrative, and managerial occupations comprise about 47 percent of Federal employment. Almost all professional specialty jobs require a 4-year college degree. Some, such as engineers, physicians and life and physical scientists require a bachelor's or higher degree in a specific field of study.

Engineers, such as chemical, civil, aeronautical, industrial, electrical, mechanical, and nuclear engineers, work in every department of the executive branch. In general, they apply physical laws toward design problems, such as building bridges or computer systems. Although most are employed in the Department of Defense, a significant number work in the National Aeronautic and Space Administration and the Department of Transportation.

Computer scientists, computer engineers, and systems analysts are employed throughout the Government. They write computer programs, analyze problems related to data processing, and keep computer systems running smoothly.

Health professionals include registered nurses and physicians, with more than 3 out of 4 of these workers employed by the Department of Veterans Affairs (VA) at one of many VA hospitals. Other professionals included life scientists, such as biologists and foresters and conservation scientists, who research problems dealing with life processes, and physical scientists, such as geologists, meteorologists, and physicists, who examine the state of the earth and research physical phenomena. The Department of Agriculture employs the vast majority of life scientists, but physical scientists are distributed evenly throughout government.

Executive, administrative, and managerial workers are primarily responsible for overseeing operations. Legislators are included in this group, and are responsible for passing and amending the Nation's laws. Because managers are generally promoted from professional occupations, most have at least a bachelor's degree. These workers include many types of managers who, at the highest levels, may head Federal agencies or programs, such as general managers, top executives, and middle managers, who oversee one activity or aspect of a program.

Other executive, administrative, and managerial workers provide management support. Accountants and auditors prepare and analyze financial reports, review and record revenues and expenditures, and check operations for fraud and inefficiency. Inspectors and compliance officers enforce Federal regulations governing everything from aircraft to food. Tax examiners determine and collect taxes. Management support workers include purchasing agents, who handle Federal purchases of supplies, and management analysts, who study Government operations and systems and suggest improvements.

Administrative support occupations

Almost one Federal worker in four falls into this category, not counting the U.S. Postal Service. Administrative support workers usually only need a high school diploma, though any further training or experience, such as a junior college degree, or at least two years of relevant work experience, is an asset. Administrative support workers aid management staff with administrative duties. They include secretaries; book keepers; accounting, auditing, stock, traffic, shipping, and receiving clerks; receptionists; and switch-board operators.

Technicians and related support occupations

Technicians make up about eight percent of the Federal workforce. They may aid professionals in research, analysis, or law enforcement. Often their tasks and skills are quite specialized, as with air traffic controllers. As a result, many technicians are required to have some vocational training or extensive work experience; many have two-year associate degrees.

Engineering technicians, who may work either directly with engineers or by themselves, are common. Other technician occupations include health technicians, such as dental hygienists and radiologists, who have specialized health service jobs, or legal assistants, who aid judges and attorneys.

Other occupations

Most Federal jobs in other occupations require no more than a high school diploma, although some departments and agencies may prefer workers with some vocational training or previous experience. For instance, some precision production workers like mechanics or machinists, or service workers such as chefs or barbers need some specific training or experience. The Federal Government also offers apprenticeship programs, which train unskilled workers on the job for some skilled occupations.

Compared to the economy as a whole, service workers are relatively scarce in the Federal Government. Nearly half of all Federal workers in these occupations are firefighters, police officers, and correctional officers. These workers protect the public from crime, oversee Federal prisons, and stand ready to intervene in emergencies.

Over half of the Federally employed precision production, craft, and repair occupations were mechanics, such as vehicle and mobile equipment mechanics, who fix and maintain all types of motor vehicles, aircraft, and heavy equipment, and electrical and electronic equipment operators. Other precision production workers are skilled in construction trades, such as painters, plumbers, and electricians.

The Federal Government employs relatively few workers in fabricator, operator, and laborer occupations; agriculture, forestry, fishing, and related occupations; and marketing and sales occupations.

OUTLOOK

Employment in the Federal Government was projected to decline by nine percent through the year 2008 due to efforts to balance the Federal budget, however, with the many new jobs now required to fight the war on terror this trend may reverse. Considerable opportunities remain in the federal sector. Uncle Sam hires an average of 305,342 new employees each year to replace workers that transfer to other federal or private jobs, retire, or stop working for other reasons. Competition will be keen for many Federal positions, especially during times of economic uncertainty when workers seek the stability of Federal Government employment. The distribution of employment will change, however, toward a higher proportion of professional, technical, and managerial workers.

Factors that influence Federal Government staffing levels are unique. Unlike any other employer in the Nation, the Congress and President determine the Government's payroll budget prior to each fiscal year, which runs from October 1 through September 30 of the following year. Whether operating at a surplus or a deficit, the Federal Government generally adheres to its payroll budget. As a result, Federal employment is not affected by cyclical fluctuations in the economy, as are employment levels in many construction, manufacturing, and other private sector industries; employment levels tend to be relatively stable in the short run.

Each Presidential administration and Congress may have different public policy priorities, resulting in greater levels of Federal employment in some programs and declines in others. Layoffs, called "reductions in force", have occurred in the past; however, they are uncommon and generally affect relatively few workers.

After major decreases following the dissolution of the Soviet Union, Department of Defense civilian employment, which makes almost 40 percent of Federal civilian employment, is expected to level-off. Employment in many other agencies is expected to decrease. However, there will be numerous employment opportunities even in agencies in which employment is contracting due to the need to replace workers who leave the workforce, retire or obtain employment elsewhere. Furthermore, some occupations, especially professional, technical, and managerial occupations, will be in demand even as employment in other occupations is being reduced.

Employment of blue-collar workers will decrease the most because many of their functions will be contracted out to private companies. As in other industries, employment of some administrative support and clerical workers in the Federal Government will also be adversely affected by the growing use of private contractors for many functions. In addition, computerization will continue to eliminate many clerical positions.

GETTING STARTED

The Book Of U.S. Government Jobs walks you through the federal hiring process. This book also steers you to highly informative government and private sector Internet web sites, electronic bulletin boards, self-service job information centers, telephone job hotlines, and it explores all facets of the federal job search.

Readers will find up-to-date information on how the federal employment system works from an insiders perspective, how to locate job announcements through various methods, and complete a thorough application package. You'll learn about special hiring programs for the physically challenged, veterans, students, and scholars, thousands of job opportunities, Civil Service Exam requirements, overseas jobs, Postal Service jobs, how to complete your employment application, and much more. Appendix A provides a comprehensive checklist that will take you through the entire federal employment process. Use Appendix A throughout your job search.

The three appendices include an easy to use federal job check list, complete lists of federal occupations, and comprehensive agency summaries and contact lists including employment office addresses and phone numbers.

This book will guide you step-by-step through the federal employment process, from filling out your first employment application to locating job announcements, networking resources and hiring agencies. Follow the guidelines set forth in this book to dramatically improve your chances of landing a federal job.

PAY & BENEFITS

Job security and excellent pay are among the top reasons most seek federal employment. There are eight predominant pay systems. Approximately half of the workforce is under the *General Schedule (GS)* pay scale, twenty percent are paid under the *Postal Service rates,* and about ten percent are paid under the *Prevailing Rate Schedule (WG) Wage Grade classification.* The remaining pay systems are for the *Executive Schedule, Foreign Service, Special Salary Rates, Nonappropriated Fund Instrumentalities pay scales,* and *Veterans Health Administration.*

General Schedule (GS) pay for locality area "Rest of U.S." pay varies from the GS-1 level at $14,757 per annum to $107,357 per annum at the top GS-15 grade (not including locality pay adjustments). The Senior Executive Service salary tops out at $130,000 per annum. The president adjusts federal salaries to levels that are competitive with the private sector. The average annual salary for full time non-postal employees increased to $51,000 in 2001.[1] Starting pay depends on the level of experience, education and complexity of the position applied for. A complete General Schedule (GS) pay schedule is printed in Chapter Two.

Each GS grade has ten pay steps. Currently, a GS-9 starts at $34,451 for step one and reaches $44,783 per year at step ten (not including locality pay adjustments). At the GS-9 grade, each pay step adds $1148.00 to the annual salary. Pay steps are earned based on time in service and the employee's work performance. General Schedule employees are referred to as white collar workers under the federal classification system. Approximately 13.3 percent of total federal non-postal employment is classified under the Wage Grade (WG) blue collar pay schedules. See Appendix D for a complete list of occupations.

---

[1] Profile of Federal Civilian Employees, January 2002, Central Personnel File.

There are a number of special compensation systems that augment the general schedule. Physicians receive signing bonuses for a one year continued-service agreement and additional bonuses for two years. The Federal Aviation Administration pays employees in safety related careers under a "Core Compensation" multi payband system. Organizations such as the General Accounting Office (GAO), NASA, and the Commerce Department's National Institute of Standards and Technology are either exempt from or have exceptions to the GS pay system.

Pay reform has been implemented to offset competitive hiring pressures from private industry and local governments. Agencies can now offer allowances and bonuses when recruiting, match salary within certain limits, and they are authorized to pay interview travel expenses under certain conditions.

> A number of agencies have implemented new pay systems. These new systems place employees in pay bands instead of steps and they are not classified under the GS system. The Federal Aviation Administration uses a multi band Core Compensation system. Pay under these systems are adjusted annually through various processes.

VACATION & SICK LEAVE

All employees receive: 10 paid holidays, 13 days of vacation for the first three years, twenty days of vacation with three to fifteen years service and after fifteen years twenty-six days. Additionally, 13 sick days are accrued each year regardless of length of service. Military time counts towards benefits. If you have 3 years of military service you begin with 4 weeks paid vacation and 3 years towards retirement.

HEALTH BENEFITS & LIFE INSURANCE

Medical health plans and the *Federal Employees' Group Life Insurance* (FEGLI) program are available to all employees. The medical plan is an employee-employer contribution system and includes HMO and Blue Cross and Blue Shield programs. There are hundreds of plans to choose from. The FEGLI program offers low cost term life insurance for the employee and basic coverage for the family. FEGLI offers up to five times the employee's salary in death benefits.

One of the primary benefits of federal employment is the satisfaction you experience from working in a challenging and rewarding position. Positions are available with the level of responsibility and authority that you desire.

RETIREMENT

The federal retirement system is now based on Social Security contributions and an employee contribution system fashioned after a 401k defined contribution plan. Currently you can elect to contribute up to 12 percent of your salary into a *THRIFT savings 401k plan*. This amount will increase 1 percent for the next three years to a maximum of 15 percent in 2004. The government will match your contribution up to 5 percent. This is effectively a 5 percent pay increase. Your contributions are tax deferred and reduce your taxable income by the amount contributed. The retirement benefit is determined by the amount that has accumulated during the employee's career. This includes the interest earned and capital gains realized from the retirement fund.

There are many withdrawal options including lump sum and various fixed term annuities. The contribution plan payout is in addition to the social security benefits that you will be eligible for at retirement.

The Employee Benefit Research Institute indicates that people retiring in 2010 will derive 37.7% of their retirement income from Social Security, 36.6% from employer sponsored pensions, and 25.7% from savings and investments.

TRAINING & CAREER DEVELOPMENT

Each department or agency determines what training best meets its needs, and offers workers training opportunities to improve job skills or become qualified to advance to other jobs. These include technical or skills training, tuition assistance or reimbursement, fellowship programs, and executive leadership and management training programs, seminars, and workshops. In general, training may be offered on the job, by another agency, or at local colleges and universities.

The Federal Government also offers college or graduate students employment training in the Presidential Management Intern program; college students may apply for one of the numerous independent agency internships. More information on these programs is available from college financial aid and placement offices.

Every occupation employed by the Federal Government has associated with it a range of pay levels, or "grades." Workers enter the Federal civil service at the starting grade for an occupation and begin a "career ladder" of promotions until they reach the full-performance grade for that occupation. This system provides for non-competitive promotions, which usually are awarded at regular intervals, assuming job performance is satisfactory. Although these promotions may not occur more than once a year, they sometimes are awarded in the form of two-grade increases. The exact pay grades associated with a job's career track depend upon the occupation. For example, the pay grades in the career track for an attorney are significantly higher than those associated with a secretary.

Once workers reach the full-performance level of the career track, they must compete for subsequent promotions, and advancement becomes more difficult. At this point, promotions occur as vacancies arise, and these promotions are based solely on merit.

The top managers in the Federal civil service belong to the Senior Executive Service (SES), the highest positions Federal workers can reach without being specifically nominated by the President and confirmed by the U.S. Senate. Only a few workers attain SES positions, and competition is keen. SES positions are concentrated at headquarters for most Federal agencies. Opportunities to advance to upper level managerial and supervisory jobs are more prevalent in the Washington, D.C. metropolitan area.

TYPES OF TRAINING

- Orientation Training (New Employees)
- Technical and Administrative Skills Training
- Professional Training
- Supervisory Training
- Executive And Management Training
- Career Development Training

Career development programs are offered by most agencies for target positions and personal long term career goals. Each agency offers its own unique programs. However, they are all authorized by the same federal regulations and many similarities exist between agencies. The following is a sampling of currently offered career development programs.

CAREER DEVELOPMENT PROGRAMS

● **Upward Mobility Program** - This program allows employees (below GS-9 or equivalent), who are in dead-end jobs, to obtain positions with greater career advancement potential. Extensive training is provided to eligible employees to gain the necessary qualifications for higher paying positions.

● **Individual Development Plans (IDP)** - This program offers employees the opportunity to sit down with their supervisor and design a career development program. Training is provided to help the employee reach his/her goal. Training programs can include formal college courses at government expense. (The amount of tuition reimbursement depends on availability of funds.) Correspondence programs are available and lateral work assignments are encouraged to provide exposure to diverse aspects of the target position.

Federal employees will benefit from the book titled *"Take Charge of Your Federal Career,"* published by Federal Employees News Digest. This book is a practical, action-oriented career management workbook for all federal employees that guides you step-by-step through the IDP process. It's available for $17.95 plus shipping with all major credit cards by calling 1-800-782-7424. Complete information about this title is available in the back of this book.

● **The Presidential Management Intern Program (PMI)** - The PMI program provides a career starting point in the federal government for high potential graduate students who have demonstrated a commitment to the management or analysis of public programs and policies. Graduate students must be nominated by their college or university and undergo an extensive screening process to be chosen as an intern. Those selected enter at the GS-9 level, receive 2 years of formal and on-the-job training and career planning. Those who successfully complete the program are eligible for career appointments at the GS-12 level.

● **Seminar for Prospective Women Managers** - (Offered by the Department of Transportation). This seminar provides opportunities for women who demonstrate high abilities and motivation to enter a management position.

LOCATING A JOB

Fourteen cabinet departments and over 100 independent agencies comprise the federal government system. These departments and agencies have offices in all corners of the world. The size of each agency varies considerably. The larger the agency the more diverse the opportunities. These large agencies hire a broad spectrum of occupations, professional and blue collar.

If you desire to travel, the government offers abundant opportunities to relocate within the 50 states and throughout the world.

If you desire to travel, the government offers abundant opportunities to relocate within the 50 states and throughout the world. Chapter 7 provides information on thousands of overseas employment opportunities. Twelve federal agencies and departments offer employment abroad for over 60,000 U.S. citizens. The Department of Defense Dependent Schools system employees hundreds of teachers for military dependent schools overseas.

Washington DC has the largest number of federal workers, 322,633, and Vermont the least with 2,853 workers. All of the 315 (MSA) Metropolitan Statistical Areas in the U.S. and Puerto Rico have federal civilian employment as listed in the Central Personnel Data File. Small towns and rural areas outside of MSA's had approximately 18 percent of total non-Postal federal workers.[1] The actual number of federal civilian employees is greater than the above figures. The Defense Intelligence Agency, Central Intelligence Agency, and the National Security Agency do not release this data. Chapter Three provides job resources including Internet web sites, magazines and newspapers that list thousands of national job openings and job placement services. Special hiring programs are explained for *Outstanding Scholars,* and student employment oppor-tunities. Appendix C provides a comprehensive agency contact list that includes national and regional personnel office contacts.

---

[1]Federal Civilian Employment By State & Metropolitan Areas (CPDF)

TABLE 1-2
FEDERAL EMPLOYMENT BY STATE MARCH 2000
Non-Postal

STATE	TOTAL	STATE	TOTAL
Alabama	36,203	Nevada	7,234
Alaska	11,170	New Hampshire	3,094
Arizona	28,169	New Jersey	25,782
Arkansas	10,959	New Mexico	20,936
California	141,377	New York	57,456
Colorado	33,138	North Carolina	30,294
Connecticut	7,130	North Dakota	4,970
Delaware	2,478	Ohio	42,376
Florida	60,220	Oklahoma	32,212
Georgia	62,345	Oregon	17,044
Hawaii	19,084	Pennsylvania	61,448
Idaho	7,336	Rhode Island	5,771
Illinois	40,696	South Carolina	15,880
Indiana	21,884	South Dakota	6,768
Iowa	6,950	Tennessee	35,309
Kansas	14,669	Texas	102,361
Kentucky	19,407	Utah	24,166
Louisiana	19,767	Vermont	2,853
Maine	7,893	Virginia	114,436
Maryland	101,425	Washington	41,775
Massachusetts	24,905	Washington DC	143,751
Michigan	21,348	West Virginia	11,775
Minnesota	12,926	Wisconsin	10,967
Mississippi	16,591	Wyoming	4,354
Missouri	32,295	OVERSEAS	89,431
Montana	7,780	*Unspecified	19,577

EDUCATION REQUIREMENTS

In the federal government 59 percent of all workers do not have a college degree. The level of required education is dependent upon the job that's applied for. Each job announcement lists needed skills and abilities including education and work experience. However, the more education and work experience that you have the more competitive you will be when ranked against other applicants. A sample qualification statement is presented in chapter 2 for Administration and Management Positions. The majority of positions within the government have a published qualifications standard similar to the provided example.

You can review and down-load a specific qualification standard on-line at **FederalJobs.Net**, (http://federaljobs.net) or visit your local Federal Depository Library. Many large college and private libraries are designated depository status and they can help you locate specific government publications including the Qualification Standards Handbook For General Schedule Positions.

CAREER SEARCH

If you are uncertain about which career to enter or if government jobs are right for you *The Book of U.S. Government Jobs* is a good place to start. Chapter Four outlines detailed informational interviewing techniques that will help you investigate primary and alternate career paths and the all new and expanded 7th edition provides over a thousand resources to help you make a connection. The Federal Jobs Checklist in Appendix A guides job seekers through the federal employment system from beginning to end.

There are many excellent resources available to assist you with your job hunt. A few select books and software programs are offered for sale by the publisher in the back of this book for your convenience. Books and services that we mention but don't offer for sale will have ordering information printed with the notation.

CIVIL SERVICE EXAMS

Tests are required for specific groups including secretarial/clerical, air traffic control, law enforcement and for certain entry level jobs. Chapter Four provides sample test questions and offers detailed information on testing requirements. *Outstanding Scholars,* college graduates with top grades, can be hired on the spot. Entry-level professional and administrative job applicants that graduate from a four year college with a grade point average of 3.5 or above — on a 4.0 scale — can be hired without competition if the applicant impresses agency recruiters with experience and technical abilities during an interview.

Chapter Two
Understanding The
Federal Employment System

$\mathbf{M}$ost government personnel specialists do not have the time to counsel the majority of the job seekers who call government offices weekly. Examples of common questions are: Must all applicants take extensive written exams? What is a federal register, appointment, series and announcement? What training and experience is required? Who in government is currently hiring? What jobs are available state-side, overseas and with the U.S. Postal Service, and what can he/she expect to achieve? There are too many questions and too few counselors to answer them.

COMPETITIVE SERVICE

About 12 percent of all federal jobs are in the Washington D.C. metropolitan area. Government employees work in offices, shipyards, laboratories, national parks, hospitals, military bases and many other settings across the country and overseas. Approximately 50 percent of civilian jobs are in the *competitive service*, which means that people applying for them must be evaluated by the Office of Personnel Management (OPM) either directly or through agency personnel offices that are delegated direct hire or case hire authority. Chapter Three explains the various services into which you can be hired.

Approximately 80%, of government jobs are filled through a competitive examination of your background, work experience, and education, not through a written test.

COMPETITIVE EXAMINATIONS

Hiring for federal jobs is generally through a competitive *"examination."* Don't be intimidated by the word examination. The majority— approximately 80%— of government jobs are filled through a competitive examination of your background, work experience, and education, not through a written test. There are exceptions to this rule, and non-competitive appointments are available for certain veterans, the physically challenged or handicapped, and other groups. New employees are hired for their ability to perform the work advertised in the job announcement. An applicant's ability is determined through an evaluation of educational background, work experience, and skills testing for certain job series.

DETERMINING YOUR ELIGIBILITY

Eligibility is determined through evaluating an applicant's education **AND/OR** work experience. For example, an entry level radio operator would start at a GS-2 pay grade, $16,592 per year if he/she was a high school graduate **OR** had at least three months of *general experience*. That same radio operator could start at a GS-4, $20,322 per year, if he/she had six months of general experience and six months of *specialized experience*, **OR** two years of education above high school with courses related to the occupation. You would add from 8.64% or more to these salary figures depending on the Locality Pay area that the job is located in.

GENERAL EXPERIENCE

This is any type of work which demonstrates the applicant's ability to perform the work of the position, or experience which provided a familiarity with the subject matter or process of the broad subject areas of the occupation. Specialized experience can be substituted for general experience.

SPECIALIZED EXPERIENCE

This is experience which is in the occupation of the position to be filled, in a related occupation, or in one of the specialized areas within that occupation, which has equipped the applicant with the particular *knowledge, skills, and abilities* (KSA's) to perform the duties of the position.

WRITTEN TESTS

An *examination announcement (job opening notice)* may or may not require a written test. In many cases the examination consists of a detailed evaluation of your work experience, education, and schooling listed on your employment application. OPM eliminated the reliance on a written test as a single examining method and now provides agencies with additional examining options. Under this program, applicants apply for specific vacancies rather than broad occupational groups. While written tests will continue to be used for some jobs, taking a test is no longer the compulsory first step in the hiring process. Applicants now can complete one of several optional forms including the new Federal resume format. OPM or the hiring agency then scores the applicants' responses to determine the most highly qualified candidates. Hiring offices receive a list of the best qualified applicants from either OPM or the agency's Human Resource department for each vacancy. Agencies may require qualified applicants to take a written test for specific occupations.

Approximately 110 entry level professional and administrative jobs originally required written tests under the Administrative Careers With America (ACWA) program. A centralized list of qualified applicants was maintained by OPM until the program changed in late 1994. Individuals now apply for individual openings that are announced on USAJOBS or individual agency web sites. Agencies may use the ACWA test to rate the best qualified applicants. Sample test questions are featured in Chapter Five for entry level professional and administrative applicants to study. Additionally, jobs in Air Traffic Control, various security agencies, and other specialized fields require written tests.

The federal government evaluates each candidate strictly for his/her ability to perform the duties of the position. **Ability is obtained through education AND/OR experience.** Even engineering positions are rated this way. For example, there are several alternative non-degree paths that allow applicants to rate eligible for engineering positions. OPM qualifications for engineering positions require either a four-year engineering degree OR four year college level education, and/or technical experience. Chapter Three provides specific details on the *Engineering Conversion Program*.

JOB SERIES

Each job announcement describes the required experience, education, job location, pay and miscellaneous details needed to apply for a position within a *job series*. A complete occupational job series listing is provided in Appendix D. These series are from the General or Wage Schedules that are in the competitive service. Excepted Service job series are designated with different alpha characters, however most follow the General Series Qualification Standards.

JOB SERIES EXAMPLES

TITLE	SERIES
Accountant	GS-510
Secretary	GS-318
Engineer-Electrical	GS-801
Computer Specialist	GS-334
System Specialist	GS-2101
Equipment Mechanic	WG-5800
Laboring	WG-3502

THE FEDERAL REGISTER

Most *federal registers* were abolished in the mid 1990s. Applicants who passed an examination with a score of 70 out of a maximum of 100 points were added to a register and agencies would hire from this listing as vacancies developed. Applicants for the most part no longer apply for general consideration. They now apply for specific vacancies. Federal registers created problems for employer and employee alike. Agencies had to purge the registers of applicants no longer seeking employment and applicants who scored high on the entrance tests could not understand why they didn't get called. Some agencies, especially those in the Excepted Service including the U.S. Postal Service, still maintain lists of eligible candidates. When job vacancies exist those agencies select from active lists.

EXAMINATION ANNOUNCEMENTS

Examination announcements are issued by the Office of Personnel Management and by individual agencies that have *direct hire* or *case examining* authority. The Office of Personnel Management (OPM) operates a network of Employment Service Centers, Federal Jobs Touch Screen Computers, USAJOBS by phone local telephone numbers and an extensive Internet web site at http://www.usajobs.opm.gov that you can use to locate **"Federal Job Announcements"** for anticipated job vacancies within their servicing area. OPM does not advertise all jobs for all agencies. To locate all available jobs you must contact individual agencies in your area. A comprehensive list of federal agency employment web sites is located on **http://federaljobs.net**. You can also locate job vacancies through many other sources today. Refer to Chapter Three to locate Internet sites, electronic bulletin boards, job hotlines, and other services that offer federal job listings. A sample announcement is located in Chapter Six.

Visit the web site federaljobs.net for links to over 200 agency employment web sites.

Examination announcements are advertised for periods from several days to months depending on the agency's critical needs. Exceptions to these rules apply to Vietnam Era and recently discharged veterans, disabled veterans, and the handicapped. You must obtain examination announcements through the resources mentioned above and in Chapter Three.

CASE EXAMINING

The Office of Personnel Management implemented case examining hiring procedures to assist agencies that have critical hiring needs. Applicants can apply directly to various agencies for positions that meet specific qualifications. Under these procedures, when an agency has a vacancy they issue a vacancy announcement, not OPM. This announcement lists the title, series and grade of the position; gives the opening/closing dates and duty location; provides information concerning the duties, responsibilities and qualification requirements of the position; and gives the name and phone number of a contact person in the recruiting agency. To obtain announcements applicants must contact the agency where the vacancy exists.

The agency reviews the applicant's basic eligibility. The final ratings are done by OPM and the candidates are ranked according to total score. OPM does maintain a centralized listing of open case examinations through USAJOBS. See Chapter Three for complete information on how to obtain current announcement information for case examinations.

DIRECT HIRE AUTHORITY

Direct hire authority is granted to agencies with specific hiring needs in one or several job series. The Office of Personnel Management allows agencies with this authority to advertise job openings, rate applicants, establish their own eligibility lists and registers, conduct interviews and hire. Job seekers can contact individual agencies to identify direct hire job openings or subscribe to one of several private companies' federal jobs listing services. OPM is encouraging agencies to list their job openings on the USAJOBS (see Chapter three resources).

*O*ver 80% of all job vacancies are now advertised through either Case Examining or Direct Hire authority.

APPLYING FOR FEDERAL JOBS

The application process changed significantly over the past Six years. Prior to these changes, the SF-171, "*Application for Federal Employment*," a six page document, was required when applying for most jobs. The SF-171 is now optional and it was replaced with a process that allows applicants to use a Federal style resume or other form of written application.

It is important to remember that **YOU MUST SUBMIT ALL REQUIRED INFORMATION AND FORMS**. You now have the option to use a resume format, other standard forms including the OF-612 Optional Application for Federal Employment, or the SF-171. If you don't include all required information as presented in Chapter Six, your application may **not** be considered.

There are vast differences between industry's standard brief **RESUME** format and the detailed information you must supply on the new approved Federal job resume format. The resume that most are accustomed to is a short one to two page introduction. Uncle Sam's resume must be highly structured with specific data or the resume may not be considered. I consider the optional OF-612 form the safest application process. All required information is placed on these forms and you don't have to worry about whether or not you included all of the required information.

*I*nadequately prepared application forms prevent many highly qualified candidates from making the eligible list.

An excellent and comprehensive set of tools for obtaining a federal job, called *Quick & Easy Federal Jobs Kit* by DataTech Software, is available. It includes the new optional forms, the original SF-171 application, it generates resumes from data that you entered on your forms, provides for KSAs, and it includes spell check and various formatting options. The updated software includes 9 additional employment forms as well and it is Windows 95, 98, NT, ME, 2000 and XP compatible. This program is available from the publisher's catalog in the back of this book or you can call to order toll free at 1-800-782-7424.

The federal government rates applicants on their work experience and education. The personnel specialist rating your application generally knows little about the specific job you bid on. This administrative specialist will rate you either eligible or ineligible by referring to the *Federal Qualification Standards*. (See a sample qualification standard on the following pages.) These standards break most job series down to general and specialized qualifying work experience and required education. You must have a certain number of years of both general and specialized experience for various starting pay grades. Past work experience and training must be noted on your application. If your application is rated eligible you will be ranked against all applicants and the best qualified candidates will be referred to the selecting official. The selecting official must pick from the top rated applicants. Interviews are optional; however, if one applicant is interviewed generally all of the top rated applicants will be interviewed. Refer to Chapter Six for guidance on how to complete your application.

LITTLE KNOWN FACTS

If you visit USAJOBS on-line or use one of the Federal Job Touch Screen Computers located at Federal buildings around the country and view their current list of job vacancies, the list may not be all inclusive for that area. Agencies in your area may have direct hire or case hiring authority for specific job skills and many agencies can hire college graduates non-competitively under the *Outstanding Scholars Program*. These agencies may not advertise openings through OPM. See Chapter Three for details.

To locate other potential job openings and networking resources contact individual agency's personnel or human resource departments at locations that you wish to work. Also, contact OPM or your local Federal Executive Board (FEB) to obtain a list of agencies in your area. There are 28 FEBs located in cities that are major centers of Federal activity. Many now have web sites that you can access with a computer and modem. For a complete list of FEB web sites visit http://federaljobs.net/feblist.htm. You will also find a list of FEBs in the Appendix B. Most FEBs publish a comprehensive area federal agency directory that you can use to identify where the agency offices are located in your area. Many agencies have multiple staffed facilities in major metropolitan areas.

Review the blue pages in your white page directory. Blue pages list government agencies in your area. The yellow pages also offer comprehensive government listings.

To obtain specific information about a particular agency, first refer to Appendix C and then look up the *United States Government Manual* at your library for additional details. This highly informative book is published and revised yearly and lists each department and agency. Contact names, addresses, and a brief agency description are provided along with some employment information.

Don't overlook your local state employment office. The Office of Personnel Management supplies current employment lists to all state employment offices and direct hire agencies may forward their lists to state agencies.

HOW JOBS ARE FILLED

Selecting officials can fill positions through internal promotions or reassignments, reemploying former employees, using special noncompetitive appointments such as the *Veterans Readjustment Act program*, or by appointing a new employee through a vacancy announcement.

NONCOMPETITIVE APPOINTMENTS

If you can qualify for a special noncompetitive appointment, you should contact agencies directly. The following chapters explain the various special appointments that are available.

Agencies often hold off on hiring until close to the end of the fiscal year, September 30th. They evaluate their attrition, projected retirements, and staffing allowances throughout the year. However, they often hold off hiring because of budgetary concerns. Agencies are able to use the funds they save for positions that go unfilled for that fiscal year, however they must be staffed at 100% by September 30th or they risk losing that position next fiscal year. One of the best times of the year to look for employment is from July through September.

Adding to the confusion, many federal employees are eligible to retire at age 55 with 30 years service or at age 60 with 20 years service. Some job series offer early retirement with as little as 20 years service. Many eligible employees opt to remain long after their retirement anniversary date. After age 55 is reached, agencies don't know when employees will elect to retire. One day agencies are fully staffed and the next day they could have 50 people submit their retirement paperwork. Over 28% of the federal work force is now eligible for retirement.

Federal managers fear that if they don't hire up to their authorized employment ceiling in the current fiscal year, congress will, with the stroke of a pen, reduce their em-ployment ceiling next year.

All of this uncertainty causes agencies to go begging for new employees at or close to the end of a fiscal year, September 30. Unfortunately, if agencies advertise through the Office of Personnel Management it can take from several weeks to months before the job is advertised, applicants rated, and the selection made.

Noncompetitive appointments and former employees can be selected and picked up the same day. If you qualify for any noncompetitive program, multiply your chances by going direct to each agency in your area. Send them a signed copy of your application, preferably the OF-612 or SF-171, and write a cover letter explaining who you are, what program you qualify for, and when you can start working. Be tactful and don't demand employment. Agencies don't have to hire anyone non-competitively if they choose not to.

The term *"noncompetitive"* is misleading. It should be noted that individuals within noncompetitive groups do compete for jobs. If there are three Veterans Readjustment Appointment candidates vying for the same position, the best qualified candidate will be selected from this group, generally through the interview process.

REINSTATEMENT

Reinstatement is the noncompetitive re-entry of a former federal employee into the competitive service. Formal federal employees are not required to compete with applicants for federal employment. Reinstatement is a privilege accorded in recognition of former service and not a "right" to which the formal employee is entitled. Reinstatement is completely at the discretion of the appointing agency.

Former employees entitled to veterans preference who served, or who were serving, under appointment that would lead to career status and nonveteran employees with career tenure may be reinstated regardless of the number of years since their last appointment. Career status is obtained when an employee works for three full years with the federal government in a career position.

Former nonveteran career-conditional employees, those who worked less than three years with the federal government, may be reinstated only within three years following the date of their separation. Certain types of service outside the competitive service may be used to extend this limit.

Employees seeking reinstatement should apply directly to the personnel offices of the agency where they wish to work. Refer to the current edition of the Federal Employees Almanac, published by Federal Employees News Digest, P.O. Box 8550, Reston, VA 20195-9907 for additional information on reinstatement and all other personnel issues or call toll free 1-800-989-3363.

The following pay table may be misleading. There are 32 locality pay areas that increase the base salary for employees working in those areas. Also, agencies offer jobs to new employees typically at step one of each grade. However, for certain critical jobs, agencies may be able to match your current salary up to but not over step 10 for that grade. If you are currently making more than step one of the advertised grade ask if they can match your current salary if you accept the position.

TABLE 2-1
ANNUAL SALARY RATES
2002 General Schedule (GS)

There are 32 locality pay areas. Visit **http://federaljobs.net** for specific locality pay information for all areas. This chart is the base pay chart. All of the 32 locality pay areas adjust the base chart salary by at least 8.64% or more depending on the metropolitan area that the job is located in. Updated pay charts will be posted at federaljobs.net each year.

STEP INCREASES 1-10									
GRADE	1	2	3	4	5	6	7	8	9	10
GS 1	14,757	15,249	15,740	16,228	16,720	17,009	17,492	17,981	18,001	18,456
2	16,592	16,985	17,535	18,001	18,201	18,736	19,271	19,806	20,341	20,876
3	18,103	18,706	19,309	19,912	20,515	21,118	21,721	22,324	22,927	23,530
4	20,322	20,999	21,676	22,353	23,030	23,707	24,384	25,061	25,738	26,415
5	22,737	23,495	24,253	25,011	25,769	26,527	27,285	28,043	28,801	29,559
6	25,344	26,189	27,034	27,879	28,724	29,569	30,414	31,259	32,104	32,949
7	281,614	29,103	30,042	30,981	31,920	32,859	33,798	34,737	35,676	36,615
8	31,191	32,231	33,271	34,311	35,351	36,391	37,431	38,471	39,511	40,551
9	34,451	35,599	36,747	37,895	39,043	41,191	41,339	42,487	43,635	44,783
10	37,939	39,204	40,469	41,734	42,999	44,364	45,529	46,794	48,059	49,324
11	41,684	43,073	44,462	45,851	47,240	48,629	50,018	51,407	52,796	54,185
12	49,959	51,624	53,289	54,954	56,619	58,284	59,949	61,614	53,279	64,944
13	59,409	61,389	63,369	65,349	67,329	69,309	71,289	73,269	75,249	77,229
14	70,205	72,545	74,885	77,225	79,565	81,905	84,245	86,585	889,259	91,266
15	82,580	85,333	88,086	90,839	93,592	96,345	99,098	101,851	104,604	107,357

SENIOR EXECUTIVE SERVICE

GRADE	BASE
ES-1	$113,000
ES-2	$118,300
ES-3	$123,700
ES-4	$129,800
ES-5	$130,000
ES-6	$130,000

PAY REFORM

The pay charts listed on the previous page cover General Schedule employees and executives who do not work in one of 32 high cost of living areas such as New York City, Los Angeles, and Pittsburgh. High cost areas receive premium pay over the basic rates specified. For example, if you were hired to work in Los Angeles at a GS-10 pay grade you would start at $44,028 per year. The starting pay for the same position in Pittsburgh, Pennsylvania would be 41,551 for a GS-10 step 1 as noted on the pay schedule printed on the previous page.

Locality pay adjustments were instituted to provide pay comparability between federal employees and the private sector. Typically, government agencies in high cost areas have had a difficult time recruiting. These differentials were designed to attract new employees and to encourage existing employees to stay with the government.

SAMPLE QUALIFICATION STANDARD

The following qualification standard example will give you an idea of what raters look for and how all job series standards are written:

GROUP COVERAGE QUALIFICATION STANDARD FOR ADMINISTRATIVE AND MANAGEMENT POSITIONS

This qualification standard covers positions in the General Schedule that involve the performance of two-grade interval administrative and management work. It contains common patterns of creditable education and experience to be used in making qualifications determinations. Section IV-B of the Qualifications Handbook contains individual occupational requirements for some occupations that are to be used in conjunction with this standard. Section V identifies the occupations that have test requirements.

A list of the occupational series covered by this standard is provided on pages IV-A-13 and IV-A-14 of the Qualification Standard Handbook. This standard may also be used for two-grade interval positions other than those listed if the education and experience pattern is determined to be appropriate.

EDUCATION AND EXPERIENCE REQUIREMENTS

Table 2-2 on the next page shows the amount of education and/or experience required to qualify for positions covered by this standard.

		EXPERIENCE	
GRADE	**EDUCATION**	**GENERAL**	**SPECIALIZED**
GS-5	4-year course of study to a bachelor's degree	3 years, 1 year equivalent to at least GS-4	None
GS-7	2 full years of graduate level education or superior academic achievement	None	1 year equivalent to at least GS-5
GS-9	2 full years of progressively higher level graduate education or master's or equivalent graduate degree (such as an L.L.B. or J.D.)	None	1 year equivalent to at least GS-7
GS-11	3 full years of progressively higher education or Ph.D. or equivalent doctoral degree	None	1 year equivalent to at least GS-9
GS-12 & above	None	None	1 year equivalent or at least next grade level

TABLE 2-2
EDUCATION OR EXPERIENCE

Some of the occupational series covered by this standard include both one-and two-grade interval work. The qualification requirements described in this standard apply only to those positions that typically follow a two-grade interval pattern. While the levels of experience shown for most positions covered by this standard follow the grade level progression pattern outlined in the table, users of the standard should refer to the "General Policies and Instructions" (Section 11 of the Qualifications Handbook) for guidance on crediting experience for positions with different lines of progression.

Undergraduate Education: Successful completion of a full 4-year course of study *in any field* leading to a bachelor's degree, in an accredited college or university, meets the GS-5 level requirements for many positions covered by this standard. Others have individual occupational requirements in Section IV-B that specify that applicants must, in general, (1) have specific course work that meets the requirements for a major in a *particular field(s)*, or (2) have at least 24 semester hours of course work in the field(s) identified. Course work in fields closely related to those specified *may* be accepted if it clearly provides applicants with the background of knowledge and skills necessary for successful job performance. One year of full-time undergraduate study is defined as 30 semester hours or 45 quarter hours, and is equivalent to 9 months of general experience.

Superior Academic Achievement: The superior academic achievement provision is applicable to all occupations covered by this standard. See the "General Policies and Instructions" for specific guidance on applying the superior academic achievement provision.

Graduate Education: Education at the graduate level in an accredited college or university in the amounts shown in the table meets the requirements for positions at GS-7 through GS-11. Such education must demonstrate the knowledge, skills, and abilities necessary to do the work.

One year of full-time graduate education is considered to be the number of credit hours that the school attended has determined to represent one year of full-time study. If that information cannot be obtained from the school, 18 semester hours should be considered as satisfying the one year of full-time study requirement.

Part-time graduate education is creditable in accordance with its relationship to a year of full-time study at the school attended.

For certain positions covered by this standard, the work may be recognized as sufficiently technical or specialized that graduate study alone may not provide the knowledge and skills needed to perform the work. In such cases, agencies may use selective factors to screen out applicants without actual work experience.

General Experience: For positions for which individual occupational requirements do not specify otherwise, general experience is three years of progressively responsible experience (one year of which was equivalent to at least GS-4) that demonstrates the ability to:

1.   Analyze problems to identify significant factors, gather pertinent data, and recognize solutions;
2.   Plan and organize work; and
3.   Communicate effectively orally and in writing.

Such experience may have been gained in administrative, professional, technical, investigative, or other responsible work. Experience in substantive and relevant secretarial, clerical, or other responsible work may be qualifying as long as it provided evidence of the knowledge, skills, and abilities (KSA's) necessary to perform the duties of the position to be filled. Experience of a general clerical nature (typing, filing, routine procedural processing, maintaining records, or other nonspecialized tasks) is not creditable. Trades or crafts experience appropriate to the position to be filled may be creditable for some positions.

For some occupations or positions, applicants must have had work experience that demonstrated KSA's in addition to those identified above. Positions with more specific general experience requirements than those described here are shown in the appropriate individual occupational requirements,

Specialized Experience: Experience that equipped the applicant with the particular knowledge, skills, and abilities to perform successfully the duties of the position, and that is typically in or related to the work of the position to be filled. To be creditable, specialized experience must have an equivalent to at least the next lower grade level in the normal line of progression for the occupation in the organization. Applicants who have the one *year* of appropriate specialized experience, as indicated in the table, are not required by this standard to have general experience, education above the high school level, or any additional specialized experience to meet the minimum qualification requirements.

Combining Education and Experience: Combinations of successfully completed post-high school education and experience may be used to meet total qualification requirements for the grade levels specified in the table. They may be computed by first determining the applicant's total qualifying experience as a percentage of the experience required for the grade level; then determining the applicant's education as a percentage of the education required for the grade level; and then adding the two percentages. (See examples below.) The total percentages must equal at least 100 percent to qualify an applicant for that grade level. Only graduate education in excess of the amount required for the next lower grade level may be used to qualify applicants for positions at grades GS-9 and GS-11. (When crediting education that requires specific course work, prorate the number of hours of related courses required as a proportion of the total education to be used.)

The following are examples of how education and experience may be combined. They are examples only, and are not all-inclusive.

• The position to be filled is a Quality Assurance Specialist, GS-1910-5. An applicant has two years of general experience and 45 semester hours of college that included nine semester hours in related course work as described in the individual occupational requirements in Section IV-B. The applicant meets 67 percent of the required experience and 38 percent of the required education. Therefore, the applicant exceeds 100 percent of the total requirement and is qualified for the position.

● The position to be filled is a Management Analyst, GS-343-9. An applicant has six months of specialized experience equivalent to GS-7 and one year of graduate level education. The applicant meets 50 percent of the required experience but none of the required education, since he or she does not have any graduate study beyond that which is required for GS-7. Therefore, the applicant meets only 50 percent of the total requirement and is not qualified for the position. (The applicant's first year of graduate study is not qualifying for GS-9.)

● The position to be filled is a Music Specialist, GS-1051-11. An applicant has nine months of specialized experience equivalent to GS-9 and 2 ½ years of creditable graduate level education in music. The applicant meets 75 percent of the required experience and 50 percent of the required education, i.e., the applicant has ½ year of graduate study beyond that required for GS-9. Therefore, the applicant exceeds the total requirement and is qualified for the position. (The applicant's first 2 years of graduate study are not qualifying for GS-11.)

SELECTIVE FACTORS FOR COVERED POSITIONS

Selective factors must represent knowledge, skills, or abilities that are essential for successful job performance and cannot reasonably be acquired on the job during the period of orientation/training customary for the position being filled. For example, while the individual occupational requirements for Recreation Specialist provide for applicants to meet minimum qualifications on the basis of education or experience in any one of a number of recreational fields, a requirement for knowledge of therapeutic recreation may be needed to perform the duties of a position providing recreation services to persons with physical disabilities. If that is the case, such knowledge could be justified as a selective factor in filling the position.

TABLE 2-3
The "TYPICAL" Federal Civilian Employee

INDIVIDUAL CHARACTERISTICS	1990	2000
Average Age	42.3	46.3
Average Length of Service	13.5	17.1
Retirement Eligible		
CSRS	8.0%	17.0%
FERS	3.0%	11.0%
College Educated	35%	41%
Gender		
Men	57%	55%
Women	43%	45%
Race & National Origin		
Minority Total	27.4%	30.4%
Black	16.7%	17.1%
Hispanic	5.4%	6.6%
Asian/Pacific Islander	3.5%	4.5%
Native American	1.8%	2.2%
Disabled	7.0%	7.0%
Veterans Preference	30.0%	24.0%
Vietnam Era Veterans	17.0%	14.0%
Retired Military	4.9%	3.2%
Retired Officers	0.5%	0.5%

Sources: "The 'typical' Federal Civilian Employee"; Office of Workforce Information, 2001

Chapter Three
What Jobs Are Available

The Internet has simplified locating federal job vacancies. Job seekers can connect direct to OPM's internet employment web site (http://www.usajobs.opm.gov) or visit hundreds of agency employment web sites through **federaljobs.net** (http://federaljobs.net). You can also call OPM's **USAJOBS** hotline 24 hours a day, seven days a week, for updated job information at 1-912-757-3000. Federal Career Opportunities publishes a consolidated list of thousands of federal job vacancies bi-weekly. You can also subscribe to Federal Jobs Central's on-line government job vacancy listings at **http://www.fedjobs.com** or you can search their on-line jobs database for specific occupations in your area.

Additional avenues are also available to locate open job announcements including; OPM and agency sponsored job hot lines, internet web sites, computer generated data bases, employment services, directories, and periodicals that publish job listings. These resources are listed in this chapter under *Common Job Sources*. Specific hiring programs are discussed following the job resource listings such as; the Outstanding Scholars Program, student hiring, and engineering conversion paths.

> Use the links listed on
> **http://Federaljobs.net**
> to visit over 200 federal agency
> employment web sites.

Individual agency personnel offices should also be contacted to obtain job announcements. Regional offices are the most productive and an agency directory is included in Appendix C. I also suggest that you contact your local Federal Executive Board, see listing in Appendix B. They publish federal office directories for their area. A consolidated listing of Washington, D.C. Federal Personnel Departments is provided following the *Common Job Sources* section in this chapter. If an agency has direct hire or case examining authority, and most do today, they advertise jobs independently from the Office of Personnel Management (OPM). OPM doesn't maintain a consolidated list of direct hire job announcements. Occasionally OPM conducts job fairs throughout the country and they are announced on USAJOBS.

Chapter Seven explains the Veteran Readjustment Appointment (VRA) Program and Veterans Preference. Postal Service jobs are covered separately in Chapter Nine. The U.S. Postal Service (USPS) doesn't advertise job openings through OPM. The federal Handicapped Hiring Program is presented in Chapter Ten and we added a comprehensive Chapter on Law Enforcement occupations including the new Federal screeners that are now at airports nationwide. The new Chapter Eleven focuses on this large occupational group.

IMPROVING YOUR CHANCES

The more contacts you make the greater your chances. **Don't get lost in the process.** Too many job seekers pin all their hopes on one effort. They find an open announcement, send in an application, then forget about the process until they receive a reply. Federal jobs are highly competitive. The more jobs you apply for the better your chances.

Good things come to those who wait, as long as they work like hell while they wait.

If you're not using a computer program to generate your application or new resume format, before sending in your first application have it duplicated at a local print shop. Then you can send copies to bid on other announcements. Copies are acceptable as long as you have an original signature on the copy you submit. Don't sign the original. Use the original as a master and sign each copy.

Use the list of OPM Service Centers, Federal Executive Boards and Regional Offices in Appendix B and C and the common job resources listed in this chapter to improve your chances. If you're willing to relocate, obtain job announcements from other areas to improve your chances.

Several of the job resources listed in this chapter publish comprehensive national federal job listings. USAJOBS and individual agencies Each maintain job listings, most are accessible on-line databases. Also, contact local agency offices and find out what is currently available, what's coming up, and how to apply. This is especially true since the abolishment of centralized federal job registers. Now over 80% of all jobs are advertised through individual agencies. OPM does not list vacancies from Excepted Service agencies or for many agencies with direct hire authority.

> Resumes and optional job application forms are now accepted by Uncle Sam. Job seekers need to learn how to write a professional federal resume and application and develop job search strategies that work under the new federal hiring guidelines. Chapter Six will guide you step-by-step through the application process.

The informational interviewing methods presented in Chapter Four will help you develop agency contacts that may be able to help you land a job with Uncle Sam. You aren't locked into the first job or, for that matter, location that you are originally selected for. Once hired, you'll have opportunities to bid for jobs in-house. Many agencies have offices at hundreds of locations and you can bid to any one of those locations for future promotions or to enter a related field under your job series. Check with employing agencies to see if they have offices located in or close to the area you want to eventually live. If so, more than likely you will have an opportunity to bid on future openings at that location.

Our business in life is not to get ahead of others, but to get ahead of ourselves — to break our own records, to outstrip our yesterdays by our today.

Susan B. Johnson

COMMON JOB SOURCES

This section presents resources that can be used to locate federal job announcements. After reviewing the listed resources, refer to Appendix D for a complete list of federal occupations. Appendix B lists OPM Service Centers and FEB offices throughout the country. A number of the periodicals and directories listed in this chapter are available at libraries. Many publishers will send complimentary review copies of their publications upon request.

Resource headings include job openings, internet web sites, directories, and general information. Job openings include publications with job ads and job hotlines. The general information section lists related books, pamphlets, informational services, brochures, and computer software. All job sources are listed alphabetically.

JOB OPENINGS

PERIODICALS & NEWSPAPERS WITH FEDERAL JOB ADS

Equal Opportunity Publications - 445 Broad Hollow Rd., Suite 425, Melville, NY 11747; 631-421-9421, E-mail info@eop.com. This company publishes a number of excellent publications including **Minority Engineer, Woman Engineer, Equal Opportunity, CAREERS & The disABLED,** and **Hispanic Career World** magazines. Display ads feature national employers, including the federal government, seeking applicants for many varied fields. Each issue offers a dozen to sixty or more display job ads. Call for subscription rates or visit their Internet web site for complete information at http://www.eop.com/contact.html.

Federal Career Opportunities - Federal Research Service, PO Box 1059, Vienna, VA 22183; 1-800-822-5027 or 703-281-0200; E-mail *info@fedjobs.com*. A biweekly publication listing thousands of currently available federal jobs, $49 for a 3 month subscription, 6 bi-weekly issues or $19.97 for a one month subscription. Their vacancy listings are available in the printed version or through an on-line service at http://fedjobs.com.

Federal Jobs Digest - Breakthrough Publications, P.O. Box 594, Millwood, NY 10546; 1-800-824-5000, http://jobsfed.com, publishes a bi-weekly listing of federal job vacancies in a newspaper format, $34 for 6 bi-weekly issues. They offer a Job Matching Service for $35. The recommendation covers Job Titles and Grade Levels, not vacancies. Typically takes three to four weeks for analysis.

Federal Times - 6883 Commercial Dr., Springfield, VA 22159; 800-368-6718, http://www.federaltimes.com, weekly; $52/year subscription rate, $29.25 for six months. Publishes some vacancies with brief descriptions starting at the GS-7 level.

Federal Practitioner - Quandrant Health Com, Inc., 105 Raider Blvd., Belle Meade, NJ 08502; 800-976-4040, monthly, $44.95 for annual subscription. Generally includes up to a dozen or so ads for Veterans Administration hospital nurses and physicians under the "Classifieds" section.

Internships in the Federal Government - Graduate Group, P.O. Box 370351, West Hartford, CT 06137; 860/233-2330, $27.50. Provides information on internships and a few permanent positions, published annually.

Internships in Congress - Graduate Group, P.O. Box 370351, West Hartford, CT 06137; 860/233-2330, $27.50. Provides information on internships and a few permanent positions with members of the Congress, published annually. There web site is www.graduategroup.com.

SPOTLIGHT - National Association of Colleges and Employers, 62 Highland Ave., Bethlehem, PA 18042; 800-544-5272, 610-868-1421, annual subscriptions free to members. Call for subscription rates. A newsletter to keep up with the latest trends in the job market; get up-to-the-minute information changes in hiring laws; and learn about what the technology professionals use to perform their jobs more efficiently. Get the latest job openings within the profession. Twelve issues a year. Job listings provided on their web site at http://www.naceweb.org.

The Black Collegian Magazine - Black Collegiate Services, 909 Poydas St., New Orleans, LA 70130; 504-821-5694, http://www.black-collegian.com, published semiannual. Student Subscription Rate : $4.00 per year or $8.00/2 years. Non-Student Subscription Rate : $8.00 per year or $16.00/2 years. Your one year subscription entitles you to two Super Issues, which are published in October(*Career Planning and Job Search Issue*) and February(*Top 100 Employers and African American History Issue*).

The Employment Bulletin - American Sociological Association, 1307 New York Avenue, NW, Suite 700, Washington, DC 20005; 202-383-9005, monthly, Individual subscriptions (calendar year) are: ASA members, $10; non-members, U.S., $40. The Employment Bulletin contains current position vacancy listings in academic and in practice settings, and fellowship announcements. Also available free on-line at http://www.asanet.org. Applicants should contact employers for more complete information or changes. It is mailed first class to all subscribers (air mail overseas). Published monthly.

FEDERAL JOB HOTLINES

USA JOBS Automated Telephone System - Federal government job national hotline 1-478-757-3000, TDD 478-744-2299. You can also call one of the 14 OPM Service Centers located throughout the country for information on federal employment. These centers provide support to agencies in their geographical area. However, if you have a problem with an announcement or can't get the information you need from various Internet sites call them for assistance. You can also email or fax your questions. Complete contact information is provided in Appendix B.

USA JOBS is operated by the Office of Personnel Management. The hotline Phone answers 24 hours a day and provides federal employment information for most occupations. Callers can leave messages to receive forms and announcements by mail. Requested job announcements and applications are mailed within 24 hours. Easy to use on-line voice prompts and voice commands allow access with any touch tone or rotary dial telephone. **Note** - *Not all vacancies are listed on this service. Excepted agencies and agencies with direct hire authority announce vacancies through their individual human resources departments.*

Department of Veteran's Affairs - Delegated Examining Unit. Hot line for VA job information announcement requests only. Call 1-800-368-6008. Voice prompts guide you through the process. You must have the job announcement number, title of the position and job location before you call.

United States Postal Service - The Postal Service has a comprehensive employment web site at http://www.usps.gov for vacancies including management, supervisory, administrative, professional and technical positions. Craft or bargaining unit positions such as: clerk, carrier, custodian, mail handler, and maintenance technician or any postal position, which requires an individual to be tested, cannot be accessed at this site. You can also call **1-800-276-5627** to obtain general information about Postal job opportunities by phone.

WEB SITES

There are thousands of internet web sites now available to assist you with your job search. Many agencies have searchable on-line job databases available. Not all federal jobs are listed on OPM's USAJOBS web site. You must contact individual agency personnel offices in your area or visit that Department's internet jobs database for complete job listings. The internet has simplified the process. The larger key sits are listed in this section. For direct links to over 200 federal agency employment web sites visit our web site at **http://federaljobs.net**. Links are updated monthly and you can find direct links to many helpful sites. You can review on-line job vacancy announcements as they are posted, print them out and apply for vacancies nationwide.

federaljobs.net (http://federaljobs.net) This career center will assist you with your federal government job search and guide you step-by-step through the process. You can search this site for key words and phrases. Includes a listing of over 200 federal agency employment web sites that you can visit for up-to-date job listings and agency information. You will also find current pay scales and updates to the 8th edition of The Book of U.S. Government Jobs. If you find a changed URL (Internet address) or contact information in this book visit Federaljobs.net for the updated information. E-mail contact information changes to (update@federaljobs.net). We will research and post updates as needed.

Federal On-Line Job Search by FRS - (http://fedjobs.com) Federal Research Service, Inc., P.O. Box 1059, Vienna, VA 22180-1059; 1-800-822-JOBS or 703-281-0200. A searchable database of thousands of federal job vacancies updated each weekday. Search thousands of federal job vacancies by GS series, grade, location, eligibility, agency or any combination of the above. Subscriptions are available. Call or visit their Internet web site for rates.

Federal Web Locator (http://www.infoctr.edu/fwl) The Federal Web Locator is a service provided by the Villanova Center for Information Law and Policy and is intended to be the one stop shopping point for federal government information on the World Wide Web. I found this site to be very useful with full links to hundreds of sites. If you are looking for anything in the federal sector visit this site and just click on the agency, department, or anyone of hundreds of selections that may interest you.

FeDWorld - (http://www.fedworld.gov/) The FedWorld Federal Job Search uses files created by the Office of Personnel Management. FedWorld downloads source files from USAJOBS which also operates a web site with this data at http://www.usajobs.opm.gov/. This site allows job searches by various key words such as occupational title, series, grade and by state. Each Job Announcement on FedWorld has a link to the same announcement at USAJOBS. This site's job search capability is excellent and when you find the USAJOBS site overloaded and slow go to Fedworld for job lists.

FirstGov - (http://www.firstgov.gov) This site was developed by the administration to be the federal government's Internet directory. It provides abundant information on all aspects of federal government including a jobs page that offers extensive links that you can explore. Includes numerous employment resources.

Health Care Jobs (Career Center) - (http://healthcarejobs.org)Explore health care services occupations or use this career center to locate jobs in all specialties including jobs with Uncle Sam. You will find a tremendous amount of up-to-date information and resources that you can use to explore lucrative and fast growing careers in the health care industry.

Jobsfed.com - Breakthrough Publications, P.O. Box 594, Millwood, NY 10546; 1-800-824-5000, http://jobsfed.com, on-line job search database available for registration fee. They also publish a bi-weekly listing of federal job vacancies in newspaper format. Visit their web site for registration fees and to view their site features.

Student Jobs - (http://studentjobs.gov) Use this site to explore student job vacancy announcements and draft your resume. This excellent site also provides active links to agencies that recruit students since a number of excepted agencies do not advertise on USAJOBS.

USAJobs - (http://www.usajobs.opm.gov) Operated by the Office of Personnel Management (OPM). This site provides access to the national federal jobs database; full text job announcements; answers to frequently asked employment questions; and access to electronic and hard copy application forms. Listings are divided into professional career, entry level professional, senior executive, worker-trainee, clerical and technician, trades and labor, and summer positions. An email job notification feature is available at this site. Registered users can create and store up to three searches on this service. When jobs are announced you will be notified by email.

This site offers a resume builder that you can use to create a federal style resume that can be printed, saved, and edited. They also offer resume electronic transfers via email. Agencies may choose to accept electronic resumes on a job-by-job basis.

Many Federal job announcements don't make it into this database and many agencies have their own job web sites. A good place to start looking for agency listings that are not hosted on this site is to visit http://federaljobs.net/.

FEDERAL DEPARTMENT INTERNET WEB SITES

Generally you can link to each the Agencies of each Department from the listed home page. For example, when you visit the Department of Transportation's web site you will find links to the Federal Aviation Administration and other affiliated agency links. Visit http://federaljobs.net for a comprehensive and updated listing of agency employment sites.

Appendix C includes wed site addresses for most agencies and major departments.

Executive Departments:

Department of Agriculture (http://www.usda.gov)
Department of Commerce (http://www.doc.gov)
Department of Defense (http://www.hrsc.osd.mil/empinfo.htm)
Department of Education (http://www.ed.gov)
Department of Energy (http://www.energy.gov)
Department of Health & Human Services (http://www.hud.gov)
Department of Interior (http://www.doi.gov)
Department of Justice (http://www.usdoj.gov)
Department of Labor (http://www.dol.gov)
Department of State (http://www.state.gov)
Department of Transportation (http://www.dot.gov)
Department of Treasury (http://www.ustreas.gov)
Department of Veteran's Affairs (http://www.va.gov)
Whitehouse (http://www.whitehouse.gov)

Independent Establishments and Government Corporations:

Central Intelligence Agency (http://www.cia.gov)
Environmental Protection Agency (http://www.epa.gov)
Federal Communications Commission (http://www.fcc.gov)
Office of Personnel Management (http://www.opm.gov)
United States Postal Service (http://www.usps.gov)

DIRECTORIES

Congressional Staff Directory - CQ Staff Directories, Inc., P.O. Box 62, Mt. Vernon, VA 22121; 703-739-0900. Three volume set costs $227. Lists 20,000 Congressional employees. Includes biographies of 3,200 key staff. Available at many libraries.

Directories In Print - Gale Research Company, Book Tower, Detroit, MI 48226; 800/877-4253, request current edition. This two volume set costs around $400 and is a directory of directories. It lists over 14,000 published directories worldwide. Available at most libraries.

Federal Employees Almanac (Published in January of each year) Federal Employees News Digest, PO Box 8550, Reston, VA 20195, 1-800-989-3363, E-mail: info@fedforce.com. A comprehensive guide to federal pay, benefits, retirement and more. Includes complete pay scales, detailed information about special emphasis hiring programs, veterans benefits, with detailed contact information. Visit their highly informative web site at http://www.fedforce.com for more information.

Federal Personnel Guide - (Published February 1, of every year) - Key Communications Group, Inc., P.O. Box 42578, Dept. US8, Washington, DC 20015-0578, 1-800-705-5353, 192 pages, $11.95 plus shipping. This guide is a useful, accurate, time-saving source of valuable information on government organization, compensation, promotion, retirement, insurance, benefits, and other important and interesting subjects for Civil Service, Postal Service, and all other employees of the federal government. Also available on-line at http://www.fedguide.com/. Available in print, CD and on-line versions.

Federal Yellow Book: Who's Who in Federal Departments and Agencies - Leadership Directories Inc., 104 Fifth Ave, 2nd floor, New York, NY 10011; 212-627-4140, quarterly, $340 for one year subscription. This is one of the most up-to-date directories of federal departments and agencies. It lists thousands of key contacts in all branches including regional offices, 1,000 pages. Available at many libraries. Includes thousands of E-mail and fax numbers. Visit their web site at http://www.leadershipdirectories.com/.

Guide to Military Installations In The U.S - Army Times Publishing Company, Springfield, VA 22159; 800-424-9335, 703-750-8900, published annually in November for a small charge including shipping and handling. A comprehensive guide that includes base realignment information due to base closings and other major impacts. One of the largest employers in the federal government is the Department of Defense with over 700,000 federal civilian workers of which many are employed at or around military bases.

Military Facilities Directory - Carroll Publishing Company, 1058 Thomas Jefferson St., NW, Washington, DC 20007; 800-336-4240, 202-333-8620. Call for pricing information for this two edition set. Includes contact information for thousands of decision makers at over 500 military installations.

Washington Information Directory - Congressional Quarterly Inc., 1414 22nd St., NW, Washington, DC 20037; 800-638-1710, 202-887-8500, published June of each year, $120, approximately 1000 pages. Discusses 18 federal government subject categories and provides abundant information on federal departments and agencies. Their web site is www.cqpress.com.

The United States Government Manual - 2001/2002 edition. Superintendent of Documents, P.O. Box 371954, Pittsburgh, PA 15250-7954, 693 pages, $40.00. Available at many libraries. The official handbook of the Federal Government provides comprehensive information on all agencies of the legislative, judicial, and executive branches. The manual also includes information on quasi-official agencies; international organizations in which the United States participates; and boards, commissions, and committees.

A typical agency description includes a list of principal officials, a summary statement of the agency's purpose and role in the federal government, a brief history of the agency, including its legislative or executive authority, a description of its programs and activities, and a "Sources of Information" section. This last section provides information on consumer activities, contracts and grants, employment, publications, and many other areas of public interest.

GENERAL INFORMATION

Books, Services, & Software

Campus-Free College Degrees, 9th edition by Marcie Kisner Thorson. Available through Amazon.com for $27.95. This book will help you qualify for targeted jobs. Colleges have developed non-traditional programs to meet the demand for alternative approaches to learning.

Over 200 regionally accredited colleges and universities across the U.S. offer college degrees through distance learning, and these programs are fully described in this excellent book. This guidebook also includes chapters on accreditation, state higher education agencies, methods for earning credits, high school diplomas, the Regents Credit Bank, an index of study concentrations and more.

General Test Practice For 101 U.S. Jobs - by Hy Hammer, 2000, 226 pgs, 5th edition, $12.95. This workbook has helped hundreds of thousands of federal job seekers to prepare for the general clerical and administrative tests. Includes hundreds of sample test questions and answers, practice in all the most common exam subjects, and inside information on working for the U.S. Government. Available toll free at 1-800-782-7424.

Government Job Finder (3rd edition) - by Daniel Lauber, 1997 - 2000, 322 pages, $16.95. If you are interested in exploring state and local government jobs this is a must have resource. Written by one of the leading experts in the field, Mr. Lauber provides abundant resources for you to land jobs in every state and overseas. This highly informative book introduces readers to over 2,000 resources and tools for finding jobs and getting hired in local, state, and federal government. Designed for professional, labor, trade, technical, and office staff in local, state, and federal government in the U.S. and overseas. Available from Bookhaven's back-of-book catalog.

Guide to Careers in Federal Law Enforcement - by Thomas H. Ackerma, 1999, 257 pages, $29.95. Provides profiles of 225 law enforcement occupations with tactics on how to land a job. Provides concise profiles of 225 careers with more than 130 agencies. It gives readers time-saving information on how to locate the agencies, including addresses, phone numbers, web site and email addresses. A must for those interested in law enforcement careers. Order toll free at 1-800-782-7424.

Health Care Job Explosion! High Growth Health Care Careers and Job Locator (2nd edition) - by Dennis V. Damp, 1998, 320 pages, $17.95. The perfect book for anyone seeking work in the health care industry. Bursting with details on over 1,000 sources for locating health care jobs including jobs with the federal government, this comprehensive career guide and job finder steers readers to where they can actually find job openings. Lists hundreds of internet web sites and E-mail addresses. Appendices include extensive guidance on health care careers with the federal government. Available from the publisher's back-of-book catalog or order by phone toll free at 1-800-782-7424.

Non-Profits & Education Job Finder - by Daniel Lauber, 1997 - 2000, 340 pages, $16.95. Introduces readers to over 2,200 tools for finding jobs and getting hired in education and the rest of the non-profit sector. Available fromPlanning/Communications, 7215 Oak Avenue, River Forest, IL 60305-1935; toll-free: 888-366-5200. This is the only career book that gets you to all the places where jobs and internships in education and with non-profit organizations are advertised, not just on the internet but also in print and on job hotlines that all job seekers can use.

Post Office Jobs - (2nd edition 2000) by Dennis V. Damp, 224 pages, $17.95. Call 1-800-782-7424 to order. The USPS employs over 800,000 workers in 300 job categories for positions at 39,000 post offices, branches, stations, and community post offices throughout the United States. Approximately 40,000 postal workers are hired each year to backfill for retirements, transfers, deaths and employees who choose to leave. This book presents eight steps to successfully landing a high paying job with the postal service. It includes sample tests to help you pass the 470 Battery Exam, prepares you for the interview, and show you how to apply.

Summer Jobs 2003 - Peterson's Guides,P.O. Box 67005, Lawrenceville, NJ 08648; 800-338-3282 or 609-896-1800. This publication along with Peterson's *Internship 2003* is updated annually. Lists over 55,000 summer job openings. Visit their web site for pricing information at http://www.petersons.com/.

The Resume Place, Inc. - www.resume-place.com, 888-480-8265 or E-mail at resume@resume-place.com/. This service offers expert federal and electronic resume, KSA, SES, and federal application writing services. Customers: Both federal employees seeking advancement and private industry people seeking their first federal job. President: Kathryn Troutman, Author, Federal Resume Guidebook & PC disk.

Take Charge of Your Federal Career: by Dennis V. Damp, 224 pages, $17.95. Call 1-800-782-7424 to order. A Practical, Action-Oriented Career Management Workbook for Federal Employees. Packed with proved tips and valuable assessment and evaluation tools, this unique workbook provides federal workers with the know-how and guidance they need to identify, obtain, and successfully demonstrate the skills and experience required to qualify for new and better federal jobs.

Computer Software

Quick & Easy Federal Jobs Kit — by DataTech, $49.95 plus shipping. Call 1-800-782-7424 to order. This Windows 95/98/NT/ME/2000 & XP compatible system offers an excellent and comprehensive set of tools for obtaining a federal job. Includes the new 2000 Resume Processor and allows you to search the internet for federal jobs automatically. This program extracts vacancy announcements and stores them on your computer.

This software includes the **new optional forms**, the **original SF-171 application**, and it **generates federal resumes** from data that you entered on your forms. It also includes the VA 10-2850 application, AID 1420-17 forms, OPM 1170/17 supplemental Qualifications Statement, SF-181, DA-3433, AD-799 and the SF-172 Amendment to Application for Federal Employment.

Quick & Easy is designed to be easy to use, even for the person with little or no computer experience. You simply enter your information into the computer using a series of screens that look just like the forms that you want to fill out. The program is completely menu driven with advanced help at the touch of a button. It is a complete system with word processing and spell check specifically designed to fill in and manage the new optional forms (OF-612), resume, and the original SF-171. The *Quick & Easy Federal Jobs Kit* prints all forms on any Windows compatible system. Includes the new RESUMIX technology to scan resumes that are submitted. This program is available from the publisher's back-of-book catalog.

TABLE 3-1
WASHINGTON D.C. AGENCY
OFFICE NUMBERS (September 1999)

TDD (Telephone Device for the Deaf)
Main office number ● *Job Hotline* ■ *Personnel Office*

References: Government Manual 2001-2002 / The Federal Blue Pages
www.bp.fed.gov / Federal Phone listings at www.info.gov/phone.htm

Agriculture Department	■ 202/720-2791	Mineral Mgmt. Service	202/208-3985
Research Services	301/504-1638	National Parks Service	■ 202/208-5074
Farmers Services	202/720-5237	Office of Surface Mining	■ 202-208-6702
Food/consumer Service	703-305-2351	U.S. Geological Survey	■ 703/648-6131
Foreign Service	202/720-7115		
Forest Service	202/205-8333	**Justice Dept.**	● 202/514-3397
Inspector General	■ 202/720-5781	Attorney Applications	■ 202-514-1432
		Bureau of Prisons	■ 202/307-3082
Commerce Department	■ 202/482-5138		● 800/347-7744
Bureau of Census	301/457-8353	Drug Enforcement Admin.	202-307-1000
International Trade	202/482-3809	FBI	202/324-2727
Nat'l Oceanic & Admin.	■ 206-526-6294	Immigration/Naturalization	202/514-2530
Patent/Trademark Office	703/305-8341	US Marshall Service	202/307-9000
Defense Department	■ 703-617-7211	**Labor Department**	● 800/366-2753
Defense Logistics Agency	■ 703/767-7150		
Dept. of the Air Force	703/697-6061	**State Department**	202/647-4000
Dept. of the Army	703/695-2442	Foreign Service	■ 202/261/8888
Navy Department	■ 703/545-6700	Civil Service Positions	● 202/647-7284
Marine Corps	■ 703/697-7474		
Nation al Security Agency	301/688-6524	**Transportation**	● 800/525-2878
		Coast Guard	202-267-2229
Education	■ 202/401-0553		● 800/438-8724
TDD	202/260-8956	Federal Aviation Admin.	202/267-8521
		Federal Highway Admin.	202/366-0534
Energy	■ 202/586-1234	Federal Transit Admin.	202/366-4043
		Maritime Administration	202/366-5807
Health & Human Services	■ 301/443-3201	Surface Transportation	202/565-1594
Substance Abuse &			
Mental Health	■ 301/443-3408	**Treasury**	304/480-6144
Food & Drug Admin.	■ 301/827-4120	Bureau of Public Debt	■ 202/219-3300
Indian Health Service	■ 301/443-2650	Bureau of Alcohol, Tobacco	
National Inst. of Health	301/496-4000	& Firearms	■ 202/927-8500
Housing & Urban Dev.	■ 202/708-0408	Comptroller of Currency	■ 202/874-5000
		Engraving & Printing	■ 202/874-3019
Interior	■ 303/445-2670	Financial Mgmt. Service	■ 202/874-6740
Bureau of Reclamation	■ 202/208-6702	IRS	■ 202/622-5000
Fish & Wildlife Service	■ 202/208-5634	Thrift Supervision	■ 202/906-6000
		US Customs Service	■ 202/927-6724

US Mint	■ 202/354-7200	National Labor Relations Bd	202/273-1000
US Secret Service	202/435-5708	TDD	202/273-4300
		National Mediation Board	202/692-5000
Veterans Affairs	202/273-4800	National Archives/Records ●	800/827-4898
		TDD	314/538-4799
INDEPENDENT AGENCIES		National Capital Planning	202/482-7200
		National Credit Union Admin.	703/518-6300
African Development Found-		National Foundation of the	
ation	202/673-3916	Arts and the Humanities	202/682-5400
Central Intelligence Agency	703/482-1100	National Science Foundation ■	703/292-8180
Commodity Trading Comm.	201/418-5000	●	202/306-0080
Consumer Product Safety	301/504-0580	●	800/628-1487
Defense Nuclear Facilities	202/694-7000		
EEO Commission	■ 202/663-4306	National Transportation	
Environmental Protection	■ 202/260-3300	Safety Board	■ 202/314-6239
Export-Import Bank of US	800/565-EXIM	Nuclear Regulatory Comm.	■ 301/415-7516
Farm Credit Administration	■ 703/883-4135	Occupation Safety & Health	202/606-5100
Federal Comm. Commission	■ 202/418-0134	Office of Government Ethics	202/208-8000
Federal Deposit Ins. Corp	202/393-8400	Office of Mgmt & Budget	202/395-3080
Federal Emergency Mgmt.	800/424-9530	Office of Personnel Mgmt.	■ 202/606-2400
Federal Housing Finance	202/408-2500	Peace Corps	■ 202/692-1200
Federal labor Relations	■ 202/482-6660		● 800/818-9579
Federal Maritime Comm.	■ 202/523-5773	Postal Rate Commission	202/789-6800
Federal Mediation and Con-		Securities & Exch. Comm.	■ 202/942-4070
ciliation Service	202/606-8100	Selective Service System	■ 703-605-4056
Federal MineSafety & Health	202/653-5625	Small Business Admin.	202/205-6600
Federal Trade Commission	■ 202/326-2021	Social Security Admin.	800/772-1213
Federal Reserve System	202/452-3000	Tennessee Valley Authority ■	865/632-3222
General Accounting Office	202/512-3000	Trade & Development	703/875-4357
General Services Admin.	■ 202/501-0370	US Comm. On Civil Rights	■ 202/376-8464
Government Printing Office	202/512-1124	US International Trade	
Inter-American Foundation	703/306-4301	Commission	■ 202/205-2651
Merit Systems Protection Bd.	202/653-7200	US Postal Service	202/268-2000
NASA	■ 202/358-1543		● 800/562-8777

NOTE

The numbers listed noted above are subject to change. Approximatley 50% of the numbers changed from the 7th edition printing in early 2000 to early 2002 when we were researching the 8th edition, just under a two year period. If you try a number and it is incorrect go to the federal blue page listings on the Internet at **http://bp.fed.gov** and search for an updated number. You can also obtain updated numbers at **www.info.gov/phone.htm**. If you are trying to locate TDD (Telephone Device for the Deaf) visit this excellent site; **www.fts.gsa.gov.frs/ttydir/**.

EMPLOYMENT TYPES

The government offers *Competitive and Excepted Service jobs*. There are a multitude of employment options within these groups. Competitive Service means individuals compete for positions and the most qualified applicant is selected. Hiring is based on the applicant's knowledge, skills, and ability as compared to all other applicants. Excepted Service job benefits, pay, etc. are identical in most cases to Competitive Service positions. Certain jobs are excepted by statute or by OPM. The Federal Courts, Library of Congress, the Federal Reserve System, the U.S. Foreign Service, the Tennessee Valley Authority, the FBI, the CIA, and other federal intelligence agencies are Excepted Service by statute. OPM uses the Excepted Service to fill positions that are extremely difficult to fill through normal competitive processes.

The U.S. Postal Service, Veterans Readjustment Act Appointments, attorneys, teachers in dependents' schools overseas, the CIA and FBI, Secret Service, and most positions in the legislative and judicial branches are also in the Excepted Service. Foreign nationals that hold jobs overseas are excepted by Executive Order.

One disadvantage of the Excepted Service is the inability to transfer directly into a Competitive Service position. Excepted Service employees who want to apply for a Competitive Service job must compete for jobs with all other applicants.

For example, technicians working for the Air National Guard are in the Excepted Service. The same technician position with the Air Force Reserve is in the Competitive Service. If the Reserve base would close down the Competitive Service Technician would have first rights to any similar technician position in any competitive job around the country. The Air National Guard technician would not have this right and would have to bid on competitive federal positions.

Individuals do not have a choice between Competitive or Excepted Service when applying for employment. The job announcement will specify which service the job is in. However, you should be aware of the differences and if you can choose between two jobs, it may be to your benefit to accept the competitive position. Less than 19 percent of all Federal Civil Service jobs are in the Excepted Service.

TABLE 3-2
THE TYPICAL FEDERAL CIVILIAN EMPLOYEE

(NON-POSTAL EMPLOYMENT)

JOB CHARACTERISTICS	1990	2000
Annual Base Salary	$32,026	$51,618
Pay System		
General Schedule (GS)	73%	72%
Wage Grade	17%	13%
Other	10%	15%
Occupations		
White-Collar	83%	87%
Professional	21%	24%
Administrative	24%	31%
Blue-Collar	17%	13%
Work Schedule		
Full-Time	93%	94%
Part-Time	4%	3%
Intermittent	3%	3%
Service		
Competitive	80%	77%
Excepted & SES*	20%	23%

* - The SES is the Senior Executive Service

Source: The Office of Workforce Statistics, publication OWI-606-1817, July 2001.

EQUAL EMPLOYMENT OPPORTUNITY

The federal government is an Equal Opportunity Employer. Hiring and advancement in the government are based on qualifications and performance regardless of race, color, creed, religion, sex, age, national origin, or disability.

EMPLOYMENT OPTIONS

There are numerous employment paths available: full time, part time and job sharing positions, cooperative education hiring programs, Presidential Management Internships, student employment, job opportunities for veterans and the handicapped, the Outstanding Scholar, and summer work programs. Military dependents and veterans can be hired under special appointment through the *Family Member Preference, Military Spouse Preference Programs, or the Veterans Readjustment Appointment (VRA) Program.* Military dependent and veteran's programs are explained in Chapter Six.

The majority of applicants will seek federal employment through announcements from listed on USAJOBS or individual agency sites. Alternate routes are categorized into special emphasis groups, such as student employment, military dependent, veteran and handicapped hiring programs.

ADMINISTRATIVE CAREERS WITH AMERICA (ACWA EXAMINING PROGRAM)

This program was originally a dual-track method of entry into approximately 90 professional and administrative occupations. A complete list of the 90 occupations is presented in Chapter Five. One track allowed agencies to recruit and hire candidates on-the-spot who have a 3.5 grade-point average (GPA). This track is often referred to the *Outstanding Scholars Program.* Agencies can still use this recruitment method. The second track, significantly modified in 1994, consisted of a set of six examinations developed for each of six occupational groupings. A seventh job grouping was rated on education and experience rather than a written examination.

Effective November 16, 1994, OPM eliminated registers (central lists) of applicants maintained by OPM and used to refer job candidates to agencies needing to fill entry-level jobs. The reliance on a written test as a single examining method was also eliminated, providing agencies with additional examining options based on specific needs. Under the new modified examination, applicants will apply for specific job openings rather than broad occupational groups. While written tests will continue to be used for some jobs, taking a test will no longer be the compulsory first step, or hurdle, in the examination process. Instead, applicants will complete computer-scanable questionnaires detailing their qualifications and job-related experience. OPM will score the questionnaire responses to determine the most highly qualified candidates. Hiring agencies will then receive from OPM a list of the best qualified applicants for the job. In addition, agencies may require qualified applicants to take the written test for specific occupations.

Applicants should prepare for the tests since the best qualified candidates may be tested by the hiring agency. ACWA testing information, including sample test questions, are available for your review in chapter five.

STUDENT EMPLOYMENT OPPORTUNITIES

Student Employment Programs are available to attract students into the public sector. These programs offer on-the-job experience that could lead to a full-time career with the government after graduation. Industry and government utilize student programs to identify prospects for future hiring. The web site http://www.studentjobs.gov/ and the USAJOBS Hotline hotline provide updates on what agencies are hiring students and for which specialties. The recently established web site, Studentjobs.gov, is very helpful and provides direct access to student opportunities on-line.

*V*isit the web site *Studentjobs.gov for current job lists and links to key recruitment sites.*

The *Student Education Employment Program* is open to students pursuing a diploma, academic or vocational certificate, or degree.This program replaced familiar student employment programs such as the Stay-in-School and summer employment programs and consolidated 13 student hiring authorities into one streamlined authority consisting of two components.

You may be hired under these programs if you are working at least half-time for a:

❶   high school diploma or general equivalency diploma (GED),

❷   vocational or technical school certificate, or

❸   degree (associate, baccalaureate, graduate or professional).

The first component, the *Student Temporary Employment Program* (STEP), introduces students to the work environment and teaches basic workplace skills. The second component, the *Student Career Experience Program* (SCEP), provides experience that is related to the academic and career goals of the student. Approximately 50,687 students nationwide were employed at some point in 2000 by the federal government.

Students in the Career Experience Program may qualify for conversion to a career or career-conditional appointment. Eligibility for conversion requires that students graduate from an accredited school, complete at least 640 hours of career-related work in the Career Experience Program, and be hired into a position related to their academic training and career work experience. No competition is required.

Appointments to jobs under the Student Temporary Employment Program can last up to one year; extensions in one-year increments are possible. Employing agencies, at their discretion, may establish academic and job performance standards that students must meet to continue in the program. There is no conversion element under the Temporary Employment Program.

Students interested in the Temporary Employment Program or the Career Experience Program can find out about job opportunities through their high school or college cooperative education office. In addition, information on job openings nationwide are available via telephone or personal computer through OPM's electronic bulletin boards—see resources printed earlier in this chapter..

The following table lists current student employment summaries and provides insight into the various student hiring programs.

STUDENT HIRING PROGRAMS

- Federal Junior Fellowship Program

- Federal Cooperative Education Program — changed to the Student Career Experience Program in 1994

- Presidential Management Intern Program (P.I.)

- Stay-in-School Program — Changed to Student Temporary Employment Program in 1994

- Summer Employment Program — Program now falls under either of the two new programs

- Student Volunteer Services

PRESIDENTIAL MANAGEMENT INTERNSHIP (P.I.) PROGRAM

This program is targeted for graduate students who would like to enter management within the federal government. Entry into this program is considered an honor and recognized throughout the government. In 2000 there were 344 PMI selections made to over 27 major universities. Harvard, JFK School of Government had 27 finalists and Columbia University had 25.

Professional, entry-level positions are available that provide exposure to a wide range of public management issues and offer considerable chances for career progression. P.I. candidates are appointed for a two year period and most positions are located in the Washington, D.C. area. At the end of your two-year appointment you will be converted to a permanent position as long as your performance was satisfactory during your internship.

Qualifications

Typical study areas that qualify include finance, economics, accounting, criminal justice, business administration, health administration, urban planning, social services, public administration, information systems management, law, political science, and information systems management. This list is not all inclusive.

❶   You must be scheduled to receive or have received a graduate degree.

❷   During your studies you must have demonstrated an outstanding ability and personal interest in a government career in management of public policies and programs.

❸   You are currently a U. S. citizen or will soon become a citizen before being appointed to a P.I.

Your graduate school's dean, director, or chairperson must nominate you for the program. Nominations are made by the first of December of each year. Selections from each school are highly competitive and are based on skills, abilities, and knowledge.

The final selections from all nominees are made through a comprehensive individual and group interview, application assessment, writing samples, and a review of your school's recommendations.

P.I. announcements are mailed in September to graduate schools nationwide. If interested, contact your career placement and guidance office. Call the Career America Hotline for additional information and specific appointment details.

STUDENT VOLUNTEER SERVICES

Students can volunteer to work with local agencies to gain valuable work experience. These jobs are not compensated. Schools coordinate participation and high school and college students are eligible for this program. A number of colleges include volunteer service internships. Interested students can contact agencies directly.

The Student Volunteer program is an excellent path for students to develop agency contacts, work experience, and gain insight into various government careers. Often, participants receive career counseling and acquire first hand information on upcoming paid student and full time openings.

All agencies are permitted to utilize this program. However, many don't participate for various reasons. Interested students should ask their career counselor for assistance when contacting agencies. Often, a counselor can persuade a manager to try out the program on a test basis. Student Volunteer Service is an excellent opportunity for aggressive students to get their foot in the door.

THE LARGEST OCCUPATIONS

White-collar workers are classified into 442 different occupations. Refer to Appendix D for a complete list of white-collar occupational groups and their descriptions. Average worldwide annual base salary for this group reached $51,618 in 2001. The following table lists the twenty-three white-collar occupations with at least 13,000 employees.

Occupations ranged in size from several occupations with fewer than 10 employees each to 64,433 employees in series 303 Miscellaneous Clerk and Assistant.

Certain white-collar occupations are concentrated in particular federal agencies. The Department of Agriculture employed 62.2 percent of Biological Science employees and 91.6 percent of Veterinary Medical Science workers. The Social Security Administration was the major employer of the Social Science, Psychology and Welfare Group (37.4 percent). The Department of Veterans Affairs employed 71.2 percent of the Medical Hospital, Dental and Public Health group. The Department of Defense and Treasury combined employed 72.3 percent of the Accounting and Budget group. The Social Security Administration and Departments of Treasure and Justice altogether employed 64.9 percent of the Legal and Kindred group. The Department of Transportation had 68.6 percent of the Transportation Group employees. The Departments of the Justice and Treasure together employed 73.3 percent of the Investigative Group.[1]

---

[1] Excerpted from Occupations of Federal White-Collar & Blue Collar Workers, 9/30/99.

TABLE 3-5
WHITE-COLLAR OCCUPATIONS WITH
13,000 OR MORE EMPLOYEES

SERIES	TITLE	EMPLOYMENT 1999
0303	Misc. Clerk & Assistant	64,433
0301	Misc. Administration	57,697
0334	Computer Specialist	56,216
0318	Secretary	54,404
0343	Management/Program Analysis	41,770
0610	Nurse	39,654
1811	Criminal Investigation	35,840
1102	Contracting	27,021
0905	General Attorney	26,321
0105	Social Insurance Administration	25,092
2152	Air Traffic Controller	23,926
0962	Contact Representative	23,250
0855	Electronics Engineering	21,612
1101	General Business & Industry	21,004
0801	General Engineering	18,171
0802	Engineering Technicians	17,552
0525	Accounting Technician	15,844
2005	Supply Clerical & Technician	14,252
0592	Tax Examining	13,643
0326	Office Automation Clerical	13,470
0512	Internal Revenue Agent	13,276
0462	Forestry Technician	13,293
0007	Correctional Officer	13,097

SOURCE: Office of Workforce Statistics, Central Personnel File, September 30, 1999

Blue-collar workers are classified into 410 different occupations and organized into 37 job family groups. Refer to Appendix D for a complete list of blue-collar occupational groups and their descriptions. The occupational survey for 1999 covered 229,485 full-time federal civilian employees in trades and labor occupations. The Department of Defense employed over two-thirds of all blue-collar workers.

TABLE 3-6
BLUE-COLLAR OCCUPATIONS WITH
3,000 OR MORE EMPLOYEES

SERIES	TITLE	EMPLOYMENT 1999
6907	Materials Worker	13,308
4749	Maintenance Mechanic	11,631
3566	Custodial Workers	11,374
8852	Aircraft Mechanic	11,121
5803	Heavy Mobile Equipment Mechanic	9,493
2604	Electronics Mechanics	7,410
5703	Motor Vehicle Operator	6,715
3806	Sheet Metal Mechanic	6,541
7408	Food Service Worker	6,463
2805	Electrician	5,392
5823	Automotive Mechanic	5,374
3502	Laborer	4,936
3414	Machinist	4,616
4204	Pipefitter	4,171
2610	Electronic Integrated System Mechanic	3,978
7404	Cook	3,869
4102	Painter	3,751
8602	Aircraft Engine Mechanic	3,728
5716	Engineering Equipment Operator	3,333
2810	Electrician (High Voltage)	3,262

SOURCE: Office of Workforce Statistics, Central Personnel File

Three of every four blue-collar employees worked in these 12 job families: Warehousing and Stock Handling (22,647); General maintenance and Operation (17,992); General Services Support Work (17,783); Transportation/Mobile Equipment Maintenance (15,879); Electronic Equipment Installation and Maintenance (14,682); Aircraft Overhaul (13,536); Electrical Installation and Maintenance (12,074); Food Preparation and Serving (11,851); Industrial Equipment Maintenance (10,713); Industrial Equipment Operation (9,631); and Metal Work (9,585).

In September of 1999 blue-collor average salaries in major geographic areas were: $38,171 in the Washington, DC-MD-VA-WV Metropolitan Statistical Area (MSA); $36,433 in the remaining United States; and $30,503 overseas. The highest average salaries were in the printing job family: $50,353 for men and $41,534 for women.

ENGINEERING CONVERSIONS

Many professional engineering jobs are open to non degree applicants that meet the Office of Personnel Management's Engineering Conversion criteria. This is good news to those who have over 60 semester hours of college in specific areas of study. Federal regulations state that to qualify for professional engineering positions, GS-5 through GS-15, a candidate must meet basic requirements for all professional engineering positions. The *Engineering Position Qualification Standard* provides an alternate and primary conversion path.

PRIMARY PATH

There are two paths to achieving professional engineering status. The primary path consists of having an engineering degree from a four-year accredited college. The curriculum must be accredited by the Accreditation Board for Engineering and Technology (ABET) or include the specific courses and five of the specific study areas listed in Note 1 below.

ALTERNATE PATHS

Alternate paths are available to those who don't have a four-year engineering degree but have the specific knowledge, skills, abilities, and work experience for an engineering position.

Four years of college level education, training, and/or technical experience is required and can be obtained through the following paths:

A. Professional Engineering Registration Exam
B. Engineering-in-Training-Examination
C. 60 semester hours in an accredited college
   including the courses and areas of study
   listed in Note 1 below.

D. A degree in related curriculum

The first three alternate programs require appropriate training and work experience. If an applicant has the engineering experience and completed A, B, or C above, OPM will rate them as Professional Engineers.

The fourth alternate program is a related degree. For example, applicants who have a four-year degree in civil engineering and bid on a mechanical engineering job can be rated eligible if they have at least one year of experience under a professional mechanical engineer.

NOTE 1. Curriculum must include differential and integral calculus and courses (more advanced than first year physics and chemistry) in five of the seven following areas:

a.   Statics: Dynamics

b.   Strength of Materials

c.   Fluid Mechanics, Hydraulics

d.   Thermodynamics

e.   Electrical Fields and Circuits

f.   Nature and Properties of Materials

g.   Other fundamental engineering subjects including

       Optics, Heat Transfer, Electronics

Chapter Four
The Interview Process

Their are two primary interview types that you will encounter during your job search—the *informational interview* and the *employment interview*. The informational interview—initiated by the job seeker—is a valuable networking tool used to explore job opportunities. Employment interviews are initiated by prospective employers to assess your ability and weigh your strengths and weaknesses with other applicants. The person with acceptable qualifications and the ability to impress the interview panel gets the job.

INFORMATIONAL INTERVIEWS

The first step is to call agencies in your area and ask to talk with a supervisor who works in your specialty, i.e.; administration, technical, computer operations, etc. If an immediate supervisor isn't willing to talk with you in person, ask to talk with someone in the Human Resource Department. Briefly explain to this individual that you are investigating government careers and ask if he/she would be willing to spend ten minutes talking with you in person about viable federal career paths with their agency.

If you're uncertain whether or not your job skills are needed by an agency, contact the personnel or Human Resources Department. Secretaries can often answer this question.

If an informational interview is granted take along a signed copy of your employment application or federal resume and a cover letter describing your desires and qualifications. The informational interview will help you investigate available employment opportunities in many diverse agencies. You will need to identify candidates to interview through the methods mentioned above. You don't have to limit your informational interviews strictly to supervisors. Any individual currently employed in a position you find attractive can provide the necessary information. The outcome of these interviews will help you make an objective career decision for specific positions. There is one key element you must stress when requesting an informational interview:

When asking for the interview make them aware
that you only desire information and
are not asking for a job.

This should be brought to their attention immediately after requesting an interview. Many supervisors and employees are willing to talk about their job even when no vacancies exist. These interviews often provide insight into secondary careers and upcoming openings that can be more attractive than what you were originally pursuing.

Place a time limit on the interview. When contacting supervisors, request the interview by following the above guidelines but add that you will only take 15 minutes of their time. Time is a critical resource that most of us must use sparingly. When going for the interview you should be prepared to ask specific questions that will get the information you need. The following questions will help you prepare:

INFORMATIONAL INTERVIEW QUESTIONS

EXPERIENCE AND BACKGROUND

1. What training and education is needed for this type of work?

2. How did you personally prepare for your career?

3. What experience is absolutely essential?

4. How did you get started?

5. What do you find most and least enjoyable with this work?

CREDENTIALS

Of the items listed below which do you consider most important?

1. Education   4. Personality

2. Special skills   5. Organizational knowledge

3. Former work experience   6. Other

GENERAL QUESTIONS

1. What advice would you give to someone interested in this field?

2. How do I find out more about available jobs and how are they advertised?

3. Does this agency hire directly from regional offices or do they hire through the Office of Personnel Management?

4. Does this position have career development potential and if so what is the highest grade I could achieve?

5. Is there considerable or moderate travel involved with this line of work?

6. Are you required to work shifts?

REFERRAL

1. As a result of our conversation today, are there others I should talk to?

2. May I use your name when I contact them?

If an interview is not granted ask permission to send a resume or the new optional application forms for their prospective employee file. In many cases agencies cannot hire you directly unless you qualify for a direct appointment. However, if upcoming positions open they can notify you when the job will be advertised. Positions created through these methods bring aboard highly desirable employee prospects under future competitive announcements.

Certain agencies do have the authority to hire directly. To determine if an agency has this ability you must contact their regional Human

Resources or Personnel Department. When agencies hire directly you must apply through their personnel office. Send direct hire agencies a cover letter and application for their prospective employment file. Office addresses and phone numbers can be obtained by calling local area agency offices and asking for the address and phone number of that agency's regional office. For example, most agencies now hire and advertise jobs directly.

It is hard to imagine the diversity of jobs needed by most agencies. Don't exclude any agency in this process. Most agencies hire a broad spectrum of skills and professions. When going for the interview dress appropriately for the position applied for. You can expect numerous rejections while pursuing these methods. Don't get discouraged. A good manager in industry or the federal government is always on the lookout for talent he/she will be needing. If you present yourself in a professional manner and have a good work and educational history for the position applied for you will make a connection. Persistence pays when dealing with the government. Many promising candidates give up prematurely before giving their efforts a chance to work. It can sometimes take years to get the job you desire.

Most government job openings are first advertised within the agency and current employees have the first chance to bid for a higher paying position. If the job can't be filled in-house then it is advertised in the private sector by the Office of Personnel Management or in certain cases by the agency itself. These are the jobs you will be bidding on. The reason for going to the private sector is that no qualified in-house bidders applied for the positions.

EMPLOYMENT INTERVIEWING

There are several different types of interviews which you may encounter. You probably won't know in advance which type you will be facing. Below are some descriptions of the different types of interviews and what you can expect in each of them.[1]

Types of Interviews

- Screening Interview. A preliminary interview either in person or by phone, in which an agency or company representative determines whether you have the basic qualifications to warrant a subsequent interview.

- Structured Interview. In a structured interview, the interviewer explores certain predetermined areas using questions which have been written in

---

[1] Excerpted from the Job Search Guide, U.S. Department of Labor.
This excellent guide is available from the Government Printing Office.

advance. The interviewer has a written description of the experience, skills and personality traits of an "ideal" candidate. Your experience and skills are compared to specific job tasks. This type of interview is very common and most traditional interviews are based on this format.

- Unstructured Interview. Although the interviewer is given a written description of the "ideal" candidate, in the unstructured interview the interviewer is not given instructions on what specific areas to cover.

- Multiple Interviews. Multiple interviews are commonly used with professional jobs. This approach involves a series of interviews in which you meet individually with various representatives of the organization. In the initial interview, the representative usually attempts to get basic information on your skills and abilities. In subsequent interviews, the focus is on how you would perform the job in relation to the company's goals and objectives.

  How you do in the interview can often determine whether you get the job.

  After the interviews are completed, the interviewers meet and pool their information about your qualifications for the job. A variation on this approach involves a series of interviews in which unsuitable candidates are screened out at each succeeding level.

- Stress Interview. The interviewer intentionally attempts to upset you to see how you react under pressure. You may be asked questions that make you uncomfortable or you may be interrupted when you are speaking. Although it is uncommon for an entire interview to be conducted under stress conditions, it is common for the interviewer to incorporate stress questions as a part of a traditional interview. Examples of common stress questions are given later in this chapter.

- Targeted Interview. Although similar to the structured interview, the areas covered are much more limited. Key qualifications for success on the job are identified and relevant questions are prepared in advance.

- Situational Interview. Situations are set up which simulate common problems you may encounter on the job. Your responses to these situations are measured against pre-determined standards. This approach is often used as one part of a traditional interview rather than as an entire interview format.

- Group Interview. You may be interviewed by two or more agency or company representatives simultaneously. Sometimes, one of the interviewers is designated to ask "stress" questions to see how you respond under pressure. A variation on this format is for two or more company representatives to interview a group of candidates at the same time.

NOTE: Many agencies have initiated quality of worklife and employee involvement groups to build viable labor/management teams and partnerships. In this environment agencies may require the top applicants to be interviewed by three groups. There are generally three interviews in this process, one by the selection panel, and the other two by peer and subordinate groups. All three interview groups compare notes and provide input to the selection committee.

The interview strategies discussed below can be used effectively in any type of interview you may encounter.

BEFORE THE INTERVIEW

Prepare in advance. The better prepared you are, the less anxious you will be and the greater your chances for success.

- Role Play. Find someone to role play the interview with you. This person should be someone with whom you feel comfortable and with whom you can discuss your weaknesses freely. The person should be objective and knowledgeable, perhaps a business associate.

- Use a mirror or video camera when you role play to see what kind of image you project.

Assess your interviewing skills.

- What are your strengths and weaknesses? Work on correcting your weaknesses, such as speaking rapidly, talking too loudly or softly and nervous habits such as shaking hands or inappropriate facial expressions.

- Learn the questions that are commonly asked and prepare answers to them. Examples of commonly asked interview questions are provided later in this chapter. Career centers and libraries often have books which include interview questions. Practice giving answers which are brief but thorough.

- Decide what questions you would like to ask and practice politely interjecting them at different points in the interview.

Evaluate your strengths

- Evaluate your skills, abilities and education as they relate to the type of job you are seeking.

- Practice tailoring your answers to show how you meet the federal agency's needs, if you have details about the specific job before the interview.

Assess your overall appearance.

- Find out what clothing is appropriate for your job series. Although some agencies now allow casual attire, acceptable attire for most federal professional positions is conservative.

- Have several sets of appropriate clothing available since you may have several interviews over a few days.

- Your clothes should be clean and pressed and your shoes polished.

- Make sure your hair is neat, your nails clean and you are generally well groomed.

Research the federal department and agency. The more you know about the company and the job you are applying for, the better you will do on the interview. Get as much information as you can before the interview. (See Chapter 3 and review Appendix C and D.)

Have extra copies of your resume, optional forms, or SF-171 application available to take on the interview. The interviewer may ask you for extra copies. Make sure you bring along the same version of your resume or application that you originally sent the agency. You can also refer to your resume to complete applications that ask for job history information (i.e., dates of employment, names of former employers and their telephone numbers, job responsibilities and accomplishments.)

Arrive early at the interview. Plan to arrive 10 to 15 minutes early. Give yourself time to find a restroom so you can check your appearance.

It's important to make a good impression from the moment you enter the reception area. Greet the receptionist cordially and try to appear confident. You never know what influence the receptionist has with your interviewer. With a little small talk, you may get some helpful information about the interviewer and the job opening. If you are asked to fill out an application while you're waiting, be sure to fill it out completely and print the information neatly.

Don't make negative comments about anyone or anything, including former employers.

DURING THE INTERVIEW

The job interview is usually a two-way discussion between you and a prospective employer. The interviewer is attempting to determine whether you have what the company needs, and you are attempting to determine if you would accept the job if offered. Both of you will be trying to get as much information as possible in order to make those decisions.

The interview that you are most likely to face is a structured interview with a traditional format. It usually consists of three phases. The introductory phase covers the greeting, small talk and an overview of which areas will be discussed during the interview. The middle phase is a question-and-answer period. The interviewer asks most of the questions, but you are given an opportunity to ask questions as well. The closing phase gives you an opportunity to ask any final questions you might have, cover any important points that haven't been discussed and get information about the next step in the process.

Introductory Phase. This phase is very important. You want to make a good first impression and, if possible, get additional information you need about the job and the company.

- Make a good impression. You only have a few seconds to create a positive first impression which can influence the rest of the interview and even determine whether you get the job.

  The interviewer's first impression of you is based mainly on non-verbal clues. The interviewer is assessing your overall appearance and demeanor. When greeting the interviewer, be certain your handshake is firm and that you make eye contact. Wait for the interviewer to signal you before you sit down.

  Once seated, your body language is very important in conveying a positive impression. Find a comfortable position so that you don't appear tense. Lean forward slightly and maintain eye contact with the interviewer. This posture shows that you are interested in what is being said. Smile naturally at appropriate times. Show that you are open and receptive by keeping your arms and legs uncrossed. Avoid keeping your briefcase or your handbag on your lap. Pace your movements so that they are not too fast or too slow. Try to appear relaxed and confident.

- Get the information you need. If you weren't able to get complete information about the job and the agency or department in advance, you should try to get it as early as possible in the interview. Be sure to prepare your questions in advance. Knowing the following things will allow you to present those strengths and abilities that the employer wants.

✎ Why does the company need someone in this position?

✎ Exactly what would they expect of you?

✎ Are they looking for traditional or innovative solutions to problems?

■ When to ask questions. The problem with a traditional interview structure is that your chance to ask questions occurs late in the interview. How can you get the information you need early in the process without making the interviewer feel that you are taking control?

Deciding exactly when to ask your questions is the tricky part. Timing is everything. You may have to make a decision based on intuition and your first impressions of the interviewer. Does the interviewer seem comfortable or nervous, soft spoken or forceful, formal or casual? These signals will help you to judge the best time to ask your questions.

The sooner you ask the questions, the less likely you are to disrupt the interviewer's agenda. However, if you ask questions too early, the interviewer may feel you are trying to control the interview.

Try asking questions right after the greeting and small talk. Since most interviewers like to set the tone of the interview and maintain initial control, always phrase your questions in a way that leaves control with the interviewer. Perhaps say, "Would you mind telling me a little more about the job so that I can focus on the information that would be most important to the agency?" If there is no job opening but you are trying to develop one or you need more information about the agency, try saying, "Could you tell me a little more about where the company is going so I can focus in those areas of my background that are most relevant?"

You may want to wait until the interviewer has given an overview of what will be discussed. This overview may answer some of your questions or may provide some details that you can use to ask additional questions. Once the middle phase of the interview has begun, you may find it more difficult to ask questions.

Middle Phase. During this phase of the interview, you will be asked many questions about your work experience, skills, education, activities and interests. You are being assessed on how you will perform the job in relation to the agency objectives.

All your responses should be concise. Use specific examples to illustrate your point whenever possible. Although your responses should be prepared in advance so that they are well-phrased and effective, be sure they do not sound rehearsed. Remember that your responses must always be adapted to the present interview. Incorporate any information you obtained earlier in the interview with the responses you had prepared in advance and then answer in a way that is appropriate to the question.

Below are frequently asked questions and some suggested responses:

"Tell me about yourself."

Briefly describe your experience and background. If you are unsure what information the interviewer is seeking, say, "Are there any areas in particular you'd like to know about?"

"What is your weakest point?" (A stress question)

Mention something that is actually a strength. Some examples are:

　　"I'm something of a perfectionist."

　　"I'm a stickler for punctuality."

　　"I'm tenacious."

Give a specific situation from your previous job to illustrate your point.

"What is your strongest point?"

　　"I work well under pressure."

　　"I am organized and manage my time well,"

If you have just graduated from college you might say,

　　"I am eager to learn, and I don't have to unlearn old techniques."

Give a specific example to illustrate your point.

"What do you hope to be doing five years from now?"

"I hope I will still be working here and have increased my level of responsibility based on my performance and abilities."

"Why have you been out of work for so long?" (A stress question)

"I spent some time re-evaluating my past experience and the current job market to see what direction I wanted to take."

"I had some offers but I'm not just looking for another job; I'm looking for a career."

"What do you know about our agency? Why do you want to work here?'"

This is where your research on the agency will come in handy.

"You are a small/large agency and a leading force in government."

"Your agency is a leader in your field and growing." "Your agency has a superior reputation."

You might try to get the interviewer to give you additional information about the agency by saying that you are very interested in learning more about the agency objectives. This will help you to focus your response on relevant areas.

"What is your greatest accomplishment?"

Give a specific illustration from your previous or current job where you saved the company money or helped increase their profits. If you have just graduated from college, try to find some accomplishment from your school work, part-time jobs or extra-curricular activities.

"Why should we hire you?" (A stress question)

Highlight your background based on the company's current needs. Recap your qualifications keeping the interviewer's job description in mind. If you don't have much experience, talk about how your education and training prepared you for this job.

"Why do you want to make a change now?"

"I want to develop my potential."

"The opportunities in my present company are limited."

"Tell me about a problem you had in your last job and how you resolved it."

The employer wants to assess your analytical skills and see if you are a team player. Select a problem from your last job and explain how you solved it.

Some Questions You Should Ask.

✎   "What are the agency's current challenges?"

✎   "Could you give me a more detailed job description?"

✎   "Why is this position open?"

✎   "Are there opportunities for advancement?"

✎   "To whom would I report?"

Closing Phase. During the closing phase of an interview, you will be asked whether you have any other questions. Ask any relevant question that has not yet been answered. Highlight any of your strengths that have not been discussed. If another interview is to be scheduled, get the necessary information. If this is the final interview, find out when the decision is to be made and when you can call. Thank the interviewer by name and say goodbye.

ILLEGAL QUESTIONS

During an interview, you may be asked some questions that are considered illegal. It is illegal for an interviewer to ask you questions related to sex, age, race, religion, national origin or marital status, or to delve into your personal life for information that is not job-related. What can you do if you are asked an illegal question? Take a moment to evaluate the situation. Ask yourself questions like:

✎   How uncomfortable has this question made you feel?

✎   Does the interviewer seem unaware that the question is illegal?

✎   Is this interviewer going to be your boss?

Then respond in a way that is comfortable for you.

If you decide to answer the question, be succinct and try to move the conversation back to an examination of your skills and abilities as quickly as possible. For example, if asked about your age, you might reply, "I'm in my forties, and I have a wealth of experience that would be an asset to your company." If you are not sure whether you want to answer the question, first ask for a clarification of how this question relates to your qualifications for the job. You may decide to answer if there is a reasonable explanation. If you feel there is no justification for the question, you might say that you do not see the relationship between the question and your qualifications for the job and you prefer not to answer it.

AFTER THE INTERVIEW

You are not finished yet. It is important to assess the interview shortly after it is concluded. Following your interview you should:

- Write down the name, phone number, e-mail address, and title (be sure the spelling is correct) of the interviewer.

- Review what the job entails and record what the next step will be.

- Note your reactions to the interview; include what went well and what went poorly.

- Assess what you learned from the experience and how you can improve your performance in future interviews.

Make sure you send a thank-you note within 24 hours. Your thank-you note should:

- Be hand-written only if you have a very good handwriting. Most people type the thank-you note.

- Be on good quality white or cream colored paper.

- Be simple and brief.

- Express your appreciation for the interviewer's time.

- Show enthusiasm for the job.

- Get across that you want the job and can do it.

Here is a sample thank-you letter:

(Current Date)

Dear Mr. Adams:

I really appreciated your taking the time to meet with me this afternoon. I believe that my experience in law enforcement would fit right in with your agency's criminal investigation unit. I am very interested in working for your agency.

As we agreed, you will hear from me next Thursday.

Sincerely,

PHONE FOLLOW-UP

If you were not told during the interview when a hiring decision will be made, call after one week.

At that time, if you learn that the decision has not been made, find out whether you are still under consideration for the job. Ask if there are any other questions the interviewer might have about your qualifications and offer to come in for another interview if necessary. Reiterate that you are very interested in the job.

- If you learn that you did not get the job, try to find out why. You might also inquire whether the interviewer can think of anyone else who might be able to use someone with your abilities, either in another department or at another agency.

- If you are offered the job, you have to decide whether you want it. If you are not sure, thank the employer and ask for several days to think about it. Ask any other questions you might need answered to help you with the decision.

- If you know you want the job and have all the information you need, accept the job with thanks and get the details on when you start. Ask whether the employer will be sending a letter of confirmation, as it is best to have the offer in writing.

Who Gets Hired?

In the final analysis, the agency will hire someone who has the abilities and talents which fulfill their needs. It is up to you to demonstrate at the interview that you are the person they want.

Chapter Five
Civil Service Exams

Tests are required for specific groups including secretarial and clerical, air traffic control, and for certain entry level jobs. The majority — approximately 80% — of government jobs are filled through a competitive examination of your background, work experience, and education, not through a written test.

Mandatory testing for administrative careers has been eliminated. OPM and individual agencies announce professional and administrative job vacancies and interested people request and receive application material through the mail or internet. Applicants must return a simple questionnaire and a resume or optional application forms. Personnel offices score applications and generate hiring lists within two weeks of the job announcement's closing date. Agencies have the option to use a written test if they wish. Table 5-1 provides a complete list of professional and administrative occupations that may be tested. Sample test questions are provided in this chapter. Additionally, Table 5-3 lists over 60 clerical positions that require written tests.

Approximately 80% of government jobs are filled through a competitive examination of your background, work experience, and education, not through a written test.

PROFESSIONAL AND ADMINISTRATIVE POSITIONS

About 100 professional and administrative job series were originally filled using one of two options:

- A written examination; (no longer mandatory) or
- An application based on scholastic achievement, reflected by your grade point average (GPA), and work experience.

Entry level grades generally start at the GS-5 and GS-7 levels. College graduates with top grades can still be hired on the spot at OPM college fairs or by agencies under the *Outstanding Scholar Program*. Applicants who meet the requirements of the Outstanding Scholar Program are not required to take a written test and they may apply directly to agencies.

Applicants who meet the requirements of the *Bilingual/Bicultural Program* may apply directly to agencies at any time, but they may be required to take a written test. This program permits federal agencies to hire directly individuals who are proficient in Spanish language or have knowledge of the Hispanic culture when public interaction or job performance would be enhanced by this skill or knowledge.

Entry-level professional and administrative job applicants now earn eligibility by either:

- [1]Earning a college **grade point average of 3.5 or above** on a 4.0 scale or having graduated in the upper 10 percent of your class or major university subdivision, and impressing agency recruiters with experience and technical abilities during an interview. This method is referred to as the *Outstanding Scholar Program.*

- Passing an examination of your education and/or experience for a specific job vacancy. Agencies may use the original written tests to assess an applicants' abilities prior to appointment.

---

[1] Your GPA can be rounded in the following manner: a 3.44 is rounded down to 3.4; a 3.45 is rounded up to 3.5.

TABLE 5-1
SEVEN OCCUPATIONAL GROUPS

Group 1-Health, Safety and Environmental Occupations

Series	Title
0018	Safety & Occupational Health Management
0023	Outdoor Recreational Planning
0028	Environmental Protection Specialist
0673	Hospital Housekeeping Management
0685	Public Health Program Specialist

Group 2-Writing and Public Information Occupations

Series	Title
1001	General Arts & Information
1035	Public Affairs
1082	Writing & Editing
1083	Technical Writing & Editing
1147	Agricultural Market Reporting
1412	Technical Information Services
1421	Archives Specialist

Group 3-Business, Finance and Management Occupations

Series	Title
0011	Bond Sales Promotions
0106	Unemployment Insurance
0120	Food Assistance Program Specialist
0346	Logistics Management
0393	Communications Specialist
0501	Financial Administration
0560	Budget Analysis
0570	Financial Institution Examining
1101	General Business & Industry
1102	Contract Specialist
1104	Property Disposal
1130	Public Utilities
1140	Trade Specialist
1145	Agricultural Program Specialist
1146	Agricultural Marketing
1149	Wage and Hour Law Administration
1150	Industrial Specialist
1160	Financial Analysis
1163	Insurance Examining
1165	Loan Specialist
1170	Realty
1171	Appraising & Assessing
1173	Housing Management
1176	Building Management
1910	Quality Assurance Specialist
2001	General Supply
2003	Supply Program Management
2010	Inventory Management
2030	Distribution Facilities & Storage Management
2032	Packaging
2050	Supply Cataloging
2101	Transportation Specialist
2110	Transportation Industry Analysis
2125	Highway Safety Management
2130	Traffic Management
2150	Transportation

Group 4-Personnel, Administration and Computer Occupations

Series	Title
0142	Manpower Development
0201	Personnel Management
0205	Military Personnel Management
0212	Personnel Staffing
0221	Position Classification
0222	Occupational Analysis
0223	Salary & Wage Administration
0230	Employee Relations
0233	Labor Relations
0235	Employee Development
0244	Labor Management Relations Examining
0246	Contractor Industrial Relations
0301	Misc. Admin & Program
0334	Computer Specialist (Trainee)
0341	Admin Officer
0343	Management Analysis
0345	Program Analysis
1715	Vocational Rehabilitation

Group 5-Benefits Review, Tax & Legal Occupations

Series	Title
0105	Social Insurance
0187	Social Services
0526	Tax Technician
0950	Paralegal Specialist
0962	Contact Representative
0965	Land Law Examining
0967	Passport & Visa Examining
0987	Tax Law Specialist
0990	General Claims Examining
0991	Worker's Compensation Claims Examining
0993	Social Insurance Claims Examining
0994	Unemployment Compensation
0995	Claims Examining
0996	Veteran Claims Examining
0997	Civil Service Retirement Claims Examining

Group 6-Law Enforcement & Investigation

Series	Grade
0025	Park Ranger
0080	Security Administration
0132	Intelligence
0249	Wage & Hour Compliance
1169	Internal Revenue Officer
1801	Civil Aviation Security Specialist
1810	General Investigator
1811	Criminal Investigator
1812	Game Law Enforcement
1816	Immigration Inspector
1831	Securities Compliance Examining
1854	Alcohol, Tobacco, and Firearms Inspection
1864	Public Health Quarantine Inspection
1889	Import Specialist
1890	Customs Inspector

Group 7-Positions with Positive Education Requirements

Series	Title
0020	Community Planning
0101	Social Science
0110	Economist
0130	Foreign Affairs
0131	International Relations
0140	Manpower Research & Analysis
0150	Geography
0170	History
0180	Psychology
0184	Sociology
0190	General Anthropology
0193	Archeology
1015	Museum Curator
1420	Archivist
1701	General Education & Training
1720	Education Program

BASIC QUALIFICATIONS

It's important to note that a college degree isn't required to qualify for most of these jobs. Equivalent experience is acceptable as an alternative to a college degree. For example, to qualify for a GS-5 position you would require four years of education leading to a bachelor's degree, 3 years of *responsible experience,* or an equivalent combination of education and experience.

Applicants have three avenues to explore. If you don't have three years of experience or a bachelor's degree you can use a combination of education and experience to qualify.

RESPONSIBLE EXPERIENCE

You can combine education and experience to meet the qualification requirements. One academic year of full-time study (30 semester hours or 45 quarter hours) is equivalent to nine months of responsible experience. A bachelor's degree is equivalent to three years of responsible experience. To be considered as qualifying experience, your experience must be related to the position applied for.

COURSES TAKEN AT NONACCREDITED INSTITUTIONS ARE ACCEPTABLE IF THEY MEET THE QUALIFYING CONDITIONS:

- The courses are accepted for advanced credit at an accredited institution.
- The institution is one whose transcript is given full credit by a State University.
- The courses have been evaluated and approved by a State Department of Education.
- The course work has been evaluated by an organization recognized for accreditation by the Council of Postsecondary Accreditation.

OUTSTANDING SCHOLAR PROGRAM

If your GPA is 3.45 or higher or you graduated in the upper ten (10) percent of your class or major subdivision you can apply for entry-level positions in 116 career fields. Applicants who meet these provisions can locate jobs online through OPM's USAJOBS website. This special hiring authority is restricted to grade levels GS-5 and GS-7 and positions in

Accounting and Auditing, Engineering, Physical Sciences, Biological Science, and Mathematics are not covered by this program. Agencies are authorized to make immediate offers of employment to candidates who meet the requirements of this program. Visit federaljobs.net for additional information and direct links to federal regulations that govern this program. This site also provides downloadable application forms.

SAMPLE QUESTIONS

The following sample questions are excerpted from the original administrative and professional testing background information guides. They are provided to assist those entering the administrative and professional job series. Agencies have the option to use a written test to assess the skills of those who may be appointed to a position. Tests consist of:

- Vocabulary
- Reading
- Tabular Completion
- Arithmetic Reasoning
- The Individual Achievement Record (IAR)

* NOTE: The Careers in Writing and Public Information Occupations do not have an arithmetic reasoning section.

VOCABULARY QUESTIONS:

The following questions present a key word and five suggested answers. Your task is to find the suggested answer that is closest in meaning to the key word. Wrong answers may have some connection with the word, but the meanings will be essentially different from that of the key word. Sample questions 1,2 and 3 are examples of the vocabulary questions in the test.

1. *Stipulation* means most nearly

A) essential specification
B) unnecessary addition
C) unnecessary effort

D) required training
E) required correction

The word *stipulation* refers to a required condition or item specified in a contract, treaty, or other official document. Therefore, response A, *essential specification* is the best synonym. A *stipulation* could be an addition to a contract or other document, but even without the word *unnecessary*, response B is incorrect. Response C and D are clearly unrelated to the meaning of *stipulation*. Response E, *required correction*, shares with *stipulation* the idea of being necessary, as well as an association with something written. However, a correction is an alteration made to remedy or remove an error or fault, so its basic meaning is completely different from that *of stipulation.*

2. *Allocation* means most nearly

A) prevention   D) assignment
B) site   E) ointment
C) exchange

An *allocation* is the act of setting something apart for a particular purpose. Response D, *assignment*, refers to the act of specifying or designating something exactly or precisely, and is, therefore, the best synonym for *allocation*. Response A,C, and E are clearly unrelated to the meaning of *allocation*. Response B, *site*, means to put something in a location or position; however, the emphasis with *site* is on the physical location given to an object, rather than on the purpose of the object.

3. To *collaborate* means most nearly to work

A) rapidly   D) overtime
B) together   E) carefully
C) independently

The word *collaborate* means to work with another, especially on a project of mutual interest. Therefore, response B, *together*, is the best answer. Response A,D, and E are clearly unrelated to the meaning of *collaborate*, and response C, *independently*, is opposite meaning.
NOTE: Question 1 and 2 relates to the Careers in Benefit Review, Tax, and Legal Occupations. Question 3 deals with Careers in Personnel, Administrative, and Computer Occupations.

READING QUESTIONS:

In each of the questions you will be given a paragraph which contains all the information necessary to infer the correct answer. Use only the information provided in the paragraph. Do not speculate or make assumptions that go beyond this information. Also, assume that all information in the paragraph is true, even if it conflicts with some fact known to you. Only one correct answer can be validly inferred from the information contained in the paragraph.

Pay special attention to negative verbs (for example, "are <u>not</u>") and negative prefixes (for example "<u>in</u>complete" or "<u>dis</u>organized"). Also pay special attention to qualifiers, such as "all," "none," and "some." For example, from a paragraph in which it is stated that "it is not true that all contracts are legal," or that "some illegal things are contracts," but one **cannot** validly infer that "no contracts are legal" and "all contracts are two sided agreements," one can infer that "some two-sided agreements are legal," but one **cannot** validly infer that "all two-sided agreements are legal."

Bear in mind that in some tests, universal qualifiers such as "all" and "none" often give away incorrect response choices. That is not the case in these tests. Some correct answers will refer to "all" or "none" of the members of a group.

Be sure to distinguish between essential information and unessential, peripheral information. That is to say, in a real test question, the example above ("all contracts are legal" and "all contracts are two-sided agreements") would appear in a longer, full-fledged paragraph. It would be up to you to separate the essential information from its context and then to realize that a response choice that states "some two-sided agreements are legal" represents a valid inference and hence the correct answer.

4. Personnel administration begins with the process of defining the quantities of people needed to do the job. Thereafter, people must be recruited, selected, trained, directed, rewarded, transferred, promoted and perhaps released or retired. However, it is not true that all organizations are structured so that workers can be dealt with as individuals. In some organizations, employees are represented by unions, and managers bargain only with these associations.

A) no organizations are structured so that workers cannot be dealt with as individuals.
B) some working environments other than organizations are structured so that workers can be dealt with as individuals
C) all organizations are structured so that employees are represented by unions.
D) no organizations are structured so that managers bargain with unions
E) some organizations are not structured so that workers can be dealt with as individuals

The correct answer is response E. This conclusion can be derived from information contained in the third sentence of the paragraph, which states that *it is not true that all organizations are structured so that workers can be dealt with as individuals.* From this statement, it can be inferred that some organizations are not structured so that workers can be dealt with as individuals.

Note that in this question, the correct answer follows basically from one sentence in the paragraph--the third sentence. The rest of the paragraph presents additional information about personnel administration which is relevant to the discussion, but not necessary to make the inference. Part of your task in the Reading section is to understand what you read, and then discern what conclusions follow logically from statements in the paragraph. Consequently, in the test, you will find some questions in which it is necessary to use all or most of the statements presented in the paragraph, while in others, such as this one, only one statement is needed to infer the correct answer.

5) One use of wild land is the protection of certain species of wild animals or plants in wildlife refuges or in botanical reservations. Some general types of land use are activities that conflict with this stated purpose. All activities that exhibit such conflict are, of course, excluded from refuges and reservations.

A) all activities that conflict with the purpose of wildlife refuges or botanical reservations are general types of land use
B) all activities excluded from wildlife refuges and botanical reservations are those that conflict with the purpose of the refuge or reservation
C) some activities excluded from wildlife refuges and botanical reservations are general types of land use
D) no activities that conflict with the purpose of wildlife refuges and botanical reservations are general types of land use
E) some general types of land use are not excluded from wildlife refuges and botanical reservations

The correct answer is response C. The answer can be inferred from the second and third sentences in the paragraph. The second sentence tells us that *some general types of land use are activities that conflict with* the purpose of wildlife refuges and botanical reservations. The third sentence explains that *all activities that exhibit such conflict are... excluded from refuges and reservations.* Therefore, we can conclude that *some activities excluded from refuges and reservations* (the ones that conflict with the purpose of refuges an reservations) *are general types of land use.*

NOTE: Question 4 directly relates to the Careers in Personnel, Administrative, and Computer Occupations. Question 5 deals with the Careers in Health, Safety, and Environmental Occupations.

TABULAR COMPLETION QUESTIONS

These questions are based on information presented in tables. Only two sample questions of this type appear below, although, in the actual test, you will have to find five unknown values in each table. You must calculate these unknown values by using the known values given in the table. In some questions, the exact answer will not be given as one of the response choices. In such cases, you should select response E, "none of these." Sample questions 5 and 6, which are based on the accompanying table, are examples of the tabular completion questions in this test.

LOCAL GOVERNMENT EXPENDITURES OF FINANCES:
1996 TO 1999 *(In millions of dollars)*

ITEM	1996	1997	1998	1999	
				TOTAL	PERCENT*
Expenditures	(I)	432,328	485,174	520,966	100.0
Direct General Expenditures	326,024	367,340	405,174	(IV)	83.2
Utility and Liquor Stores	30,846	(II)	43,016	47,970	9.2
Water and electric	20,734	24,244	28,453	31,499	6.0
Transit and other	10,112	11,947	14,563	16,471	3.2
Insurance Trust Expenditure	23,504	28,797	36,582	39,466	(V)
Employee retirement	12,273	14,008	(III)	17,835	3.4
Unemployment compensation	11,231	14,789	20,887	21,631	4.2

Hypothetical data.   * Rounded to one decimal place

6. What is the value of I millions of dollars?

    A) 380,374
    B) 377,604
    C) 356,870
    D) 349,528
    E) none of these

The answer is A. It can be calculated by adding the values for Direct General Expenditures, Utility and Liquor Stores, and Insurance Trust Expenditure. Numerically, 326,024 + 30,846 + 23,504 = 380,374.

7. What is the value of II in millions of dollars?

    A) 338,543   D) 40,744
    B) 64,988   E) none of these
    C) 53,041

The answer is E. The correct value (not given as an answer) is calculated by adding the value for water and electric and the value for transit and other. Numerically, 24,244 + 11,947 = 36,191.

NOTE: Questions 6 and 7 relate to the Careers in Benefits Review, Tax, and Legal Occupations.

ARITHMETIC REASONING QUESTIONS

In this part of the test you have to solve problems formulated in both verbal and numeric form. You will have to analyze a paragraph in order to set up the problem, and then solve it. If the exact answer is not given as one of the response choices, you should select response E, "none of these."

8. An investigator rented a car for four days and was charged $200. The car rental company charged $10 per day plus $.20 per mile driven. How many miles did the investigator drive the car?

    A) 800
    B) 950
    C) 1,000
    D) 1,200
    E) none of these

The correct answer is A. It can be obtained by computing the following: 4 (10) + .20X = 200.

9. In a large agency where mail is delivered in motorized carts, two tires were replaced on a cart at a cost of $34.00 per tire. If the agency had expected to pay $80 for a pair of tires, what percent of its expected cost did it save?

    A) 7.5%
    B) 17.6%
    C) 57.5%
    D) 75.0%
    E) none of these

The answer is E. The correct answer is not given as one of the response choices. The answer can be obtained by computing the following:

$$(80/2 - 34)/40 = X$$

$$X = 6/40 = .15$$
$$.15 \times 100 = 15\%$$

The expected $80 cost for a pair of tires would make the cost of a single tire $40. The difference between the actual cost of $34 per tire and the expected cost of $40 per tire is $6, which is 15% of the $40 expected cost.

10. It takes two typists three 8-hour work days to type a report on a word processor. How many typists would be needed to type two reports of the same length in one 8-hour work day?

A) 4   D) 12
B) 6   E) None of these
C) 8

The correct answer is D. It can be obtained by computing the following:

$$3 \times 2 \times 2 = X.$$

The left side of the equation represents the total number of 8-hour work days of typing required for two reports: three days times two typists times two reports equals 12 8-hour work days of typing. If all of this had to be accomplished in on 8-hour work day, 12 typists would be needed.

NOTE: Question 8 deals with Careers in Law Enforcement and Investigation Occupations. Question 9 relates to the Careers in Business, Finance, and Management Occupations and question 10 relates to the Careers in Benefit Review, Tax, and Legal Occupations.

CLERICAL TESTS

The Office of Personnel Management has implemented a pilot project at the Newark, NJ area office and in the New York area which waives clerical testing. Applicants submit a SF-171 and comprehensive Supplemental Qualifications Statement and OPM rates bidders on education and/or experience. Most OPM area offices administer a multiple choice clerical test.

The written test measures the clerical and verbal abilities needed to:

✎ Design, Organize, & Use a Filing System
✎ Organize Effectively the Clerical Process in an Office
✎ Make Travel, Meeting, & Conference Arrangements
✎ Locate & Assemble Information for Reports & Briefings
✎ Compose Non-technical Correspondence
✎ Be Effective in Oral Communication
✎ Use Office Equipment

TABLE 5-2
QUALIFICATION REQUIREMENTS

For Clerk Typist positions:

GRADE	GENERAL EXPERIENCE		EDUCATION	PROFICIENCY
GS-2	3 months	OR	High school or equivalent	40 wpm typing
GS-3	6 months	OR	1 year above high school	40 wpm typing
GS-4	1 year	OR	2 years above high school	40 wpm typing

For Clerk Stenographer positions:

GRADE	GENERAL EXPERIENCE		EDUCATION	PROFICIENCY
GS-3	6 months	OR	High school or equivalent	40 wpm typing
GS-4	1 year	OR	2 years above high school	40 wpm typing
GS-5	2 years	OR	4 years above high school	40 wpm typing

For all other clerical and administrative support positions covered:

GRADE	GENERAL EXPERIENCE		EDUCATION
GS-2	3 months	OR	High school or equivalent
GS-3	6 months	OR	1 year above high school
GS-4	1 year	OR	2 years above high school

Some clerical and administrative support positions also require typing and/or stenography proficiency.

GENERAL EXPERIENCE: High school graduation or the equivalent may be substituted for experience at the GS-2 level for all listed occupations except Clerk-Stenographer, where it may be substituted for experience at the GS-3 level. Equivalent combinations of successfully completed education and experience requirements may be used to meet total experience requirements at grades GS-5 and below.

Table 5-3 lists all of the positions and grades covered under the Clerical and Administrative Support Positions test. Positions at higher grade levels in listed occupations are covered under separate examinations.

TABLE 5-3
Clerical and Administrative Support Positions
Clerk GS 2/3, Clerk Typist GS-2/4
Clerk Stenographer GS-3/5
Secretary GS-3/4

Business
Business Clerk GS-2/4
Procurement Clerk GS-2/4
Production Control Clerk GS-2/4
Property Disposal Clerk GS-2/4
Purchasing Agent GS-2/4

Communications
Communications Clerk GS-2/4
Communications Technician GS-2/4
Communications Relay Operator GS-2/4
Cryptographic Equip. Operator GS-2/4
Teletypist GS-2/4

Finance
Accounting Clerk GS-2/4
Budget Clerk GS-2/4
Cash Processing Clerk GS-2/4
Financial Clerk GS-2/4
Insurance Accounts Clerk GS-2/4
Military Pay Clerk GS-2/4
Payroll Clerk GS-2/4
Tax Accounting Clerk GS-2/4
Time & Leave Clerk GS-2/4
Voucher Examining Clerk GS-2/4

Legal
Claims Clerk GS-2/4
Legal Clerk GS-2/4
Legal Records Clerk GS-2/4

Office Clerk
Correspondence Clerk GS-2/4
Information Reception Clerk GS-2/4
Mail and File Clerk GS-2/4

Office Clerk (continued.)
Office Equipment Operator GS-2/4
Personnel Clerk GS-2/4
Personnel (Military) Clerk GS-2/4
Printing Clerk GS-2/4
Statistical Clerk GS-2/4
Supply Clerk GS-2/4
Telephone Operator GS-2/4

Transportation
Dispatching Clerk GS-2/4
Freight Rate Clerk GS-2/4
Passenger Rate Clerk GS-2/4
Shipping Clerk GS-2/4
Transportation Clerk GS-2/4
Travel Clerk GS-2/4

Miscellaneous
Archives Clerk GS-2/4
Arts & Information Clerk GS-2/4
Coding Clerk GS-2/4
Compliance Inspection Clerk GS-2/4
Computer Clerk GS-2/4
Editorial Clerk GS-2/4
Electronic Accounting Machine Operator GS-2/4
Environmental Protection Assistant GS-2/4
Fingerprint Identification Clerk GS-2/4
Intelligence Clerk GS-2/4
Language Clerk GS-2/4
Library Clerk GS-2/4
Management Clerk GS-2/4
Messenger GS-2/4 *
Security Clerical & Assistant GS-2/4

* Under 5 U.S.C 3310, appointment to a messenger position is restricted to persons entitled to veterans preference as long as such persons are available.

TYPING PROFICIENCY

Typing proficiency is determined one of several ways. You can present a speed certification statement from a typing course, take a typing test with OPM, or personally certify that you type 40 or more words per minute and later take a test upon reporting for duty.

TESTING PROCESS

The written clerical test consists of two parts, clerical aptitude and verbal abilities. To pass the written test, applicants must make a minimum score of 33 on the verbal abilities and a minimum combined total score of 80 on both the clerical and verbal parts. A score of 80 converts to a numerical rating of 70. In addition to written tests, applicants must complete the *Occupational Supplement for Clerical Positions* (OPM Form 1203-A1). With this form OPM will be able to determine an applicants' minimum qualifications based on a review of their education and work experience.

A final rating results from the written examination and Form 1203-A1, with 5 or 10 additional points added for veterans preference. After taking the exam and filling out the additional forms OPM will send you a *Notice of Rating* (NOR) within 5 to 10 work days of testing.

SAMPLE CLERICAL TESTS

There are several books on the market that provide sample tests for government clerical positions. You can find test preparation manuals published by *ARCO* at most book stores. When you apply to take an OPM test, they generally send out sample questions and explain the test in detail. The tests are multiple choice in the areas described above.

The following sample questions were provided by OPM.

SAMPLE QUESTIONS (Clerical Test)

The following sample questions show types of questions found in the written test you will take. Your answers to the questions are to be recorded on a separate answer sheet. The questions on the test may be harder or easier than those shown here, but a sample of each kind of question on the test is given.

Read these directions, then look at the sample questions and try to answer them. Each question has several suggested answers lettered A, B, C, etc. Decide which one is the best answer to the question. During the test you will be provided with an answer sheet. When taking the actual test, find the answer space that is numbered the same as the number of the question, and darken completely the oval that is lettered the same as the letter of your answer. All questions are multiple choice. The answers to the sample questions are provided on the following pages. For some questions an explanation of the correct answer is given.

Vocabulary. For each question like 1 through 3, choose the one of the four suggested answers that means most nearly the same as the word in *italics*.

1. *Option* means most nearly
    A) use   C) value
    B) choice   D) blame

2. *Innate* means most nearly
    A) eternal   B) well-developed
    C) native   D) prospective

3. To *confine* means most nearly to
    A) restrict   C) eliminate
    B) hide   D) punish

Grammar. In questions 4, 5, and 6, decide which sentence is preferable with respect to grammar and usage suitable for a formal letter or report.

4. A) If properly addressed, the letter will reach my mother and I.
    B) The letter had been addressed to myself and my mother.
    C) I believe the letter was addressed to either my mother or I.
    D) My mother's name, as well as mine, was on the letter.

The answer to question 4 is D). The answer is not A because the word me (reach . . . me) should have been used, not the word I. The answer is not B. The expression, to myself, is sometimes used in spoken English, but it is not acceptable in a formal letter or report. The answer is not C, because the word I has been used incorrectly, just as it was in A.

5. A) Most all these statements have been supported by persons who are reliable and can be depended upon.
    B) The persons which have guaranteed these statements are reliable.
    C) Reliable persons guarantee the facts with regards to the truth of these statements.
    D) These statements can be depended on, for their truth has been guaranteed by reliable persons.

6. A) Brown's & Company employees have recently received increases in salary.
    B) Brown & Company recently increased the salaries of all its employees.
    C) Recently Brown & Company has increased their employees' salaries.
    D) Brown & Company have recently increased the salaries of all its employees.

Spelling. In questions 7 through 9, find the correct spelling of the word among the choices lettered A, B, or C and darken the proper answer space. If no suggested spelling is correct, darken space D.

7. A) athalete   C) athlete
    B) athelete   D) none of these

In question 7 an extra letter has been added to both A and B. The fourth letter in A makes that spelling of *athlete* wrong. The fourth letter in B makes that spelling of *athlete* wrong. Spelling C is correct.

8. A) predesessor   C) predecesser
    B) predecesar   D) none of these

All three spellings of the word are wrong. The correct answer, therefore, is D because none of the printed spellings of *predecessor* is right.

9. A) occassion   C) ocassion
    B) occasion   D) none of these

Correct Answers to Sample Questions

1. B   6. B
2. C   7. C
3. A   8. D
4. D   9. B
5. D

Word Relations. In questions like 10, 11, and 12 the first two words in capital letters go together in some way. The third word in capital letters is related in the same way to one of the words lettered A, B, C, or D).

10. PLUMBER is related to WRENCH as
     PAINTER is related to
     A) brush   C) shop
     B) pipe   D) hammer

The relationship between the first two words in capital letters is that a PLUMBER uses the tool called the WRENCH in doing his work. A PAINTER uses the tool called the BRUSH in doing his work. Therefore, the answer to question 10 is A. The answer is not B because a pipe is not a tool. The answer is not C for two reasons. A *shop* could be used by either a plumber or a painter and a shop is not a tool. The answer is not D. A hammer is a tool but it is not a tool used by a painter in his work.

11. BODY is related to FOOD as ENGINE is related to
     A) wheels   C) motion
     B) smoke   D) fuel.

You soon saw that the relationship between the words in question 10 does not fit the words in question 11. The relationship here is that the first runs on the second-the BODY runs on FOOD; and ENGINE runs on D) fuel.

12. ABUNDANT is related to CHEAP as SCARCE is related to
     A) ample   C) costly
     B) inexpensive   D) unobtainable

Reading. In questions like 13, 14, and 15, you will be given a paragraph, generally from 4 to 10 lines long. Read the paragraph with great care for you will have to decide which one of four statements is based on the' information in the paragraph. The statement may not be based on the main thought of the paragraph.

13. What constitutes skill in any line of work is not always easy to determine; economy of time must be carefully distinguished from economy of energy, as the quickest method may require the greatest expenditure of muscular effort and may not be essential or at all desirable.

The paragraph best supports the statement that
     A)   the most efficiently executed task is not always the one done in the shortest time
     B)   energy and time cannot both be conserved in performing a single task

C) a task is well done when it is performed in the shortest time
D) skill in performing a task should not be acquired at the expense of time

The answer is A. You can see that the paragraph points out that the task done most quickly is not necessarily the task done best. The paragraph does not compare energy and time although it mentions both, so B is not an answer. The paragraph does not support C, which is almost the opposite of the answer, A. The statement in D may be true, but it is not contained in the paragraph.

14. The secretarial profession is a very old one and has increased in importance with the passage of time. In modern times, the vast expansion of business and industry has greatly increased the need and opportunities for secretaries, and for the first time in history their number has become large.

The paragraph best supports the statement that the secretarial profession

     A) is older than business and industry
     B) did not exist in ancient times
     C) has greatly increased in size
     D) demands higher training than it did formerly

15. It is difficult to distinguish between bookkeeping and accounting. In attempts to do so, bookkeeping is called the art, and accounting the science, of recording business transactions. Bookkeeping gives the history of the business in a systematic manner; and accounting classifies, analyzes, and interprets the facts thus recorded.

The paragraph best supports the statement that

     A) accounting is less systematic than bookkeeping
     B) accounting and bookkeeping are closely related
     C) bookkeeping and accounting cannot be distinguised from one another
     D) bookkeeping has been superseded by accounting

Correct Answers to Sample Questions
10. A
11. D
12. C
13. A
14. C

Sample questions 16 through 20 require name and number comparisons. In each line across the page there are three names or numbers that are very similar. Compare the three names or numbers and decide which ones are exactly alike. On the sample answer sheet, mark the answer -

A   if ALL THREE names or numbers are exactly ALIKE
B   if only the FIRST and SECOND names or numbers are exactly ALIKE
C   if only the FIRST and THIRD names or numbers are exactly ALIKE
D   if only the SECOND and THIRD names or numbers are exactly ALIKE
E   if ALL THREE names or numbers are DIFFERENT

16. Davis Haven	David Hexane	David Haven
17. Lois Appal	Lois Appal	Lois Apfel
18. June Allan	Jane Allan	Jane Allan
19. 10235	10235	10235
20. 32614	32164	32614

In the next group of sample questions, there is an underlined name at the left, and four other names in alphabetical order at the right. Find the correct space for the underlined name so that it will be in alphabetical order with the others, and mark the letter of that space as your answer.

A) →
   Goodyear, G. L.
B) →
   Haddon, Harry
21. Jones, Jane   C) →
   Jackson, Mary
D) →
   Jenkins, Williams
E) →

A) →
   Olsen, C. A.
B) →
   Olsen, C. D.
23. Olsen, C. C.   C) →
   Olsen, Charles
D) →
   Olsen, Christopher
E) →

A) →
   Kessel, Carl
B) →
   Kessinger, D. J.
22. Kessler, Neilson   C) →
   Keesler, Karl
D) →
   Kessner, Lewis
E) →

A) →
   DeLong, Jesse
B) →
   DeMatteo, Jesse
24. DeMattia, Jessica   C) →
   Derbie, Jessie S.
D) →
   DeShazo, L. M.
E) →

Correct Answers to
Sample Questions

16. E
17. B
18. D
19. A
20. C
21. E
22. D
23. B
24. C

In questions like 25 through 28, solve each problem and see which of the suggested answers A, B, C, or D is correct. If your answer does not exactly agree with any of the first four suggested answers, darken space E.

Answers

25. Add:
22
+33

A) 44   B) 45
C) 54   D) 55
E) none of these

27. Multiply:
25
x5

Answers

A) 100   B) 115
C) 125   D) 135
E) none of these

26. Subtract:
24
-3

Answers

A) 20   B) 21
C) 27   D) 29
E) none of these

28. Divide

6√126

Answers

A) 20   B) 22
C) 24   D) 26
E) none of these

There is a set of 5 suggested answers for each of the groups of sample questions appearing below. Do not try to memorize these answers, because there will be a different set on each page in the test.

To find the answer to each question, find which one of the suggested answers contains numbers and letters all of which appear in that question. These numbers and letters may be in any order in the question, but all four must appear. If no suggested answers fits, mark E for that question.

29. 8 N K 9 G T 4 6

30. T 9 7 Z 6 L 3 K

31. Z 7 G K 3 9 8 N

32. 3 K 9 4 6 G Z L

33. Z N 7 3 8 K T 9

34. 2 3 P 6 V Z 4 L

35. T 7 4 3 P Z 9 G

36. 6 N G Z 3 9 P 7

37. 9 6 P 4 N G Z 2

38. 4 9 7 T L P 3 V

Suggested Answers

A = 7, 9, G, K
B = 8, 9, T, Z
C = 6, 7, K, Z
D = 6, 8, G, T
E = none of these

Suggested Answers

A = 3, 6, G, P
B = 3, 7, P, V
C = 4, 6, V, Z
D = 4, 7, G, Z
E = none of these

Correct Answers to Sample Questions	
25. D	32. E
26. B	33. B
27. C	34. C
28. E	35. D
29. D	36. A
30. C	37. E
31. A	38. B

Chapter Six
Completing Your
Employment Application

This chapter guides you through the application process step-by-step so that you can write an application or federal resume that will get results. The SF-171, "*Application for Federal Employment,*" was originally required when applying for most jobs. The SF 171 is now optional and it was replaced with a process that allows applicants to use a *federal resume,* or other form of written application. Applicants must prepare their resumes and applications in accordance with the specific federal guidelines that are presented in this chapter. OPM has developed the following enhanced application services:

    ✎   Diverse methods for agencies to collect information from job applicants, written, telephone, and automated techniques
    ✎   Applicant choices in how they submit written applications
    ✎   Two new optional forms and an acceptable resume format
    ✎   USAJOBS Internet web site for job vacancy announcements
    ✎   OPM Service Centers (See Appendix B)
    ✎   Online resume writer at http://www.opm.gov/

It is misleading to assume that a standard resume will land you a job with Uncle Sam.

Individuals may still use the SF-171 to apply for jobs; however, agencies can not require SF-171 applications. The SF-171 application is very comprehensive and many federal workers choose to use this form to bid on job vacancies.

All of the required information is currently included in the SF-171 application. If you have your SF-171 completed, or a computer program that generates this form, you can submit it in many cases when applying for employment. The exception is when applying for jobs with agencies that use automated application processes like RESUMIX referral system which is deployed throughout the Department of Defense and other federal agencies. With RESUMIX formatted resumes, you submit one resume electroncially either on line, included in an e-mail message, or by fax for scanning. The RESUMIX application process is discribed later in this chapter.

REQUIRED INFORMATION

It is misleading to assume that a standard resume will land you a job with Uncle Sam. Most private industry resumes are loosely structured and simply introduce the applicant to the company. Follow the guidance in this chapter to write successful applications and resumes for the job you want in government. The application is one of the keys to successfully landing a federal job. You must write a professional application or federal resume and develop job search strategies that work. This book will help you achieve those goals.

> If your application or resume doesn't include all of the information that is requested in the job vacancy announcement, you may not be considered for that job.

In addition to information requested in the job vacancy announcement your application or resume **MUST** contain the following information:[1]

JOB INFORMATION

❑   Announcement number, title and grade(s) of the job for which you are applying.

PERSONAL INFORMATION

❑   Full name, mailing address *(with Zip Code)* and day and evening phone numbers.

❑   Social Security Number

❑   Country of citizenship *(Most federal jobs require United States citizenship.)*

---

[1] Reprinted from OPM brochure OF 510

❑   Veterans' Preference

  ✔   If you served on active duty in the United States military and were separated under honorable conditions, you may be eligible for veterans' preference. To receive preference if your service began after October 15, 1976, you must have a Campaign Badge, Expeditionary Medal, or a service-connected disability. For further details, call on of the OPM Service Centers listed in Appendix B or visit OPM's USAJOBS internet web site at http://www.opm.gov/.

  ✔   Veterans' preference is not a factor for Senior Executive Service Jobs or when competition is limited to status candidates *(current former federal career or career-conditional employees).*

  ✔   To claim 5-point veterans' preference, attach a copy of your DD-214, *Certificate of Release* or *Discharge from Active Duty* or other proof of eligibility.

  ✔   To claim 10-point veterans' preference, attach an SF-15, *Application for 10-Point Veterans' Preference,* plus the proof required by that form.

❑   Reinstatement eligibility *(If requested, former federal employees must attach a SF-50 proof of your career or career-conditional status.)*

  ✔   Highest federal civilian grade held *(Also give job series and dates held.)*

EDUCATION

❑   High School

  ✔   Name, city, and State *(Zip Code if known)*
  ✔   Date of diploma or GED

❑   Colleges and universities

  ✔   Name, city, and state *(Zip Code if known)*

✔ Majors

✔ Type and year of any degrees received (*If no degree, show total credits earned and indicate whether semester or quarter hours.*)

❑ Send a copy of your college transcript only if the job vacancy announcement requests it.

WORK EXPERIENCE

❑ Give the following information for your paid and nonpaid work experience related to the job for which you are applying. (*Do not send job descriptions.*)

✔ Job title (*include series and grade if federal job*)
✔ Duties and accomplishments
✔ Employer's name and address
✔ Supervisor's name and phone number
✔ Starting and ending dates (month and year)
✔ Hours per week
✔ Salary

❑ Indicate if we may contact your current supervisor.

OTHER QUALIFICATIONS

❑ **Job-related** training courses (*title and year*)

❑ **Job-related** skills; for example, other languages, computer software/hardware, tools, machinery, typing speed.

❑ **Job-related** certificates and licenses (*current only*)

❑ **Job-related** honors, awards, and special accomplishments; for example, publications; memberships in professional or honor societies; leadership activities; public speaking; and performance awards. (*Give dates but do not send documents unless requested.*)

AGENCY FORMS

Two optional forms are available. The *"Optional Application for Federal Employment"* is a simplified application for individuals who prefer a form. This optional application contains information considered to be the minimum necessary to determine an applicant's qualifications. Federal agencies do not require all applicants to use the optional application, except where the agency had developed a computer-compatible version of the optional application.

If you elect to use the OF-612 form you will discover that the OF-612 only includes space to enter work history from your current and previous employer. **DON'T STOP THERE**. To earn a rating as high as possible include all related work experience as far back as necessary, including your military time. Many applicants do not add supplemental sheets to include related work experience that can earn them a higher rating for the job. Programs like *Quick & Easy Federal Jobs Kit Version 4.0* automatically expands to capture additional work experiences. This software will also convert your application to any approved format, the OF-612, SF-171, federal resume, or RESUMIX. The Sample OF-612 Application included in this chapter was created with *Quick & Easy software*. If you are not using a software program add supplemental sheets to capture **ALL** previous employment, see examples in this chapter.

The second form, *"Declaration for Federal Employment"*, is used primarily to collect information on conduct and suitability, and also on other matters, such as receipt of a government annuity. Agencies have the option of asking applicants to complete this optional form at any time during the hiring process, but it is required by all appointees — those selected for a job. It is anticipated that only the final few applicants who have a good chance of receiving a job offer would complete this form. This form also warns applicants of the consequences of submitting fraudulent information and by signing it you are certifying the accuracy of your application materials.

OPM Form 1203, Form C, assists agencies when computer-assisted techniques are used to rate job applicants. Applicants must complete OPM Form 1203, an optical scan form designed to collect applicant information and qualifications in a format suitable for automated processing. The form is a standard computer graded form. However, the questions on the from are tailored to the job announcement and vary by occupation and agency. You could actually bid on the same job series with two different agencies and the qualification questions will be different.

A sample blank OF-612 form is included in this chapter. Use this form to draft your application while waiting for official copies from OPM. You can also download forms from http://federaljobs.net.

Agency-specific Forms

It is anticipated that agencies may need agency-specific forms; for example, when necessary for an electronic application system or for unique occupations with highly specialized requirements. To prevent a proliferation of government application forms, OPM encourages agencies to use the new process. In addition, agency-specific questions are permitted in one of three areas. These items are unique to certain agencies or positions and, therefore, are not included on the optional forms.

Optional Job Application Methods

Applicants now have several avenues available that greatly improve the application and rating processes. These methods streamline the submission of federal job applications. For selected jobs, applicants can apply to Agencies or OPM by telephone, online at OPM or agency internet web sites, or via e-mail or by fax with electronic resumes. For other jobs, job seekers will complete a questionnaire that is read and scored by computer. Both methods drastically reduce the time it takes to produce a list of ranked candidates. Where automation is not used, applicants are given a choice in how they handle job applications.

Computer Generated Applications

DataTech Software offers a comprehensive set of tools for obtaining a federal job, called ***Quick & Easy Federal Jobs Kit***. Thousands of people each month find a federal job using the internet. Resumes are scanned by a computer rather than read by a person. There are more forms than ever before.

This valuable software package includes a built-in browser with a built-in list of internet web sites that have federal job listings. With a click, you can go instantly to any of these sites, find a job, and save the vacancy announcement on your computer.

It includes the new optional forms, the original SF-171 application, seven new agency-specific employment forms and it generates resumes from data that you entered on your forms. You can also upload your resume to their extensive on-line federal resume database. This software includes the new **Fed Res 2000(tm) Resume Processor**, a powerful federal resume design tool that optimizes your resume for **RESUMIX**, scanning, OCR, and e-mailing. *Quick & Easy* is designed to be easy to use—even for the person with little or no computer experience. You simply enter your information into the computer using a series of screens that look just like the forms that you want to fill out. The program is completely menu driven with advanced help at the touch of a button. It is a complete system with word processing and spell check specifically designed to fill in and manage the new optional forms, resume, and the original SF-171.

Quick & Easy Federal Jobs Kit prints all forms on any Windows compatible system including Windows 95, 98, 2000, NT, ME and XP systems. If your federal application was completed on an earlier version of *Quick & Easy* software, this new version imports your application file and generates all new forms. This program is available for $49.95 plus shipping at 1-800-782-7424 or from the publisher's back of book catalog.

INSTRUCTIONS FOR COMPLETING
OPTIONAL APPLICATION FORM OF-612

Job Title Sought and Personal Information (Questions 1 - 7)

1. and 2. Job Title and Grade(s) Applying For

In block 1, fill in the job title listed in the announcement. Grade is the level of difficulty. If you aren't sure what grade you're qualified for, put in the entire range indicated on the announcement. EXAMPLE: Electronic Technician, GS-856-9/11

3. Announcement Number

Fill in the number on the job announcement.

4-7. Full Name, Social Security Number, Mailing Address, and Phone Numbers

Fill in all blanks with the requested information.

Work Experience

8. Describe your paid and nonpaid work experience related to the job for which you are applying.

The optional form includes two job blocks. You may need additional space to describe your duties and accomplishments or additional jobs that relate to the position you are applying for. You can add as many work experiences that you determine to be relevant by simply adding additional pages to your application. Make sure you include all of the required information on the supplemental pages for each job that you describe. Refer to the OF-612 sample application starting on page 126. Examples of typical duties, responsibilities and accomplishments are outlined for your review.

Many applicants only provide work experience for their current and previous job because the new forms only have two work experience blocks included on the form. This is a mistake and it can cost you valuable rating points. One of the major benefits of the *Quick and Easy Federal Jobs Kit* job application software is that it automatically expands the application forms to include all of your work experience.

I suggest that you include **ALL** work experience that is relevant as far back as necessary and don't forget to include your military experience as well. If you were on active duty or in the military reserves and you are applying for a job that requires the skills you learned in the military, include that work experience.

Read the job announcement for the position you are applying for thoroughly and pay attention to the kind and amount of experience that is required. Look for special skills or other evaluation factors that are needed. You must provide examples of the work experience you have that is relevant to the job you are bidding on.

Another error is to use the same exact application for all jobs that you apply for. The key is to read the job announcement and then tailor your application to that specific job. Jobs within the same series can often have different skill sets or required experience. Read the announcement and insure that your application includes the required knowledge, skills and abilities. Software such as *Quick and Easy Federal Jobs Kit* will help you tailor your application easily to each job announcement.

9. May we contact your current supervisor?

Answer *yes* only if you have discussed your interest in other employment with your supervisor.

10-12. Education

List all requested information completely, including zip codes. You may need to add supplemental pages for schools you attended. The standard form only provides space for three schools.

If you anticipate graduating within the next year, list the year and note "EXPECTED" next to the year. EXAMPLE: B.S., 2000 (EXPECTED). If you are rated eligible for the position based on your education you will be required to furnish an official transcript. Some positions may require a transcript or a list of courses. Job announcements indicate whether or not a transcript is required.

13. Other Qualifications

The categories under other qualifications call for training, skills, licenses, honors, awards and special accomplishments as they relate to the job you've targeted. Limit this to related qualifications and it isn't recommended to send unnecessary attachments with your application. Don't send samples of your work unless requested. Your application should be thorough but not full of unrelated material or material that will cause the reviewer to search through a mountain of papers to find the information he/she needs.

14. Are you a U.S. citizen?

Answer yes or no; if no, give country of citizenship. Generally speaking, you must be a citizen to get a federal job.

15. Do you claim Veterans' Preference?

Answer yes or no. Veterans' Preference is the special consideration given to qualified veterans. Refer to Chapter Seven for complete details.

16. Were you ever a federal civilian employee?

Answer yes or no. Give the job series number for the highest grade held during your federal civilian service, the grade level and the dates you held that grade. Example: *GS 856* (series), *12* (grade), *11/89 - 9/94* (from, to). Remember that the question asks for "highest," not last or your present grade.

17. Are you eligible for reinstatement (based on career or career-conditional federal status)?

Answer yes or no. Previous federal employees who are eligible for reinstatement must attach a copy of their last Standard Form SF-50 as proof of employment.

18. Applicant Certification

First read the certification thoroughly, then sign and date in ink. Applicants must submit this page with an original signature (not a photocopy) to the personnel office.

JOB ANNOUNCEMENTS

The following posted job announcement was available October 1, 1999 online at http://www.usajobs.opm.gov/. Reviewing this job announcement, and the sample OF-612 application that follows, will help you understand the federal job application process. This process is considerably more complex than what you would typically find in the private sector. Applicants that fully understand this process have the greatest chance of successfully landing a job. This job announcement is for a GS-0343-7 Management Analyst. You can review the *Qualification Standard* for the GS-0343 in Chapter Two starting on page 41.

Each announcement is typically a little different, however the process is the same. You must submit **ALL** required applications and supporting information including transcripts if required. You will find shadow boxes located throughout the following documents that clarify specific issues and guide you through the procedures needed to successfully apply for positions. Underlined text also points out key information that you should review.

I applied for this job using a fictitious name and information and I followed the checklist supplied in the announcement on page 118. This announcement permits partial online application submissions which does simplify the process. Many jobs now allow applicants to at least submit the Qualifications and Availability Form C, OPM Form 1203-AW, online. Form C is often misunderstood and many don't realize its importance. If you don't complete Form C you won't be considered for the job.

Form C

Form C in it's hard copy format is simply an answer sheet that the applicant marks — fills in the blanks — with a number 2 lead pencil. The form is scanned by a computer to retrieve and compile the results. There are 25 sections and each section has multiple questions. The form supplies availability information such as geographic preferences, contact information, and social security number. However agencies also provide up to 160 *Supplemental Qualification Questions* that focus on core competencies for the job.

The Job Announcement that follows was downloaded from the internet. You will find the first 8 of 23 total pages reproduced here. The remaining 15 pages include the entire Form C instructions including 160 questions about experiences you may have had that are related to the requirements of the job for which you are applying. The first 16 questions are about your educational and work experience background and they are multiple choice, you answer A, B, C, D, or E. The remaining questions focus on your accomplishments and require an answer YES or NO to each question, A for YES and B for NO. Several examples of the types of questions follow. These questions were excerpted from the entire bid package.

1. Outstanding Scholar Eligibility - Do you possess a bachelor's degree and possess a cumulative grade point average of at least a 3.5 on a 4.0 point scale?   A. Yes   B. No

10. I have been employed in work similar to that of the job covered by this examination:
A. = never employed in a similar job
B. = less than 1 year
C. = 1 - 2 years
D. = 3 - 4 years
E. = over 5 years

17. Have you successfully done work where your primary responsibility was to help others work out their problems (for example, worked as a therapist)?
A. = Yes   B. = No

51. Have you been given additional responsibilities because of your ability to organize and complete your regular work more quickly than expected?
A. = Yes   B. = No

106. Have you successfully done work that regularly involved verifying the accuracy of information or the relevance of information to a problem or a situation (for example, investigative work)?   A. = Yes   B. = No

---

CAUTION

I submitted Form C online through OPM's web site and it took 30 minutes to complete. When I first submitted the form it came back with an error statement. It read, "Response to an Occupational Question is invalid. Valid responses are A through I or blank." When answering Yes or No questions it's easy to forget that A = Yes and B = No. I had entered Y and N in several responses. After correcting my errors the application was accepted. **Secondly,** before starting your online application, print out the job announcement. Follow the step-by-step instructions. If you start to fill out the form without referencing the instructions you will be confused because the first few question's answers must be exactly as noted from the announcement instructions.

Typically, the government adds a checklist at the end of a job announcement. I like to pull them out and put them in the front. Use the checklist as your guide to completing your application. It will help to insure that you comply with all requirements of the bid.

APPLICANT CHECKLIST

To ensure that you file a correct and complete application package, please see the list below. Each of these is explained in detail in the announcement, so be sure to refer to the corresponding section of the announcement for complete instructions.

❑   Submit answers to the Supplemental Qualifications Statement. This can be done in either of the following ways:

Form C - Explained in detail under the "Hard Copy" section of the announcement. DO NOT FAX THIS FORM - IT MUST BE MAILED.

-OR-

Electronic Filing - Explained in detail under the "Electronic Application Options" section of the announcement. REMEMBER: Print out your "Thank You Message" or "Notice of Applicant Responses" as confirmation of your filing status; and write "Electronic Filer" at the top of your written application.

❑   Submit written application of your choice. You may submit an OF-612, SF-171, or personal resume. Whichever you choose, please be sure it contains all of the information outlined in the "Written Application" section of the announcement. NOTE: Electronic resumes are not being accepted for this vacancy.

❑   Transcripts. If you qualify and/or claim to qualify for this position based on education, you must submit transcripts or a list of college courses detailing for each course, the course number and department, course title, number of credit hours, and grade earned.

❑   Proof of Veterans Preference. If you are claiming 5-point veterans reference, please submit a DD-214. If claiming 10-point veterans preference, submit a Standard Form 15 and any other documentation required on the reverse of the Standard Form 15.

❑   Proof of Eligibility for Priority Consideration. See the "Special Selection Priority Consideration Provisions for Surplus and Displaced Federal Employees" section at the end of the announcement.

USAJOBS   **CONTROL NO CK0916**

MANAGEMENT ANALYST   **OPEN PERIOD 09/15/1999 - 10/05/1999**
SERIES/GRADE: GS-0343-07/07
SALARY: $ 27,508 TO $ 35,760, ANNUAL   PROMOTION POTENTIAL: GS-09
ANNOUNCEMENT NUMBER: 99-0916 LV

> **SALARY** - The starting salary may be negotiable. GS-09 salary ranges from $27,508, step 1, to $35,760, step 10. Your initial offer will be at the lowest step or $27,508. If you are currently earning more than $27,508 ask them to match your current salary and give them a copy of your most recent pay stud for verification. Your starting salary can't exceed the maximum step 10 pay. **You MUST ask for this prior to accepting an offer**. An agency can't adjust your salary after you accept the position.
>
> **PROMOTION POTENTIAL** - Generally this means that you are hired into a position that has promotion potential to a specified grade, GS-9 in this bid, if you performance is acceptable.

HIRING AGENCY: NAT ARCHIVES AND RECORDS ADMINISTRATION

DUTY LOCATIONS: 0001 SUITLAND, MD

REMARKS: APPLICATION RECEIPT **DEADLINE: 10/13/99.**

> **DEADLINE:** The closing date is 10/5/99. They will accept your application if it is post marked by no later than 10/5/99 and if it is received on or before 10/9/99.

CONTACT: USAJOBS BY PHONE
                  PHONE: (816) 426-5702
                    INTERNET ADDRESS: http://www.usajobs.opm.gov

                  NTNL ARCHIVES & RECORDS ADMIN
                  C/O US OFC OF PERSONNEL MGMT
                  601 EAST 12TH STREET, ROOM 131
                  KANSAS CITY, MO 64106-

FEDERAL EMPLOYMENT OPPORTUNITY ANNOUNCEMENT
U.S. Office of Personnel Management
Kansas City Service Center
601 East 12th Street
Kansas City, MO 64106

POSITION: MANAGEMENT ANALYST
PUBLIC NOTICE NUMBER: 99-0916 LV
SERIES: GS-0343
GRADE: GS-07, $27,508 to $35,760 per annum
PROMOTION POTENTIAL: GS-09

OPENING DATE: 09-15-99   CLOSING DATE: 10-05-99

Candidates' requests to obtain the appropriate application forms must be postmarked no later than the closing date. In order to be accepted, completed application packages must be RECEIVED in this office by 10-13-99.

IMPORTANT -Post mark by closing date.

PLACE OF EMPLOYMENT: National Archives & Records Administration;
                      Office of Records Services - Washington, DC
                      Modern Records Program
                      Washington National Records Center
                      Suitland, Maryland

SPECIAL PROVISIONS: This position may be filled through competitive procedures or through the Outstanding Scholar appointment authority. Please see the Outstanding Scholar section of this vacancy announcement for further details.

IMPORTANT NOTE: Relocation costs **WILL NOT be paid**. In accordance with 5 USC 3303, recommendations by a Senator or Representative may not be considered except as to the character or residence of the applicant. Enrollment in Direct Deposit/Electronic Funds transfer is required as a condition of employment for all new employees. Position requires a background investigation.

DUTIES - I underlined words that identify the key duties of the position and that are an integral part of the Qualification Standard. Do this with all job announcements and then include these key words and duties in your OF-612 or Resume work descriptions. If you have that skill or a related skill include it in your application. The more you focus your application to key duties and responsibilities the higher your rating will be.

DUTIES: The incumbent analyzes elements of the Center's program and office automation systems and recommends improvements. Conducts analytical and management studies related to program and office automation applications and their effect on operational efficiency. Acts as technical expert on, analyzes and advises management on all aspects of the manpower tracking system, TASK; the records location system, NARS-5; and the space information system, SIS. Provides training to users and managers. Gives training on accessing and using the systems, and interpreting management reports. Makes recommendations concerning the desirability and feasibility of automating manual processes. Develops written reports which describe findings, describe scope of study, and include statistical and cost/benefit. Develops systems products to facilitate programs and administration. Designs office automation applications. Coordinates with Center branches on office automation applications. Analyzes hardware and software requirements; identifies data elements, input and output requirements; and designs data entry screens and report formats. Tests applications prior to implementation. Creates and maintains appropriate user and technical documentation. Provides office automation training. Prepares annual ADP training plan. Maintains a technical reference library. Acts as a System Administrator for the Center's Information Processing System(CIPS). Provides system maintenance.

QUALIFICATION REQUIREMENTS: Applicants will not be required to take a written examination, but will be rated on the extent and quality of their education and/or experience according to information provided in their application forms. To be rated eligible, applicants must meet one of the requirements described below, AND the Selective Factor, which follows.

> **QUALIFICATION REQUIREMENTS** - In most cases you **DON'T** need a degree to qualify. Even engineers can qualify using alternative non-degree avenues. At first glance it appears that a 4-year bachelor's degree is required. Uncle Sam permits substitution of 3 years of general work experience at an equivalent GS-4 to be eligible for this position. This is another reason why you must be thorough when describing your work experience and include all key duties and responsibilities in your write-up. See the sample OF-612.

Specialized Experience: One year of specialized experience equivalent to the GS-5 level of the Federal service that provided the applicant with the knowledge, skills, and abilities to successfully perform the work of this position as described above. Specialized experience is experience analyzing and evaluating the effectiveness of line program operations; or developing life cycle cost analyses; or performing cost benefit evaluations of projects or automated equipment; or advising on the distribution of work; or analyzing new or proposed legislation or regulations for their impact on a program; or developing new or modified administrative policies or regulations.

> Underline key **Specialized Experience** requirements and focus your written application on these requirements as well as the functional duties of the position.

OR

Education: One full year of graduate level study, or a master's or higher degree in a field that provided the knowledge, skills, and abilities necessary to do the work of this position. Such fields include business administration, industrial management, industrial engineering, industrial psychology, public administration, political science, or government.

OR

<u>Combination of Experience and Education</u>: Combinations of successfully completed college level education and specialized experience may be used to meet the total experience requirements of this position. NOTE: Only graduate level education may be combined with experience.

OR

Alternative Requirement: Completion of all requirements for a bachelor's degree that, by itself, is fully qualifying for the position which meets one of the following Superior Academic achievement standards:

1. A standing in the upper third of your class or major subdivision (e.g., school of business) at the time you apply;
2. A grade average of "B" (3.0 of a possible 4.0) or its equivalent for all courses completed: (a) at the time of application; or (b) during the last two years of your undergraduate curriculum;
3. A "B+" (3.5 of a 4.0) average or its equivalent for all courses completed in a qualifying major field of study, either: (a) at the time of application; or (b) during the last 2 years of your undergraduate curriculum;
4. Election to membership in one of the national honorary societies (other than freshman societies) that meet the requirements of the Association of College Honor Societies.

**If more than 10 percent of your courses were taken on a pass/fail basis, your claim must be based on class standing or membership in an honorary society.

SELECTIVE FACTOR: (ALL APPLICANTS MUST MEET)You MUST provide a narrative in your written application describing your experience/education in relation to the following Selective Factor: <u>Demonstrated ability to identify, analyze, and solve problems, especially those related to office automation by conducting management studies and issuing findings</u>.

SPECIAL PROVISIONS FOR OUTSTANDING SCHOLAR ELIGIBILITY This position may be filled through the Outstanding Scholar appointment authority. All persons with a bachelor's degree and a cumulative grade point average of at least 3.5 on a 4 point scale will be referred as Outstanding Scholar eligibles. To be considered under this authority, applicants MUST INCLUDE A COPY OF THEIR COLLEGE TRANSCRIPT(S), and must follow the instructions for Outstanding Scholars in the <u>Supplemental Qualifications Statement on Form C</u>.

BASIS OF RATING: Applicants will be rated on their responses to items in the Supplemental Qualifications Statement as recorded on the Qualifications and Availability Form (Form C) or through the electronic application process.

HOW TO APPLY: Please read and follow the 2-Step process described below to ensure that you submit a complete application package. Applicants will be evaluated on the basis of information provided in their initial application forms only. This office will not solicit information which is missing or seek clarification of unclear information, nor will additional information be accepted after the final receipt date. Failure to provide complete information and/or supporting documentation may result in receipt of a lower or ineligible rating.

STEP 1) WRITTEN APPLICATION

Submit a resume, Optional Application for Federal Employment(OF-612), or other written application format of your choice. E-mailed resumes are not being accepted for this vacancy. Please mail or fax your written application to the address below. Be sure your resume contains all of the information requested below:

> The resume outline must be followed. If you leave out requested data your application may not be considered. The OF-612 Form includes all of the information and if you fill in the blanks you will be providing all required data. Use of one of the computer programs mentioned above will also insure that your resume is complete.

- Job Information: Public Announcement Number, title, and grade(s) for which you are applying.

- Personal Information: Full name, mailing address (with zip code) and day/evening telephone numbers (with area code); Social Security Number; and country of citizenship. If ever employed by the Federal Government, please show the highest civilian grade held, job series, and dates of employment in the grade.

- Education: High School name, city, state, and zip code, date of diploma or GED; colleges and/or Universities attended, city, state, and zip code; major field(s) of study; and type and year of degree(s) received. If no degree received, show total credit hours received in semester or quarter hours. If you qualify and/or claim to qualify for this position based on education, or if you are applying as an Outstanding Scholar, YOU MUST SUBMIT A COPY OF YOUR COLLEGE TRANSCRIPTS OR A LIST OF COLLEGE COURSES DETAILING FOR EACH COURSE, THE COURSE NUMBER AND DEPARTMENT (I.E., BIO 101, MATH210, ETC.), COURSE TITLE, NUMBER OF CREDIT HOURS, AND GRADE EARNED. Failure to do so will result in an ineligible rating.

- Work Experience: Provide the following for each paid and non-paid position held related to the job for which you are applying (do not provide job descriptions): job title; duties and accomplishments; employers name and address; supervisor's name and phone number; starting and ending dates of employment (month and year); hours per week; and salary. Indicate if your current supervisor may be contacted.

- Other Qualifications: job-related training courses (title and year); job-related skills (e.g., other languages, computer software/hardware, tools, machinery, typing speed, etc.); job-related certificates and licenses; job-related honors, awards, and special accomplishments (e.g., publications, memberships in professional or honor societies, leadership activities, public speaking, performance awards, etc.). Do not send documents unless specifically requested.

- Veterans Preference: If you are applying for 5-point Veterans Preference, submit a copy of your DD-214. If you are applying for 10-point Veterans Preference, submit a Standard Form 15, Application for 10-Point Veteran Preference, and the proof requested by the form. More information on veterans' preference is available in the Vets' Guide that can be found on the Internet at www.opm.gov.

- Federal employees: If you are or have been a Federal employee, please submit a copy of your latest Notification of Personnel Action, Form SF-50, and your most recent or last performance appraisal. If you are applying for priority consideration under the Agency Career Transition Assistance Program (CTAP) or the Interagency Career Transition Assistance Program (ICTAP), you must submit additional documentation. See the Special Selection Priority Consideration Section on this Announcement for further information, instructions, and requirements.

STEP 2) SUPPLEMENTAL QUALIFICATIONS STATEMENT Respond to the questions on the attached SupplementalQualifications Statement (SQS). This may be done either electronically or by completing OPM Form 1203-AW, Qualificationand Availability Form "C", in hard copy format.

i.   Electronic Application Options: This is the most convenient option if you have access to a computer with communications and/or Internet capability. If you choose to file electronically, you must do so by the CLOSING DATE of this announcement (10-05-99). If this equipment is not available to you, or you fail to file electronically by the CLOSING DATE, you must submit a hard copy (Form C) with your written application (refer to the "Hard Copy" section below).

a) **World Wide Web**

1.   Connect to the USAJOBS web site at http://www.usajobs.opm.gov
2.   Click on On-line Application from the USAJOBS logo or the text line below the logo
3.   Click on "Complete On-line Supplemental Qualifications Statement"
4.   Scroll down the on-line application screen until the "Enter Control Number" box appears
5.   Enter Control Number CK0916 and click on "Submit" to begin the on-line application
6.   Follow the instructions on the Supplemental Qualifications Statement Question naire for the rest of the items

OR

b) **USAJOBS** Computer Bulletin Board

1.   Dial the USAJOBS Computer Bulletin Board at (912) 757-3100
2.   Select <2 at the Main Menu for "Conferences and System Functions"
3.   Select <1 at the next screen for "Conferences"
4.   Enter <26 for "Applications On-Line" and press return
5.   Enter "O" for OPM's Electronic Application
6.   Enter Control Number CK0916

7. Enter "Y" to the question "Do you wish to complete an application now (Y/N)?
8. Enter Vacancy ID Number CK90916 in the first block
9. Follow the instructions on the Supplemental Qualifications Statement Question naire for the rest of the items

NOTE FOR ELECTRONIC FILERS: After completing the on-line application, you will know if your electronic submission through the World Wide Web has been successful when you receive a "Thank You" message stating that your on-line application for the Control Number has been received. If you applied through the USAJOBS Bulletin Board, you will receive a message indicating that you can receive a Notice of Applicant Responses through that system's E-mail, which you can then view or download. IF YOU DO NOT RECEIVE SUCH MESSAGES, PLEASE TRY AGAIN, AS THIS INDICATES THAT YOUR RESPONSES HAVE NOT BEEN ENTERED INTO THE OPM DATABASE. When you do receive these messages, please print or save them, as they are your only confirmation of a timely submission.

THIS IS THE REPLY I RECEIVED ON 10/1/99 AFTER APPLYING

> **Thank you. Your online application for CK90916 has been received. Please be sure to review the "How to Apply" information on the vacancy announcement for this position to see if additional application steps are required. Once you have submitted your complete application, you can usually expect to receive a Notice of Results in about 4 - 8 weeks. We are sorry, but we are unable to respond to requests to verify receipt of individual applications at the USAJOBS web site. If you have questions concerning this vacancy, please write to the Office of Personnel Management Service Center shown on the job announcement.**

After filing your SQS responses on-line, your resume and any other requested documentation must be faxed to 816-426-5104 or mailed to the address below. Your resume must be received in our office by the filing deadline and must include the written notation "ATTN: ELECTRONIC FILER."

ii.   Hard Copy: Complete the hard copy Form "C" and mail it (the Form C cannot be faxed) and all other requested forms (resume, etc.) to the mailing address listed below. You may request a Form "C" by phone in the following manner:

1. Call USAJobs by Phone at 816-426-5702.
2. Press 1 for the main menu
3. At the main menu, select 3 to request application forms
4. Press 1 to continue (indicating you are sure of the application material you need to request)
5. Follow the prompts to ASK THAT A FORM "C" BE MAILED TO YOU, and to record your name and address.

Mailing Address: U.S. Office of Personnel Management
                                    ATTN: 99-0916 LV
                                    601 East 12th Street, Room 131
                                    Kansas City, Missouri 64106

Where to Get Forms: If you **DO NOT** have all of the required application forms listed above under the "Basis of Rating" and "How to Apply" sections, you may write to our office at the address listed above or request them by phone in the following manner:

1.   Call USAJOBS by Phone at 816-426-5702.
2.   Press 1 for the main menu
3.   At the main menu, select 3 to request application forms
4.   Press 1 to continue (indicating you are sure of the application material you need to request)
5.   Follow the prompts to ASK FOR ANNOUNCEMENT NUMBER 99-0916 LV, and to record your name and address.

Eligibility: <u>Applicants will not be considered for other positions on the basis of this application.</u>

SPECIAL SELECTION PRIORITY CONSIDERATION PROVISIONS FOR SURPLUS AND DISPLACED FEDERAL EMPLOYEES:

Individuals who have special selection priority rights under the Agency Career Transition Assistance Program (CTAP) or the Interagency Career Transition Assistance Program (ICTAP) must be well qualified for the position to receive consideration for special priority selection. CTAP and ICTAP eligibles will be considered well qualified if they receive a score of 90 or above (excluding veterans preference points).

Current or former Federal employees seeking priority selection consideration under CTAP/ICTAP provisions must submit proof that they meet the requirements of 5 CFR 330.605(a) for CTAP and 5 CFR 330.704(a) for ICTAP. This includes a copy of the agency notice, a copy of their most recent Performance Rating and a copy of their most recent SF-50 noting current or last position, grade level, and duty location. Please annotate your application to reflect you are applying as a CTAP or ICTAP eligible.

THE FEDERAL GOVERNMENT IS AN EQUAL OPPORTUNITY EMPLOYER
IMPORTANT!!

SAMPLE OF-612 APPLICATION

The following sample OF-612 application was completed in *Quick and Easy Federal Jobs Kit Version 4.0*. This software allows you to complete any application form and convert easily between standard forms, federal resumes, or the new RESUMIX formats. Once you complete your application with this software program it can be updated in a matter of minutes to apply for other jobs. This software automatically expands forms to include all related past job work experiences that are relevant to the job you are applying for. If you are using the hard copy forms, they only include two work experience blocks. When using the hard copy forms be sure to add supplemental sheets to capture **ALL** past work experience relevant to the job. *Quick and Easy* can also instantly convert your application format to any other format including standard forms OF-612, OF-171, Federal resumes or RESUMIX.

This application was used to apply for the Management Analyst job in Announcement Number 99-0916-LV. Read this announcement, starting on page 117, and then thoroughly review the following OF-612 application to see how the key duties and specialized experience is integrated into the application. You need to capture as many skills, duties and accomplishments to obtain a high ranking and to be referred to a selecting official for an interview. The more time you spend refining your application, and insuring that your application includes required key duties and specialized experience, the higher your rating.

Include job related training and other related skills, awards, licenses and certifications that you have in block 13. In the application, under the Work Experience block 8, use bullets to get the reviewers attention. If you simply write out a long narrative it's hard for them to pick out the required key duties and specialized experience. Using bullets and focusing on the job announcement will earn you a higher rating, possibly a higher entry level pay grade, and it should help you get your foot in the door. If the job is advertised as a GS-7/9, and you have the required work experience and/or education, your chances of being hired at the GS-9 grade is much better if you follow the guidance in this chapter.

Be sure to use the checklist that most job announcements include to insure that you submit all required forms and documentation. Also use the check list in Appendix A to take you step-by-step through the entire process. If your education is used to rate you eligible for the position the agency will request that you submit official transcripts for their review and verification.

Form Approved
OMB No. 3206-0219

OPTIONAL APPLICATION FOR FEDERAL EMPLOYMENT - OF 612

You may apply for most jobs with a resume, this form, or other written format. If your resume or application does not provide all the information requested on this form and in the job vacancy announcement, you may lose consideration for a job.

1 Job title in announcement

Management Analyst, GS-0343-07

2 Grade(s) applying for

GS-07

3 Announcement number

99-0916 LV

4 Last name

SMITH

First and middle names

John Q.

5 Social Security Number

123-45-6789

6 Mailing address

3401 Main Street

City	State	ZIP Code
Hyattsville	MD	20782

7 Phone numbers (include area code)

Daytime 202-123-2456

Evening 301-234-5678

WORK EXPERIENCE

8 Describe your paid and nonpaid work experience related to the job for which you are applying. Do **not** attach job descriptions.

1) Job title (if Federal, include series and grade)

Computer Analyst

From (MM/YY)	To (MM/YY)	Salary	per	Hours per week
04-23-96	Present	$27,958	year	40

Employer's name and address	Supervisor's name and phone number
Hendricks Inc	Gene Porter
435, Smithfield Drive, Smithfield, MD 20782	202-123-2456, Ext. 410

Describe your duties and accomplishments

Summary

Currently serve as the lead automation analyst for a large wholesaler that distributes products to retail outlets and services a four state area. Hendricks' employs 797 workers that are located at 7 offices in Maryland, Virginia, Pennsylvania and Delaware. Position includes providing a full range of continuing automation technical and advisory services to our operating offices, system users, company officials and warehouse managers, as well as technical expertise, Novell System Certified and LAN/WAN management.

Continued on a Separate Page

2) Job title (if Federal, include series and grade)

Computer Specialist

From (MM/YY)	To (MM/YY)	Salary	per	Hours per week
04-12-94	04-22-96	$17,547	year	40

Employer's name and address	Supervisor's name and phone number
National Rental Corp	Charles Massie
101 Fifth Street, Silver Spring, MD 20901	202-234-2345

Describe your duties and accomplishments

Summary

As a computer specialist I was responsible for user terminal maintenance and new software training at their branch office in Silver Spring Maryland There were 47 specialist and 5 managers stationed at this facility. I maintained and serviced over 67 desk top and lap top terminals for the organization. Worked closely with the department managers to insure systems were functional and that specialists were able to perform needed automation functions. I had several collateral responsibilities including researching the potential for LAN deployment at our branch office and new system integration vendor training. I attended a number of strategy sessions with vendors and managers to explore the feasibility of expanding our automation system capabilities.

Continued on a Separate Page

50612-101   NSN 7540-01-351-9178   Optional Form 612 (September 1994)
U.S. Office of Personnel Management

9 May we contact your current supervisor?

YES [X] NO [   ] ▸ If we need to contact your current supervisor before making an offer, we will contact you first.

EDUCATION

10 Mark highest level completed. **Some HS** [   ] **HS/GED** [X] **Associate** [   ] **Bachelor** [   ] **Master** [   ] **Doctoral** [   ]

11 Last high school (HS) or GED school. Give the school's name, city, State, ZIP Code (if known), and year diploma or GED received.

Northwestern S.H., Baltimore MD

12 Colleges and universities attended. Do **not** attach a copy of your transcript unless requested.

Name			Total Credits Earned		Major(s)	Degree - Year
			Semester	Quarter		(if any) Received
1) Community College of Baltimore Maryland					IRM Automation	
City	State	ZIP Code				
Baltimore	MD	16652				A.A. 1991
2)						
3)						

OTHER QUALIFICATIONS

13 **Job-related** training courses (give title and year). **Job-related** skills (other languages, computer software/hardware, tools, machinery, typing speed, etc. **Job-related** certificates and licenses (current only). **Job-related** honors, awards, and special accomplishments (publications, memberships in professional/honor societies, leadership activities, public speaking, and performance awards). Give dates, but do **not** send documents unless requested

Awards
In 1989, I was selected for an award by the U.S. Army for developing a communication deployment strategy that was accepted by the DOD for worldwide implementation. Received the Dickens Award for Outstanding Achievement.
In 1998, I developed the Frederick Company's internet web site. I received a substantial cash bonus for developing this site.

Licenses/Certifications
FCC Radio Telephone Communications License with Ship Radar Endorsement (Current)
NOVEL Certified

Recent Reading
"The Seven Habits of Highly Effective People" by Stephen R. Covey
"Lincoln on Leadership"
"Networking in the 21st Century? by Bill Gates

Additional Training (job related)

Continued on a Separate Page

GENERAL

14 Are you a U.S. citizen?   YES [X] NO [   ] ▸ Give the country of your citizenship. _____

15 Do you claim veterans' preference? **NO** [   ] **YES** [X] ▸ Mark your claim of 5 or 10 points below.

5 points [X] ▸ Attach your DD 214 or other proof. **10 points** [   ] ▸ Attach an *Application for 10-Point Veterans' Preference* (SF 15) and proof required.

16 Were you ever a Federal civilian employee?

	Series	Grade	From (MM/YY)	To (MM/YY)
NO [ ] **YES** [X] ▸ For highest civilian grade give:	0050	GS-02	09/93	03/94

17 Are you eligible for reinstatement based on career or career-conditional Federal status?

NO [X] YES [   ] ▸ If requested, attach SF 50 proof.

APPLICANT CERTIFICATION

18 I **certify** that, to the best of my knowledge and belief, all of the information on and attached to this application is true, correct, complete and made in good faith. **I understand** that false or fraudulent information on or attached to this application may be grounds for not hiring me or for firing me after I begin work, and may be punishable by fine or imprisonment. **I understand** that any information I give may be investigated.

SIGNATURE   **DATE SIGNED**

ADDITIONAL WORK EXPERIENCES

SMITH, John Q.   123-45-6789
Management Analyst, GS-0343-07   99-0916 LV   GS-07

3) Job title (if Federal, include series and grade)

Computer Specialist Intern, GS-02

From (MM/YY)	To (MM/YY)	Salary	per	Hours per week
9/1/93	3/15/94	$ 14,021	year	40

Employer's name and address	Supervisor's name and phone number
Internal Revenue Service	Eric Savage
Office of TPS & Compliance, Baltimore MD 20910	301-222-2222

Describe your duties and accomplishments

Summary

Worked with the IRS as a Computer Specialist Intern to satisfy the internship requirement for my Computer Specialist Associate Degree from the Community College of Baltimore Maryland. I worked on various IRS terminals and individual computer systems to resolve problems and to return the terminals to service. Worked with Microsoft Office desktop software applications used by the IRS. Performed data entry tasks in Excel and Access for operational managers. Worked with the IRM staff to restore systems and assisted with day-today automation tasks such as system backup, resetting the LAN, configuration control, and administrative functions.

Towards the end of the internship I was able to maintain the specialist's desktop units unassisted and had full responsibility for the office's daily system backup, email account management, coordination with automation vendors, and IRM parts ordering for the office.

Continued on a Separate Page

4) Job title (if Federal, include series and grade)

Communications System Repairman U.S.ARMY

From (MM/YY)	To (MM/YY)	Salary	per	Hours per week
05/30/89	06/01/91	$ 9,789	year	40

Employer's name and address	Supervisor's name and phone number
United Stated Army (Active Duty) National Training Center	Msgt Don Riley
11th Armored Cavalry Regiment, Operations Group, Fort Irwin, CA 92310-5067	760-999-9999

Describe your duties and accomplishments

Summary

Attained the rank of Sargent and was responsible for maintained and servicing the training center's field communications systems such as FM handsets, VHF and UHF transmitters and receivers used to communicate with air support and armored cavalry command units. I was assigned collateral duties to maintain field computers used to direct and coordinate troop movements with headquarters command.

Duties

- ➤ Repair and service FM hand held transceivers
- ➤ Repair VHF/UHF Transceivers
- ➤ Program field computers used for troop movement
- ➤ Work with computer specialists to repair field computers
- ➤ Order supplies to insure sufficient stock of parts on hand
- ➤ Troubleshoot telephone systems and switching equipment

Continued on a Separate Page

OF 612 Continuation Page

SMITH, John Q.	Page 1	123-45-6789
Management Analyst, GS-0343-07	99-0916 LV	GS-07

Question 13 - Other Qualifications

4/93 Microsoft Word
5/93 Microsoft Excel
2/94 Quality Worklife & Team Work (1 week)
7/94 Work Station Integration & LAN Connectivity (1 week)
7/95 NOVEL Certification Course (2 weeks)
6/96 Microsoft Office Professional (1 week)
9/97 LAN/WAN Office Configuration management Course (6 weeks) Sponsored by employer

In addition to the courses I have taken to acquire further knowledge for the positions I have held, I also have experience and expertise in the following areas:

Interpersonal Relations
I deal effectively and professionally with all people. I am a team player as evidenced by my military background and success at Frederick Corp to integrate and consolidate branch offices. I enjoy working in groups and have been trained in Quality Worklife and Partnership initiatives.

Communications Skills
I am experienced in dealing successfully with all types of people at all educational levels.I am a member of Toastmaster's **International** and have achieved the level of *"Competent Toastmaster."*

Writing Skills
I have an excellent grasp of the English language and have experience in a variety of different writing styles including reports, grants, informational material, speeches, brochures and promotional materials.I have authored several automation software articles that have been published in major journals and national magazines.

Training Skills
I have demonstrated my abilities in the area of training by developing and conducting classes for office software for over 200 employees. I have taught in a class room environment and provided on-the-job training to individual users on an as needed basis. I use the *Job Centered Training* methods that were used by the IRS when I was an intern their in 1991.

Computer Skills
Since 1985 my interest in computers has led to experience with all types of personal computers, and I have expertise in word processing, database management, spreadsheets, desk top publishing, form design and BASIC programming. I have an Associates degree in IRM Automation and have taken numerous evening courses in all facets of automation. During my tenure with Fredrick's I designed and was their web master for the corporation's internet web site. I also develop internet web sites in the evenings for small companies.

Office Skills
I am knowledgeable in all aspects of office operations and am proficient in operating a wide variety of office machinery including calculators, word processors, copiers, postage meters, telephone systems (including PBX), fax machines, electronic mail and computer modems as well as all types of audiovisual equipment such as slide and film projectors, tape recorders, and video recorders and cameras. I have an in depth knowledge of Powerpoint and have developed and fielded 5 major presentations for upper management in this format.

Work Experience Continuation

SMITH, John Q.   1) Computer Analyst - Page 1   123-45-6789
Management Analyst, GS-0343-07   99-0916 LV   GS-07

I am **Novell Certified** and proficient in most Microsoft software applications including but not limited to:
Word, Excel, Powerpoint, Scheduler, Project, Frontpage 98 and Access. I have trained over 127 users in these applications over the past two years. I also develop web sites at home for small companies and my sites have won several internet design awards. Over the past two years I have had 3 articles published in major national magazines on NOVELL upgrades and system integration issues.

DUTIES

- Technical automation expert for our Leesburg Virginia headquarters Novell LAN operation
- Analyze and advise management on all aspects of LAN operations and WAN integration
- Train detached staff office warehouse managers on system integration and LAN applications
- Perform feasibility studies concerning support staff automation needs at field facilities
- Maintain IBM NT computer work stations at headquarters for 127 employees
- Maintained company lotus ccmail for the entire organization. Updated address databases and worked with vendors concerning major problems and software failures
- Train 127 users on new system functions and software applications
- Maintain the company's internet web site
- Performed cost/benefit evaluation for work station NT Upgrade.
- Recommended field system upgrade and LAN integration through Wynnframe deployment
- Develops the company's annual (IRM) Information *Resource Management* budget
- Site automation administrator maintaining all user data, access levels, and system security passwords and documentation.
- Initiate daily backups for LAN data
- Maintain a comprehensive technical and software application library for users
- Debug, repair and service operating systems and software/hardware throughout the organization

ACCOMPLISHMENTS

- Developed written automation configuration reports to upper management to consolidate three field offices and personnel into a central hub facility at Baltimore Maryland.
- Management accepted my Wynnframe LAN field integration recommendation after I performed a cost/benefit analysis and feasibility study for the upgrade. I developed Gant and Milestone charts to accomplish upgrade, then provided training and integration after field installations were completed.
- Developed the company's internet web site on my own time. Management accepted first proposal after viewing an interactive Powerpoint presentation that I developed and viewing a live online demonstration that featured the web site's functionality. I received a substantial cash bonus for developing this site.
- A member of the company's strategic planning committee. I researched and performed a cost/benefits analysis for our automation needs through 2005 and developed Y2K strategies for the year 2000. All systems are now Y2K compliant and we have a long term IRM plan developed for major new system integration for 2003.This is coincident with a major expansion to two additional states scheduled for 2004.

Work Experience Continuation

SMITH, John Q.
Management Analyst, GS-0343-07

2) Computer Specialist - Page 1
99-0916 LV

123-45-6789
GS-07

DUTIES

> Coordinate and maintain terminal repair for all employees and managers
> Performed daily backup of critical branch office databases
> Provided one-on-one training to staff and managers for Microsoft desk top applications
> Maintain and monitor special projects involving automation software deployment within the organization.
> Researched and developed email internet accounts for all employees
> Assigned site administrator duties that included terminal and database security, database and pass word user definitions, and virus protection upgrade deployment for all users
> Upgraded systems as new replacement equipment was purchased
> Coordinated internet accounts for all system users

Accomplishments

> Analyzed the upgrade of our server to the latest NOVELL version and lead the upgrade initiative. The upgrade went smoothly with minimal down time and impact to our users and customers.
> Wrote numerous reports on various IRM issues including NOVELL upgrade, user system upgrades, and Oracle database deployment to all branch offices.
> Developed a new IRM security directive/regulation that was accepted by headquarters for use throughout the organization.
> Required to investigate the feasibility of implementing a paperless administrative corporate office. Developed a plan that included researching options, deployment strategies, and cost/benefit analysis. Initiated plan which included OCR scanners for all incoming documents and electronic daily files for all incoming and outgoing correspondence. LAN directories were assigned to all major program areas and hourly automatic file backup procedures were initiated.

Work Experience Continuation

SMITH, John Q.   3) Computer Specialist Intern, GS-02 - Page 1   123-45-6789
Management Analyst, GS-0343-07   99-0916 LV   GS-07

Contacted taxpayer account processors to:

- ◆   Coordinate computer system restoration.
- ◆   Perform Virus computer scans.
- ◆   Initiate corrective actions based upon user complaints under supervision of a senior computer specialist.

My duties and responsibilities also included:

- ◆   IRM parts ordering and supply stock.
- ◆   System daily backup
- ◆   Assisting specialists with software familiarization
- ◆   Verified account passwords for users
- ◆   Data entry for various spreadsheets and databases
- ◆   CPU repair including hard drive replacement, SIMMs upgrade, Modem installations, Keyboard replacement, and system configuration integrity checks.

Work Experience Continuation

SMITH, John Q.   4) Communications System Repairman U.S.ARMY - Page 1   123-45-6789
Management Analyst, GS-0343-07   99-0916 LV   GS-07

- ➢   Top Secrete clearance for Crypto communications and maintenance

Accomplishments

- ➢   Coordinated the utilization of limited communication resources for field deployment at the training center for over 2,000 active duty and reserve troops. Prioritized order of delivery and level of communications needed for deployments of various types.
- ➢   Crypto trained for Top Secrete scrambled communications between command centers and senior field command officers. Responsible for safeguarding equipment and destroying it at all costs if enemy infiltration discovered.
- ➢   Prioritized critical communications with limited resources determining who or which field command unit would receive support and when.
- ➢   Evaluated and developed a communications deployment scheme with automation support that was implemented throughout the Department of Defense.

RESUMIX
AUTOMATED RANKING AND REFERRAL SYSTEM

RESUMIX® generally refers to the products of Resumix corporation. These products are designed to use software and artificial intelligence to review large amounts of resumes, index them, and determine which ones meet the requirements of a position and are suitable for further review.

Resumix is being used for filing most U.S. Appropriated Fund positions within the Department of Defense, the Air Force, and the Veteran's Administration.[2] It is designed to streamline and expedite recruiting. The system is being used successfully in many larger private sector organizations including Continental Airlines and Disney Corporation. The DOD intends to use RESUMIX for recruiting current federal employees within the DOD, transferees from other federal agencies, or former federal employees seeking reinstatement. The DOD recently announced that it will no longer accept any other forms of applications for recruitment of status employees, current federal workers. U.S. Citizens currently not employed by the U.S. Government would use the traditional competitive application methods mentioned earlier in this chapter.

With RESUMIX resumes are E-mailed to a dedicated computer where the format is reviewed. After the review, properly formatted resumes are forwarded to the RESUMIX database. The same procedure applies to resumes received via mail except those are scanned directly into the database. The computer reads your resume and identifies information such as your name, address, education, and your unique skills.

E-mail is the preferred way to send a resume since they are processed faster and are not subject to errors that are introduced through handling via surface mail. Submit your E-mail resume in the body of the E-mail message, **NOT AS AN ATTACHMENT**. If the resume is submitted as an attachment it will not be accepted. The slightest fold, crease, or faded character normally causes the system to reject hardcopy resumes during the scanning process.

Resumix can extract up to 80 skills from a resume. It is important that you list the skills most relevant to the career field in which you are interested. When describing your work experience, you should clearly explain how you obtained the skills you identified. These skills are then used to match against management criteria for vacant positions. You should also list your awards, and other pertinent information. *Quick & Easy Federal Jobs Kit* will format your Resume to Resumix standards and it evaluates the resumix format for potential scanning errors.

---

[2] Excerpted from "Resumix Resume Job Kit," April 1999. Department of Defense.

Status employees, current federal workers, may only have one resume on file at any given time within a Department or agency. In order to received consideration, you must submit your **two-page** resume along with any required supplemental data sheets and transcripts when required. Agencies that accept RESUMIX applications provide lists of occupations that require supplemental forms and transcripts. They also provide applicants with specific guidance and tailored supplemental forms for job vacancies within their department. The standard RESUMIX process requires bidders to:

- Read the agency instructions
- Follow instructions and submit resume in accordance with guidelines
- Give accurate information
- Inform the agency of any changes in your status
- Provide required forms
- Keep abreast of changes in procedures and policies (check their website frequently)
- Read announcement thoroughly
- Check the qualifications requirements carefully

The Department of the Army has an extensive internet web site for overseas employment at http://cpol.army.mil/. This site only accepts 2 page Resumix formatted resumes and they offer a complete RESUMIX (*Resume Job Kit*) that you can print out and review. They also have an online *Resume Builder* that you can use to develop your resume for submission under this program. With Resumix, current federal employees, submit only one application for the Department of the Army's resume database. You don't apply for any one job. Your resume goes into a database and the employee self nominates him/herself for job vacancies. This eliminates multiple submissions of applications and dramatically reduces personnel office workload. The employee is responsible for simply going online and updating his/her resume as changes occur and to self nominate themselves for jobs that they wish to apply for.

If you are a current federal employee who is seeking overseas employment visit the web site mentioned in the previous paragraph and explore their site. You can also use their *Resume Builder* to complete your application online. The *Resume Builder* is located at http://cpol.army.mil/resume/resume.cgi/.

Currently Resumix is limited, for the most part, to internal agency bids under the Merit Promotion Plan process. These job announcements are reserved for current federal employees within an organization that wish to bid on other higher paying jobs. However, this may spread to the competitive sector as well as the efficiencies of the system are evaluated and found economically feasible.

Form Approved
OMB No. 3206-0219

OPTIONAL APPLICATION FOR FEDERAL EMPLOYMENT - OF 612

You may apply for most jobs with a resume, this form, or other written format. If your resume or application does not provide all the information requested on this form and in the job vacancy announcement, you may lose consideration for a job.

1 Job title in announcement	**2** Grade(s) applying for	**3** Announcement number

4 Last name	First and middle names	**5** Social Security Number

6 Mailing address		**7** Phone numbers (include area code)
City	State ZIP Code	Daytime
		Evening

WORK EXPERIENCE

8 Describe your paid and nonpaid work experience related to the job for which you are applying. Do **not** attach job descriptions.

1) Job title (if Federal, include series and grade)

From (MM/YY)	To (MM/YY)	Salary per	Hours per week
		$	
Employer's name and address			Supervisor's name and phone number

Describe your duties and accomplishments

2) Job title (if Federal, include series and grade)

From (MM/YY)	To (MM/YY)	Salary per	Hours per week
		$	
Employer's name and address			Supervisor's name and phone number

Describe your duties and accomplishments

9 May we contact your current supervisor?

YES [   ]   NO [   ] ▶ If we need to contact your current supervisor before making an offer, we will contact you first.

EDUCATION

10 Mark highest level completed. **Some HS** [   ] **HS/GED** [   ] **Associate** [   ] **Bachelor** [   ] **Master** [   ] **Doctoral** [   ]

11 Last high school (HS) or GED school. Give the school's name, city, State, ZIP Code (if known), and year diploma or GED received.

12 Colleges and universities attended. Do **not** attach a copy of your transcript unless requested.

Name		Total Credits Earned		Major(s)	Degree - Year
		Semester	Quarter		(if any) Received
1)					
City	State ZIP Code				
2)					
3)					

OTHER QUALIFICATIONS

13 **Job-related** training courses (give title and year). **Job-related** skills (other languages, computer software/hardware, tools, machinery, typing speed, etc. **Job-related** certificates and licenses (current only). **Job-related** honors, awards, and special accomplishments (publications, memberships in professional/honor societies, leadership activities, public speaking, and performance awards). Give dates, but do **not** send documents unless requested

GENERAL

14 Are you a U.S. citizen?   YES [   ]   NO [   ] ▶ Give the country of your citizenship.

15 Do you claim veterans' preference? NO [   ]   YES [   ] ▶ Mark your claim of 5 or 10 points below.

5 points [   ] ▶ Attach your DD 214 or other proof. **10 points** [   ] ▶ Attach an *Application for 10-Point Veterans' Preference* (SF 15) and proof required.

16 Were you ever a Federal civilian employee?

				Series	Grade	From (MM/YY)	To (MM/YY)

NO [   ]   YES [   ] ▶ For highest civilian grade give:

17 Are you eligible for reinstatement based on career or career-conditional Federal status?

NO [   ]   YES [   ] ▶ If requested, attach SF 50 proof.

APPLICANT CERTIFICATION

18 I **certify** that, to the best of my knowledge and belief, all of the information on and attached to this application is true, correct, complete and made in good faith. **I understand** that false or fraudulent information on or attached to this application may be grounds for not hiring me or for firing me after I begin work, and may be punishable by fine or imprisonment. **I understand** that any information I give may be investigated.

SIGNATURE   **DATE SIGNED**

Knowledge, Skills and Abilities (KSAs)

KSAs are also referred to as Knowledge, Skills, Abilities, and Other Characteristics (KSAOs). They are required for the selecting official to identify the best qualified candidate for the position. Most look at writing KSAOs as drudgery, however it is a necessary part of your employment application, if requested on the job announcement. To qualify for a position you must meet two types of factors; *Selective Factors* and *Quality Ranking Factors*.

KSAOs are attributes needed to perform a specific job function that are demonstrate through qualifying training, education and experience. The following definitions will help you understand what the selecting official is looking for when reviewing your submissions:

Knowledge - An organized body of information, usually of a factual or procedural nature, which if applied, makes adequate performance on the job possible.

- Examples include knowledge of:

    Federal Regulations and Directives
    Operational systems and procedures
    Budget and accounting principals
    Engineering practices
    Environmental Compliance Law
    Administrative practices

Skill - The manipulation of date, things, or people through manual, mental or verbal means. Skills are measurable through testing, can be observed, and quantifiable. Often referred to expertness that comes from training, practice, etc.

- Examples include skill in:

    Keyboard data entry
    Motor vehicle operation
    Computer software proficiency
    Electronic or computer repair
    Carpentry, plumbing and/or HVAC repair
    Second language proficiency

Ability - The capacity to perform a physical or mental activity at the present time. Typically abilities are apparent through functions completed on the job. Abilities and skills are often interchange in KSAOs. The main difference is that ability is the capacity to perform where a skill is the actual manipulation of data, things or people.

You may have the ability but unless observed through actions that ability may not transfer to a skill set.

•   Examples include the ability to:

        Organize and plan work (observed at work)
        Analyze situations, programs and problems
        Communicate orally and in writing
        Coach and mentor others

Other Characteristics - Mental or physical attributes or characteristics that don't fall under the other areas.

•   Examples are:

        <u>Proactive</u> - takes initiative to get things done without prompting
        <u>Copes well in stressful environments</u> - handles complex tasks
        <u>Reliability</u> - assigned work is completed ahead of schedule and the quality of work is exceptional
        <u>Multiple work assignments</u> - capable of successfully handling various and sundry tasks

This factor is required for jobs that to a greater degree encounter these characteristics such as jobs with the Federal Aviation Administration in air traffic control, work at nuclear power plants, and careers in law enforcement.

SELECTIVE FACTORS

All applicants must meet the *Selective Factors* for a position which are over and above the minimum experience and education requirements in the Qualification Standards Handbook. After meeting the basic *Selective Factors* you can achieve a higher ranking score if you meet or exceed the *Quality Ranking Factors* (QRFs) as annotated on the job announcement. QRFs aren't required to meet basic eligibility, there purpose is to provide the selecting official with additional information that demonstrates how well you will perform the duties of the position.

QUALITY RANKING FACTORS

Quality Ranking Factors must be taken seriously for you to rate as high as possible. Most, feel, "Why should I have to reinvent the wheel, I've already completed a comprehensive application - Just read it - it's all in there!" Don't get discouraged. This is a natural feeling and most applicants don't want to bother. After all, when you applied in the private sector all you gave them was a short one or two page resume!

You have to remember that this is the Federal government. You have to complete the paperwork to beat out your competition. Federal government jobs are rated this way to eliminate favoritism and to provide a level playing field for all those who apply. Keep this in mind when completing your application and your chances of landing a job will increase substantially.

Each agency develops their own unique QRFs and there can be as few as one to as many as a dozen or more. The most I've had to complete during my 33 years of government service was eight. The higher the grade position you are applying for the more likely QRFs will be required. Some agencies require special forms while others only specify the factor and ask you to address each on in detail on a separate piece of paper.

There are a number of rating systems used by various agencies and the methods even differ within agencies. Some use point systems from 1 to 10, others simply evaluate the KSA as meets or exceeds the standard, still others use designations such as "Below Expectations," "Average," or "Above Average." If you call the contact person identified on the announcement, you may be able to obtain a copy of their rating guide. Follow the guidance on the announcement and provide all of the information they require. KSA's require contact information including names, phone numbers, and addresses so the personnel specialist or selecting official can verify your information.

There are often limits on the amount of data you can submit. For example, many KSAOs are limited to one typewritten page per KSAO, etc. I suggest highlighting or underline each requirement on the announcement so that you will provide all requested information.

INSTRUCTIONS FOR ADDRESSING KSAO'S

If a special form isn't required, list each KSAO title on a separate sheet of plain bond paper, and follow it with a description of what you did to meet this KSAO and include in each KSAO any of these relevant elements:

- Education
- Training
- Experience
- Volunteer work
- Outside Activities
- Awards, Licenses, etc.

You must include a narrative that indicates the degree to which you possess the KSAO and include each of the bullets listed above that apply in that narrative. For each work example or accomplishment listed, describe the situation, problem, or objective of the assignment, what was done, and the results obtained. Statements should be limited to one typewritten page per KSAO. Following the narrative, the applicant must indicate: * The duration (date) of the activity, and * The name and telephone number of a person who can verify the information provided, if available. Applicants may attach copies of any relevant documents that will help substantiate their statements, such as performance evaluations, awards, or work products. The applicant's narrative must indicate exactly how these documents relate to the KSAO. DO NOT INCLUDE SUCH DOCUMENTS UNLESS THEY ARE DIRECTLY RELEVANT.

Formatting Your KSAOs

You can format your KSAOs in a narrative form starting with "I" or use bullets that start with a forceful verb such as organized, directed, managed, coordinated, analyzed, or conducted to provide action to your statements. If you don't refer directly to an experience block be sure to summarize the experience and provide the time that you performed that function. If you are applying for a supervisory position mention the number of people that you supervised, their status such as part time or full time and pay grade if applicable.

After writing your KSAs review them a number of times asking yourself "what did I do," "When did I do it," "where did I perform these functions" and don't forget the proverbial question, "How often and how much did I do it." If you didn't answer these questions edit your work until it is included. Add examples either in the narrative or by attaching an example which is permitted in most cases.

Another factor that many overlook is the depth of training that you completed. Include correspondence study, seminars, classes, lectures, computer based instruction, on-the-job training, every facet of training that you received including software programs that you taught yourself.

Include special licenses, registration exams, or certifications that you obtained in your specialty. If you are a Medical Assistant and passed the (RMA) Registered Medical Assistant Exam, annotate that on your application and in your KSAOs. If you are in the trades and have various equipment operator's licenses list items such as "Fork Lift Operator" certification, list whatever is relevant to the job announcement.

The following KSAOs were excerpted from Announcement Number 02-ADP-156 that closed on 1/11/2002. This announcement was located on OPM's USAJOBS web site. Note that all of the KSAOs could apply to almost any position and that if you are bidding on the GS-05/07 you have only four to complete. If you bid on the higher grade positions GS-09/11 you must complete an additional two KSAOs.

Sample Supplemental Qualification Statements are provided for each of the first four elements. If special forms are not provided or if specific formats are not specified follow the sample outline to submit your narratives. Notice the use of bullets and short concise statements. You want to attract the selecting official to your key qualifications and good formatting techniques and the use of bullets, bold and underlined type will focus the readers attention to your information. If you run everything together it is difficult for the selecting official to focus on the key elements that you accomplished to satisfy the factor. Include all required information and be sure to add your name, job announcement number and position title at the top of each page.

You will find that some books suggest placing your Social Security Number (SSN) at the top of each page of your KSAOs. I suggest that you only use your SSN if it is specifically requested. Your SSN is annotated on your OF-612 or in your Federal style resume, it really isn't needed here.

SAMPLE KSAOs

GS-05/07 Level Ranking Factors

QUALIFICATION REQUIREMENTS: One year experience at/or equivalent to the next lower grade for current/former federal employees. One year experience for non-federal employees. RANKING FACTORS: These are mandatory to be considered for a position and will be used to determine who the highest qualified candidates are.

1. Demonstrated ability to organize and coordinate work within schedule constraints and handle emergent requirements in a timely manner.

2. Demonstrated ability to monitor important and complex projects concurrently.

3. Knowledge of Microsoft Word, Excel, Powerpoint, and Lotus Notes/other E-mail software.

4. Demonstrated ability to effectively communicate orally and in writing, to include writing and preparing memorandums, letters, and other official correspondence.

GS-09/11 Level Ranking Factors

QUALIFICATION REQUIREMENTS: One year experience at/or equivalent to the next lower grade for current/former federal employees. One year experience for non-federal employees.

RANKING FACTORS: In addition to the above ranking factors, applicants at the GS-9/11 level must address the following two ranking factors. These are mandatory to be considered for a position and will be used to determine who the highest qualified candidates are.

1. Demonstrated knowledge of administrative/office management skills.
2. Demonstrated ability to gather, assemble, and analyze facts to include drawing conclusions and recommending solutions.

SAMPLE KSAOs

Job Title: Administrative Officer, GS-341-05/11
Announcement Number: 02-ADP-156
Applicant's Name: John Smith

KSA #1 *Demonstrated ability to organize and coordinate work within schedule constraints and handle emergent requirements in a timely manner.*

I performed the following duties in my current position (Block A):

- Managed the office suspense lists for all office supervisors. Transcribed meeting minutes and compiled action item lists, annotated due dates and specified responsible parties. Sent reminders to responsible parties, kept list current and upward reported accomplishments to the office manager weekly.

- Planned and coordinated two annual share holders meeting for over 700 stock owners, key management and staff. Drafted the itinerary, set up the registration booth, arranged for morning breakout sessions, planned lunch and the shareholders meeting from 1:00 to 3:00 pm. Also staffed the shareholders information booth after the meeting.

Award: Received an award for exemplary service for planning and organizing the 2001 meeting, <u>copy attached</u>.

- Required to frequently complete short notice work assignments including reports, transcribing meeting minutes, and payroll accounting tasks. I am the chief headquarters Payroll clerk and I provide backup to 12 field offices. If any of the field office clerks or supervisors are not available I complete their payroll reports prior to the cutoff time.

- Responsible for notifying management of pending funding shortfalls and providing justification for additional fund requests. I analyzed budget reports for trends, calculated spend rates and recommended reallocation of funds to satisfy pending or potential shortages.

Training:

1.   Certificate : 24-hour Meeting Preparation and Planning seminar, March 1999

2.   40 - hour Time Management Course, RMC Services, April 2001

Job Title: Administrative Officer, GS-341-05/11
Announcement Number: 02-ADP-156
Applicant's Name: John Smith

KSA #2 *Demonstrated ability to monitor important and complex projects concurrently.*
Performed these duties in my present position from 1/1/99 to the present (Block A):

- Budget analyst duties - Trend tracking, monitor and control of the Office's annual budget of $350,000. Performed budget data entry, compiled reports, tracked trends, anticipated fund shortages in various program areas and drafted requests for additional funds for management's signature. Audited program areas to insure fund expenditures were justified and properly classified.

- Payroll chief clerk - Insured timely submission of all payroll data before the cutoff date each pay period, entered amendments, and researched pay problems for 37 employees. I advised management of problems and notified them when to review and approve the attendance for each pay period.

Training: 80 - hour Peachtree accounting software class, by Peachtree, January 1999.

Performed the following duties in my previous position as Administrative Officer, GS-0341-7, with the USDA from 10/4/96 to 12/31/98 (Block B):

- Organizational Charts & Staffing - Processed revisions to and generated complex organizational charts based on input from the management team. Reviewed proposed changes to insure they conformed to authorized levels and that positions were properly classified. Concurrently, prepared, and tracked personnel actions for 124 employees and provided support in various program areas including payroll, benefits, staffing, and budget areas.

- Office of Workmen Compensation Program (OWCP) Program - Conducted annual (OWCP) seminars for managers and supervisors. Seminars included guidance on procedures, claims processing and post accident interventions. Provided guidance to immediate supervisors of injured employees and maintained the OSHA 200 log for all accidents.

Award: Cash award, June 1998, for managing the OWCP program, copy attached.

Training: 60 - hours Position Management and Position Classification Course, 012-V-933, Graduate School, USDA Washington D.C., June 1997.

Job Title: Administrative Officer, GS-341-05/11
Announcement Number: 02-ADP-156
Applicant's Name: John Smith

KSA #3 *Knowledge of Microsoft Word, Excel, Powerpoint, and Lotus Notes/other email software.*
Performed these duties in my present position from 1/1/99 to the present (Block A):

- Proficient in Microsoft Office, Word, Excel, Powerpoint and Lotus and I use Lotus notes for office e-mail. Developed a 34 page powerpoint presentation (copy attached) for our CEO to use at the 2002 annual stock holders meeting in Memphis Tennessee. The presentation received rave reviews and I was asked to develop similar presentations for other meetings. Worked closely with accounting to compile the data and then integrated it into a colorful and succinct visual presentation. I use WORD for all office correspondence.

- Conducted Microsoft Word and Excel mini-training sessions for those less proficient in the office. Typically sessions ran 1-2 hours in length. Attended various software system seminars including Microsoft Office, Peachtree Accounting, and our new Lotus Notes e-mail program.

Volunteer Work: Performed these duties while working as a volunteer for United Way over past 6 years. Approximately 12 hours a week. (Block E):

- Developed our chapter's web site (http://www.HELPUnited.org) using Microsoft Frontpage 98. I consider myself very proficient in web site development and I learned Frontpage through self study and experimentation. This web site consists of 48 pages, two databases and we use a secure server for confidential assistance requests. I'm the Webmaster. Contact the United Way Chairperson, Ms. Mary Jones for verification at 890-123-4567.

Performed the following duties in my previous position as Administrative Officer, GS-0341-7, with the USDA from 10/4/96 to 12/31/98(Block B):

- Proficient in VISO. I used VISO to generate ORG Charts while at the USDA.

- Proficient in several Payroll & T&A software systems including IPPS, the USDA's Integrated Personnel and Pay System.

Training Certificates: 24-hour <u>VISO software course</u> and a 16-hour <u>IPPS software course</u> both completed at our Regional Office, May 1998.

Job Title: Administrative Officer, GS-341-05/11
Announcement Number: 02-ADP-156
Applicant's Name: John Smith

KSA #4 *Demonstrated ability to effectively communicate orally and in writing, to include writing and preparing memorandums, letters, and other official correspondence.*

Performed these duties in my present position from 1/1/99 to the present (Block A):

- **Written Guidance** - Developed Standard Operation Procedures (SOPs) for program areas including payroll administration, office suspense tracking, monitor and control, and general office procedures. Adopted by the Regional Office for use throughout the organization, sample attached. I also wrote numerous internal memorandums within my program areas that provided direction for specific functions and clarified company policy issues.

  I also Prepare transmittal forms for project files, letters to share holders, fax cover letters, e-mail messages to team leads and customers, flip charts for meetings, Power Point presentations, proof and edit management draft correspondence, and prepare replies to organizational reports.

- **Oral Communications** - In current capacity I teach office software to small groups, brief management team of progress at meetings, give presentations at inter-office meetings and to small groups of share holders.

Volunteer Work

- I speak at various fund raisers for our local United Way and prepare written presentations to our work group and Chairperson. I organized and hosted a dozen fund raisers since 1994. Contact the United Way Chairperson, Ms. Mary Jones for verification at 890-123-4567.

Education: Completed 12 semester hours, 3 courses in communications, at Duguesne University in 1997; Report Writing, Oral Communications I and Effective Writing Techniques.

Training:
1) **Competent Toastmaster.** Joined Toastmasters International in 1995. Obtained Competent Toastmaster status in 1997. Chapter President, Dan McCormick, 321-6543-0987. Certificate attached.
2) **Certificate;** Constructive Communications With The Public, USDA Course 01501, June 1996. Interpersonal Communications, Seminar 1996, sponsored by OPM.

KASOs CHECKLIST

Use this list to insure that you have included key information. It's important to consider these areas when drafting your KSAO statements. When you first start to draft your KSAOs don't worry about the specifics such as exact dates, contact information, etc. You can add that later. It is best to simply write down any and everything, even the least significant events. After you get it all down then add specifics and put them in logical sequence. Review and rewrite your KSAOs at least three times and more if needed. Let your draft sit overnight and review it again the next day. You will be surprised at what you left out on the first draft.

❑ **Experience** - Include experience for all offices, departments or agencies that you worked for to show depth and range of experience. For example, include that you tracked inter-office correspondence at multiple locations, or that you tracked budgets for headquarters. Also show expertise in what you do well such as having A++ certification, maintain LANS/WANS for several locations, thoroughly familiar with Peachtree accounting software, proficient at office organization, etc.

❑ **Supervision** - If you don't have a supervisory background, did you work independently with minimal supervision and make decisions for your program areas? If so state that in your KSAOs. Were you assigned to be an acting supervisor on several occasions? Do you draft memorandums and letters for your supervisor's signature? Do you manage/supervise programs or projects?

❑ **ComplexityFactors** - Did you write reports or work on large projects coordinating activities for various groups? Does your job impact the safety of others and what standards do you follow and utilize in your present and past jobs? Do you have certifications, licenses, specific training, or accreditation that would help you land this job?

❑ **Achievements and Impact** - How did you show initiative and creativity in your office while working under adverse conditions? Where you responsible for major programs, product, or activity? If so list them. What did you do to save time, money, resources or to improve the work environment?

❑ **Awards/Recognition** - Include all awards, monetary, letters of achievement, time-off awards, or write-ups in your office newsletter. Include scholastic nominations as well and any service awards or recognition received from volunteer work.

❑ **Contacts** - If you dealt with headquarters staff, the general public, EPA or OSHA inspectors, local authorities, or government officials, list them in your KSAOs.

❑ **Fashionable Trends** - Mention current trends such as "BPE" Business Process Engineering, Model Work Environment initiatives, MBO - Management by Objectives, Partnership, Quality Work Groups, etc. If you have exposure to there and other initiatives list them in your write-up.

Chapter Seven
Veterans and Military
Dependent Hiring Programs

There are several special emphasis civil service employment programs available to veterans. *Veterans Preference*[1] and the *Veterans Readjustment Act (VRA)* are two of the better known programs. Unknown to many, military dependents and spouses of active duty personnel receive hiring preference for government jobs under the *Military Spouse Preference Program and the Family Member Preference Program.*

Over 24% of all federal employees are veterans.

When vacancies are announced by an agency, the selecting official can fill the position by:

✎ Internal promotions or reassignments of existing federal workers;

✎ Reemploying former employees;

✎ Using approved special purpose noncompetitive appointments such as the VRA, Spouse Preference, and Military Dependent programs; and,

✎ Appointing a new employee who has successfully completed an examination. The examination can be either written or an extensive examination of your past work experience and education as listed on a Federal Employment Application.

---

[1] Authorized by Law Title 5 USC, Section 2108 and Section 3501.

VETERANS PREFERENCE

When an agency advertises job vacancies through the Office of Personnel Management or locally through direct hire authority the agency must select from the top rated eligible applicants. The official may not pass over a Veterans Preference eligible, however, and appoint a nonpreference eligible lower on the list unless the reasons for passing over the veteran are sufficient.

Veterans preference gives special consideration to eligible veterans looking for federal employment.[2] Veterans who are disabled or who served on active duty in the United States Armed Forces during certain specified time periods or in military campaigns are entitled to preference over nonveterans both in hiring into the federal civil service and in retention during *reductions in force*. There are two classes of preference for honorably discharged veterans:

Five Point Preference

Five-point preference is given to those honorable separated veterans (this means an honorable or general discharge) who served on active duty (not active duty for training) in the Armed Forces:

- During any war (this means a war declared by Congress, the last of which was World War II); **or**

- For more than 180 consecutive days, other than for training, any part of which occurred after 1/31/55 and before 10/15/76; **or**

- During the period April 28, 1952, through July 1, 1955; **or**

- During the Gulf War from August 2, 1990, through January 2, 1992; **or**

- In a campaign or expedition for which a campaign medal has been authorized, such as El Salvador, Lebanon, Granada, Panama, Southwest Asia, Somalia, and Haiti, qualifies for preference.

A campaign medal holder or Gulf War veteran who originally enlisted after September 7, 1980, or entered on active duty on or after

---

[2] Reference OPM's "Vet Info Guide" available online at http://www.opm.gov/veterans/html/vetsinfo.htm.

October 14, 1982, without having previously completed 24 months of continuous active duty, must have served continuously for 24 months or the full period called or ordered to active duty.

Effective on October 1, 1980, military retirees at or above the rank of major or equivalent, are not entitled to preference unless they qualify as disabled veterans.

Ten Point Preference

Ten-point preference is given to:

- Those honorably separated veterans who 1) qualify as disabled veterans because they have served on active duty in the Armed Forces at any time and have a present service-connected disability of 10% or more or are receiving compensation, disability retirement benefits, or pension from the military or the Department of Veterans Affairs; or 2) are Purple Heart recipients;

- The mother, widow, widowers, or spouses of a veteran who died in service or who is permanently and totally disabled. This is called "derived preference."

When applying for Federal jobs, eligible veterans should claim preference on their application or resume. Applicants claiming 10-point preference must complete **form SF-15**, Application for 10-Point Veteran Preference. This form is included in the *Quick & Easy Federal Jobs Kit* Software program. See the back-of-book catalog for complete information. Veterans who are still in the service may be granted 5 points tentative preference on the basis of information contained in their applications, but they must produce a DD Form 214 prior to appointment to document entitlement to preference.

Note: Reservists who are retired from the Reserves but are not receiving retired pay are not considered "retired military" for purposes of veterans' preference.

The Veterans' Preference Advisor system allows Veterans to examine the preferences for which they might be entitled with regard to Federal jobs. This Advisor was developed by the Veterans' Employment and Training Service.

To find out whether you qualify for veterans' preference, visit America's Job Bank, operated by the Department of Labor (DOL). The Internet address for the veterans' preference program is:

(http://www.dol.gov/dol/vets/public/programs/programs/preference/main.htm)

The Department of Labor's Office of the Assistant Secretary for Policy (OASP) and Veterans' Employment and Training Service (VETS) developed this "expert system" to help veterans receive the preferences to which they are entitled. This system is designed to help veterans determine the type of preference to which they are entitled, the benefits associated with the preference and the steps necessary to file a complaint due to the failure of a Federal agency to provide those benefits.

(State employment service offices have veteran representatives available to assist veterans in gaining access to this information.)

> ## PURPLE HEART RECIPIENTS ARE CONSIDERED TO HAVE A SERVICE CONNECTED DISABILITY

VETERANS EMPLOYMENT OPPORTUNITIES ACT

This law was passed in 1998 and it gives veterans access to Federal job opportunities that might otherwise be closed to them. The law requires that:

- Agencies allow eligible veterans to compete for vacancies advertised under the agency's merit promotion procedures when the agency is seeking applications from individuals outside its own workforce.

- All merit promotion announcements open to applicants outside an agency's workforce include a statement that these eligible veterans may apply.

- OPM create an appointing authority to permit the appointment of these individuals if they are selected.

The law also establishes a new redress system for preference eligibles and makes it a prohibited personnel practice for an agency to knowingly take or fail to take a personnel action if that action or failure to act would violate a statutory or regulatory veterans' preference requirement (more about this later).

How Preference Applies In Competitive Examination

Veterans who are eligible for preference and who meet the minimum qualification requirements of the position, have 5 or 10 points added to their passing score on a civil service examination. For scientific and professional positions in grade GS-9 or higher, names of all eligibles are listed in order of ratings, augmented by veterans' preference points, if any. For all other positions, the names of 10-point preference eligibles who have a service-connected disability of 10 percent or more are placed ahead of the names of all other eligibles. Other eligibles are then listed in order of their earned ratings, augmented by veterans' preference points. A preference eligible is listed ahead of a nonpreference eligible with the same score.

WHAT DOES THIS MEAN!!!

If you apply for a federal job, your knowledge, skills and abilities will be rated on a point system. You will receive points for related education, experience, special skills, awards, and written test if required. To qualify for a position you must have a score of 70 to 100 points. If an eligible five-point preference candidate accumulates 90 points, five additional points are awarded on preference for a total score of 95. Therefore, the preference veteran, in most cases, must be hired before an agency can hire anyone with 95 points or less in this example. If that same vet accumulated 100 points their final score with preference would be 105 points. A 10-point preference vet would have a total score of 100.

Vets who ace the exam will go to the top of the list since only veteran preference veterans can exceed 100 points on the exams. For example, a disabled vet can earn a maximum score of 110 points if they accumulate 100 points on the exam.

The agency must select from the top 3 candidates (known as the Rule of 3) and may not pass over a preference eligible in favor of a lower ranking non-preference eligible without sound reasons that relate directly to the veteran's fitness for employment. The agency may, however, select a lower-ranking preference eligible over a compensably disabled veteran within the Rule of 3.

A preference eligible who is passed over on a list of eligibles is entitled, upon request, to a copy of the agency's reasons for the pass over and the examining office's response.

If the preference eligible is a 30 percent or more disabled veteran, the agency must notify the veteran and OPM of the proposed passover. The veteran has 15 days from the date of notification to respond to OPM. OPM then decides whether to approve the passover based on all the facts available and notifies the agency and the veteran.

> **_Entitlement to veterans' preference does not guarantee a job. There are many ways an agency can fill a vacancy other than by appointment from a list of eligibles._**

Filing Applications After Examinations Close

A 10-point preference eligible may file an application at any time for any position for which a nontemporary appointment has been made in the preceding 3 years; for which a list of eligibles currently exists that is closed to new applications; or for which a list is about to be established. Veterans wishing to file after the closing date should contact the agency that announced the position for further information.

SPECIAL APPOINTING AUTHORITIES FOR VETERANS

The following special authorities permit the noncompetitive appointment of eligible veterans. Use of these special authorities is entirely discretionary with the agency; no one is **entitled** to one of these special appointments:

The Veterans' Readjustment Appointment (VRA)

The VRA is a special authority by which agencies can appoint an eligible veteran without competition at any grade level through General Schedule (GS) 11 or equivalent. The VRA is an excepted appointment to a position that is otherwise in the competitive service. After 2 years of satisfactory service, the veteran is converted to a career-conditional appointment in the competitive service. (Note, however, that a veteran may be given a noncompetitive temporary or term appointment based on VRA eligibility. These appointments do not lead to career jobs.)

When two or more VRA applicants are preference eligibles, the agency must apply veterans' preference as required by law. (While all VRA eligibles have served in the Armed Forces, they do not necessarily meet the eligibility requirements for veterans' preference under section 2108 of title 5, United States Code.)

Eligibility Requirements

To be eligible for a VRA appointment the veteran must:

- have served in the Armed Forces on active duty (not active duty for training or inactive duty as a Reservist) for more than 180 days, any part of which occurred after August 4, 1964, (or February 28, 1961, for those who actually served in the Republic of Vietnam) and been separated under conditions other than dishonorable.

  The 180-day requirement does not apply to veterans who were discharged or released from active duty because of a service connected disability, or members of the Reserve or National Guard ordered to active duty under 10 United States Code (U.S.C.) 12301(a), (d), or (g), 12302, or 12304 for service during a period of war as defined in 38 U.S.C. 101(11) or in a campaign or expedition for which a campaign badge is authorized. "Period of war" includes World War II, the Korean conflict, Vietnam era, the Persian Gulf War, or the period beginning on the date of any future declaration of war by the Congress and ending on the date prescribed by Presidential proclamation or concurrent resolution of the Congress; **and**

  meet the qualification requirements for the position. The individual's military service is considered qualifying for positions at GS-3 and below. For positions above GS-3, the   appointee must meet the qualification requirements, but the agency may waive any written test requirement. If a test is required, a designated agency examiner may administer the test noncompetitively.

Time Limits

To be eligible for a VRA appointment, an otherwise eligible veteran must be appointed within 10 years of his or her last discharge from active duty. This time limit does not apply to a veteran with a 30 percent or more service-connected disability.

Making Appointments

Ordinarily, an agency may simply appoint any VRA eligible who meets the basic qualifications requirements for the position to be filled without having to announce the job or rate and rank applicants. However, as noted, veterans' preference applies in making appointments under the

VRA authority. This means that if an agency has 2 or more VRA candidates and 1 or more is a preference eligible, the agency must apply veterans' preference. Furthermore, an agency must consider all VRA candidates on file who are qualified for the position and could reasonably expect to be considered for the opportunity; it cannot place VRA candidates in separate groups or consider them as separate sources in order to avoid applying preference or to reach a favored candidate.

How to Apply

Complete a Federal Employment Application, resume, or SF-171 and forward it to selected agencies. Refer to the resources listed in Chapter Three and the Appendices for specific agency addresses and telephone numbers. Also visit http://federaljobs.net for direct links to over 200 federal agency recruiting sites. **Blank standard forms are printed in Chapter Six with complete line by line instructions**. You can also request blank forms from any local federal government office or download forms from federaljobs.net or the OPM web site.

Send a cover letter with your application explaining that you are a VRA candidate and would like to be considered for an appointment with that agency. Send a copy of your DD-214 form with your cover letter and application.

Follow up each application with a phone call. Often it helps to call an agency first and obtain a name and address to which you can send an application. Send applications to every office and department that interests you. You can send copies of your application. However, each copy must be personally signed.

Agencies **do not have to hire through the VRA program**. Only if your education and work experience meets their requirements, they have openings, and like what they see, will they make you an offer. Be tactful and don't be demanding.

30 PERCENT OR MORE DISABLED VETERANS

These veterans may be given a temporary or term appointment (not limited to 60 days or less) to any position for which qualified (there is no grade limitation). After demonstrating satisfactory performance, the veteran may be converted at any time to a career-conditional appointment.

Terms and conditions of employment

Initially, the disabled veteran is given a temporary appointment with an expiration date in excess of 60 days. This appointment may be converted to at any time to a career conditional appointment. Unlike the VRA, there is no grade limitation.

How To Apply

Veterans should contact the Federal agency Personnel office where they are interested in working to find out about opportunities. Veterans must submit a copy of a letter dated within the last 12 months from the Department of Veterans Affairs or the Department of Defense certifying receipt of compensation for a service-connected disability of 30% or more.

Disabled Veterans Enrolled in VA Training Programs

Disabled veterans eligible for training under the Department of Veterans Affairs' (VA) vocational rehabilitation program may enroll for training or work experience at an agency under the terms of an agreement between the agency and VA. The veteran is not a Federal employee for most purposes while enrolled in the program, but is a beneficiary of the VA.

The training is tailored to individual needs and goals so there is no set length. If the training is intended to prepare the individual for eventual appointment in the agency (rather than just work experience), OPM must approve the training plan. Upon successful completion, the veteran will be given a Certificate of Training showing the occupational series and grade level of the position for which trained. This allows any agency to appoint the veteran noncompetitively for a period of 1 year. Upon appointment, the veteran is given a Special Tenure Appointment which is then converted to career-conditional with OPM approval.

EXCEPTED APPOINTMENT UNDER SCHEDULE B

Authorized by the Veterans Employment Opportunities, this authority permits an agency to appoint an eligible veteran who has applied under an agency merit promotion announcement that is open to candidates outside the agency.

To be eligible for a Schedule B appointment, a candidate must be a preference eligible or veteran separated after 3 years or more of continuous active service performed under honorable conditions.

Terms and conditions of employment

Veterans given a Schedule B appointment are in the excepted service. The appointment does not lead to competitive status. However, these appointees may be promoted, demoted, or reassigned at their agency's discretion, and may apply for jobs (whether in their own or other agencies) under the same terms and conditions that applied to their original appointment -- i.e., they may apply only when the agency has issued a merit promotion announcement open to candidates outside the agency.

Veterans interested in applying under this authority should seek out agency merit promotion announcements open to candidates outside the agency. Applications should be submitted directly to the agency.

Positions Restricted To Preference Eligibles

Examinations for custodian, guard, elevator operator and messenger are open only to preference eligibles as long as such applicants are available.

VETERAN'S COMPLAINTS

Veterans who believe they have not been afforded their rights have several avenues to pursue, depending upon the nature of the complaint and the individual's veteran status. Any veteran with a legitimate complaint may contact any OPM Service Center. Service Centers are listed in Appendix B.

MILITARY DEPENDENT HIRING PROGRAMS

Dependents of military and civilian sponsors and spouses of active duty military personnel receive hiring preference when applying for civilian employment with Department of Defense Agencies. The Military Family Act expanded hiring preference to many jobs previously not available to this program and for jobs within the states, territories, and U. S. Possessions.[3]

The U.S. Army in Europe hires the majority of civilian employees. Most are either residents of the host country or family members of military and civilians officially stationed in Europe. The largest number of European vacancies were in Germany with additional vacancies in Belgium, Italy, Saudi Arabia, the Mid-East, and Africa. The majority of jobs in the Pacific region are in Korea, Japan, and the Philippines. A limited number of positions are also available in the states.

Family Member Employment Assistance Programs are available at most large bases. These programs are sponsored by local Civilian Employ-

---

[3] DOD Instruction (DODI) 1400.23 (Appendix 3)

ment Offices and Family Support Centers to provide employment information, career assistance and counseling, job skills training, and personal development workshops.

MILITARY SPOUSE PREFERENCE PROGRAM

Military Spouse Preference Programs concentrate on placement into competitive civil service vacancies in the 50 states, the territories, the possessions, the District of Columbia, and in foreign areas. Noncompetitive positions for spouse preference are generally Excepted Service and *Nonappropriated Fund Instrumentality (NAFI)* positions.[4] NAFI jobs are in service clubs, exchanges, retail stores, snack bars, base services, and related activities.

Preference is given for employment in Department of Defense (DOD) civilian positions for which a military spouse is *best-qualified* at pay grades GS-1 through GS/GM-15 or equivalent.[5]

Best qualified doesn't mean the highest rated candidate. This term is used to identify anyone who meets the basic requirements for the position. Generally, the only candidates with a higher preference are veterans and career civil service employees displaced from their jobs through a reduction in force.

COMPETITIVE POSITIONS

NONSTATUS applicants are those who have never worked for the government and must establish eligibility. Individuals can also establish eligibility at overseas Department of Defense (DOD) locations.

Previous federal employees, called *STATUS* applicants, may have reinstatement eligibility. They must submit a current application and a copy of their most recent (SF) 50, Notification of Personnel Action, and a copy of their last government performance appraisal to the appropriate *Civilian Personnel Office* (CPO).

EXCEPTED SERVICE AND NAFI POSITIONS

The majority of overseas positions are *Excepted Service*. Each employing CPO maintains a list of qualified and available candidates. Excepted Service applicants must complete an employment application and supplemental forms required by the CPO. Applicants for NAFI positions require a service application form such as the Army's DA-3433. All required forms are provided by local CPOs.

---

[4] DOD Instruction (DODI) 1401.1 "Personnel Policy for NAFI.

[5] Public Law 99-1435 "DOD Authorization Act" 11/8/85, Section 806.

ELIGIBILITY

A spouses' eligibility begins 30 days before the military sponsor's overseas reporting date. A spouse with less than six months time remaining in the area may be non-selected for permanent continuous positions. Also, preference entitlement ends when the spouse accepts or declines (whichever occurs first) any position expected to last longer than 12 months at any acceptable grade level. Preference is limited to positions in the same commuting area as that of the new duty station. However, a spouse may compete for positions, without preference, outside the commuting area. Spouse preference can be exercised only once for each permanent relocation of the military member.

HOW TO APPLY

Spouses can apply for preference at any armed forces or defense agency facility within the commuting area of the military member's duty station. You can apply at any service branch in your area. Contact your local CPO for employment information and application forms.

FAMILY MEMBER PREFERENCE

Most family member positions are clerical. However, family members are eligible to apply for any position for which they qualify. Family members of both military and civilian sponsors are given equal preference for positions designated for U. S. citizen occupancy, after military spouse and veteran's preference, for employment in nonsupervisory positions at pay grades of GS-8 or below.

Normally, family members are appointed under Excepted appointments which cannot extend longer than 2 months beyond the sponsor's departure or separation date. Family members hired under this program do not acquire competitive civil service status, but may gain eligibility for Federal Civil Service re-employment (under Executive Order 12362) when returning to the States.

EXECUTIVE ORDERS 12362 and 12721

Eligible family members who worked overseas may be non-competitively appointed on a career-conditional basis to a competitive position in the United States including Guam, Puerto Rico, and the Virgin Islands. Eligible family members can apply to any position in the United States for which they meet all qualification requirements and time-in-grade restrictions provided that he or she:

1) Is a citizen of or owes permanent allegiance to the United States;

2) Accumulated 52 weeks of creditable overseas service in an appropriated fund position(s) under an overseas local hire appointment(s) within any 1--year period beginning after January 1, 1980. The service of regularly-scheduled employees, whether employed on a permanent, part-time basis, is computed on the basis of the calendar time the employee spent in the position;

3) Received a fully successful or better performance rating for the period of creditable overseas service;

4) Was a family member of a Federal civilian employee, a non-appropriated fund employee, or of a member of a uniformed service (the civilian or uniformed sponsor) who was officially assigned to the overseas areas during the period of creditable overseas service.

5) Accompanied the civilian or uniformed sponsor on official assignment in the overseas areas while serving in the overseas position during the period of creditable overseas service.

6) Is appointed by March 31, 1998 or three years from the date of their return to the United States (whichever is later) from the overseas tour of duty during which he or she acquired eligibility; and

7) Meets the qualification requirements for the position in the United States for which he or she is applying.

The appointment can be made to any occupation and grade for which you are qualified. Non-competitive means you can apply for a position advertised on a local vacancy announcement which is open to transfer and reinstatement eligibles. An agency may waive any requirement for a written test after determining that the duties and responsibilities of the overseas position were similar enough to make the written test unnecessary.

Executive Order eligibility entitles you to register in the DOD Priority Placement Program (PPP) when you return to the United States.

APPLICATION PROCEDURES

Most Excepted Service and NAFI stateside and overseas vacancies are filled by local Civilian Personnel Offices (CPOs). Stateside competitive positions are controlled by OPM in most cases while overseas competitive positions are often handled by CPOs that have direct hire authority.

Army, Air Force, Navy and Marine installation Family Support Centers work with local CPOs to offer family members employment assistance, career counseling and in some cases skills training. Family Support Centers have slightly different names within each military branch. In the Army they are called Army Community Service (AWS) offices. Contact your local Support Center for additional information.

If a military sponsor is relocating to a new duty station, family members should contact the CPO or Family Support Center at the new location and request employment information. CPOs provide detailed job information and often provide the names of other federal agencies in the commuting area, as well as non-federal personnel offices.

Family member counseling is provided by local CPO Recruitment and Placement offices upon request and at least thirty days prior to departing an area.

SPOUSE PREFERENCE APPLICATION PROCEDURES

You are encouraged to call the Human Resource Office (HRO) for an appointment to pre-register within 30 days of your departure. For pre-registration, you will need to bring a copy of your Permanent Change of Station orders and application. Contact the local HRO for application details. You typically must submit an employment application along with a detailed statement that includes: your name; the name of the installation or activity at which you are applying; a statement that you have not been offered and declined a position for which you applied under spousal preference during your current PCS; the position title or number for which you are applying; and a copy of the service member's official orders, attached to the statement and application.

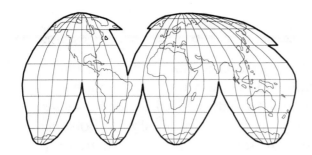

Chapter Eight
Overseas Employment Opportunities

Thousands of United States citizens work for the federal government in foreign countries, in the United States territories, Alaska, and Hawaii.[1] The positions that are most often available are administrative, technical and professional, accountants, auditors, foreign service officers, budget and program officers, management analysts, nurses, procurement officers, shorthand reporters, equipment specialists, engineers, social workers, housing officers, teachers, and alcohol and drug abuse specialists. Clerical (clerk-typist, stenographer) and secretary positions are normally filled locally overseas.

> In 2001 there were 89,431 federal employees stationed overseas in over 140 countries. The Defense Department is the largest overseas employer with 53,796 workers. The State Department is the #2 overseas employer with 17,468 employees stationed abroad.

Positions are filled in several ways. In the U.S. territories, Hawaii, and Alaska most positions are filled through competitive civil service announcements. Various positions overseas are filled through Excepted Service and Nonappropriated Fund Instrumentality (NAFI) hiring programs. Excepted Service positions are described in Chapter Three. Nonappropriated Fund positions are paid using money generated within the Department of the Army and other military branches through sales revenues. These positions are primarily governed by military regulations.

---

[1] ARMY Civilian Personnel Office Online

When positions are filled locally overseas, U.S. citizens living abroad, dependents of citizens employed or stationed overseas, or foreign nationals, can be hired. Most countries have agreements with United States installations that require the hiring of local nationals whenever possible to bolster the local economy. All positions held by foreign nationals are in the Excepted Service. Excepted Service positions are not subject to OPM's competitive hiring requirements.

Of the 89,431 overseas civilian federal employees, 63,248 are U.S. citizens as of July 2001.[1] Since 1999, total overseas federal civilian employment dropped by 14,490 positions.

The drop in total overseas employment can be attributed to military downsizing. The Department of Defense is the largest employer of civilians overseas. Consequently, the majority of lost jobs were associated with military base closings.

Most of the upper-and mid-level positions are filled through internal placement. Internal placement allows government employees wanting to work overseas to first apply for the positions in-house. If there are no in-house bidders, agencies then advertise through competitive announcements. Overseas applicants should contact individual Agency and OPM web sites for job listings.

CONDITIONS OF EMPLOYMENT

Overseas workers must meet various requirements: physical, security, qualifications, tour of duty, etc. Announcements list specific restrictions, conditions, and special qualifications.

PHYSICAL EXAMINATIONS

Individuals wanting to work overseas must meet certain stringent requirements. Thorough physical exams for both the applicant and, in many cases, accompanying dependents require physicals. You must be able to physically adapt to the conditions at various locations that may not have adequate health care facilities. Individuals on medication or who require special care will not be considered for certain positions. Any physical impairment that would create a hazard to others or to yourself, or would reduce performance level, will disqualify the applicant.

SECURITY CLEARANCE CHECKS

All applicants considered for appointment must pass a comprehensive security clearance, character and suitability check. These investiga-

---

[1] Federal Publication OMSOE-OWI-07-01, Federal Civilian Workforce Statistics, July 2001.

tions take from a few weeks to several months to complete. If you are selected for a position you will be appointed conditionally, pending the results of the investigation.

TRANSPORTATION AGREEMENTS

Individuals selected for overseas assignment are generally required to sign a transportation agreement. Typically, overseas tours last from twelve to thirty-six months.

FOREIGN LANGUAGE REQUIREMENTS

A foreign language that would not be a position requirement in the States may be required for certain overseas positions. The job announcement will specify if a language is required. Several agencies appoint candidates without the required language skill and give them a period of time to develop acceptable language proficiency.

DEPENDENTS

Most agencies permit professional employees to take dependents with them. Professional positions are generally considered to be mid-level positions and above. Other employees can often arrange for dependents to follow them at a later date.

Government employees' dependents are often given priority employment consideration at U.S. overseas facilities. Your spouse may receive hiring preference.

PAY AND BENEFITS

Pay is generally the same overseas for the comparable stateside position. Additional allowances such as a post differential, cost-of-living and quarters allowance, are provided where conditions warrant. Military base privileges are authorized in many circumstances and Department of Defense schools are available for dependent children through grade 12.

Basic benefits are the same for all civil service employees. Overseas employees also receive free travel, transportation and storage of household goods, and extra vacation with free transportation to stateside homes between tours of duty.

COMPETITION

There are a limited number of overseas positions and competition is keen. However, if you are well qualified and available for most locations, there are opportunities available. The normal rotation of current employees back to the United States creates a large number of recurring vacancies.

CITIZENSHIP

Applications are accepted only from U.S. citizens and American Samoans.

APPLYING FOR AN OVERSEAS JOB

Apply early. It pays to apply for federal jobs well in advance of the time you will be available for employment. Many overseas jobs, especially jobs with the Department of Defense, now require submission of a RESUMIX (resume) application. Complete guidance on the RESUMIX application process is included in Chapter Six. Applications use to take six to eight weeks for processing. The new RESUMIX online application has dramatically reduced the application processing time. It may take longer if written tests are required, especially in overseas areas. Many jobs limit the number of applications available and the time allowed for filing. Applications are given out until the limit is reached or until the closing date of the announcement. Refer to Chapter Six for detailed Federal Employment Application guidance.

TEMPORARY EMPLOYMENT

Federal agencies often hire temporary employees. You may be considered for both temporary and permanent positions. If you accept a temporary appointment, your name will remain on the register for consideration for permanent positions. Temporary employment is usually for one year or less, but may be extended for up to four years.

NAFI JOBS

Department of Defense agencies employ over 140,000 *Non Appropriated Fund Instrumentalities (NAFI)* workers in post exchanges, military clubs and recreation services. These positions are not in the competitive service and they are funded by the revenue generated by the exchanges and clubs. Applications for these jobs must be submitted to the individual agencies or personnel offices. The NAF Personnel office can assist you with locating NAFI jobs worldwide:

- NAF Personnel Policy Office
  1400 Key Boulevard, Suite B200
  Arlington, VA 22209-5144
  (703) 696-3318 or (703) 696-3310
  Web Site: http://www.cpms.osd.mil/nafppoindex.html

OVERSEAS FEDERAL JOB SOURCES

This section presents resources that can be used to locate federal job announcements for overseas jobs. Refer to Chapter Three's Common Job Source lists for additional resources. Appendix D provides a complete list of federal occupations. Also refer to Appendix C for detailed descriptions of government agencies and departments.

A number of the periodicals and books listed in this chapter are available at libraries. Many publishers will send complimentary review copies of periodicals upon request.

Resource headings include job openings, *Hiring Agency Directory*, and general information. The Hiring Agency Directory lists addresses of many agencies that offer overseas employment. Job openings include publications with job ads, job hotlines, and internet web sites. The general information section lists related books, pamphlets, brochures, and computer software. All job sources are listed alphabetically.

JOB OPENINGS

Periodical with job ads

Federal Career Opportunities - Federal Research Service, PO Box 1059, Vienna, VA 22183; 1-800-822-5027 or 703-281-0200; E-mail *info@fedjobs.com*. A biweekly publication listing thousands of currently available federal jobs, $49 for a 3 month subscription, 6 bi-weekly issues or $19.97 for a one month subscription. Their vacancy listings are available in the printed version or through an on-line service at http://fedjobs.com.

Federal Jobs Digest - Breakthrough Publications, P.O. Box 594, Millwood, NY 10546; 1-800-824-5000, http://jobsfed.com, publishes a bi-weekly listing of federal job vacancies in a newspaper format, $34 for 6 bi-weekly issues. They offer a Job Matching Service for $35. The recommendation covers Job Titles and Grade Levels, not vacancies. Typically takes three to four weeks for analysis.

Federal Jobs.Net (http://federaljobs.net)
This career center helps anyone who is actively seeking government employment and current federal employees looking for career progression. Visit this site for the latest updates to this book and to locate information on all government jobs including positions overseas, jobs with the U.S. Postal Service, special appointments for people with disabilities, job application guidance, student hiring programs, veterans preference and direct links to hundreds of locations that provide guidance to job seekers. Use the direct links to over 200 agency employment sites to locate job vacancies.

Job Hotlines

Department of Defense Dependent Schools (DODDS)
(http://odedodea.edu/pers) The processing of requests for teaching positions is handled by the Department of Defense Education Activity, ATTN: Teacher Recruitment, 4040 North Fairfax Drive, Arlington, VA 22201-1634, phone: **(703) 696-3067.**

USA JOBS by Phone - Federal government job hotline **1-912-757-3000** or **202-606-2700.** Operated by the Office of Personnel Management. Phone answers 24 hours a day. Provides federal employment information for most occupations. Callers can leave voice-mail messages with their name, address, and phone number. Requested job announcements and applications are mailed within 24 hours. Easy to use on-line voice prompts and voice commands allow access with any touch tone or rotary dial telephone. (Note - Not all vacancies are listed on this service. Agencies with direct hire authority announce vacancies through their individual human resources departments.)

Peace Corps Recruiting Contacts (http://www.peacecorps.gov) The Peace Corps has numerous university programs, including: *The Peace Corps Preparatory Program, The Master's Internationalist Program, The Community College Model, Campus Compact Internships, Student Internships, Cooperative Education, Volunteer Partners,* and *Research Collaboration* programs. For specific information contact the Peace Corps, Office of Human Resource Management, Washington, D.C. 20526, phone **1-800-424-8580.**

U.S. Department of State Jobs (http://www.state.gov/m/dghr/hr). Inquires about employment in the Foreign Service should be directed to: PER/REE/REC, P.O. Box 9317, Arlington, VA 22210, phone: **703-875-7490.** Employment 24 hour hot line: **202-647-7284.** Call this number for current Foreign Service Specialist job openings. The State Department employs 28,054 employees of which 17,466 work overseas.

Internet Web Sites

Army Civilian Personnel Online (http://www.cpms.osd.mil/) Very helpful with links to the Atlantic and Pacific employment web sites. Includes RESUMIX application online forms, job listings, and much more.

Army CPO Links (http://cpol.army.mil/main/links.html)This page provides direct links to job vacancies in the Pacific, Atlantic, Korea, and all Army stateside regions as well.

Central Intelligence Agency (http://www.cia.gov/) Complete information on CIA employment opportunities with job lists.

Federal agencies that employ individuals overseas include, but are not limited to, the following agencies:

Department of Agriculture	(http://www.usda.gov)
Department of Commerce	(http://www.doc.gov)
Department of Defense	(http://www.cpms.osd.mil)
Department of Energy	(http://www.hr.doe.gov/pers/doejobs.htm)
Department of Justice	(http://www.usdoj.gov)
Department of State	(http://www.state.gov/m/dghr/hr)
Department of Transportation	(http://www.dot.gov)
Department of the Treasury	(http://www.ustreas.gov/jobs)
Department of Veteran Affairs	(http://www.va.gov)

FBI (http://www.fbi.gov/employment/employ.htm) Visit this site for complete information on job opportunities and vacancy announcements.

National Security Agency (http://www.nsa.gov:8080) Visit their employment page for vacancy announcements and for complete information on the agency and its mission.

USAJOBS - Sponsored by OPM (http://www.USAJOBS.opm.gov)
This site provides a comprehensive listing with full search capability for many federal job vacancies, general employment information, with on-line applications for some jobs and a resume builder.

HIRING AGENCY DIRECTORY

The following list of agency personnel offices that hire overseas is not complete. Some agencies employ small numbers of workers for overseas assignments.

TABLE 8-1 OVERSEAS EMPLOYMENT BY DEPARTMENT	
Department	Overseas Employment
State	17,468
Treasury	1,376
Defense	53,796
Justice	2,549
Interior	381
Agriculture	1,287
Commerce	770
Labor	43
Health & Human Services	259
Housing & Urban Development	90
Transportation	502
Energy	8
Education	5
Veterans Affairs	3,273

Department of Agriculture (FAS) http://usajobs.opm.gov/a9ag.htm

Contact the Information Division, Ag Stop 1004, 1400 Independence Avenue SW., Washington, DC 20250-1004. Phone, 202-720-7115.

The Foreign Agricultural Service (FAS) was established in 1953 to encourage foreign countries to import American farm products. Over 500 employees work at the Washington, D.C., headquarters. Another 275 employees are stationed at posts throughout the world.

This agency staffs 75 foreign posts covering 130 countries to maintain a worldwide agricultural intelligence and reporting service. Most overseas employees are members of the Foreign Service. They are selected from among agricultural economists in FAS who have passed a rigorous examination process for entry into the Foreign Service. FAS Foreign Officers are rotated between Washington assignments and 2-to-4-year assignments at overseas locations.

Positions are generally filled from the Professional and Administrative Career Examination and various agricultural occupations:

Agricultural Program Specialist	GS-1145
Agricultural Marketing Series	GS-1146
Agricultural Market Reporting	GS-1147
Agricultural Engineering	GS-0890

Economists start at the GS-9 pay grade and have promotion potential to the GS-12 grade.

The Service carries out its tasks through its network of agricultural counselors, attaches, and trade officers stationed overseas.

Department of Commerce - http://persec.whs.mil/hrsc/index.html

Employment information is available electronically through the internet or phone, 202-482-5138.

Department of Defense - http://persec.whs.mil/hrsc.osd.mil/

Human Resource Services Center, Washington Headquarters Services, Room 2E22, 5001 Eisenhower Avenue, Alexandria, VA 22233-0001,. Phone, 703-617-7434. The DOD is the largest overseas employer and provides hiring support to other federal agencies, including the Department of the Air Force and Navy, through its Overseas Employment Program (OEP). The OEP gives first consideration to qualified employees currently working at federal installations overseas. Former employees with reinstatement rights and current government employees should contact DOD

Civilian Personnel Offices (CPOs) at DOD installations. When positions can't be filled in-house, Human Resources opens a competitive register to fill the position.

Department of the Army - http://www.cpol.army.mil

The Department of the Army generally hires locals for trades, laborers, equipment operators, crafts and clerical positions. Dependents of military and civilian U.S. citizens assigned abroad receive hiring preference for many of these positions. Contact CPOs at local Army posts vacancies.

Contact their employment web site, Army Civilian Personnel Online (http://www.cpol.army.mil). This site is links to their Atlantic and Pacific over-seas employment web sites. Includes RESUMIX application online forms, job listings, and much more.

PACIFIC Opportunities - http://pacific-cpoc.ak.pac.army.mil

Civilian Personnel Operations Center, Pacific Region, ATTN: APPE-CP-OC-PS (RESUMIX), Bldg. 56, 600 Richardson Drive #6700, Fort Richardson, AK 99505-6700. There are federal civil service employees in Hawaii, Guam, Japan, Korea, the Philippines, and American Samoa.

Most federal jobs in the Pacific overseas areas are with the Department of Defense. Many positions in DOD agencies are currently filled under a special appointment authority for hiring family members of U.S. military or civilian personnel stationed in foreign areas. Jobs not filled by the special appointment authority are frequently filled by federal employees that transfer overseas or are filled by U.S. citizens living in the local areas on a temporary or time-limited basis. Generally, the greatest demand is for experienced engineering, administrative, educational, technical, and scientific occupations. Federal employees in Hawaii and Guam receive cost-of-living allowances (COLAs) in addition to their basic pay.

ATLANTIC Opportunities - http://www.chrma.hqusareur.army.mil

The majority of positions are in Germany, Belgium, Italy, and Africa. Germany is the largest employer. The majority of these jobs are filled by residents of the host country or by family members of military and civilians officially stationed in Europe. Approximately 5% are U.S. citizens who were recruited outside of Europe.

Local Army Civilian Personnel Offices (CPOs) have primary responsibility within Europe for most noncareer, technical and administrative positions.

If you seek employment with the Department of the Army, Navy or Air Force, or any other federal agency in the Atlantic region, the U.S. Army,

Europe and Seventh Army (USAREUR), located in Leiman, Germany, has been delegated the examining authority by the Office of Personnel Management for certain positions above the GS-7 grade level.

Status and Nonstatus applicants, who are seeking employment in the Atlantic Overseas Area for GS-7 and above positions, should apply through the online system listed on their web sites. You can fax applications but they prefer online applications through the RESUMIX system.

A status applicant is one who previously worked for the federal government and obtained career status. Nonstatus applicants have never worked for the federal government and must establish eligibility with the Office of Personnel Management or with an agency that has been delegated examining authority, such as the USAREUR.

Department of Defense Schools (DODDS)

Elementary and secondary schools have been operating on U.S. military bases overseas since 1946 for children of military and civilian personnel. The DODDS provides educational opportunities comparable to those offered in the better school systems in the United States. This segment of U.S. public education consists of around 224 elementary, middle, junior high, and high schools and a community college. [1]The schools are located in 13 foreign countries and in seven states, Puerto Rico and Guam, with an enrollment of approximately 106,430 students, and are staffed with approximately 15,000 employees. In comparison with the largest school systems in the United States, the overseas school system enrollment is among the top ten.

School Locations:
European Region - Belgium, England, Iceland, Netherlands, Norway, Scotland, Germany, Azores, Bahrain, Greece, Italy, Spain, Turkey
Pacific Region - Japan, Korea, Okinawa (Japan)
Americas Region - Stateside, Puerto Rico, Cuba and Guam

Salary:
Overseas salaries are comparable to the average of the range of rates for similar positions in urban school jurisdictions in the U.S. having a population of 100,000 or more.

The school year consists of 190 duty days, with a minimum of 175 days of classroom instruction. Teachers are presently paid on several

---

[1]Reference Overseas Employment Information for Teachers, http://www.usajobs.opm.gov/b1c.htm/.

different pay bands (bachelor's degree, bachelor's degree plus 15 semester hours, master's degree plus 30 semester hours, and doctor's degree).

Housing and Living Conditions

In some areas, living quarters are provided by the United States government. These quarters may be in dormitories, apartments, old hotels, converted office buildings, or new modern facilities. These U.S. government quarters are usually provided without charge.

Visit their website at http://www.odedodea.edu/pers for complete employment information or write to: Department of Defense, Education Activity, ATTN: Teacher Recruitment, 4040 North Fairfax Drive, Arlington, VA 22201-1634, phone: **(703) 696-3067.**

Department of Justice - http://www.usdoj.gov

Rm 6150, Tenth Street & Constitution Avenue, NW, Washington, DC 20530. Phone, 202-514-1432. Agency wide employment job line available at 202-514-3397.

> **Drug Enforcement Administration** (DEA) - Recruitment Division, 600-700 Army-Navy Drive, Arlington, VA 22202. Phone 202-307-1000. Employs several hundred workers overseas.
> *Drug enforcement agents and administrative.*

Department of Transportation (DOT) - http://www.dot.gov

Transportation Administrative Service Center (TASC) DOT Connection, Room PL-402, 400 Seventh Street SW., Washington, DC 20590. Phone, 202-366-9391.

Employees work in hundreds of occupations including many professional and technical categories. Employs a large number of electronics technicians and engineers. The majority of overseas employment, 460 specialists, work for the Federal Aviation Administration (FAA).

> Federal Aviation Administration (http://www.faa.gov). Visit their web site for complete employment listings for both stateside and overseas jobs.
> *Aviation safety inspectors, pilots, electronics technicians.*

Department of State - http://www.state.gov

Foreign service employees include approximately 4,500 Foreign Service Officers and over 3,400 Foreign Service Specialists who serve in more than 170 countries and in the United States. Inquires about employment in the Foreign Service should be directed to : Office of Recruitment, Examination and Employment, HR/REE, SA-1, 2401 E. St., NW, 5H, Washington, DC 20522. Phone, 202-262-8888, Fax: 202-262-8841. Inquires about civil service positions should be directed to: PER/CSP/POD, P.O. Box 18657, Washington, DC 20036-8657. A 24 hour job information line is available at 202-647-7284.

Foreign service officers, enforcement specialists, technical specialists, medical care specialists, administrative specialists, advisors, building operations, and internships.

The Foreign Service of the United States is America's diplomatic, commercial, and overseas cultural and information service. This agency assists the President and Secretary of State in planning and carrying out American foreign policy at home and abroad. Some 5,000 Foreign Service Officers of the Department of State serve as administrative, consular, economic, and political officers in more than 240 American Embassies and Consulates in over 140 countries.

The United States Information Agency (USIA) deploys 950 Foreign Service Officers abroad as public affairs, information, and cultural affairs officers.

Personnel in this agency spend an average of 60% of their careers abroad, moving at two-to four-year intervals. Many overseas posts are in small or remote countries where harsh climates, health hazards, and other discomforts exist, and where American-style amenities frequently are unavailable.

ENGLISH LANGUAGE SKILLS

The Foreign Service requires all employees to have a strong command of the English language. All Foreign Service Officers must be able to speak and write clearly, concisely, and correctly. The Departments of State and Commerce and USIA give high priority to English-language skills in selecting officers and evaluating their performance.

FOREIGN LANGUAGE SKILLS

Knowledge of a foreign language is not required for appointment. Candidates without such knowledge are appointed as language probationers and must acquire acceptable competency in at least one foreign language before tenure can be granted. Officers can attend classes at the *National Foreign Affairs Training Institute*, which offers training in over 40 languages. These agencies particularly seek persons with knowledge of Arabic, Chinese, Japanese, or Russian.

Department of the Treasury - http://www.treas.gov

1500 Pennsylvania Avenue NW., Washington, DC 20220. Phone, 202-622-2000. Almost every major field of study has some application to the work of this Service. A substantial number of positions are filled by persons whose major educational preparation was accounting, business administration, finance, economics, criminology, and law. There are, however, a great number of positions that are filled by persons who's college major was political science, public administration, education, liberal arts, or other fields not directly related to business or law.

Department of Veterans Affairs - http://www.va.gov

The VA headquarters is Located at 810 Vermont Avenue NW., Washington, DC 20420. Phone, 202-273-4800. The Department operates programs to benefit veterans and members of their families. Benefits include compensation payments for disabilities or death related to military service; pensions; education and rehabilitation; home loan guaranty; burial; and a medical care program incorporating nursing homes, clinics, and medical centers. Most overseas employment is located in Hawaii, Alaska, and Puerto Rico.

Employs most medical specialties. This system does not require civil service eligibility.

Chapter Nine
The U.S. Postal Service

The U. S. Postal Service (USPS) employs 856,550 workers in 300 job categories for positions at 39,000 post offices, branches, stations, and community post offices throughout the United States. Approximately 40,000 postal workers are hired each year to backfill for retirements, transfers, deaths and employees who choose to leave the Postal Service.

Vacancies are advertised internally by the USPS and not by the Office of Personnel Management. In 1971, the Postal Service became independent. Pay scales are determined by the Postal Pay Act and are not a part of the General Pay Schedule.

Pay starts at $22,559 per year for full time career employees at the PS-1-BB pay grade and increases to $46,947 at the PS-10-P top pay grade. The median annual salary for bargaining unit Postal Service clerks was $39,010 or $18.75 per hour. Adding benefits, overtime, and premiums, the average bargaining unit hourly rate was $24.08, yielding an effective annual compensation rate of $50,103.[1] The PS pay scale is the largest pay system in the USPS and is predominately for bargaining unit employees. There are also Executive and Administrative Schedules for nonbargaining unit employees that range from $20,875 up to an authorized maximum of $161,200 for the Postmaster General.

Adding benefits, overtime, and premiums, the average bargaining unit hourly rate was $24.08, yielding an effective annual compensation rate of $50,103.

EMPLOYEE CLASSIFICATIONS

Initial appointments are either casual (temporary) or Part-Time Flexible (Career). Hourly rates for Part-Time Flexible employees vary

---

[1]Comprehensive Statement on Postal Operations, 2000 — USPS

depending upon the position's rate schedule. Some positions are filled full-time such as the Maintenance (Custodial) classification.

Full-Time and Part-Time Flexible (career) employees comprise the *Regular Work Force*. This category includes security guards. Part-Time Flexible employees are scheduled to work fewer than 40 hours per week and they must be available for flexible work hours as assigned. Part-Time Flexible employees are paid by the hour. Hourly rates vary from $11.28 at the P1 Postal Service Schedule STEP BB 1 to $23.47 for step P Grade 10.

A *Supplemental Work Force* is needed by the Postal Service for peak mail periods and offers casual (temporary) employees two 89-day employment terms in a calendar year. During Christmas an additional 21 days of employment can be offered to Supplemental Work Force employees.

College students may be considered for casual (temporary) employment with the Postal Service during the summer months. The rate of pay is up to $11.50 per hour. Tests are not required and appointments cannot lead to a career position. Apply early for summer work. Contact Post Offices in your area by no later than February for summer employment applications.

EMPLOYMENT RESOURCES

There are several resources that provide abundant information for those interested in working for the Postal Service. Visit these sites or call the listed numbers for additional information:

http://usps.gov/hrisp (Official Postal Service Human Resources site)
http://postalemployeenetwork.com/index.htm (This site provides resources for Postal workers and they offer a free electronic newsletter subscription.)
Post Office Jobs Hotline: 1-800-276-5627 (Sponsored by the USPS)

QUALIFICATION REQUIREMENTS

Various standards from age restrictions to physical requirements must be met before you can take one of the Postal Service exams.

Age Limit

You must be eighteen to apply. Certain conditions allow applicants as young as sixteen to apply. Carrier positions, requiring driving, are limited to age 18 or older. High school graduates or individuals that terminated high school education for sufficient reason are permitted to apply at age 16.

Entrance Exams

Clerk, carrier and other specific postal job applicants must pass an entrance exam. Specialties such as mechanic, electronic technician, machinist, and trades must also pass a written test. The overall rating is based on the test results and your qualifying work experience and education. Professionals and certain administrative positions don't require an entrance exam or written test. They are rated and hired strictly on their prior work experience and education.

The **NEW 470 Battery examination** covers seven major entry level positions including:

✔ **Carrier**   ✔ **Mail handler**
✔ **Clerk**   ✔ **Mail Processor**
✔ **Distribution Clerk, Machine**   ✔ **Mark-Up Clerk, Automated**
✔ **Flat-Sorting Machine Operator**

The *470 Battery Examination* covers the majority of entry level hiring although some offices also maintain custodial registers, which by law, are reserved for veteran preference eligibles. The USPS also maintains *motor vehicle* and *tractor trailer registers* and some highly skilled maintenance positions such as *Building Equipment Mechanic, Engineman, Electronics Technician, and General Mechanic.* All of the skilled maintenance positions require examination 931. A separate announcement, examination number 932, is required for Electronics Technician positions.

Six sample exams are presented in Chapter Five and a sample *470 Battery Test* is included in Chapter Six to help you prepare for this test. The 470 examination and completion of forms will require approximately two hours and fifteen minutes. Jobs with the U.S. Postal Service are highly competitive due to the excellent salary and benefits offered. It's essential that you pass the test with the highest score possible to improve your chances. Applicants scoring between 95-100% have a better chance of being hired. An excellent study guide for the 470 Battery Test is Norman Hall's *Postal Exam Preparation Book.*

Citizenship

Applicants do not have to be U.S. citizens. If you have permanent alien resident status in the United States of America or owe allegiance to the United States of America you can apply for Postal Service Jobs.

Physical Requirements

Physical requirements are determined by the job. Carriers must be able to lift a 70-pound mail sack and all applicants must be able to efficiently perform assigned duties. Eyesight and hearing tests are required. Applicants must have at least 20/40 vision in the good eye and no worse than 20/100 in the other eye. Eyeglasses are permitted.

State Drivers License

Applicants must have a valid state driver's license for positions that require motor vehicle operation. A safe driving record is required and a Postal Service road test is administered for the type of vehicle that you will operate.

DRUG TESTING (SUBSTANCE ABUSE)

The Postal Service maintains a comprehensive program to insure a drug-free workplace. A qualification for postal employment is to be drug free, and this qualification is determined through the use of a urinalysis drug screen. When you are determined to be in the area of consideration for employment, you will be scheduled for a drug screening test.

APPLICATION PROCEDURES

Positions Requiring Written Examinations

The USPS does not maintain a national directory or register of openings. The Postal Service has a decentralized hiring process for personnel and examination related matters. The examinations are administered by examination center personnel from local Customer District Human Resources offices located in most large cities. A comprehensive listing of Customer Service District offices is provided in Chapter Four of *Post Office Jobs*.

To apply for postal positions you must contact a Management Sectional Center (MSC), Bulk Mail Center, General Mail Facilities, Customer Service District Office or a Sectional Center Facility to register for the postal workers civil service exam. Contact your local post office to find out where the tests are administered in your area. A complete listing of Postal facilities is available from the USPS in their National Five-Digit Zip Code and Post Office Directory (two volumes). A copy of this publication is usually available for use in the post office lobby.

A passing score of 70 percent or better on an exam will place the applicant's name on an eligible *register* for a period of two years. Registers are lists of job applicants that have passed an exam or evaluation process. Your score determines your placement on the register. Applicants can write to the Postal Examination office for a one-year extension. Requests for extension must be received between the eighteenth-and twenty-fourth month of eligibility. Most people hired have a score of between 90% and 100%. There is a separate register for each job classification. To improve your chances, test for as many different positions that you can qualify for.

Positions That Don't Require a Written Exam

Vacancies in these positions—generally professional and administrative—are announced (advertised) first within the Postal Service. Postal employees who have the knowledge, education, credentials, and skills may apply for these openings. If there aren't any qualified applicants (called bidders in the federal sector), then the postal service will advertise the vacancies to the general public and accept resumes and applications for rating. All applicants must pass an entrance examination and/or an evaluation process to be placed on a register in numerical score order.

VETERANS PREFERENCE

Veterans receive five or 10 point preference. Those with a 10% or greater compensable service-connected disability are placed at the top of the register in the order of their scores. All other eligibles are listed below the disabled veterans group in rank order. The Veterans Preference Act applies to all Postal Service positions. Refer to Chapter Eight for detailed information on Veterans Preference.

Custodial exams for the position of cleaner, custodian, and custodial laborer are exclusively for veterans and present employees. This exam is open only to veterans preference candidates.

POSTAL CLERKS AND MAIL CARRIERS
(The Largest USPS Occupations)

Nature of the Work

Each day, the United States Postal Service receives, sorts, and delivers millions of letters, bills, advertisements, and packages. To do this, it employs 853,300 workers. Almost three out of four of these workers are either mail handlers or clerks , who sort mail and serve customers in post offices, or mail carriers, who deliver the mail.[2]

Clerks and carriers are distinguished by the type of work they do. Clerks are usually classified by the mail processing function they perform, whereas carriers are classified by their type of route, city or rural.

About 350 mail processing centers throughout the country service post offices in surrounding areas and are staffed primarily by postal clerks. Some clerks, more commonly referred to as mail handlers, unload the sacks of incoming mail; separate letters, parcel post, magazines, and newspapers; and transport these to the proper sorting and processing area. In addition, they may perform simple canceling operations and rewrap packages damaged in processing after letters have been put through stamp-canceling machines. They are taken to other workrooms to be sorted according to

---

[2]Occupational Outlook Handbook, 2002-2003 Edition, U.S. Department of Labor

destination. Clerks operating electronic letter-sorting machines push keys corresponding to the ZIP code of the local post office to which each letter will be delivered; the machine then drops the letters into the proper slots. A growing proportion of clerks operate optical character readers (OCRs) and bar code sorters, machines that can "read" the address and sort a letter according to a code printed on the envelope. Others sort odd-sized letters, magazines, and newspapers by hand. Finally, the mail is sent to local post offices for sorting according to delivery route and delivered.

Postal clerks at local post offices sort local mail for delivery to individual customers and provide retail services such as selling stamps and money orders, weighing packages to determine postage, and checking that packages are in satisfactory condition for mailing. Clerks also register, certify, and insure mail and answer questions about postage rates, post office boxes, mailing restrictions, and other postal matters. Occasionally, they may help a customer file a claim for a damaged package.

Once the mail has been processed and sorted, it is ready to be delivered by mail carriers. Duties of city and rural carriers are very similar. Most travel established routes delivering and collecting mail. Mail carriers start work at the post office early in the morning, where they spend a few hours arranging their mail for delivery and taking care of other details.

Carriers may cover the route on foot, by vehicle, or a combination of both. On foot, they carry a heavy load of mail in a satchel or push it in a cart. In some urban and most rural areas, they use a car or small truck. Although the Postal Service provides vehicles to city carriers, most rural carriers use their own automobiles. Deliveries are made house-to-house, to roadside mailboxes, and to large buildings such as offices or apartments, which generally have all the mailboxes on the first floor.

Besides delivering and collecting mail, carriers collect money for postage-due and C.O.D. (cash on delivery) fees and obtain signed receipts for registered, certified, and insured mail. If a customer is not home, the carrier leaves a notice that tells where special mail is being held.

After completing their routes, carriers return to the post office with mail gathered from street collection boxes, homes, and businesses. They turn in the mail receipts and money collected during the day and may separate letters and parcels for further processing by clerks.

The duties of some city carriers may be very specialized; some deliver only parcel post while others collect mail from street boxes and receiving boxes in office buildings. In contrast, rural carriers provide a wide range of postal services. In addition to delivering and picking up mail, they sell stamps and money orders and accept parcels, letters, and items to be registered, certified, or insured.

All carriers answer customers' questions about postal regulations and services and provide change-of-address cards and other postal forms when requested. In addition to their regularly scheduled duties, carriers often participate in neighborhood service programs in which they check on elderly or shut-in patrons or notify the police of any suspicious activities along their route.

Postal clerks and mail carriers are classified as casual, part-time flexible, part-time regular, or full time. Casual workers help process and deliver mail during peak mailing or vacation periods. Part-time flexible workers do not have a regular work schedule or weekly guarantee of hours; they replace absent workers and help with extra work as the need arises. Part-time regulars have a set work schedule of less than 40 hours per week. Full-time postal employees work a 40-hour week over a 5-day period.

Working Conditions

Postal clerks usually work in clean, well-ventilated, and well-lit buildings. However, other conditions vary according to work assignments and the type of labor saving machinery available. In small post offices, mail handlers use hand trucks to move heavy mail sacks from one part of the building to another and clerks may sort mail by hand. In large post offices and mail processing centers, chutes and conveyors move the mail, and much of the sorting is done by machines. Despite the use of automated equipment, the work of mail handlers and postal clerks can be physically demanding. These workers are usually on their feet, reaching for sacks and trays of mail or placing packages and bundles into sacks and trays.

Mail handlers and distribution clerks may become bored with the routine of moving and sorting mail. Many work at night or on weekends because most large post offices process mail around the clock, and the largest volume of mail is sorted during the evening and night shifts.

Window clerks, on the other hand, have a greater variety of duties, frequent contact with the public, and rarely have to work at night. However, they may have to deal with upset customers, and they are held accountable for the assigned stock of stamps and for postal funds.

Most carriers begin work early in the morning, in some cases as early as 4:00 a.m. if they have routes in the business district. A carrier's schedule has its advantages, however: Carriers who begin work early in the morning are through by early afternoon, and they spend most of the day on their own, relatively free from direct supervision.

Carriers spend most of their time outdoors, and deliver mail in all kinds of weather. Even those who drive often must walk when making deliveries and must lift heavy sacks of parcel post items when loading their vehicles. In addition, carriers always must be cautious of potential hazards on their routes. Wet roads and sidewalks can be treacherous, and each year numerous carriers are bitten by unfriendly dogs.

Employment

The U.S. Postal Service employed 74,000 clerks; 324,000 mail carriers; and 289,000 mail sorters, processors, and processing-machine operators in 2000. Most of them worked full time. While some postal clerks provided window service, most processed mail. Many distribution clerks and mail processors sorted mail at major metropolitan post offices; others worked at mail-processing centers. The majority of mail carriers worked in cities and suburbs, while the rest worked in rural areas.

Postal Service workers are classified as casual, part-time flexible, part-time regular, or full time. Casuals are hired for 90 days at a time to help process and deliver mail during peak mailing or vacation periods. Part-time flexible workers do not have a regular work schedule or weekly guarantee of hours but are called in as the need arises. Part-time regulars have a set work schedule of fewer than 40 hours per week, often replacing regular full-time workers on their scheduled day off. Full-time postal employees work a 40-hour week over a 5-day period.

Training, Other Qualifications, and Advancement

Postal clerks and mail carriers must be U.S. citizens or have been granted permanent resident-alien status in the United States. They must be at least 18 years old (or 16, if they have a high school diploma). Qualification is based on a written examination that measures speed and accuracy at checking names and numbers and ability to memorize mail distribution procedures. Applicants must pass a physical examination as well, and may be asked to show that they can lift and handle mail sacks weighing up to 70 pounds. Applicants for jobs as postal clerks operating electronic sorting machines must pass a special examination that includes a machine aptitude test. Applicants for mail carrier positions must have a driver's license, a good driving record, and a passing grade on a road test.

Applicants should apply at the post office or mail processing centers where they wish to work in order to determine when an exam will be given. Applicants' names are listed in order of their examination scores. Five points are added to the score of an honorably discharged veteran, and 10 points to the score of a veteran wounded in combat or disabled. When a vacancy occurs, the appointing officer chooses one of the top three applicants; the rest of the names remain on the list to be considered for future openings until their eligibility expires, usually two years from the examination date.

Relatively few people under the age of 25 are hired as career postal clerks or mail carriers, a result of keen competition for these jobs and the customary waiting period of 1-2 years or more after passing the examination. It is not surprising, therefore, that most entrants transfer from other occupations.

New postal clerks and mail carriers are trained on the job by experienced workers. Many post offices offer classroom instruction. Workers receive additional instruction when new equipment or procedures are introduced. They usually are trained by another postal employee or, sometimes, a training specialist hired under contract by the Postal Service.

A good memory, good coordination, and the ability to read rapidly and accurately are important. In addition, mail handlers should be in good physical condition. Mail handlers and distribution clerks work closely with other clerks, frequently under the tension and strain of meeting dispatch transportation deadlines. Window clerks and mail carriers must be courteous and tactful when dealing with the public, especially when answering questions or receiving complaints.

Postal clerks and mail carriers often begin on a part-time flexible basis and become regular or full time in order of seniority as vacancies occur. Full-time clerks may bid for preferred assignments such as the day shift, a window job, or a higher level nonsupervisory position as expediter or window service technician. Carriers can look forward to obtaining preferred routes as their seniority increases, or to higher level jobs such as carrier technician. Both clerks and carriers can advance to supervisory positions.

Job Outlook

Those seeking a job in the Postal Service can expect to encounter keen competition. The number of applicants for postal clerk and mail carrier positions is expected to continue to far exceed the number of openings. Job opportunities will vary by occupation and duties performed.

Overall employment of postal clerks is expected to grow more slowly than the average through the year 2005. In spite of the anticipated increase in the total volume of mail, automation will continue to increase the productivity of postal clerks. Increasingly, mail will be moved using automated materials-handling equipment and sorted using optical character readers, bar code sorters, and other automated sorting equipment. In addition, demand for window clerks will be moderated by the increased sales of stamps and other postal products by grocery and department stores and other retail outlets.

Conflicting factors also are expected to influence demand for mail carriers. Despite competition from alternative delivery systems and new forms of electronic communication, the volume of mail handled by the Postal Service is expected to continue to grow. Population growth and the formation of new households, coupled with an increase in the volume of third class mail, will stimulate demand for mail delivery. However, increased use of the "ZIP + 4" system, which is used to sort mail to the carrier route, should decrease the amount of time carriers spend sorting their mail. In addition, the Postal Service is moving toward more centralized mail delivery, such as the use of more cluster boxes, to cut down on the number of door-to-door deliveries. Although these trends are expected to increase carrier productivity, they will not significantly offset the growth in mail volume, and employment of mail carriers is expected to grow about as fast as the average for all occupations.

In addition to jobs created by growth in demand for postal services, some jobs will become available because of the need to replace postal clerks and mail carriers who retire or stop working for other reasons. The factors that make entry to these occupations highly competitive - attractive salaries, a good pension plan, steady work, and modest educational requirements contribute to a high degree of job attachment, so that replacement needs produce relatively fewer job openings than in other occupations of this size. In contrast to the typical pattern, postal workers generally remain in their jobs until they retire; relatively few transfer to other occupations.

Although the volume of mail to be processed and delivered rises and falls with the level of business activity, as well as with the season of the year, full-time postal clerks and mail carriers have, to date, never been laid off. When mail volume is high, full-time clerks and carriers work overtime, part-time clerks and carriers work additional hours, and casual clerks and carriers may be hired. When mail volume is low, overtime is curtailed, part-timers work fewer hours, and casual workers are discharged.

Earnings

Median annual earnings of postal mail carriers were $38,420 in 2000. The middle 50 percent earned between $33,620 and $41,930. The lowest 10 percent had earnings of less than $26,140, while the top 10 percent earned over $44,040. Rural mail carriers are reimbursed for mileage put on their own vehicles while delivering mail.[3]

Median annual earnings of Postal Service clerks were $39,010 in 2000. The middle 50 percent earned between $36,140 and $41,870. The lowest 10 percent had earnings of less than $31,980, while the top 10 percent earned more than $43,590.

Median annual earnings of mail sorters, processors, and processing-machine operators were $32,080 in 2000. The middle 50 percent earned between $22,560 and $39,300. The lowest 10 percent had earnings of less than $18,940, while the top 10 percent earned more than $42,570.

Postal Service workers enjoy a variety of employer-provided benefits similar to those enjoyed by Federal Government workers. The American Postal Workers Union or the National Association of Letter Carriers, both of which are affiliated with the AFL-CIO, represent most of these workers.

---

[3] Occupational Outlook Handbook, 2002 - 2003 Edition

ADDITIONAL REFERENCE MATERIAL

Post Office Jobs: **How To Get A Job With The U.S. Postal Service**
$17.95 (Second edition)
by Dennis V. Damp

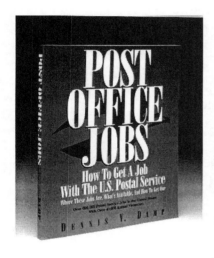

A one-stop resource for those interested in working for the Postal Service. Updated with all new contact information including new Postal Service internet sites and phone hot lines. It presents what jobs are available, where they are, and how to get one. *Post Office Jobs* dispels the myth that everyone in the postal service is a mail carrier or clerk. About a third of the 852,000 Postal Service workers are employed in hundreds of occupations—from janitors and truck drivers to accountants, personnel specialists, electronics technicians, and engineers. Many professional and administrative jobs do not require written examinations.

This book includes sample exams for most job categories with study tips by Norman Hall for the 470 Battery Test's four key testing areas. Mr. Hall has scored 100% on the United States Postal Exam four times.

Post Office Jobs presents eight steps to successfully landing a job and helps Job seekers:

❶ Identify job openings.
❷ Match skills correctly to hundreds of postal job classifications.
❸ Determine when postal exams are scheduled in their area.
❹ Prepare for exams and score between 90% and 100%.
❺ Thoroughly complete job applications and resumes.
❻ Prepare and practice for job interviews.
❼ Apply for jobs that don't require written tests.
❽ Pass the pre-employment drug screening test.

This book is available at bookstores or from the publisher's back-of-book catalog. You can also order it by phone toll free with most credit cards including Visa, Master Card, and American Express at **1-800-782-7424**.

OCCUPATIONS LIST
(Partial Listing)

Craft & Wage per hour positions:

Administrative Clerk
Auto Mechanic
Blacksmith-Welder
Building Equipment Mechanic
carpenter
Carrier
Cleaner, Custodian
Clerk Stenographer
Data Conversion Operator
Distribution Clerk
Electronic Technician
Elevator Mechanic
Engineman
Fireman
Garageman-Driver

General Mechanic
Letter Box Mechanic
Letter Carrier
LSM Operator
Machinist
Mail Handler
Maintenance Mechanic
Mark Up Clerk
Mason
Mechanic Helper
Motor Vehicle Operator
Painter
Plumber
Scale Mechanic
Security Guard

Professional

Accounting Technician
Architect/Engineer
Budget Assistant
Computer Programmer
Computer System Analyst

Electronic Engineer
Transportation Specialist
Industrial Engineer
Technical Writer
Stationery Engineer

Management

Administrative Manager
Foreman of Mail
General Foreman
Labor Relations Representative
Manager Bulk-Mail
Manager-Distribution
Manager-Station/Branch

Postmaster-Branch
Safety Officer
Schemes Routing Officer
Supervisor-Accounting
Supervisor-Customer Service
System Liaison Specialist
Tour Superintendent

Chapter Ten
Employment Opportunities
For People With Disabilities

Seven percent of the total federal civilian workforce, 189,280 people with disabilities, work for the federal government.[1] Opportunities exist at all levels of government and in hundreds of occupations. Total disabled federal employment has remained constant at seven percent since 1980. The enactment of The *Americans With Disabilities Act* (ADA) and Executive Order 13217, issued in 2001, will increase awareness of hiring options by federal managers. These programs along with numerous Office of Personnel Managment (OPM) initiative should expand total disabled employment opportunities throughout government.

Agencies have direct hire authority for trial appointments.

The federal government offers special noncompetitive appointments (special emphasis hiring options) for people with physical or mental disabilities. There are distinct advantages for managers to hire individuals under special emphasis hiring appointments. Managers are able to hire individuals under special appointments within days where it may take as long as three to six months to fill positions under the competitive process. Secondly, federal managers are tasked with specific performance targets, called *"critical job elements (CJEs)"*, for maintaining workforce diversity. All agencies are required by law to develop outreach efforts to identify qualified candidates to meet agency workforce diversity goals.

This chapter explains the various hiring options for people with disabilities. Individuals seeking appointments with the federal government must be proactive and begin networking with local agencies, contacting listed resources, and aggressively seeking out all available federal employment opportunities.

---

[1]Reported by the Office of Workforce Information 2001 FACT BOOK OWI-01-05

FEDERAL MANAGER's RESPONSIBILITES

Federal agency managers and supervisors are responsible for the employment and advancement of people with disabilities.[2] This includes recruitment, hiring, training, career development, mentoring support and considering reasonable accommodations when requested.

Career development and promotion opportunities, training, awards, and other similar programs must be an integral part of an agency's responsibilities towards employees with disabilities. Federal employers are required to make reasonable accommodations to the known physical or mental limitations of a qualified applicant or employee with a disability, unless the agency can demonstrate that the accommodation(s) would impose an undue hardship on the agency. Absent undue hardship, agencies must remove physical barriers as a matter of reasonable accommodation to particular employees for whom necessary facilities are inaccessible.

Agencies are requried to establish procedures to ensure that the employment and advancement of people with disabilities meet affirmative action program objectives, diversity planning, emphasis, and accountability. They must also ensure that there are no personnel or management policies, practices or procedures which unnecessarily restrict hiring, placement and advancement of people with disabilities.

It is illegal for a Federal agency to discriminate in employment against qualified individuals with disabilities. Anyone who believes he or she has been subjected to discrimination on the basis of disability may file a complaint with the employing agency's equal employment opportunity (EEO) office.[3]

Agencies have direct hire authority for Schedule A appointments. Therefore interested parties must contact individual agencies to determine what's available. Refer to the agency lists in Appendix C and the common resources listed in Chapter Three. Additional special hiring programs exist for disabled veterans. Refer to Chapter Six for complete details.

HIRING OPTIONS

The federal government provides opportunities for qualified persons with physical and mental disabilities. Applicants with handicaps must be considered fairly for all jobs in which they are able to perform the job duties efficiently and safely.

---

[2] Employment Guide for People With Disabilities in the Federal Government (1999)

[3] EEOC's MD-110 and 29 CFR, Part 1614. EEO complaint process.

Agency Human Resource Management departments encourage federal managers to give people with disabilities full and fair consideration, and to make accommodations when necessary. Although the majority of employees with handicaps obtain their jobs through competitive procedures, there are some for whom ordinary procedures do not function fairly or accurately. The competitive process is explained in Chapters Two and Three. To meet the needs of those with severe impairments, agencies may use the following special appointing techniques:

PEOPLE WITH SEVERE PHYSICAL DISABILITIES

This option has two different appointments:

- **Option 1 -** *Leading to Continuing Positions:* This program is designed to help qualified physically impaired people obtain employment in positions consistent with their level of skills and abilities, at grades GS-1 to GS-15 or under the Federal Wage System. (5 CFR213.3102(u))

    Requirements: Persons may be appointed if (1) they have already demonstrated their ability to perform the position duties satisfactorily on a temporary trial appointment or (2) they have been certified by counselors of State Vocational Rehabilitation Agencies or the Department of Veterans Affairs as likely to succeed in the performance of the position duties.

    Type of Appointment: Excepted service.

    Conversion to Permanent Position: After completing two years of satisfactory performance, employees may be converted to appointments in the competitive service. (5CFR 315.709)

- **Option 2 -** *Time-Limited Positions*: This authority is designed to help qualified people with physical disabilities obtain time-limited employment in positions consistent with their level of skills and abilities at grades GS-1 to GS-15 or under the Federal Wage System. (5 CFR 213.3102 (i)(3))

    Requirements: Persons may be appointed when OPM has determined that examining is impracticable.

    Type of Appointment: Excepted service.

Conversion to Permanent Position: There is no provision under this authority for conversion to a permanent appointment when the time-limited appointment expires.However, conversion to appointments which lead to continuing positions, as described above, is possible.

PEOPLE WITH MENTAL RETARDATION

This program is designed to promote the full consideration of people with mental retardation for employment in positions where they meet the performance requirements or where the performance requirements can be modified to take advantage of their abilities. (5 CFR 213.3102 (t))

Requirements: Persons may be appointed based on certification from the appropriate State Vocational Rehabilitation Agency that they have the ability to perform the position duties, are physically qualified to do the work without risk to themselves or others, and are competent to maintain themselves in a work environment.

Type of Appointment: Excepted service.

Conversion to Permanent Position: After completing two years of successful service, employees may be converted to appointments in the competitive service. (5 CFR315.709)

PEOPLE WITH PSYCHIATRIC DISABILITIES

This program is designed to help persons who are certified as at a severe disadvantage in obtaining employment because of disrupted employment due to hospitalization or outpatient treatment for psychiatric disabilities. (5 CFR 213.3202(k))

Requirements: Persons may be appointed to positions at grades GS-15 and below if they are individuals who meet two specific criteria. First, that they are placed at a severe disadvantage in obtaining employment because of a psychiatric disability evidenced by hospitalization or outpatient treatment and have had a significant period of substantially disrupted employment because of the disability. Secondly, they must be certified to a specific position by a State vocational rehabilitation counselor or a Veterans Administration counseling psychologist (or psychiatrist) who indicates that they meet the severe disadvantage criteria stated above, that they are capable of functioning in the positions to which they will be appointed, and that any residual disability is not job related.

Type of Appointment: Excepted service.

Conversion to Permanent Position: Employment of any individual under this authority may not exceed 2 years following each significant period of mental illness. There is no provision under this authority for conversion to a permanent appointment.

Note: OPM has proposed regulations that will provide individuals with psychiatric disabilities the same opportunities for conversion into the competitive civil service as employees with other disabilities. OPM plans to issue final regulations on this subject. Until the regulations are final, agencies may continue to use 5 CFR 213.3202(k) and other appropriate excepted service appointing authorities for persons with psychiatric disabilities.

TEMPORARY LIMITED APPOINTMENTS

Temporary appointments are made when the need for the position is short-term and not expected to last for more than one year. Temporary jobs are filled through competitive procedures with a requirement for public notice. Under limited circumstances, agencies may use "outside-the-register" procedures. Agencies may also give noncompetitive temporary appointments to individuals who qualify for positions and have a specific noncompetitive eligibility such as reinstatement or veterans readjustment appointment (VRA) (5 CFR 316.402).

Time Limits: Appointments are not-to-exceed 1 year; a 1-year extension is allowed.

Conversion to Permanent Position: There is no provision under this authority for conversion to a permanent appointment when the temporary appointment expires.

TERM APPOINTMENTS

Term appointments are made when the need for an employee's services will last for a period of more than one year, but no more than four years. Reasons for term appointments may include, but not be limited to, project work, extraordinary workload, and uncertainty of future funding. Term positions are filled through competitive procedures with the requirement for public notice.

These positions may also be filled by qualified individuals based on specific noncompetitive eligibility such as reinstatement and veterans readjustment appointment (VRA) (5 CFR Part 316.302).

Time Limits: Appointments are made for more than one year but not more than four years.

Conversion: This authority does not contain a provision for conversion to a permanent appointment when the term expires.

STUDENT VOLUNTEER PROGRAM

Agencies may provide educationally-related work assignments for student volunteers on a non-pay basis. (5 CFR 308.103)

Requirements: The student is enrolled at least half-time in a high school, trade school, vocational institute, university, or other accredited educational institution, and the school permits the participation of the student in a program established to provide educational experience.

Time Limits: No time limits have been established for these appointments, as long as the student continues to meet program requirements.

COMPETITIVE VERSUS EXCEPTED SERVICE

People with disabilities may start their federal career in the Excepted Service while most federal jobs are in the Competitive Service.

Congress excepted certain jobs and groups from the Competitive Service. In the competitive service individuals must compete for positions through examination. The end result is that individuals are placed on a competitive register in rank order of their rating. Agencies then can select from the top three candidates on the list when vacancies arise.

The Excepted Service includes a number of agencies such as the CIA, FBI, National Security Agency, Federal Aviation Administration, and about a dozen or so others. Specific jobs are also excepted and include the Stay-in-school program, student interns, veterans readjustment appointments, and the physically and mentally impaired programs discussed above. Excepted Service employees on permanent excepted appointments are eligible for all benefits including health insurance, life insurance, leave, retirement, and they are eligible for promotion and reassignment just like those in the Competitive Service. The first year of employment is a trial period similar to the one-year probationary period for the Competitive Service.

There are some differences between these two appointments. First, excepted service employees are not eligible for transfer to other agencies or for noncompetitive reinstatement that is afforded to competitive service employees. Excepted Service employees are also placed in a separate category when agencies go through a reduction in force, typically referred to as layoffs in private industry.

These differences cease to exist after the two year period of acceptable performance is achieved. Workers with physical or mental impairments may be converted to the Competitive Service upon supervisory recommendation as noted above for many appointments.

UNPAID WORK EXPERIENCE

Most rehabilitation organizations include on-the-job training and job placement programs for participants. Vocational rehabilitation centers work with federal agencies to place people with disabilities in jobs that provide meaningful work experience. Agencies benefit from the services provided by these workers and they get an opportunity to evaluate a prospective employee.

Federal regulations limit unpaid services from a person with disabilities to those who are clients of a State *Office of Vocational Rehabilitation* (OVR). Applicants must be enrolled in an OVR programs. Signed agreements must be initiated between the rehabilitation center and the federal agency. Agencies can negotiate these agreements individually with local Vocational Rehabilitation Facilities. Once an agreement is initiated the agreement covers all participants. Individuals accepted into these programs don't receive any compensation from the government; however, many sponsors provide a small stipend to the worker.

SPECIAL ACCOMMODATIONS

When appropriate, OPM uses special examination (testing) procedures for applicants who are physically handicapped to assure that their abilities are properly and fairly assessed.[4] Special testing arrangements are determined on an individual basis depending on the applicant's disability. For example: readers, examinations in Braille, tape, or large print for visually impaired competitors; and interpreters for test instructions and modifications of parts of tests for hearing impaired competitors.

Accommodations on the job

When federal agencies hire a person with disabilities, efforts are made to accommodate the individual to remove or modify barriers to their ability to effectively perform the essential duties of the position. Agencies may, for example: (1) provide interpreter service for the hearing impaired, (2) use readers for the visually impaired, (3) modify job duties, (4) restructure work sites, (5) alter work schedules, and (6) obtain special equipment or furniture.

APPOINTMENT CRITERIA

These procedures apply to those with severe disabling conditions or to those who have a number of minor conditions. All others are subject to the usual competitive hiring process.

Applicants establish eligibility by:

- Meeting the experience and/or education requirements in the qualification standards, including any written test requirement, or:

- Certification by state Office of Vocational Rehabilitation (OVR) or the Veterans Administration.

The OVR certification option permits agencies to waive the established qualification requirements. Employment may begin under a trial temporary appointment. If the applicant doesn't meet the qualification requirements, agencies need a certification letter from an OVR or the VA and a report of medical examination. If the applicant meets the qualification

---

[4]U.S. OPM, Office of Affirmative Employment Programs, ES-5 (GPO 0-157-269).

requirements, including any applicable exam, a medical report is the only requirement.

When the trial period performance is satisfactory the agency may convert the trial appointment to an excepted appointment. No further documentation is needed, except agency personnel actions are required to initiate this change.

In the event an agency chooses to permanently appoint a person with disabilities without a trial period, OVR or VA certification is mandatory regardless of whether the applicant meets the qualification standards. A certification letter contains the following:

1.   A statement from the applicant's counselor indicating that he/she is familiar with the duties of the position, and certification that the applicant, in the counselor's judgment, is capable of performing the duties without hazard to him or herself or others.

2.   A medical examination report or summary of one which fully describes the extent and nature of the disability.

OVR counselors should also describe any limitations, suggest job or worksite modifications, and provide any other information which could help in accommodating the applicant and making a sound judgment. Agency selective placement coordinators will assist the counselor and explain the agency's requirements.

COMMON JOB SOURCES

This section presents resources that can be used to locate federal job announcements for people with disabilities. After reviewing the listed resources refer to Appendix D for a complete list of federal occupations. A number of the periodicals and directories listed in this chapter are available at libraries. Many newsletter and periodical publishers will send complimentary review copies of their publications upon request.

Resource headings include job openings, placement services, directories, and general information. Job openings include publications with job ads, job hot lines, and internet web sites. The general information section lists related books, pamphlets, and internet fact sheets. All job sources are listed alphabetically. For additional resources refer to Chapter Three's listings.

JOB OPENINGS

Periodicals & Newspapers with Federal Job Ads

ABILITY Magazine - Jobs Information Business Service, 1001 West 17th St., Costa Mesa, CA 92627; 949-854-8700, Fax 949-548-5966. ABILITY Magazine provides information on new technologies, the "Americans with Disability Act", travel and leisure, employment opportunities for people with disabilities, human interest stories, national and local resource centers and more. ABILITY Magazine helps remove the misunderstandings and erase the stereotypes that surround disability issues. Call or visit their web site for subscription rates. Ability also offers an electronic classified system, **JobAccess**, which allows employers to recruit qualified individuals with disabilities. The goal of **JobAccess** is to enable people with disabilities to enhance their professional lives by providing a dedicated system for finding employment. People with disabilities can locate viable employment opportunities either through their print magazine or visit their excellent internet web site at **http://www.jobaccess.org/**.

CAREERS & The DisAbled (Equal Opportunity Publications) - 445 Broad Hollow Road, Suite 425, Melville, NY 11747, 631-421-9421, E-Mail: info@eop.com, internet: http://eop.com/, web site: http://eop.com. This company publishes a number of excellent target audience publications including **CAREERS & The DisAbled, Workforce Diversity, Minority Engineer, Woman Engineer and Equal Opportunity** magazines. Display ads feature national employers including the federal government seeking applicants for many varied fields. Each issue offers a dozen to sixty or more display job ads. Call for subscription rates. A resume matching service is also available to subscribers.

Internet Web Sites

Disability Direct http://disabilitydirect.gov

This New Freedom Initiative for People with Disabilities is a part of President George W. Bush's administration goals, which calls for government to use information technology to deliver government services anytime, anywhere. The site supports the adminstrations efforts to reduce barriers to the employment of people with disabilities.

The scope of DisabilityDirect.gov is comprehensive and currently includes and a comprehensive section on employment. DisabilityDirect.gov highlights current events of general interest, such as Americans With Disabilities Act (ADA) success stories, and information about employment trends, including the ever growing demand for technology workers.

Diversity Direct http://www.diversitydirect.com

Diversity Direct is an ally in the search for your next career opportunity. A free service to job seekers, this site links quality candidates with prominent companies who need their talents.

Diversity Services http://www.diversity-services.com

Diversity Services was created to address the issues of diversity in today's ever changing workplace. Diversity Services builds bridges to create workforce inclusion of all qualified individuals regardless of race, age, sexual orientation, or disability.

Federaljobs.net http://federaljobs.net

This career center will assist you with your federal government job search and guide you step-by-step through the process. You can search this site for key words and phrases. Includes a listing of over 200 federal agency employment web sites that you can visit for up-to-date job listings and agency information.

Healthcarejobs.org http://healthcarejobs.org

If you are interested in the healthcare field explore this web site for information on all heathcare career fields. Networking internet links and references are included.

JAN - Job Accommodation Network http://janweb.icdi.wvu.edu

The Job Accommodation Network (JAN) is a service of the U.S. Department of Labor Office of Disability Employment Policy hosted by West Virginia University. This highly informative site is a welath of information for those seeking employment. You can also call their toll free number at **1-800-526-7234, voice and TTY..**

JobAccess http://www.jobaccess.org
Helps employers recruit qualified individuals with disabilities. The goal of JobAccess is to enable people with disabilities to enhance their professional lives by providing a dedicated system for finding employment. People with disabilities can locate viable employment opportunities at this web site.

National Business & Disability Council http://www.business-disability.com

The National Business and Disability Council links employers and college graduates with disabilities.

State Vocational & Rehabilitation Agencies
http://jan.wvu.edu/sbses/VOCREHAB.htm

State vocational and rehabilitation agencies coordinate and provide a number of services for disabled persons. These services can include counseling, evaluation, training and job placement. There are also services for the sight and hearing impaired. Visit this site for direct links to State Vocational and Rehabilitation Agencies. You will find complete contact information including names, phone numbers, TDD numbers, addresses, internet web sites, E-mail addresses and much more. **Well worth the visit.** Call or write the office nearest you.

Unemployment Offices Listings by State http://jobhunt.com/ui/ui.shtml

This site offers internet web links to all 50 state unemployment offices. Visit this site to find the unemployment office nearest you.

Job Hotlines

Department of Veterans Affairs 800-827-1000
The Department of Veterans Affairs supports a nationwide employment training program for veterans with service-connected disabilities who qualify for vocational rehabilitation. Regional or local offices are listed under federal government agencies in the telephone directory. Social Security Administration

JAN - Job Accommodation Network 800-526-7234 & 800-ADA-WORK (V/TTY)
The Job Accommodation Network (JAN) is *not* a job placement service, but an international toll-free consulting service that provides information about job accommodations and the employability of people with disabilities. JAN is a service of the President's Committee on Employment of People with Disabilities. It also provides information regarding the Americans with Disabilities Act (ADA). Visit their web site at http://janweb.icdi.wvu.edu/.

The ARC National Employment & Training Program 800-433-5255
500 East Border, Suite 300, Arlington, TX 76010. National Organization that you may find helpful in seeking job leads, placement, training, or assistance in the employment finding process such as resume writing and interviewing techniques.

USA JOBS by Phone - Federal government job hotline **478-757-3000.** Operated by the Office of Personnel Management. Phone answers 24 hours a day. Provides federal employment information for most occupations. Callers can leave voice-mail messages with their name, address, and phone number. Requested job announcements and applications are mailed within 24 hours. Easy to use on-line voice prompts and voice commands allow access with any touch tone or rotary dial telephone. (Note - Not all vacancies are listed on this service. Agencies with direct hire authority announce vacancies through their individual human resources departments.)

PLACEMENT SERVICES

National Center For Learning Disabilities - 381 Park Ave. South, Suite 1401, New York, NY 10016; 212-545-7510, http://www.ncld.org/. Provides information, referral, public education and outreach programs on learning disabled. Offers job placement and publishes a quarterly newsletter.

State Vocational & Rehabilitation Agencies
http://jan.wvu.edu/sbses/VOCREHAB.htm
State vocational and rehabilitation agencies coordinate and provide a number of services for disabled persons. These services can include counseling, evaluation, training and job placement.

NOTE: Many of the OVR and VA rehabilitation centers offer job placement services. Many associations also offer valuable services including job placement to their members. Refer to the associations lists that follow and contact local OVR and VA facilities in your area to identify available job placement services.

DIRECTORIES

ADA Technical Assistance & Resource Manual - U.S. Equal Employment Opportunity Commission, 1801 L St., N.W., Washington, D.C. 20507; 800-669-EEOC (Voice) or 800-800-3302 (TDD). Visit their web site at http://www.eeoc.gov/ for ordering information and cost.

Encyclopedia of Associations 2001 - The Gale Group, Inc., P.O. Box 95501, Chicago, IL 60694-5501; 800-877-GALE, internet http://www.gale.com/. Lists thousands of associations and it is available at most larger libraries. Use this resource to identify associations for your specific disability. This resource is also available in two additional formats including CD ROM and online.

GENERAL INFORMATION

Associations & Organizations

The following list of associations and organizations offer numerous services to people with physical or mental impairments. Many offer job placement services, provide on-site accessibility surveys, job analysis and offer advice and support to the group represented. Contact individual listings for details of services provided.

American Cancer Society - 1-800-ACS-2345; http://www.cancer.org. Refers employers to organizations offering help in recruiting qualified individuals with disabilities, and community programs offering consultation and technical assistance to cancer patients, survivors, and their families. Publishes information on the employment of cancer patients and survivors.

American Council of the Blind - 1155 15th St., N.W., Ste. 1004, Washington, D.C. 20005; 202-467-5081 or 800-424-8666, http://www.acb.org/. Provides information on topics affecting the employment of individuals who are blind, including job seeking strategies, job accommodations, electronic aids, and employment discrimination. Provides information on job openings for individuals who are blind and visually impaired. Offers free legal assistance in employment discrimination cases.

American Speech-Language-Hearing Association - 10801 Rockville Pike, Rockville, MD 20852; 301-897-5700, 1-800-638-8255, http://www.asha.org/. Provides information and technical assistance on overcoming communication barriers.

The ARC -1010 Wayne Ave., Suite 650, Silver Spring, MD 20910, 301-565-3842, http://www.thearc.org/. (formerly Association for Retarded Citizens of the United States). This organization is the country's largest voluntary organization committed to the welfare of all children and adults with mental retardation and their families.

Arthritis Foundation - 1330 West Peachtree Street, Atlanta, GA 30309; 404-965-7537, http://Arthritis.org/. Helps people with arthritis and lupus obtain and retain employment.

Disabled American Veterans - 807 Maine Ave., SW, Washington, DC 20024; 202-554-3501, http://www.dav.org/. Provides information on recruitment sources for veterans with disabilities. Offers a broad range of services to disabled veterans.

Epilepsy Foundation of America - 4351 Garden City Dr., Landover, MD 20785; 800-332-1100 (Voice/TDD), http://www.efa.org/. Maintains a network of local employment assistance programs, which provide education and support to employers on epilepsy and employment issues including employment referrals.

Helen Keller National Center for Deaf-Blind Youths and Adults - 111 Middle Neck Rd., Sands Point, NY 11050; 516-944-8900 (Voice/TDD). Visit their web site at http://www.helenkeller.org/. Provides job placement for deaf-blind individuals, and on-site support services for employers and employees.

National Center For Learning Disabilities - 381 Park Ave. South, Suite 1401, New York, NY 10016; 888-575-7373, http://www.ncld.org/. Provides information, referral, public education and outreach programs on learning disabled. Offers job placement and publishes a quarterly newsletter.

National Down's Syndrome Congress - 7000 Peachtree-Dunwoody Road, N.E. Lake Ridge, 400 Office Park, Atlanta, GA 30328. Phone, 800-232-NDSC, http:/www.ndsccenter.org/. Provides general information on Down's Syndrome and the employment of individuals with Down's Syndrome. Provides supported employment programs for individuals with Down's Syndrome.

National Mental Health Association - 1021 Prince St., Alexandria, VA 22314; 800-969-NHMA, TTY line 800-433-5959. Web site http://www.nmha.org.

National Multiple Sclerosis Society - 6701 Democracy Blvd., Ste. 300-9, Bethesda, MD 20817. Phone: 301-588-6959, http://nationalmssociety.org.

National Spinal Cord Injury Association - 8701 Georgia Avenue., Suite 500, Silver Spring, MD 20910. Phone, 301-588-6959, visit their web site at http://www.spinalcord.org/.

Spina Bifida Association of America - 4590 MacArthur Blvd., NW, Suite 250, Washington, DC 20007-4226. Phone, 1-800-621-3141, 202-944-3285. Visit their web site at http://www.sbaa.org/.

United Cerebral Palsy Association, Inc. - 3185 8th St., NE, Washington, DC 20017; 202-269-1500, http://www.ucpa.org/.

Books, Pamphlets, & Brochures

ADA Technical Assistance & Resource Manual - U.S. Equal Employment Opportunity Commission, 1801 L St., N.W., Washington, D.C. 20507; 800-669-EEOC (Voice) or 800-800-3302 (TDD). Visit their web site at http://www.eeoc.gov/ for ordering information and cost.

JAN (Job Accommodation Network) - They will send out an informational brochure upon request. Most of the pamphlets can be reviewed online at their web site http://janweb.icdi.wvu.edu. Call 1-800-526-7234 for free consulting and information about job accommodations and the employability of people with disabilities.

Chapter Eleven
Law Enforcement Careers

Uncle Sam employs over 188,000 law enforcement personnel in over 40 job series, see table 11-1. This number includes the 26,000 new Inspectors that were created to screen and search passengers and luggage at airports nationwide. Most Federal agencies employ law enforcement specialists in some capacity or another. It's important to realize that work in law enforcement is not limited to specific investigative, police, compliance and security positions. There are tens of thousands of Federal employees working in occupations that provide direct support to these groups.

> *Over 188,000 law enforcement personnel work for Uncle Sam.*

Many of the investigative jobs have age requirements and applicants must be at least 21 years of age, and under the age of thirty seven at the time of appointment. Other positions only state that you must be 21 years of age and be a U.S. Citizens. Each job announcement will provide all of the qualifications required for that position. The point is that if you want to work in law enforcement and you are over age 37 your options are more limited and you may have to consider a support position that does not have an age requirement.

The Federal government maintains a high profile in many areas of law enforcement. The U.S. Department of Justice is the largest employer of sworn Federal officers. Federal Bureau of Investigation (FBI) agents are the Government's principal investigators, responsible for investigating violations of more than 260 statutes and conducting sensitive national security investigations. Agents may conduct surveillance, monitor court-authorized wiretaps, examine business records, investigate white-collar crime, track the interstate movement of stolen property, collect evidence of espionage activities, or participate in sensitive undercover assignments. The FBI investigates organized crime, public corruption, financial crime, fraud against the government, bribery, copyright infringement, civil rights violations, bank robbery, extortion, kidnapping, air piracy, terrorism, espionage, interstate criminal activity, drug trafficking, and other violations of Federal statutes.[1]

U.S. Drug Enforcement Administration (DEA) agents enforce laws and regulations relating to illegal drugs. Not only is the DEA the lead agency for domestic enforcement of Federal drug laws, it also has sole responsibility for coordinating and pursuing U.S. drug investigations abroad. Agents may conduct complex criminal investigations, carry out surveillance of criminals, and infiltrate illicit drug organizations using undercover techniques.

U.S. marshals and deputy marshals protect the Federal courts and ensure the effective operation of the judicial system. They provide protection for the Federal judiciary, transport Federal prisoners, protect Federal witnesses, and manage assets seized from criminal enterprises. They enjoy the widest jurisdiction of any Federal law enforcement agency and are involved to some degree in nearly all Federal law enforcement efforts. In addition, U.S. marshals pursue and arrest Federal fugitives.

U.S. Immigration and Naturalization Service (INS) agents and inspectors facilitate the entry of legal visitors and immigrants to the United States and detain and deport those arriving illegally. They consist of border patrol agents, immigration inspectors, criminal investigators and immigration agents, and detention and deportation officers. Nearly half of sworn INS officers are border patrol agents. U.S. Border Patrol agents protect more than 8,000 miles of international land and water boundaries. Their missions are to detect and prevent the smuggling and unlawful entry of undocumented foreign nationals into the United States, apprehend those persons found in violation of the immigration laws, and interdict contraband, such as narcotics. Immigration inspectors interview and examine people seeking entrance to the United States and its territories. They inspect passports to determine whether people are legally eligible to enter the United States. Immigration inspectors also prepare reports, maintain records, and process applications and petitions for immigration or temporary residence in the United States.

Special agents and inspectors employed by the U.S. Department of the Treasury work for the Bureau of Alcohol, Tobacco, and Firearms; the Customs Service; and the Secret Service. Bureau of Alcohol, Tobacco, and Firearms (ATF) agents regulate and investigate violations of Federal firearms and explosives laws, as well as Federal alcohol and tobacco tax regulations. Customs agents investigate violations of narcotics smuggling, money laundering, child pornography, customs fraud, and enforcement of the Arms Export Control Act. Domestic and foreign investigations involve the development and use of informants, physical and electronic surveillance,

---

[1]Occupational Outlook Handbook 2002/2003 (OHH)

and examination of records from importers/exporters, banks, couriers, and manufacturers. They conduct interviews, serve on joint task forces with other agencies, and get and execute search warrants.

Customs inspectors inspect cargo, baggage, and articles worn or carried by people and carriers including vessels, vehicles, trains and aircraft entering or leaving the United States to enforce laws governing imports and exports. These inspectors examine, count, weigh, gauge, measure, and sample commercial and non-commercial cargoes entering and leaving the United States. Customs inspectors seize prohibited or smuggled articles, intercept contraband, and apprehend, search, detain, and arrest violators of U.S. laws. U.S. Secret Service special agents protect the President, Vice President, and their immediate families, Presidential candidates, former Presidents, and foreign dignitaries visiting the United States. Secret Service agents also investigate counterfeiting, forgery of Government checks or bonds, and fraudulent use of credit cards.

The U.S. Department of State Bureau of Diplomatic Security special agents are engaged in the battle against terrorism. Overseas, they advise ambassadors on all security matters and manage a complex range of security programs designed to protect personnel, facilities, and information. In the United States, they investigate passport and visa fraud, conduct personnel security investigations, issue security clearances, and protect the Secretary of State and a number of foreign dignitaries. They also train foreign civilian police and administer a counter-terrorism reward program.

Other Federal agencies employ police and special agents with sworn arrest powers and the authority to carry firearms. These agencies include the U.S. Postal Service, the Bureau of Indian Affairs Office of Law Enforcement under the U.S. Department of the Interior, the U.S. Forest Service under the U.S. Department of Agriculture, the National Park Service under the U.S. Department of the Interior, and Federal Air Marshals under the U.S. Department of Transportation. Other police agencies have evolved from the need for security for the agency's property and personnel. The largest such agency is the General Services Administration's Federal Protective Service, which provides security for Federal workers, buildings, and property.

WORKING CONDITIONS

Law enforcement work can be very dangerous and stressful. In addition to the obvious dangers of confrontations with criminals, officers need to be constantly alert and ready to deal appropriately with a number of other threatening situations. Many law enforcement officers witness death and suffering resulting from accidents and criminal behavior. A career in law enforcement may take a toll on officers' private lives.

Uniformed officers, detectives, agents, and inspectors are usually scheduled to work 40-hour weeks, but paid overtime is common. Shift work is necessary because protection must be provided around the clock. Junior officers frequently work weekends, holidays, and nights. Police officers and detectives are required to work at any time their services are needed and may work long hours during investigations. In most jurisdictions, whether on or off duty, officers are expected to be armed and to exercise their arrest authority whenever necessary.

The jobs of some Federal agents such as U.S. Secret Service and DEA special agents require extensive travel, often on very short notice. They may relocate a number of times over the course of their careers. Some special agents in agencies such as the U.S. Border Patrol work outdoors in rugged terrain for long periods and in all kinds of weather.

EMPLOYMENT

There are approximately 188,239 law enforcement workers in the Federal government. There are many more in support occupations such as Administrative Officers, Clerks, Logistics Specialists, etc. The Justice Department is the largest employer of (GS-1811) Criminal Investigators, employing 20,933. The Treasury Department is the second largest employer of this series with 10,737 on the books. Criminal investigator total employment is 35,840. Correctional Officers (GS-0007) are employed by two agencies, The Department of Justice with 13,058 officers, and the Interior hires the remaining 38. All 6,626 of the Internal Revenue Officers (GS-1169) are employed by the Treasury Department.

The table on the follow page shows the major occupations, the total number employed and the largest employing agency. Use this list to identify viable opportunities and then contact those agency's recruiting sites or call their personnel offices. A list of agency phone numbers is included in Chapter Three and Appendix C provides a description of each agency with contact information and web site addresses.

You can use the job series or titles on the following table to search for job vacancy announcement on http://www.usajobs.opm.gov. This site allows job series or title searches and they also offer email notification for specific job series announcements. You can register on this site for free email notification for job vacancies. Also, visit the specific agency web site that hire law enforcement occupations. Not all agencies advertise on OPM's web site. You will find abundant information and in some cases online testing and applications on several law enforcement agency web sites.

TABLE 11-1 Law Enforcement Employment Occupations			
Job Series (GS)	Title	Total Employment	Largest Employing Department
0006	Correctional Administration	1,693	Justice (1,660)
0007	Correctional Officer	13,097	Justice (13,059)
0025	Park Ranger	6,276	Interior (4,821)
0072	Fingerprint Identification	818	Justice (779)
0080	Security Administration	6,719	Defense (3,631)
0083	Police Officer	8,731	Defense (3,137)
0101	Social Science	6,768	Defense (2,032)
0132	Intelligence	5,407	Defense (2,791)
0180	Psychology	3,666	Vet Admin (1,926)
0249	Wage & Hour Compliance	1,120	Labor (1,120)
0390	Communications Relay	710	Defense (382)
0436	Plant Protection/Quarantine	1,635	Agriculture (1,635)
1169	Internal Revenue Officer	6,626	Treasury (6,626)
1397	Document Analysis	118	Justice (57)
1801	General Insp., Investigation	11,205	Justice (5,337)
1802	Compliance Insp.& Support	7,552	Justice (4,901)
1810	General Investigation	2,739	Defense (1,246)
1811	Criminal Investigation	35,840	Justice (20,933)
1812	Game Law Enforcement	270	Interior (218)
1816	Immigration Inspection	4,921	Justice (4,921)
1822	Mine Safety & Health	1,244	Labor (1,244)
1854	Alcohol, Tobacco & Firearms	822	Treasury (822)
1889	Import Specialist	1,189	Treasury (1,187)
1896	Border Patrol Agent	8,265	Justice (8,265)
2121	Railroad Safety	403	Transportation (391)
2151	Radio Dispatching	431	Defense (373)
2181	Aircraft Operations	2,668	Defense (1,943)

Table 11-1 does not list support occupations that are available such as a number of occupations under General Administration, Clerical, Office Services, Communications, IT Professionals, Chemistry and Biological Science. A number of positions in these occupations are recruited in support of most law enforcement organizations.

TRAINING AND QUALIFICATIONS OVERVIEW

Federal civil service regulations govern the appointment of law enforcement officers, police and detectives. Candidates must be U.S. citizens, usually at least 20 years of age, and must meet rigorous physical and personal qualifications. In the Federal Government, candidates must be at least 21 years of age but less than 37 years of age at the time of appointment. Physical examinations for entrance into law enforcement often include tests of vision, hearing, strength, and agility. Eligibility for appointment usually depends on performance in competitive written examinations and previous education and experience. Federal agencies typically require a college degree. Candidates should enjoy working with people and meeting the public.

Because personal characteristics such as honesty, sound judgement, integrity, and a sense of responsibility are especially important in law enforcement, candidates are interviewed and their character traits and backgrounds are investigated. In some agencies, candidates are interviewed by a psychiatrist or a psychologist, or given a personality test. Most applicants are subjected to lie detector examinations or drug testing. Some agencies subject sworn personnel to random drug testing as a condition of continuing employment.

Before their first assignments, officers usually go through a period of training. In Federal departments, recruits get training in their agency's academy, often for 12 to 14 weeks. Training includes classroom instruction in constitutional law and civil rights, State laws and local ordinances, and accident investigation. Recruits also receive training and supervised experience in patrol, traffic control, use of firearms, self-defense, first aid, and emergency response.

Police officers usually become eligible for promotion after a probationary period ranging from 6 months to 3 years. Promotion may enable an officer to become a detective or specialize in one type of police work, such as working with juveniles. Promotions to corporal, sergeant, lieutenant, and captain usually are made according to a candidate's position on a promotion list, as determined by scores on a written examination and on-the-job performance.

The FBI has the largest number of special agents. To be considered for appointment as an FBI agent, an applicant either must be a graduate of an accredited law school or a college graduate with a major in accounting, fluency in a foreign language, or 3 years of related full-time work experience. All new agents undergo 16 weeks of training at the FBI academy on the U.S. Marine Corps base in Quantico, Virginia.

Applicants for special agent jobs with the U.S. Department of Treasury's Secret Service and the Bureau of Alcohol, Tobacco, and Firearms must have a bachelor's degree or a minimum of 3 years' related work experience. Prospective special agents undergo 10 weeks of initial criminal investigation training at the Federal Law Enforcement Training Center in Glynco, Georgia, and another 17 weeks of specialized training with their particular agencies.

Applicants for special agent jobs with the U.S. Drug Enforcement Administration (DEA) must have a college degree and either 1 year of experience conducting criminal investigations, 1 year of graduate school, or have achieved at least a 2.95 grade point average while in college. DEA special agents undergo 14 weeks of specialized training at the FBI Academy in Quantico, Virginia.

U.S. Border Patrol agents must be U.S. citizens, younger than 37 years of age at the time of appointment, possess a valid driver's license, and pass a three-part examination on reasoning and language skills. A bachelor's degree or previous work experience that demonstrates the ability to handle stressful situations, make decisions, and take charge is required for a position as a Border Patrol agent. Applicants may qualify through a combination of education and work experience.

Postal inspectors must have a bachelor's degree and 1 year of related work experience. It is desirable that they have one of several professional certifications, such as that of certified public accountant. They also must pass a background suitability investigation, meet certain health requirements, undergo a drug screening test, possess a valid State driver's license, and be a U.S. citizen between 21 and 36 years of age when hired.

Law enforcement agencies are encouraging applicants to take postsecondary school training in law enforcement-related subjects. Many entry-level applicants for police jobs have completed some formal postsecondary education and a significant number are college graduates. Many junior colleges, colleges, and universities offer programs in law enforcement or administration of justice. Other courses helpful in preparing for a career in law enforcement include accounting, finance, electrical engineering, computer science, and foreign languages. Physical education and sports are helpful in developing the competitiveness, stamina, and agility needed for many law enforcement positions. Knowledge of a foreign language is an asset in many Federal agencies

Continuing training helps police officers, detectives, and special agents improve their job performance. Through police department academies, regional centers for public safety employees established by the States, and Federal agency training centers, instructors provide annual training in self-defense tactics, firearms, use-of-force policies, sensitivity and communications skills, crowd-control techniques, relevant legal developments, and advances in law enforcement equipment. Many agencies pay all or part of the tuition for officers to work toward degrees in criminal justice, police science, administration of justice, or public administration, and pay higher salaries to those who earn such a degree.

JOB OUTLOOK

The opportunity for public service through law enforcement work is attractive to many because the job is challenging and involves much personal responsibility. Furthermore, law enforcement officers in many agencies may retire with a pension after 20 or 25 years of service, allowing them to pursue a second career while still in their 40s. Because of relatively attractive salaries and benefits, the number of qualified candidates exceeds the number of job openings in Federal law enforcement agencies resulting in increased hiring standards and selectivity by employers. Competition is expected to remain keen for the higher paying jobs with State and Federal agencies and police departments in more affluent areas. Applicants with college training in police science, military police experience, or both should have the best opportunities.

Employment of police and detectives is expected to increase faster than the average for all occupations through 2010. A more Security-conscious society and concern about drug-related crimes should contribute to the increasing demand for police services. Employment growth at the Federal level is currently being driven by the War on Terror, however, employment will be tempered by continuing budgetary constraints faced by law enforcement agencies.

The level of government spending determines the level of employment for police officers, detectives, and special agents. The number of job opportunities, therefore, can vary from year to year and from place to place. Layoffs, on the other hand, are rare because retirements enable most staffing cuts to be handled through attrition. Trained law enforcement officers who lose their jobs because of budget cuts usually have little difficulty finding jobs with other agencies. The need to replace workers who retire, transfer to other occupations, or stop working for other reasons will be the source of many job openings.

EARNINGS

In 2000, median annual earnings of detectives and criminal investigators were $48,870. The middle 50 percent earned between $37,240 and $61,750. The lowest 10 percent earned less than $29,600, and the highest 10 percent earned more than $72,160. Median annual earnings were $61,180 in Federal Government, $46,340 in local government, and $43,050 in State government.

Federal law provides special salary rates to Federal employees who serve in law enforcement. Additionally, Federal special agents and inspectors receive law enforcement availability pay (LEAP)'s equal to 25 percent of the agent's grade and step, awarded because of the large amount of overtime that these agents are expected to work. For example, in 2001 FBI agents enter Federal service as GS-10 employees on the pay scale at a base salary of $36,621, yet earned about $45,776 a year with availability pay. They can advance to the GS-13 grade level in field non-supervisory assignments at a base salary of $57,345 which is worth almost $71,681 with availability pay. FBI supervisory, management, and executive positions in grades GS-14 and GS-15 pay a base salary of about $67,765 or $79,710 a year, respectively, and equaled $84,706 or $99,637 per year including availability pay. Salaries were slightly higher in selected areas where the prevailing local pay level was higher. Because Federal agents may be eligible for a special law enforcement benefits package, applicants should ask their recruiter for more information.

INFORMATIONAL RESOURCES

Further information about employment opportunities with specific agencies are included here. Use this information and the resources provided in Chapter Three and Appendix C of this book to research opportunities with all agencies. Also visit *http://federaljobs.net* for direct links to over 150 agency employment web sites.

Bureau of Prisons - Central Office, 320 First Street NW, Washington, DC 20534. Phone: 202-307-3082 or any regional office.

CIA Agents - Information is available from 703-482-1100 or www.cia.gov/.

Correctional Officers with the Department of Justice (GS-0007) Agency wide job line at 202-514-3397.

DEA Special Agent - Information is available from the nearest DEA office, or call **(800) DEA-4288.** *Internet:* www.usdoj.gov/dea

Deputy Marshal - Information is available from: United States Marshals Service, Employment and Compensation Division, Field Staffing Branch, 600 Army Navy Dr., Arlington, VA 22202. The web site is located at www.usdoj.gov/marshals

FBI Special Agent - Information is available from the nearest FBI office. The address and phone number are listed in the local telephone directory. *Internet:* www.fbi.gov/

Immigration Inspectors - Inspectors are stationed nationwide at air, land, and seas ports of entry. Call their 24 hour hot line number at 1-877-875-4879 or contact Immigration and Naturalization Service: Central Office, 424 I street NW., Washington, DC 20536. Phone: 202-514-2530 or contact any regional office.

Transportation Security Administration (TSA) This administration is in charge of the new Airport Security Screener program and recruits for the new Federal Security Director (FSD) positions. Visit their web site at www.dot.tsa.com.

Treasury Department Personnel Office Numbers:
    Bureaus of Alcohol, Tobacco & Firearms (202) 634-5270
    Federal Law Enforcement Training Center (912) 267-2280
    United States Mint (202) 874-9300
    Internal Revenue Service (202)-874-5850
    United States Secret Service (202-435-5636

U.S. Secret Service Special Agents - Information is available from: U.S. Secret Service, Personnel Division, Suite 7400, 950 H St. NW., Washington, DC 20223. *Internet:* www.treas.gov/usss

U.S. Bureau of Alcohol, Tobacco and Firearms operations - Contact: U.S. Bureau of Alcohol, Tobacco and Firearms, Personnel Division, 650 Massachusetts Avenue NW., Room 4100, Washington, DC 20226. *Internet:* www.atf.treas.gov/

United States Border Patrol Agents (GS-1896) - Information is available from: U.S. Border Patrol, Chester A. Arthur Building, 425 I St. NW., Washington DC 20536. Internet:
www.ins.usdoj.gov/graphics/workfor/careers/bpcareer/index.htm

SPECIFIC QUALIFICATION STANDARDS FOR THE 2 LARGEST OCCUPATIONS

This section will present the Federal Qualification Standards for three of the largest occupations; Correctional Officer, GS-0007 and Criminal Investigator GS-1811.[2] The Qualification Standards are used by agency personnel department to develop the job announcements that you will see on USAJOBS and through other listing sites. They are also the primary guides that Human Resource departments use to rate your application. Review these standards closely for the occupation you are interested in to determine if you meet the basic qualification for the position. Visit http://federaljobs.net to locate qualification standards for all other occupations.

IMPORTANT

Read the entire standard before deciding whether or not you qualify. For example, look at education in the first standard. At first glance it appears that a 4 year BS degree is required for the position. There is a qualifier and this is NOT TRUE. You must have a 4 year degree **OR** 3 years of experience and they tell you exactly what experience qualifies. It may help to have a 4 year degree but experience is also acceptable. Many applicants stop reading after they see a degree requirement and think they don't qualify.

READ THE ENTIRE STANDARD - FRONT TO BACK

Correctional Officer - GS-0007

EDUCATION AND EXPERIENCE REQUIREMENTS

EDUCATION
Undergraduate Education: Successful completion of a full 4-year course of study in any field leading to a bachelor's degree, in an accredited college or university, is qualifying for GS-5 level positions.

Graduate Education: One full academic year of graduate education with major study in criminal justice, social science, or other field related to the position is qualifying

---

[2] Excerpted from "Operations Manual, Qualifications Standards for General Schedule Positions, 2000."

for GS-7. Graduate education may be pro-rated according to the grade level of the position to be filled, however, it is not qualifying for positions above GS-7.

OR

EXPERIENCE

General Experience (for GS-5 positions): Three years of general experience, 1 year of which was equivalent to at least GS-4, are qualifying for positions at the GS-5 level. This experience must have demonstrated the aptitude for acquiring knowledge, skills, and abilities required for correctional work, and, in addition, demonstrate the possession of personal attributes important to the effectiveness of correctional officers, such as:

- Ability to meet and deal with people of differing backgrounds and behavioral patterns.
- Ability to be persuasive in selling and influencing ideas.
- Ability to lead, supervise, and instruct others.
- Sympathetic attitude towards the welfare of others.
- Ability to reason soundly and to think out practical solutions to problems.
- Ability to make decisions and act quickly, particularly under stress.
- Poise and self-confidence, and ability to remain calm during emergency situations.

Qualifying general experience may have been gained in work such as:

- Social case work in a welfare agency or counseling in other types of organizations.
- Classroom teaching or instructing.
- Responsible rehabilitation work, e.g., in an alcoholic rehabilitation program.
- Supervising planned recreational activities or active participation in community action programs.
- Management or supervisory work in a business or other organization that included directing the work flow and/or direct supervision of others.
- Sales work, other than taking and filling orders as in over-the-counter sales.

Specialized Experience (for positions above GS-5): One year of specialized experience equivalent to at least the next lower level in the normal line of progression is qualifying for positions at grade GS-6 and above. Specialized experience must have equipped the applicant with the particular knowledge, skills, and abilities to perform successfully the duties of the position to be filled. Experience may have been gained in work such as police officer, mental health counselor in a residential facility, or detention officer.

EMPLOYMENT INTERVIEW

The personal qualities and characteristics of the applicant are the most critical of all the requirements for Correctional Officer positions. The applicant must be willing to perform arduous and prolonged duties on any of three shifts. In addition, the applicant must possess certain personal qualities in order to relate to inmates effectively in a correctional setting. These include empathy, objectivity, perceptiveness, resourcefulness, adaptability and flexibility, stability, and maturity.

Before appointment, candidates may be required to appear before a panel of specialists in correctional administration for an employment interview to determine the extent to which the candidates possess these and other qualities necessary to perform Correctional Officer duties adequately. The interview will also serve to acquaint applicants with further details of, and the environment surrounding, the position. A determination by the panel that a person who is otherwise qualified does not possess such personal characteristics to the required degree may result in removal of his/her application from further consideration.

MEDICAL REQUIREMENTS

The Department of Justice, Bureau of Prisons has established the following medical requirements for Correctional Officer positions:

The duties of these positions involve unusual mental and nervous pressure, and require arduous physical exertion involving prolonged walking and standing, restraining of prisoners in emergencies, and participating in escape hunts. Applicants must be physically capable of performing efficiently the duties of these positions, and be free from such defects or disease as may constitute employment hazards to themselves or others. The duties of a Correctional Officer are arduous; and sound health as well as physical fitness is required.

Vision: Must have at least 20/30 vision with or without correction. If only one eye is present or functional, the examining health care practitioner shall determine if an applicant can safely perform the physical ability test, the firearms component, and the self-defense component at the training center.

Hearing: Must be capable of hearing conversational voice, with or without a hearing aid, in at least one ear, as measured by normal findings in the decibel ranges of 500, 1000, 2000. This determination is made via a hearing booth test.

Mental/Emotional Stability: Must display mental and emotional stability. The examining health care practitioner shall evaluate mental and emotional stability based upon a thorough medical/psychiatric history as well as a current medical/psychiatric examination. Additionally, any history of psychiatric hospitalizations and outpatient psychiatric treatments shall be considered when evaluating an applicant's mental health.

Active Disease: Active diseases that are infectious and may be spread by routine means, such as handshakes, skin contact, and breathing, preclude an applicant from employment. Once this disease is cured or is considered by the examining health care practitioner to be no longer infectious, the applicant may be considered for employment. Active disease processes or conditions cannot(solely on the basis of the existence of such process, disease, condition, impairment or disability) exclude an otherwise qualified applicant from consideration for employment(i.e. HIV positive, AIDS, cancer, epilepsy, diabetes, heart disease, and loss or injury of one or more limbs).

Disability: Similarly, history of a disease, medical condition, or impairment, particularly if deemed a permanent "disability", cannot, solely on the basis of the existence of such disease, condition, or impairment, exclude an otherwise qualified applicant from consideration for employment. If the applicant is otherwise qualified and can, with or without reasonable accommodation, safely perform the essential functions of the position, the physical ability tests, the firearms component, and the self-defense component, then the individual may be considered for employment.

Criminal Investigating Series GS-1811

Use these individual occupational requirements in conjunction with the "Group Coverage Qualification Standard for Administrative and Management Positions." Individual occupational requirements for Treasury Enforcement Agent positions are identified separately. Visit Http://federaljobs.net to view the entire Group Coverage Qualification Standard for Administrative and Management Positions.

MEDICAL REQUIREMENTS
The duties of positions in this series require moderate to arduous physical exertion involving walking and standing, use of firearms, and exposure to inclement weather. Manual dexterity with comparatively free motion of finger, wrist, elbow, shoulder, hip, and knee joints is required. Arms, hands, legs, and feet must be sufficiently intact and functioning in order that applicants may perform the duties satisfactorily. Sufficiently good vision in each eye, with or without correction, is required to perform the duties satisfactorily. Near vision, corrective lenses permitted, must be sufficient to read printed material the size of typewritten characters. Hearing loss, as measured by an audiometer, must not exceed 35 decibels at 1000, 2000, and 3000 Hz levels. Since the duties of these positions are exacting and responsible, and involve activities under trying conditions, applicants must possess emotional and mental stability. Any physical condition that would cause the applicant to be a hazard to himself/herself, or others is disqualifying.

Criminal Investigator—Treasury Enforcement Agent
Department of the Treasury

Use these individual occupational requirements in conjunction with the "Group Coverage Qualification Standard for Administrative and Management Positions."

EDUCATION
Undergraduate and Graduate Education:
All Treasury Enforcement Agent (TEA) positions in Treasury bureaus and offices, except Internal Revenue Service (IRS) Special Agent positions: Major study—any field of study in an accredited college or university.

IRS Special Agent positions: Major study—any field of study that included or was supplemented by at least 15 semester hours in accounting, and 9 semester hours from among the following or closely related fields: finance, economics, business law, tax law, or money and banking.

OR

EXPERIENCE

General Experience (for GS-5 positions):

TEA positions except IRS Special Agent: Successful, responsible experience in the criminal investigative or law enforcement fields that required knowledge and application of laws relating to criminal violations, and the ability to deal effectively with individuals or groups in stressful or controversial situations, collect and assemble pertinent facts for investigations, and prepare clear, concise written reports.

IRS Special Agent positions: Successful, responsible accounting and business experience that required knowledge and application of accounting and auditing principles and general business practices, and that demonstrated the ability to analyze and comprehend accounting and bookkeeping records, financial statements, related reports and automated systems.

Nonqualifying General Experience: Experience as a uniformed law enforcement officer where the principal duties consisted of investigations and arrests involving traffic violations, minor felonies, misdemeanors, and comparable offenses; or in which the major duties involved guarding and protecting property, preventing crimes, and/or legal research without the application of investigative techniques.

Specialized Experience (for positions above GS-5):

TEA positions except IRS Special Agent: Experience in or related to investigation of criminal violations that provided the specific knowledge, skills, and abilities to perform successfully the duties of the position. Examples of qualifying specialized experience include:

- Leadership or membership of a military intelligence or criminal investigative team or component in which the principal duties consisted of security investigation, intelligence gathering, or criminal prosecution.
- Analyzing or evaluating raw investigative data and preparing comprehensive written investigative reports.
- Investigating complex claims involving suspected crimes or alleged fraud.
- Investigating criminal cases requiring the use of recognized investigative methods and techniques and that may have included appearing in court to present evidence.
- Supervising or conducting interviews or interrogations that involved eliciting evidence, data, or surveillance information.
- Law enforcement work in which 50 percent or more of the time involved criminal investigations requiring the use of surveillance, undercover, or other criminal detection methods or techniques.
- Investigating computerized business and/or accounting systems and forming sound conclusions as to related criminal business practices and compliance with Federal laws and regulations.
- Investigative work that required rapid, accurate judgments and sound decision-making in applying regulations, instructions, and procedures.

•Successful completion of formalized programs of in service training for any of the above.

IRS Special Agent positions: Specialized experience required for IRS Special Agent positions is essentially the same as that described above for other TEA positions, except that the experience must have been acquired in investigative work related to the accounting, auditing, business, or commercial practices of subjects investigated.

CERTIFICATE AS A CERTIFIED PUBLIC ACCOUNTANT (CPA)

Proof of possession of a CPA certificate (certificate number and date of issuance) obtained through written examination in a State, Territory, or the District of Columbia meets the GS-5 level requirements for positions requiring accounting knowledge. Applicants with such certificates may also qualify for higher grade levels based on their education and/or experience.

PERSONAL QUALITIES

Appointment is conditional on a satisfactory report of character and background investigation, including a tax audit. This investigation is conducted in order to secure evidence of candidates' loyalty to the U.S. Government, honesty, and integrity. For some positions, a top secret security clearance will be required.

INTERVIEW

Applicants who pass the written test, as required, and who meet the experience or educational requirements will be required to appear for an interview at the time of consideration for appointment. The interview is to evaluate observable personal qualifications essential for successful performance of the duties of the position, such as poise, tact, and ability in oral expression. An otherwise qualified applicant who is found to lack the personal qualifications necessary for successful performance of the duties of the position will be removed from further consideration.

MOTOR VEHICLE OPERATION

Applicants must possess a valid automobile driver's license at the time of appointment. Candidates must qualify after appointment for authorization to operate motor vehicles in accordance with applicable OPM regulations and related Department of the Treasury requirements.

USE OF FIREARMS

All positions require basic and periodic qualification in the use of firearms; proficiency with standard issue firearms must be demonstrated for successful completion of training. All agents are required to carry a handgun in the performance of duties.

MAXIMUM ENTRY AGE

The date immediately preceding an individual's 37th birthday is the maximum entry age for original appointment to a position within the Department of Treasury as a law enforcement officer as defined in title 5 U.S.C. 8331(20) or in 5

U.S.C. 8401(17). Consideration will be restricted to candidates who have not yet reached age 37 at the time of referral for positions.

MEDICAL REQUIREMENTS

General: The duties of these positions require moderate to arduous physical exertion involving walking and standing, use of firearms, and exposure to inclement weather. Manual dexterity with comparatively free motion of fingers, wrists, elbows, shoulders, hips and knee joints is required. Arms, hands, legs, and feet must function sufficiently in order for applicants to perform the duties satisfactorily.

Vision: For all positions, near vision, corrected or uncorrected, must be sufficient to read larger type 2 at 14 inches. Normal depth perception and peripheral vision are required, as is the ability to distinguish shades of color by color plate tests. For all positions covered by this standard, applicants who have undergone refractive surgery (i.e., surgery to improve distant visual acuity) must meet Treasury-approved requirements which include documentation that they have passed specific exam and protocol testing. Visual acuity requirements for each bureau listed below are expressed in terms of the Snellen vision test:

U.S. Secret Service — Uncorrected distant vision must test 20/60 in each eye, and corrected distant vision must test 20/20 in each eye.

Bureau of Alcohol, Tobacco and Firearms — Uncorrected distant vision must test 20/100 in each eye, and corrected distant vision must test 20/20 in one eye, 20/30 in the other.

All other bureaus — Uncorrected distant vision must test 20/200, and corrected distant vision must test 20/20 in one eye, and 20/30 in the other.

GS-1811 Treasury Enforcement Agent (Continued)

Hearing: Hearing loss, as measured by an audiometer, must not exceed 30 decibels (A.S.A. or equivalent I.S.O.) in either ear in the 500, 1000, and 2000 Hz ranges. Applicants must be able to hear the whispered voice at 15 feet with each ear without the use of a hearing aid.

Special Medical Requirements: Since the duties of these positions are exacting and involve the responsibility for the safety of others under trying conditions, applicants must possess emotional and mental stability. Any condition that would hinder full, efficient performance of the duties of these positions or that would cause the individual to be a hazard to himself/herself or to others is disqualifying.

Appointment will be contingent upon a candidate's passing a pre-employment medical examination and drug test to ascertain possession of the physical and emotional requirements for the position. For certain positions involving particularly arduous or hazardous duties, there are specific medical requirements where a direct relationship exists between the condition and the duties of the position being filled. Certain diseases or conditions resulting in indistinct speech may be disqualifying. Any chronic disease or condition affecting the respiratory system, the cardiovascular system, the gastrointestinal, musculoskeletal, digestive, nervous, endocrine or genitourinary systems that would impair full performance of the duties of the position is disqualifying. Prior to completion of the 1-year probationary period following initial appointment, an incumbent may be required to undergo a physical examination and meet the same medical requirements as those for appointment. Supervisory positions excepted, these medical requirements must be met in service placement actions, including reinstatement of former employees and transfers from positions not covered by this standard. The presence of medical conditions that would be aggravated by the environmental conditions of these positions will ordinarily disqualify an applicant for appointment.

SECURITY SCREENING POSITIONS

These positions account for approximately 28,000 new federal positions. The Department of Transportation (DOT) established the Transportation Security Agency on November 19, 2001. It is projected that by June of 2002 the majority of screeners nationwide will be working for the FAA earning approximately $35,000 a year.

The Transportation Security Act makes airport security a direct Federal responsibility. As a result of this legislation DOT plans to hire a significant number of new Federal security screeners. The new security force will be comprised of highly qualified and well-trained U.S. citizens.

One requirement of the Transportation Security Act is to establish qualification standards for screeners to be employed by the Federal Government. In response to this requirement, on December 19, 2001 the Department of Transportation published the basic eligibility requirements for Federal security screeners.

When the TSA takes over the responsibility for passenger screening operations all newly hired screeners must:

- Possess a high school diploma or general education diploma or have one year of any type of work experience that demonstrates the applicant's ability to perform the work of the position.

- Be a U.S. Citizens.

- Pass a background and security investigation, including a criminal records check, in accordance with Federal law and standards established by the Transportation Security Administration.

- Possess certain basic aptitudes and physical abilities as measured through a medical examination. These include color perception, visual and aural acuity, physical coordination, and motor skills, to the following standards:

1) Be able to distinguish objects on the screening equipment monitor at the appropriate imaging standard as specified by the Transportation Security Administration;

2) Be able to distinguish each color displayed on every type of screening equipment and explain what each color signifies;

3) Be able to hear and respond to the spoken voice and to audible alarms generated by screening equipment in an active checkpoint environment;

4) Be able efficiently and thoroughly to manipulate and handle baggage, containers, and other objects subject to security processing; and

5) Have sufficient dexterity and capability thoroughly to conduct hand-metal detector and pat down search procedures over an individual's entire body.

- Be able to read, speak, and write English well enough to:

    1) Carry out written and oral instructions regarding the proper performance of screening duties;

    2) Read English language identification media, credentials, airline tickets, and labels on items normally encountered in the screening process;

    3) Provide direction to and understand and answer questions from English-speaking individuals undergoing screening; and

    4) Write incident reports and statements and log entries into security records in the English language.

Any applicant tentatively selected for this position will be subject to a pre-employment or pre-appointment drug screening. Persons occupying these positions will be subject to random drug and/or alcohol testing and pass a Federal Civil Aviation Security Screener Aptitude test. The test will measure:

- Aptitude necessary to conduct screening;
- Ability to deal effectively with the public; and
- English proficiency.

The federal aptitude test is being developed and should be ready for use in February 2002. This new criteria will be effective once TSA assumes contract responsibilities for the screening function. Current screening company employees will be allowed to continue to be employed until such time as the work they are performing is taken over by Federal employees.

At that time they may apply, and if qualified, be hired as new Federal screeners. In the interim, retraining of the current workforce may be required to ensure a consistent level of performance. As provided by law, the TSA will give hiring preference to Veterans. TheTSA will also recruit and give consideration to displaced aviation workers.

If you'd like to be considered for one of these critical positions, email your name and email address to: screener@ost.dot.gov or call the DOT Connection toll-free at 1-866-404-1227 to leave your name and mailing address. They will send you application information as soon as it is available, at which time they will begin accepting applications.

Visit the DOT's web site at www.dot.gov for additional information. As this new agency matures the job announcements will be posted on the FAA and DOT web sites like all other job vacancies are currently posted. You can also visit the Office of Personnel Management web site at www.usajobs.opm.gov or visit the Federal Aviation Administration web site at (www.jobs.faa.gov) for regular updates.

Chapter Twelve
Employment Secrets

Many talented job seekers are frustrated by the required paperwork and give up prematurely. If you take the time to thoroughly complete your application and seek out all available job vacancies your chances for employment will increase substantially.

The secret to success is that the harder you work the luckier you get.

APPLY EARLY

It pays to start your employment search early for federal jobs, well in advance of the time you will be available for employment. Applications can take six to eight weeks for processing. It may take longer if written tests are required. From the time you first identify an opening to actual interviews and hiring can take up to several months or longer.

All individuals interested in federal employment should start researching the system, identifying jobs, locate agency internet web sites, and prepare for tests—if required —months in advance.

> Most federal agencies have launched comprehensive internet web sites. Now, over 80% of all federal jobs are advertised direct by individual agencies instead of by OPM. It's imperative that you visit agency web sites to locate **ALL** job vacancies in your area. A comprehensive list of federal job web sites is available online at http://federaljobs.net.

YOUR APPLICATION or RESUME

Review Chapter Six and follow the guidance on how to apply for federal jobs. There are a number of new application methods now available including the RESUMIX, E-mail, on-line, and telephone application processes. You must be familiar with the optional application forms including the OF-612, OF-306, and Federal resume formats.

All forms listed in the job announcement must be submitted with your package. If you need forms, most can now be downloaded off the internet. However, you will find the software program *Quick & Easy Federal Jobs Kit* very helpful. It generates all required forms including the new RESUMIX formats and it will convert one format to another with one or two key strokes. Information about this program is available in the back- of-book catalog.

APPLY FREQUENTLY

Many job hunters send in an application for only one announcement. Seek out all available job vacancies and continue to send in applications with every opportunity. The more often you apply the greater your chances. Some agencies now allow job seekers to apply on-line. Review Appendices to identify all of the job series that you can possibly qualify for. If you are having difficulty identifying job series that fit your training, experience, and abilities, review the qualification standards for those positions and review the Skills Index in Appendix E of this book. You can review qualification standards online at http://federaljobs.net. If the specific job series isn't listed you can E-mail them for a specific job series.

You will find that you can qualify for several to twenty or more job series. Don't overlook Wage Grade (WG) positions. When requesting job announcements obtain copies of announcements that cover all of the identified job series that you are qualified. You will be surprised by just how many you qualify for.

Consider the electronics technician field, for example. All of the following job series require basic electronic technician skills:[1]

GS-856   Electronics Technician
GS-802   Electronics Engineering Technician
GS-2101 Transportation Specialist (Federal Aviation Administration's Airway Facilities System Specialists)

WG-2500 - Wire Communications Equip. Installation/Maintenance Family

WG-2502   Telephone Mechanic
WG-2504   Wire Communications Cable Splicing
WG-2508   Communications Line Installing/Repairing
WG-2511   Wire Communications Equipment Install/Repair

---

[1]Publication TS-56, March 1990, Part 3, Definitions of Trades and Labor Job Families and Occupations.

WG-2600 - Electronic Equipment Installation & Maintenance Family

WG-2602	Electronic Measurement Equipment Mechanic
WG-2604	Electronic Mechanic
WG-2606	Electronic Industrial Controls
WG-2698	Electronic Digital Computer Mechanic

WG-2800	Electrical Installation Maintenance Family (4 occupations)
WG-3300	Instrument Work Family (5 occupations)
WG-4800	General Maintenance Family (7 occupations)

> ## Over 40 Electronic Related Jobs Are Listed under Various Wage Grade Families

GETTING IN THE FRONT DOOR

Getting in is half the battle. If you want to enter a certain field with a particular agency and there are currently no openings, apply for other jobs with that agency. For instance, if you qualify for a logistics/supply position and they only have clerk openings it may be to your benefit to apply and get on board. Agencies generally advertise in-house first to offer qualified workers opportunities for advancement. You will have a good chance to bid on other jobs if you have the qualifications and a good track record.

"There are two things to aim at in life: first, to get what you want; and after that to enjoy it. Only the wisest of people achieve the second."
— **Logan Smith**

MOBILITY
LOCATE ALL JOB VACANCIES

Locate announcements from all sources including OPM's USAJOBS, and individual agency personnel offices and web sites. Even if you wouldn't consider relocating you will at least be aware of the job availability in other areas. Identify local agency offices and send them a copy of your application or federal style resume along with a short cover letter. In the letter explain what job you are interested in and provide some background information. This is a good way to introduce yourself and your qualifications to a perspective employer. Each year additional agencies apply for and receive direct hire or the Case Examining authority for specific job series. The more contacts you make the better.

If you are willing to relocate consider subscribing to *Federal Career Opportunities* (http://fedjobs.com) published by Federal Research Services or *Federal Jobs Digest* (http://jobsfed.com). Both publish a bi-weekly listing of job vacancies from over 200 federal personnel offices. **The larger the area of**

consideration the better your chances. Choice jobs with certain agencies often require an applicant to accept a job in a not so desirable location. Often, agencies have to advertise jobs to the general public because the area isn't desirable and they can't get in-house applicants. Once hired, you may have an opportunity to apply to better locations after you are trained and have the required agency experience.

During my early government career I accepted a job with an agency in a remote little town of 7,000 inhabitants. After completing the required initial training and receiving what the agency calls system certification I was able to successfully relocate to the area of my choice. It took me three years to gain the training and experience needed to apply to other areas. When I did relocate the agency paid for the complete move including real estate expenses.

One important fact to remember: In most cases **your first move is at your expense**. If you are willing to relocate you will be responsible for the cost of the move. However, if you relocate to other areas after your first year of employment the government picks up the tab. The moving allowances are generous. Agencies often buy your house from you at close to market rates, pay for the move of your household goods, and pay real estate sales commissions and closing costs at your new location. On top of this you will receive 60 to 90 days of temporary quarters expenses at your new location, 64 hours of leave for the move, and a free house hunting trip may be authorized.

CAUTION

Don't jump blindly at an employment offer. Many agencies have difficulty filling jobs in high-cost living areas such as New York, L.A., and Washington D.C. Investigate the cost of living in the area you are selected for before saying yes. If you can't afford to live in the area you may have to turn down the initial offer.

"LOOK BEFORE YOU LEAP"

TRAINING AND EXPERIENCE

Often, applicants neglect to add valuable work experience and training to their application package. Go back as many years as your related education and experience goes. For example, if you were a supply specialist in the military in 1980, and you are applying for a supply/logistics position, then by all means add your military experience and training to your application.

Many agencies require supplemental application qualification forms. If you are applying for an electronics position these forms often capture your math, electronics training and specific experience background. List all of your math training back through high school. Trigonometry and algebra are required for many electronic positions. If you only had these subjects in high school and you don't list them you may not be rated eligible for the position.

KEYS TO SUCCESS

There are three basic ingredients to successfully finding federal employment for qualified applicants:

- Invest the time and energy needed to seek out all openings.

- Correctly fill out all required application forms.

- Don't give up when you receive your first rejection.

You can learn from rejections by contacting the selecting official. Ask what training and/or experience would enhance your application package for future positions. If they specify certain training or experience, then work to achieve the desired skills.

You may discover that you did have the specific skills needed. However, you either neglected to put these facts in your application or considered them unimportant for the job applied for. This happens frequently. It doesn't pay to debate your qualifications over spilled milk. The job has already been filled. Thank the selecting official for his candor and time then revise your bid for the next opening.

Write the selecting official a BRIEF letter of thanks and explain that you neglected to incorporate the recommended skills in the original application. Send him a copy of your revised application for future reference. **Managers appreciate dealing with rational and mature individuals and you will be remembered.**

It took me two years to land my first competitive federal civil service job. I was not aware of the employment options available at that time and I simply sent written requests for bids every two weeks to the local OPM office. Today there are many options available through special emphasis hiring, case and direct hire authority, Outstanding Scholar Programs, student employment, and internships, to name a few. Add to this list the over 1,000 job resources provided throughout this book. Take advantage of as many of the programs that you qualify for to expedite your career search. Don't give up or get overly frustrated with the paperwork that is required when applying for federal employment. There are software programs available today to soften the employment application process. Finally, I must add that it is unwise to get angry with the process; instead of getting mad, **GET INVOLVED**.

NETWORKING

Networking is a term used to define the establishment of a group of individuals that assist one another for mutual benefit. You can establish your own network by talking to personnel specialists, contacting regional agency employment departments, conducting informational interviews, and by bidding on all applicable job announcements. By following the guidelines outlined in the book and using your innate common sense your chances of success are magnified ten fold.

Use the over 1,000 contacts presented in this book to begin your personal employment network. Add to this information individual contacts that you make with local agencies.

*"We grow great by dreams. All
big men are dreamers.
They see things in the soft haze of a
spring day or in the red fire of a
long winter's evening. Some of
us let these dreams die, but others
nourish and protect them, nurse
them to the sunshine and light
which come always to those who
sincerely hope that their dreams
will come true."*

— **Woodrow Wilson**

Appendix A
Job Hunter's Checklist

WHAT TO DO NOW

❑ Review the Federal Occupations Lists in Appendix D and the Skills Index in Appendix E. These appendices provide lists of specific Federal jobs that you may qualify for.

❑ Visit **USAJOBS'** web site at http://www.usajobs.opm.gov/ and call the regional OPM Service Center in your area. SEE APPENDIX B for a complete national listing. If you don't have access to the internet call **USAJOBS by Phone** at 1-912-757-3000. Obtain the following information:

  ✔ Announcements for specific job series.
  ✔ A copy of the optional application form OF-612.
  ✔ Review the application process in Chapter Six and throughly review the sample job announcement and OF-612 application.

❑ Contact regional and local agency personnel offices. See Appendix C for office addresses, web sites, and phone numbers.

  ✔ Request agency career opportunities brochures.
  ✔ Visit **http://federaljobs.net** for direct links to hundreds of agency employment web sites.
  ✔ Talk with agency personnel offices and request job announcements and information on special hiring programs.
  ✔ Obtain government office phone numbers from your phone directory. Look under "U.S. Government" in the Blue Pages. Also contact Federal Executive Boards, Appendix B.

> Applications will only be accepted for current job announcements. If you're a Clerk Typist and the government doesn't have typist openings, they will not accept your application.

❑ Visit **FEDERALJOBS.NET (http://federaljobs.net).** This web site provides updates for *The Book of U.S. Government Jobs*. If hiring programs are modified, or web site addresses or contact information change, those changes will be posted on this site. You can also link direct to hundreds of federal agency employment sites.

❑ Review Chapter Three's listings to identify job announcement resources including internet web site addresses. Also review:

   ✔ Chapter Three for Student Hiring Programs.

   ✔ Chapter Seven for Veteran's Hiring programs.

   ✔ Chapter Eight for overseas job resources.

   ✔ Chapter Nine for U.S. Postal Service jobs. (Includes the new 470 Battery Test.)

   ✔ Chapter Ten for job resources for people with disabilities.

❑ Locate your high school and college transcripts, military records, awards, and professional licenses. Collect past employment history; salary, addresses, phone numbers, dates employed, etc.

❑ Visit your local library and review these publications:

   ✔ *The United States Government Manual.* This book provides agency descriptions, addresses, contacts and basic employment information.

   ✔ *The Occupational Outlook Handbook.* If your library doesn't have this publication check with a local college placement office. This handbook is a nationally recognized source of career information and includes detailed descriptions of working conditions for over 250 jobs. It also includes salary surveys, training and other qualifications, job outlook, and related occupations.

✔ *The Occupational Outlook Quarterly*, published by the U.S. Department of Labor, Bureau of Labor Statistics. This is a highly informative quarterly publication that highlights employment trends and features interesting career articles.

WHAT'S AVAILABLE

❑ Call local agencies listed in the phone directory. Also visit local Federal Buildings. **REQUEST INFORMATIONAL INTERVIEWS** per instructions in Chapter Four.

❑ Research agencies in Appendix C of this book, internet web sites, and the United States Government Manual. Department web sites are listed in Chapter Three.

❑ Consider subscribing to Federal Research Services' *Federal Career Opportunities at* http://fedjobs.com or *visit Federal Jobs Digest's* web site at http://jobsfed.com. Both publish bi-weekly listings of job vacancies from over 200 federal personnel offices. They also have on-line database searches available.

❑ Review Chapters Three, Seven, Eight, Nine, and Ten.

APPLYING FOR A JOB

❑ You will receive requested job announcements instantly via the internet or within a week by mail. Each announcement will be accompanied by all required application forms. You can use the blank optional application form in Chapter Four to draft your application while waiting for forms by mail. You can also download forms from http://federaljobs.net and OPM's web site.

❑ Review Chapter Six and follow the guidance for completing your application and/or resume. Chapter Six provides guidance on the new RESUMIX electronic resume process and takes you step-by-step through the application process. You'll learn how to write a professional federal resume and application, and get attention by using government phrases and terminology.

❑   If no vacancies exist for your specialty, visit USAJOBS and agency web sites frequently. Jobs can be advertised for as little as one day. USAJOBS offers notification via e-mail for specific job titles. Register on USAJOBS for this service. You must locate job vacancies either through USAJOBS, direct from local agencies, at local State Employment Offices, or from various publications.

❑   Contact individual agencies. The more contacts the greater your chance of finding open announcements and special emphasis programs that may apply.

❑   Complete and sign ALL application forms received with the bid. Follow the step-by-step instructions presented in Chapter 6.

❑   Retain a copy of each job announcement that you applied for along with all application forms that you submitted with your package. You may need to review them prior to the interview.

❑   Send in the completed forms to the address specified on the announcement.

RESULTS

Your application will be processed and results returned to you within several weeks. You will receive a *Notice of Rating or Notice of Results* informing you of your eligibility by mail. If rated eligible, your name will be placed on the list of eligible applicants for that position. Your name and application will be forwarded to a selecting official for consideration.

THE INTERVIEW

❑   Prepare for the interview. Review chapter Four's Employment Interviewing section.

Appendix B
Federal Service Centers &
FEB Listings Information Centers

OPM FEDERAL SERVICE CENTERS

The Office of Personnel Management (OPM) staffs these locations to provide services to all federal agencies. These offices provide a nationwide link to the automation and assessment services provided by the Employment Service's Technology Support Center and Personnel Resources and Development Center. These centers typically service federal agencies, however, you can also call for assistance with application problems.

ATLANTA

Ms. Jacqueline Y. Moses
75 Spring Street, SW, Suite 956
Atlanta, GA 30303
(404) 331-4588
(404) 730-9738 (FAX)
Email: Atlanta@opm.gov

CHICAGO

Ms. Vera Garcia
230 South Dearborn St., DPN 30-3
Chicago, IL 60604
(312) 353-6234
(313) 353-6211 (FAX)
Email: Chicago@opm.gov

DENVER

Mr. Phong Ngo
12345 Alameda Pkwy, P.O. Box 25167
Denver, CO 80225
(303) 969-6931
(303) 969-7046 (FAX)
Email: Denver@opm.gov

HONOLULU

Mr. Paul Miller
300 Ala Moana Blvd., Box 50028
Honolulu, HI 96850
(808) 541-2795
(808) 541-2788 (FAX)
Email: Honolulu@opm.gov

HUNTSVILLE

Ms. Carol Y. Toney
150 West Park Loop
Huntsville, AL 35806-1762
(256) 837-1271
(256) 837-6071 (FAX)
Email: Huntsville@opm.gov

KANSAS CITY

Mr. James D. Witkop
601 East 12th At., Room 131
Kansas City, MO 64106
(816) 426-5705
(816) 426-5104
Email: KansasCity@opm.gov

NORFOLK

Mr. F. Alan Nelson
200 Granby St., Room 500
Norfolk, VA 23510-1886
(757) 441-3373
(757) 441-6280 (FAX)
Email: Norfolk@opm.gov

PHILADELPHIA

Mr. Joe Stix
600 Arch St., Room 3400
Philadelphia, PA 19106
(215) 861-3031
(215) 861-3030 (FAX)
Email: Philadelphia@opm.gov

RALEIGH

Mr. Allen N. Goldberg
4407 Bland Rd., Suite 200
Raleigh, NC 27609-6296
(919) 790-2817
(919) 790-2824 (FAX)
Email: Raleigh@opm.gov

SAN ANTONIO

Mr. Miguel Hernandez
8610 Broadway, Room 305
San Antonio, TX 78217

(210) 805-2423
(210) 805-2429 (FAX)
Email: SanAntonio@opm.gov

SAN FRANCISCO

Ms. Linda Peterson
120 Howard St., Room 735
San Francisco, CA 94105
(415) 281-7094
(415) 281-7095 (FAX)
Email: San Francisco@opm.gov

SAN JUAN

Mr. Luis Rodriguez
Torre de Plaza Americas, Suite 1114
525 F. F. Roosevelt Ave.
San Juan, P.R. 00918
(787) 766-5242
(787) 766-5598 (FAX)
Email: SanJuan@opm.gov

TWIN CITIES

Ms. Diane Granos
One Federal Dr., Suite 596
Fort Snelling, MN 55111-4007
(612) 725-3437
(612) 725-3725 (FAX)
Email: TwinCities@opm.gov

WASHINGTON DC

Ms. Pam T. Shivery
1900 E St., NW, Room 2469
Washington, DC 20415
(202) 606-2575
(202) 606-1768 (FAX)
Email: Washington@opm.gov

FEDERAL EXECUTIVE BOARDS (FEBs)

Federal Executive Boards (FEBs) were established to improve coordination among Federal activities and programs outside of Washington. Approximately 84 percent of all Federal employees work outside the national capital area. For job seekers the FEBs offer a wealth of information. Primarily, most compile directories of all agency offices in their area with contact information. Contact the FEB in your area to obtain a list of **ALL** Federal offices in your area. This valuable resource gives the job seeker a total picture of potential employment options that are within commuting distance to their present location.

There are currently 28 FEB's located in cities that are major centers of Federal activity. The Boards are located in the following metropolitan areas: Albuquerque-Santa Fe, Atlanta, Baltimore, Boston, Buffalo, Chicago, Cincinnati, Cleveland, Dallas-Fort Worth, Denver, Detroit, Honolulu, Houston, Kansas City, Los Angeles, Miami, Minneapolis-St. Paul, Newark, New Orleans, New York, Oklahoma City, Philadelphia, Pittsburgh, Portland, St. Louis, San Antonio, San Francisco, and Seattle. The Boards are composed of the Federal field office agency heads and military commanders in these cities.

In cities where FEB's do not exist, another organization of local principal Federal agency officials often exists. These organizations are generally entitled Federal Executive Associations or Councils, and have purposes and objectives similar to FEB's. They do not, however, function within the same formal set of parameters (e.g., officially established by Presidential Memorandum, policy direction and guidance from the Office of Personnel Management, etc.) as do the FEB's.

Address all correspondence to the Federal Executive Board at the following listed addresses. Most of the 28 FEBs have internet web sites. Use this list for networking purposes and to call or e-mail local offices for listings of agencies in your area:

FEDERAL EXECUTIVE BOARD LISTING

ALBUQUERQUE, SANTA FE, NM
James L. Toya, Chairperson
Patricia Armijo, Executive Director
P.O. Box 5400
Albuquerque, NM 87110
Phone: (505) 845-4238
FAX: (505) 248-6683
www.albuquerque-santafe.feb.gov
Email: parmijo@doeal.gov

ATLANTA, GA
Marjorie Brown, Chairperson
Gwenne Campbell, Executive Dir.
Richard B. Russell Federal Building
75 Spring Street, SW, Room 1142
Atlanta, GA 30303
Phone: (404) 331-4400
FAX: (404) 331-4270
http://r4.gsa.gov/febatlanta.htm
Email: gwenne.campbell@gsa.gov

BALTIMORE, MD
Colonel R. Mark Brown, Chairperson
Richard Howell, Executive Director
Fallon Federal Building
31 Hopkins Plaza, Room G13
Baltimore, MD 21201
Phone: (410) 962-4047
FAX: (410) 962-6198
http://www.baltimorefeb.org
Email: Execdir@baltimorefeb.org

BOSTON, MA
Diane LeBlanc, Chairperson
Kim Ainsworth, Executive Director
10 Causeway Street, Room 1075
Boston, MA 02222
Phone: (617) 565-6769
FAX: (617) 565-7648
www.boston.feb.gov
Email: kim.ainsworth@gsa.gov

BUFFALO, NY
Gregory L. Mason, Chairperson
Paul Kendzierski, Executive Director
1117 Dulski Federal Building
111 W. Huron Street
Buffalo, NY 14202
Phone: (716) 551-5655
FAX: (716) 551-3007
www.buffalo.feb.gov
Email: buffalofeb@buffalo.com

CHICAGO, IL
Phyllis Stabbe, Chairperson
Janice A. Stinson, Executive Director
230 South Dearborn St., Room 3816
Chicago, IL 60604
Phone: (312) 353-6790
FAX: (312) 353-3058
www.chicago.feb.gov
Email: jan.stinson@gsa.gov

CINCINNATI, OH
Richard Ahearn, Chairperson
Donald P. Yost, Executive Director
Cincinnati Federal Executive Board

1116 JWP Federal Office Building
550 Main Street
Cincinnati, OH 45202-3215
Phone: (513) 684-2101
FAX: (513) 684-2515
http://www.cincinnati.feb.gov
Email: don@gcfeb.com

CLEVELAND, OH
Gary M. Klingler, Chairperson
Judy Montfort, Executive Director
747 A. J. Celebrezze Federal Building
1240 E. Ninth Street
Cleveland, OH 44199-2002
Phone: (216) 433-9460
FAX: (216) 433-9463
www.grs.nasa.gov/WWW/OHR/FEB
Email: judy.Montfort@grc.nasa.gov

DALLAS-FT. WORTH, TX
Francis P. Summers, Jr., Chairperson
Gladean Butler, Executive Director
4300 Amon Carter Blvd., Suite 114
Ft. Worth, TX 76155
Phone: (817) 684-5370
FAX: (817) 684-5375
www.dallas-fortworth.feb.gov
Email: gladean.butler@sba.gov

DENVER, CO
Michael S. Hacskaylo, Chairperson
Lawrence Grandison, Executive Dir.
6760 E. Irvington Place
Denver, CO 80279-8000
Phone: (303) 676-7009
FAX: (303) 676-6666
www.denver.feb.gov
Email: larry.grandison@dfas.mil

DETROIT, MI
Dwight P. Dean, Chairperson
Vacant, Executive Director
477 Michigan Avenue, Room 956
Detroit, MI 48226
Phone: (313) 226-3534
FAX: (313) 226-2155

Email: hubbardr@tacom.army.mil

HONOLULU-PACIFIC, HI
Major General Edward L. Correa, Jr.,
Chairperson
L.A. Burke, Executive Director
300 Ala Moana Blvd, Rm 8-125
Box 50268
Honolulu, HI 96850
Phone: (808) 541-2637
FAX: (808) 541-3429
www.honolulu-pacific.feb.gov
Email: hpfeb@aloha.net

HOUSTON, TX
Robert S. Trotter, Chairperson
Mike Mason, Executive Director
1919 Smith Street, Suite 632
Houston, TX 77002
Phone: (713) 209-4524
FAX: (713) 209-3465
www.houston.feb.gov
Email: hfeb@ev1.net

KANSAS CITY, MO
Kathleen Rundle, Chairperson
Lahoma Yates, Executive Director
1500 E. Bannister Road, Suite 1176
Kansas City, MO 64131
Phone: (816) 823-5100
FAX: (816) 823-5104
http://kcfeb.gsa.gov
Email: lahoma.yates@gsa.gov

LOS ANGELES, CA
Jon Ceretto, Chairperson
Kathrene Hansen, Executive Director
501 W. Ocean, Suite 3200
Long Beach, CA 90802
Phone: (562) 980-3445
FAX: (562) 980-3448
www.losangeles.feb.gov
Kathrene.L.Hansen@usdoj.gov

MIAMI, FL
Michael Rhodes, Chairperson

Jaqueline Arroyo, Executive Director
51 S.W. First Avenue, Suite 1325
Miami, FL 33130-1608
Phone: (305) 536-4344
FAX: (305) 536-4611
www.miami.feb.gov
Email: jarroyo@doc.gov

MINNESOTA
Colonel Dean Despinoy, Chairperson
Ray Morris, Executive Director
Bishop Henry Whipple Federal
Building, Room 510
St. Paul, MN 55111-4008
Phone: (612) 713-7200
FAX: (612) 713-7203
www.minnesota.feb.gov
Email: Ray_Morris@os.doi.gov

NEWARK, NJ
Brian Tait, Chairperson
Angela A. Zaccardi, Executive Dir.
970 Broad Street , Room 1434-B
Newark, NJ 07102
Phone: (973) 645-6217
FAX: (973) 645-6218
www.newark.feb.gov
Email: Angela.Zaccardi@gsa.gov

NEW ORLEANS, LA
Dennis W. Bruhl, Chairperson
Ron Appel, Executive Director
P.O. Box 29481
New Orleans, LA 70189-0294
Phone: (504) 255-5420
FAX: (504) 255-6100
www.nfc.usda.gov/feb
Email: ronald.appel@usda.gov

NEW YORK, NY
Beatrice M. Disman, Chairperson
Cynthia Gable, Executive Director
26 Federal Plaza, Room 1713
New York, NY 10278
Phone: (212) 264-1890
FAX: (212) 264-2634

www.newyorkcity.feb.gov
Email: cynthia.gable@gsa.gov

OKLAHOMA
Lindy Ritz, Chairperson
LeAnn Jenkins, Executive Director
215 Dean A. McGee Ave., Suite 320
Oklahoma City, OK 73102
Phone: (405) 231-4167
FAX: (405) 231-4165
www.oklahoma.feb.gov
Email: LeAnnJenkins@juno.com

OREGON
Colonel Randy Butler, Chairperson
Ron Johnson, Executive Director
1220 SW Third Avenue, Suite 1776
Portland, OR 97204-2823
Phone: (503) 326-2060
FAX: (503) 326-2070
www.portland.feb.gov
Email: rjohnson@pcez.com

PHILADELPHIA, PA
Benjamin F. Rogers, Chairperson
Jack Ratcliffe, Executive Director
William J. Green, Jr., Federal Bldg.
600 Arch Street, Room 4320
Philadelphia, PA 19106
Phone: (215) 597-2766
FAX: (215) 597-4601
Email: jack.ratcliffe@gsa.gov

PITTSBURGH, PA
Marlene Ackman, Chairperson
George Buck, Executive Director
Federal Executive Board
1000 Liberty Avenue, Room 406
Pittsburgh, PA 15222
Phone: (412) 395-6220
FAX: (412) 395-6221
www.pittsburgh.feb.gov
Email: GPB920@aol.com

ST. LOUIS, MO
Captain Kevin E. Schumacher, Chairperson
Susanne Valdez, Executive Director
1520 Market Street, Room 2025
St. Louis, MO 63103
Phone: (314) 539-6312
FAX: (314) 539-6314
www.stlouis.feb.gov
susanne.valdez@stl.rural.usda.gov

SAN ANTONIO, TX
Michael R. McMillion, Chairperson
Rebecca Froboese, Executive Director
10127 Morocco, Suite 108
San Antonio, TX 78216-3947
Phone: (210) 308-4520
FAX: (210) 308-4511
www.sanantonio.feb.gov
Email: froboeser@casu.satx.disa.mil

SAN FRANCISCO, CA
Robert Miller, Chairperson
Geri Spearman, Executive Director
1301 Clay Street, Room 11120N
Oakland, CA 94612-5209
Phone: (510) 637-1103
FAX: (510) 637-1253
www.gsa.gov/r9feb
Email: geri.spearman@gsa.gov

SEATTLE, WA
Larry Andrieson, Chairperson
Anne Tiernan, Executive Director
Federal Executive Board
Jackson Federal Building, Room 2942
915 Second Avenue
Seattle, WA 98174-1010
Phone: (206) 220-6171
FAX: (206) 220-6132
http://www.seattle.feb.gov
Email: sfeb@mindspring.com

Appendix C
Federal Agency Contact List

This appendix provides a functional summary and general employment information for the three branches of the government and for eighteen federal departments under the Executive Branch. Larger independent agencies are also listed.

The information and statistics provided in this appendix was extracted from The United States Government Manual 2001/2002, Federal Civilian Workforce Statistics Employment & Trends as of June 2001, The Federal Career Directory, and the Central Personnel Data File, Office of Workforce Information. The agency summaries include internet web site addresses and specific employment contact information when available. Many listings also include a summary of occupations employed by that organization. Use this Appendix in conjunction with Appendix D to target specific agencies that employ individuals in your occupational group. Also, explore related occupations that you may be qualified for. The more occupations, job series, that you target the better your chances are for employment.

Notice

If you're unable to reach an agency at the listed number, call directory assistance in that city. Directory assistance can be reached by dialing the area code plus 555-1212. For directory assistance in the metropolitan DC area call (202) 555-1212, Virginia (703) 555-1212, and (301) 555-1212 for agencies located in Maryland in close proximity to the District of Columbia.

LEGISLATIVE BRANCH

The Congress of the United States was created by Article 1, section 1, of the Constitution. All legislative powers are vested in the Congress of the United States, which consists of a Senate and House of Representatives. The Legislative Branch has 29,961 employees.

The Senate is comprised of 100 members, two from each state. Senators are elected for a six year term. The House of Representatives is made up of 435 Representatives. Each state elects Representatives based on population distribution. The larger the state the more Representatives they have.

The Vice President of the United States is the Presiding Officer of the Senate. The following offices are under the Legislative Branch (The number employed by each office is noted in parentheses):

Congress	(17,124)
Architect of the Capital	(1,950)
United States Botanical Garden	(36)
General Accounting Office	(3,117)
Government Printing Office	(3,044)
Library of Congress	(4,268)
Congressional Budget Office	(232)

ARCHITECT OF THE CAPITOL
U.S. Capitol Building, Washington D.C. 20515
(202)-228-1793, http://www.aoc.gov

The Architect of the Capitol is responsible for the care and maintenance of the Capitol Building and nearby buildings and grounds.

UNITED STATES BOTANIC GARDENS
Office of The Director, 245 First St. SW.,
Washington D.C. 20024
(202) 226-8333

The United States Botanic Garden collects and grows various vegetable productions of this and other countries for exhibition and public display, student study, scientists, and garden clubs.

GENERAL ACCOUNTING OFFICE
Office of Public Information General Accounting Office, 441 G St. NW.
Washington DC 20548
(202) 512-3000, www.gao.gov

The General Accounting Office is the i-nvestigative arm of Congress and is charged with examining all matters related to the receipt and disbursement of public funds.

GOVERNMENT PRINTING OFFICE

Chief, Employment Branch
732 North Capitol Street NW
Washington, DC 20401
(202) 512-0000, www.access.gpo.gov

This office prints, binds, and distributes the publications of the Congress as well as the executive departments. Employment primarily in administrative, clerical and technical fields. Hires through OPM registers.

LIBRARY OF CONGRESS
Recruitment & Placement Office
101 Independence Ave. SE.
Washington, DC 20540
(202) 707-4315, www.loc.gov

The Library of Congress is the national library of the United States, offering diverse materials for research including comprehensive historical collections. Direct applications and inquiries to this office.

CONGRESSIONAL BUDGET OFFICE
Second & D Streets SW
Washington, DC 20515
(202) 226-2600

Provides Congress with assessments of the economic impact of the federal budget.

JUDICIAL BRANCH

Article III, section 1, of the Constitution of the United States provides that "the judicial power of the United States, shall be vested in one supreme Court, and in such inferior Courts as the Congress may from time to time ordain and establish." The Supreme Court was established on September 24, 1789. This Branch employs 31,568 legal professionals, clerks, administrative personnel, secretaries, and other related specialties. The following offices are under this Branch:

The Supreme Court of the United States
Lower Courts
Special Courts
Administrative Office of the United States Courts
Federal Judicial Center

THE SUPREME COURT

1 First Street NE
Washington, DC 20543
(202) 479-3000, **www.supremecourtus.gov**

Comprised of the Chief Justice and eight Associate Justices who are nominated by the President of the United States.

LOWER COURTS

Administrative Office of the U.S. Courts,
One Columbus Circle, NE
Washington, DC 20544
(202)502-2600

The twelve circuits include all states. There are 89 district offices located throughout the country. Consult your local telephone book for offices located near you.

you. Includes Court of Appeals, U.S. District Courts, Territorial Courts, and the Judicial Panel on Multidistrict Litigation.

SPECIAL COURTS

Clerk Special Courts
717 Madison Place NW., Washington, DC 20005. (202) 219-9657

Consists of the United States Claims Court, Court of International Trade, Court of Military Appeals, United States Tax Court, Temporary Emergency Court of Appeals, Court of Veterans Appeals, and Others.

ADMINISTRATIVE OFFICE OF U.S. COURTS

Human Resource Division
Thurgood Marshall Federal Judiciary Bldg.
Washington, DC 20544
(202) 502-3100

Charged with the nonjudicial, administrative business of U.S. Courts. Includes the following divisions; Bankruptcy, Court Admin., Defender Services, Financial Management, General Counsel, Magistrates, Personnel, Probation and Statistical Analysis.

EXECUTIVE BRANCH

The President is the administrative head of the executive branch and is responsible for numerous agencies as well as 14 executive departments. The administration of this vast bureaucracy is handled by the President's cabinet that includes the heads of the 14 executive departments. The Executive Branch consists of 2,704,015 employees distributed among the 14 departments and numerous independent agencies. The following offices, departments, and over 63 independent agencies are under the executive branch: (The number employed by each office is noted in parentheses)

Executive Office of the President	**(1,566)**
The White House Office	**(369)**
Office of Management and Budget	**(490)**
Council of Economic Advisors	**(30)**
National Security Council	**(47)**

Office of Policy Development	(31)
U. S. Trade Representative	(173)
Council on Environmental Quality	(11)
Office of Science & Technology Policy	(19)
Office of Administration	(182)
Office of the Vice President	(15)
Office of National Drug Control Policy	(109)

THE WHITE HOUSE OFFICE
1600 Pennsylvania Avenue NW.
Washington, DC 20500
(202) 456-1414, www.whitehouse.gov

This office assists the president in the performance of the many duties and responsibilities of the office. The staff facilitates and maintains communication with Congress, agencies and the public.

OFFICE OF MANAGEMENT & BUDGET
Executive Office Building
Washington, DC 20503
(202) 395-3080, **www.whitehouse.gov/omb**

Evaluates, formulates, and coordinates management procedures and program objectives among federal departments and agencies. Employment inquiries - (202) 395-1088.

NATIONAL SECURITY COUNCIL
Eisenhower Executive Bldg.
Washington, DC 20506
(202) 456-1414

Advises the president with respect to the integration of domestic, foreign, and military policies relating to national security.

OFFICE OF POLICY DEVELOPMENT
Eisenhower Executive Office Bldg., Rm. 216
Washington, DC 20502
(202) 456-2216

Advises the president in the formulation, evaluation, and coordination of long-range domestic and economic policy.

U.S. TRADE REPRESENTATIVE
600 Seventeenth Street NW.
Washington, DC 20508
(202) 395-3230

Responsible for the direction of all trade negotiations of the United States and for the formulation of trade policy for the United States.

COUNCIL ON ENVIRONMENTAL QUALITY
722 Jackson Place NW.
Washington, DC 20503
(202) 395-5750

Develops and recommends to the president national environmental quality policies.

OFFICE OF SCIENCE & TECHNOLOGY
Eisenhower Executive Office Bldg.
Washington, DC 20502
(202) 395-7347

Provides scientific, engineering, and technological analysis and judgement for the president in major policy, plans, and programs.

OFFICE OF ADMINISTRATION
Eisenhower Executive Building
725 Seventeenth St. N.W.
Washington, DC 20503
(202) 456-2891

Provides administrative support to all units within the Executive Office of the President. Contact their main number for information.

OFFICE OF THE VICE PRESIDENT
Eisenhower Executive Office Building
Washington, DC 20501
(202) 456-2326

The executive functions of the vice president include participation in Cabinet meetings and, by statute, membership on the National Security Council and the Board of Regents of the Smithsonian Institution.

THE 14 EXECUTIVE DEPARTMENTS

Agriculture	(100,084)
Commerce	(39,151)
Defense - nonmilitary	(670,568)
Education	(4,581)
Energy	(15,689)
Health & Human Services	(63,323)
Housing & Urban Development	(10,154)
Interior	(72,982)
Justice	(126,711)
Labor	(16,016)
State	(28,054)
Transportation	(64,131)
Treasury	(159,274)
Veterans Affairs	(223,137)

DEPARTMENT OF AGRICULTURE

Fourteenth Street and Independence Avenue SW
Washington, DC 20250
(202) 720-2791, http://www.usda.gov

This department works to maintain and improve farm income and develop and expand markets abroad for agricultural products. Helps curb and cure poverty, hunger, and malnutrition. Enhances the environment and maintains production capacity through efforts to protect the soil, water, forests, and other natural resources.

General employment inquiries may be sent to the Staffing & Personnel Information Systems Staff, Office of Personnel, Department of Agriculture, Washington, DC 20250.

EMPLOYMENT INFORMATION - Employment opportunities within the Food & Consumer Service can be researched by contacting their national headquarters in Washington, DC. Phone (703) 305-2351. Regional offices are located in Atlanta, Chicago, Dallas, San Francisco, Denver, Boston, and NJ. For these locations look up the Department of Agriculture, Food & Nutrition Services in the above cities' phone directory or obtain addresses from their headquarters in Washington, DC.

Field meat and poultry inspector units are located throughout the country in hundreds of metropolitan areas. Employment opportunities exist at hundreds of locations that are administered from the central offices listed in this appendix. Persons interested in employment in the Office of the Inspector General should contact the USDA Office of Personnel, Room 31-W, Administration Bldg., Washington, DC 20250. Phone (202) 720-5781.

DEPARTMENT OF COMMERCE (DOC)

Fourteenth Street between Constitution Ave. and E Street NW.,
Washington, DC 20230
(202) 482-2000, Employment Number:(202) 482-5138
Employment Web Site:www.doc.gov/ohrm

This department promotes the nation's international trade, economic growth, and technological advancement. The Department of Commerce provides assistance and information to increase America's competitiveness in the world economy, administers programs to prevent unfair foreign trade competition, provides research and support for the increased use of scientific engineering and technological development. Other responsibilities include the granting of patents and registration of trademarks, development of policies and conducting various research projects.

DOC OFFICES, AGENCIES AND BUREAUS

- **BUREAU OF THE CENSUS** - This bureau is a general purpose statistical agency that collects, tabulates, and publishes a wide variety of statistical data about people and the economy of the nation. For additional information contact the Public Information Office, Bureau of the Census, Dept. of Commerce, Washington, DC 20233. Phone (301) 457-8353.

- **ECONOMIC & STATISTICS ADMINISTRATION** - This bureau provides a picture of the U. S. economy. For additional information contact the Public Information Office, Bureau of Economic Analysis, Dept. of Commerce, Washington, DC 20230. Phone (800) 782-8872.

- **BUREAU OF EXPORT ADMINISTRATION** - The major functions of this agency are to process export license applications, conduct foreign availability studies, and enforce the U.S. export laws. For additional information contact the Bureau of Export Administrations, Rm. 3897, 14th St. and Constitution Ave. NW., Washington, DC 20230. Phone (202) 482-2721.

- **ECONOMIC DEVELOPMENT ADMINISTRATION** - This agency was created to generate new jobs, to help protect existing jobs, and to stimulate commercial and industrial growth in economically distressed areas. For further information contact the Economic Development Administration, Department of Commerce, Washington, DC 20230. Phone, (202) 482-2309.

- **INTERNATIONAL TRADE ADMINISTRATION** - The International Trade Administration was established to strengthen the international trade and investment position of the United States. There are 47 district offices located throughout the country. A listing of district offices and specific employment information can be obtained through The International Trade Administration, Department of Commerce, Washington, DC 20230. Phone, (202) 482-3809.

- **MINORITY BUSINESS DEVELOPMENT AGENCY** - This agency was created to assist minority enterprise in achieving effective and equitable participation in the American free enterprise system. Provides management and technical assistance to minority firms on request, primarily through a network of minority business development centers. For additional information contact the Public Information Office, Minority Business Development Agency, Dept. of Commerce, Washington, DC 20230. Phone (202) 482-5061.

- **NATIONAL OCEANIC AND ATMOSPHERIC ADMINISTRATION (NOAA)** -NOAA's mission is to explore, map, and chart the global ocean and its living resources and to manage, use, and conserve those resources. Predicts atmospheric conditions, ocean, sun, and space environment. Maintains weather stations including an electronic maintenance staff to service weather radar systems and other related weather equipment. Field employment offices:

Western Administrative Support Center, Bin C15700
7600 Sand Point Way NE
Seattle, WA 98115
206-526-6026

Mountain Administrative Support Center
325 Broadway
Boulder, CO 80303
303-497-6431

Central Administrative Support Center
601 East Twelfth St.,
Kansas City, MO 64106
816-426-2050

Eastern Administrative Support Center
200 World Trade Center
Norfolk, VA 23510
757-441-6864

- **PATENT AND TRADEMARK OFFICE** - Examines applications for patents and trademarks. Issued 122,977 patents in 1997 and registered 112,509 trademarks in that same year. Sells copies of issued patents and trademark registrations, records and indexes documents transferring ownership, maintains a scientific library and search files containing over 30 million documents. Office of Personnel, 2121 Crystal Dr., Arlington, VA 22202. Phone (703)-305-8341.

- **NATIONAL INSTITUTE OF STANDARDS AND TECHNOLOGY-** Conducts research for the nation's physical and technical measurement systems as well as scientific and technological measurement systems. Phone, 301-975-6478, E-mail: inquires@nist.gov, or visit their web site at http://www.nist.gov/.

DEPARTMENT OF DEFENSE (DOD)
The Pentagon
Washington, DC 20301-1155
(703) 545-6700, http://www.defenselink.mil

Responsible for providing the military forces needed to deter war and protect the security of the United States. Major elements are the Army, Navy, Marine Corps, and Air Force, consisting of close to 1.5 million men and women on active duty. In case of emergency, they are backed up by 1 million reserve forces members. In addition, there are about 770,000 Defense Department civilian employees.

The DOD is composed of the Office of the Secretary of Defense; the military departments and the military services within those departments; the Organization of the Joint Chiefs of Staff; the unified and specified combatant commands; the Armed Forces Policy Council; the Defense agencies and various DOD field facilities. This Executive Branch Department is the largest civilian employer. The jobs are interspersed through the United States and at several hundred installations overseas.

For overseas locations and employment contacts see Chapter Seven. The jobs in the United States are distributed throughout every state including the District of Columbia. The majority of military installations hire civilian personnel. Many are hired off of OPM's federal registers and others are special appointments for hiring veterans, spouses and family members of military personnel, the handicapped, minorities and others.

Locate military installations in your area in the yellow pages of your phone directory under GOVERNMENT. Also the blue pages in the back of the white page telephone directory provide comprehensive listings of government offices including military installations in your area.

EMPLOYMENT INFORMATION - Additional employment information can be obtained by writing to the Human Resource Service Center, Washington Headquarters Services, Room 2E22, 5001 Eisenhower Avenue, Alexandria, VA 22233-0001. Phone 703-617-7211 or visit their Internet web site at http://www.whs.mil/hrsc/index.html.

DEPARTMENT OF EDUCATION

400 Maryland Ave., SW
Washington, DC 20202
(800) USA-LEARN, http://www.ed.gov

The Department of Education is the Cabinet-level department that establishes policy for, administers, and coordinates most federal assistance to education. Total employment within this department is less than 5,000. There are ten regional offices located in: Atlanta, Boston, Chicago, Dallas, Denver, Kansas City, New York, Philadelphia, San Francisco, and Seattle.

EMPLOYMENT INFORMATION - Employment inquiries and applications should be directed to the Personnel Management Service at the above address. Phone (202) 401-0553.

DEPARTMENT OF ENERGY

1000 Independence Avenue SW
Washington, DC 20585
(202) 586-5000, http://www.doe.gov

The Department of Energy provides a balanced national energy plan through the coordination and administration of the energy functions of the federal government. The department is responsible for long-term, high-risk research and development of energy technology; the marketing of federal power, energy conservation; the nuclear weapons program, energy regulatory programs, and a central energy data collection and analysis program.

The majority of the department's energy research and development activities are carried out by contractors who operate government-owned facilities. Management and administration of these government-owned, contractor operated facilities are the major responsibility of this department.

EMPLOYMENT INFORMATION - Employment inquiries and applications should be directed to the Personnel Management Service at the above address. Phone (202)586-1234.

DEPARTMENT OF HEALTH AND HUMAN SERVICES (HHS)

200 Independence Avenue SW
Washington, DC 20201
(202) 619-0257, http://dhhs.gov

The Department of Health and Human Services employs 60,000 and touches the lives of more Americans than any other federal agency. This department advises the President on health, welfare, and income security plans, policies, and programs of the federal government. These programs are administered through five operating divisions, which include: the Social Security Administration, the Health Care Financing Administration, the Office of Human Development Services, the Public Health Service, and the Family Support Administration.

ADMINISTRATION, SERVICES AND OTHER OFFICES

- **ADMINISTRATION FOR CHILDREN AND FAMILIES** - Provides national leadership and direction to plan, manage, and coordinate the nationwide administration of comprehensive and supportive programs for vulnerable children and families. Contact the Office of Human Resource Management, Fourth Floor West, 370 L'Enfant Promenade SW., Washington, DC 20447. Phone, 202-401-9200.

- **AGENCY FOR HEALTH CARE RESEARCH** & QUALITY- The research arm of the Public Health Service. They work with the private sector and other public organizations to help consumers make better informed choices. Contact the agency at 301-594-2408. Internet, http://www.ahrG.gov/.

- **CENTER FOR DISEASE CONTROL AND PREVENTION** - CDC is the federal agency charged with protecting the public health of the nation by providing leadership and direction in the prevention and control of diseases and other conditions. Contact the CDC at 1600 Clifton Road, NE., Atlanta, GA 30333. Phone, 707-488-1725. Internet, http://www.cdc.gov/.

- **FOOD & DRUG ADMINISTRATION (FDA) -** The FDA's programs are designed to achieve the objective of consumer protection. Contact the Personnel Officer (HFA-400), phone 301-827-4120. Schools interested in the college recruitment program should contact 301-827-4120.

- **HEALTH CARE FINANCING ADMINISTRATION** - Provides oversight of the Medicare and Medicaid program. Contact 202-690-6726 for employment information.

- **INDIAN HEALTH SERVICE -** Provides a comprehensive health services delivery system for American Indians and Alaska Natives. Contact the Policy Support Staff, Room 6-34, 5600 Fishers Lane, Rockville, MD 20851. Phone 301-443-2650, www.ihs.gov/.

- **NATIONAL INSTITUTES OF HEALTH -** NIH seeks to expand fundamental knowledge about the nature and behavior of living systems, to apply that knowledge to extend the health of human lives, and to reduce the burdens resulting from disease and disability. Contact the Office of Human Resources at 301-496-2404 or visit (www.nih.gov) for employment information.

  EMPLOYMENT INFORMATION - General employment Inquiries should be directed to the Director, Human Resources Service, Program Support Center, 5600 Fishers Lane, Rockville, MD 20857. Phone 301-496-2404.

DEPARTMENT OF HOUSING AND URBAN DEVELOPMENT (HUD)
451 Seventh Street SW
Washington, DC 20410
(202) 708-1422

This department employs 10,154 and is the federal agency responsible for programs concerned with the nation's housing needs, the development and preservation of the nation's communities, and the provisions of equal housing opportunity.

The department administers the Federal Housing Administration mortgage insurance programs, rental assistance programs for lower income families; the Government National Mortgage Association mortgage-backed securities programs and other programs. Regional offices are located in Boston, New York City, Philadelphia, Atlanta, Fort Worth, Kansas City, Denver, San Francisco, and Seattle.

  EMPLOYMENT INFORMATION - General employment Inquiries should be directed to the Office of Personnel, 202-708-0408.

DEPARTMENT OF THE INTERIOR
1849 C Street NW
Washington, DC 20240
(202) 208-3100, www.doi.gov

The nation's principal conservation agency employs 72,982. The Department of the Interior has responsibility for most of our nationally owned public lands and natural resources. This includes fostering the wisest use of our land and water resources, protecting our fish and wildlife, preserving the environmental and cultural values of our national parks and historical places, and providing for the enjoyment of life through outdoor recreation.

EMPLOYMENT INFORMATION:

BUREAUS, SERVICES AND OTHER OFFICES

- **UNITED STATES FISH, WILDLIFE & PARKS SERVICE** - This service is composed of a headquarters office in Washington, DC, seven regional offices in the lower 48 states and Alaska, a regional research structure, and a variety of field units and installations. These include 450 National Wildlife Refuges and 150 Waterfowl Protection Areas, 25 major fish and wildlife laboratories and centers, 36 cooperative research units at universities, 70 National Fish Hatcheries, and a nationwide network of wildlife law enforcement agents. Division of Personnel Management, 1849 C St. NW, Mail Stop ARLSQ-100, Washington, DC 20240. Phone, (202) 208-6702. Their web site is located at http://www.fws.gov/employ.htm.

- **NATIONAL PARK SERVICE** - The National Park Service has a service center in Denver and a center for production of exhibits in Harpers Ferry, WV. There are more than 350 units in the National Parks and monuments, scenic parkways, riverways, seashores, lakeshores, recreation areas, and reservoirs; and historic sites. This service develops and implements park plans and staffs the area offices. Phone, (202) 208-6843. Internet, http://www.nps.gov/.

  > **EMPLOYMENT INFORMATION** - Direct inquiries to the Personnel Office, National Parks Service, Department of the Interior, Washington, DC, 20240. **Applications for temporary employment** must be received between September 1 and January 15 and should be sent to the Division of Personnel Management, National Parks Service, 1849 C St., NW, Washington, DC 20240. Phone, 202-208-5074.

- **LAND & MINERALS MANAGEMENT**
  This service has responsibility for programs associated with public land management; operations management and leasing for minerals on public lands. Also manages Indian lands; surface mining reclamation and enforcement functions. Contact the Land and Minerals Management, Washington, DC 20240 for additional employment information. Phone 202-208-3171.

- **GEOLOGICAL SURVEY** - The primary responsibilities of this service are to identify the nation's land, water, energy, and mineral resources. U.S. Geological Survey, Dept. of the Interior, 12201 Sunrise Valley Drive, Reston, VA 22092. Phone 703-648-6131. Internet, http://www.usgs.gov/.

- **BUREAU OF INDIAN AFFAIRS** - The principal objectives of the Bureau are to actively encourage and train Indian and Alaska Native people to manage their own affairs under the trust relationship to the federal government. For information contact the Public Information

Office, Bureau of Indian Affairs, Dept. of the Interior, Washington, DC 20240. Phone (202) 208-3710. Visit their web site at http://www.usgs.gov/doi/bureau-Indian-affairs.html/.

DEPARTMENT OF JUSTICE
950 Pennsylvania Avenue, NW
Washington, DC 20530
(202) 514-2000, http://www.usdoj.gov
Agency Wide Employment HOTLINE: 202-514-3397

The Department of Justice employs 123,498 and it is the largest law firm in the nation and serves as counsel for its citizens. It represents them in enforcing the law in the public interest. This department conducts all suits in the Supreme Court in which the United States is concerned. The Attorney General supervises and directs these activities, as well as those of the U.S. attorney and U.S. marshals in the various districts around the country.

DIVISIONS - DEPARTMENT OF JUSTICE

ANTITRUST - Responsible for promoting and maintaining competitive markets by enforcing the federal antitrust laws. This division has field offices at the federal buildings in Atlanta, GA; Chicago, IL; Cleveland, OH; Dallas, TX; New York, NY; Philadelphia, PA; and San Francisco, CA.

CIVIL - Litigation involves cases in federal district courts, the U.S. Courts of Appeals, the U.S. Claims Court, etc.. This division represents the United States, its departments and agencies, members of Congress, Cabinet officers, and other federal employees. There are three field office facilities. The Commercial Litigation Branch has two field offices. For employment information contact the Civil Division, Tenth Street & Pennsylvania Ave., Washington, DC 20530. Phone, 202-514-3301.

CRIMINAL - Formulates criminal law enforcement policies, enforces and exercises general supervision over all federal criminal laws except those assigned to the other divisions.

BUREAUS AND SERVICES

- **FEDERAL BUREAU OF INVESTIGATION (FBI)**
  935 Pennsylvania Ave.
  Washington, DC 20535
  (202) 324-3000, www.fbi.gov
  The FBI is the principal investigative arm of the United States Department of Justice. It is charged with gathering and reporting facts, locating witnesses, and compiling evidence in cases involving federal jurisdiction. The Bureau's investigations are conducted through 58 field offices.

  EMPLOYMENT INFORMATION - Direct inquiries to the Federal Bureau of Investigation, Director, Washington, DC 20535. You can also contact any of the 58 field offices. Consult your local telephone directory for the office nearest you.

- **BUREAU OF PRISONS**
  320 First St., NW
  Washington, DC 20534
  (888) 317-8455, www.bop.gov

  Responsible to maintain secure, safe, and humane correctional institutions for individuals placed in the care and custody of the Attorney General. Maintains and staffs all Federal Penal & Correctional Institutions.

EMPLOYMENT INFORMATION - Direct inquiries to the Bureau of Prisons, Central Office, Washington, DC 20534, 202-307-3082 or to any regional or field office.

- ## UNITED STATES MARSHAL SERVICE
  600 Army Navy Drive
  Arlington, VA 22202-4210
  (202) 307-9000

The presidentially appointed marshals and their support staff of just over 4,300 deputy marshals and administrative personnel operate from 427 office locations in all 94 federal judicial districts nationwide, from Guam to Puerto Rico, and from Alaska to Florida.

- ## IMMIGRATION AND NATURALIZATION SERVICE
  425 I Street NW
  Washington, DC 20536
  (202) 514-4316

This service provides information and service to the public, while concurrently exercising its enforcement responsibilities. The Immigration and Naturalization Service assists persons to the United States as visitors or as immigrants, provides assistance to those seeking permanent residence, prevents unlawful entry, and removes illegal aliens from the country. Major occupations include: Border Patrol Agent, Special Agent, Immigration Examiner, Immigration Inspector, Deportation Officer, Attorney, Computer Specialist and administrative positions. **Many jobs require employees to speak Spanish.**

EMPLOYMENT INFORMATION - Contact or direct inquiries to the Immigration & Naturalization Service, Central Office, 425 I St. NW, Washington, DC 20536. **Call 202-514-2530 or contact any regional or district office.**

- ## DRUG ENFORCEMENT ADMINISTRATION
  600-700 Army Navy Drive
  Arlington, VA 22202
  (202) 307-1000

The Drug Enforcement Administration is the lead federal agency in enforcing narcotics and controlled substances laws and regulations. The administration has offices throughout the United States and in 43 foreign countries. Special agents conduct criminal investigations and prepare for the prosecution of violators of the drug laws. Entry level is at the GS-7 or GS-9 grade with progression to GS-12 in three years.

This administration uses accountants, engineers, computer scientists, language majors, chemists, history majors, mathematicians, and other specialties for special agents. Investigators, intelligence research and administrative positions are also filled.

EMPLOYMENT INFORMATION - Contact the Office of Personnel, Drug Enforcement Administration at the address listed above.

DEPARTMENT OF LABOR
200 Constitution Avenue NW
Washington, DC 20210
(202)693-5000, www.dol.gov

The Department of Labor was created to foster, promote and develop the welfare of the wage earners of the United States, to improve their working conditions, and to advance their opportunities for profitable employment. The department administers a variety of federal labor laws guaranteeing workers the right to safe and healthful working conditions.

This department has 15,927 employees and ranks eleventh out of the fourteen departments in total numbers of employees. Yet, the Department of Labor effects every worker in the United States through one of their many internal components; the Pension and Welfare Benefits Administration, Office of Labor-Management Standards, Office of Administrative Law Judges, Benefits Review Board, Bureau of International Labor Affairs, The Bureau of Labor Statistics, Women's Bureau, Employment Standards Administration, Employment and Training Administration, Mine Safety and Health Administration, Veterans' Employment and Training Service, and Occupational Safety and Health Administration (OSHA).

> **EMPLOYMENT INFORMATION -** Personnel offices use lists of eligibles from the clerical, scientific, technical, and general examinations of the Office of Personnel Management. Inquiries and applications may be directed to the address listed above or consult your telephone directory (under U.S. Government - Department of Labor) for field offices nearest you. You can also call their job opportunity bank system at 1-800-366-2753.

DEPARTMENT OF STATE
2201 C Street NW
Washington, DC 20520
(202) 647-4000 (24-hour job vacancy hot line)

"The Department of State advises the president in the formulation and execution of foreign policy." The department's primary objective is to promote long-range security and well-being of the United States.

There were 164 U.S Embassies, 12 missions, 66 consulates general, 14 consulates, 1 U.S. Liaison office and 45 consular agencies throughout the world in April of 1998, manned by several thousand Foreign Service Officers of the Department of State. The State Department's total employment exceeds 24,727 full time employees assigned stateside and overseas in administrative, personnel, management, engineering, communications electronics, security, and career Foreign Service Officer positions. Five Regional Bureaus consist of the Bureaus of African Affairs, European & Canadian Affairs, East Asian and Pacific Affairs, and the Near Eastern and South Asian.

> **EMPLOYMENT INFORMATION - For Foreign Service Opportunities contact**: Foreign Service, Recruitment Division, HR/REE/REC, Room H-518, 2401 E Street NW, Washington, DC 20522. Phone (202) 261-8888. **For Civil Service Opportunities**: Staffing Services Division, Office of Civil Service Personnel (HR/CSP/S), Department of State, P.O. Box 58040, Washington, DC 20037. Phone 202-663-2176.

DEPARTMENT OF TRANSPORTATION
Central Employment Information Office
400 Seventh Street, SW
Washington, DC 20590
(202) 366-4000, http://www.dot.gov

"The U.S. Department of Transportation employs 64,234 and establishes the nation's overall transportation policy. There are nine administrations whose jurisdiction includes highway planning;

urban mass transit; railroads; aviation; and the safety of waterways, ports, highways, and pipelines."

ADMINISTRATIONS & OFFICES OF THE DOT

U.S. Coast Guard
Federal Aviation Administration
Federal Highway Administration
Federal Railroad Administration
National Highway Traffic Safety Administration
Federal Transit Administration
St. Lawrence Seaway Development Corporation
Maritime Administration
Research and Special Programs Administration
Bureau of Transportation Statistics

● **UNITED STATES COAST GUARD**
Civilian Personnel Division
2100 Second Street, SW
Washington, DC 20593
(202) 267-2229, http://www.uscg.mil

The U.S. Coast Guard is responsible for maritime service to the nation through search and rescue operations, preservation of navigational aids, merchant marine safety, environmental protection, maritime law enforcement, and boating safety.

● **FEDERAL AVIATION ADMINISTRATION (FAA)**
Headquarters
800 Independence Avenue, SW
Washington, DC 20591
(202) 267-8521, http://www.faa.gov

"The Administration is charged with regulating air commerce, controlling navigable airspace, promoting civil aeronautics, research and development, installing and operating air navigation facilities, air traffic control, and environmental impact of air navigation."

> **EMPLOYMENT INFORMATION:** Entry level engineers start at the FV-5/7/9 grade depending on college grades and work experience. The FAA is now an Excepted agency and their pay system is determined by a core compensation payband system. Engineers progress to the FV-11 or 12 pay grade. Air Traffic Control Specialists start at an equivalent FG-7 pay grade and can progress through an equivalent FV-14 grade and higher. Electronics technicians typically start in the F or G band (equivalent to the FV 9/11) and journeyman specialists are in the H band which is greater than a typical GS-12 grade. A large number of administrative, clerical, and personnel specialists are also needed.

● **FEDERAL HIGHWAY ADMINISTRATION**
400 Seventh Street, NW
Washington, DC 20590
(202) 366-0534

"This agency is concerned with the total operation and environment of highway systems." Civil/Highway Engineers, Motor Carrier Safety Specialists, Accountants, Contract Specialists, Computer Programmers, and administrative and clerical skills are needed.

> **EMPLOYMENT INFORMATION** - Major occupations include Civil/Highway Engineer, Motor Carrier Safety Specialists, Accountants, Contract Specialists, Computer Programmers, Administrative, Clerical and Transportation Specialists.

- **FEDERAL RAILROAD ADMINISTRATION**
  Office of Personnel
  1120 Vermont Avenue NW
  Washington, DC 20590
  (202) 493-6024

The Federal Railroad Administration enforces railroad safety, conducts research and development, provides passenger and freight services, and staffs and maintains the Transportation Test Center.

> **EMPLOYMENT INFORMATION** - Major occupations include Economist, Contract Specialist, Accountant, Attorney, Law Clerk, Administrative and Clerical.

- **NATIONAL HIGHWAY TRAFFIC SAFETY ADMINISTRATION**
  Office of Personnel
  400 Seventh Street, SW
  Washington, DC 20590 (202) 366-9550, www.nhtsa.dot.gov
  "The National Highway Traffic Safety Administration was established to reduce the number of deaths, injuries, and economic losses resulting from traffic accidents on national highways."

> **EMPLOYMENT INFORMATION** - Major occupations include Attorney Advisor, Law Clerk, Highway Safety Specialist, Mathematical Statistician, Mechanical Engineer, Safety Standard Engineer, Administrative and Clerical.

- **FEDERAL TRANSIT ADMINISTRATION**
  400 Seventh Street, SW
  Washington, DC 20590
  (202) 366-4043, http://www.fta.dot.gov

"Their mission is to assist in the development of improved mass transportation, to encourage the planning and establishment of area wide urban mass transit systems, and to provide assistance to state and local governments in financing such systems."

> **EMPLOYMENT INFORMATION** - Transportation Specialist, Civil Engineer, General Engineer, Contract Specialist, Administrative and Clerical.

- **RESEARCH & SPECIAL PROGRAMS ADMINISTRATION**
  Personnel Office, Rm 8401
  400 Seventh Street, SW
  Washington, DC 20590
  (202) 366-0656

"This administration consists of the Office of Hazardous Materials Transportation; the office of Pipeline Safety; Office of Civil Rights; Office of the Chief Council; the Transportation

Systems Center in Cambridge, Massachusetts; Office of Emergency Transportation; Office of Aviation Information Management; and the Office of Administration."

> **EMPLOYMENT INFORMATION** - Major occupations include Transportation Specialist, General Engineer (Pipeline), Mechanical Engineer, Chemical Engineer, Writer/Editor, Administrative and Clerical.

DEPARTMENT OF THE TREASURY
1500 Pennsylvania Avenue NW
Washington, DC 20220
(202) 622-2000

"The Department of the Treasury employs 151,529 and performs four basic functions: formulating and recommending economic, financial, tax, and fiscal policies; serving as financial agent for the U.S Government; enforcing the law; and manufacturing coins and currency."

BUREAUS, SERVICES, & OFFICES OF THE TREASURY

Internal Revenue Service
U.S. Customs Service
Bureau of Alcohol, Tobacco, & Firearms
Bureau of Engraving and Printing
Financial Management Service
Federal Law Enforcement Training Center
U.S. Mint
Office of the Comptroller of the Currency
Bureau of the Public Debt
U.S. Secret Service

● **INTERNAL REVENUE SERVICE (IRS)**
1111 Constitution Avenue NW
Washington, DC 20224
(202) 622-5000

"The Internal Revenue Service has more than 100,000 employees and is the largest organization in the Department of the Treasury. Approximately 7,000 of these employees work in Washington, DC. Others are employed in hundreds of offices throughout the U. S. There is an IRS Office in or near every town."

> **EMPLOYMENT INFORMATION** - "Almost every major field of study has some application to the work of the IRS. A substantial number of positions are in accounting, business administration, finance, economics, criminology, and law. There are also a great number of persons whose college major was political science, public administration, education, liberal arts, or other fields not directly related to business or law."

● **THE U.S. CUSTOMS SERVICE**
Office of Human Resources
1300 Pennsylvania Avenue, NW
Washington, DC 20229
(202) 927-6724

The Customs Service collects revenue from imports and enforces customs and related laws. Customs also administers the Tariff Act of 1930. They also enforce trademark, copyright, and patent privileges. "The 50 states, plus the Virgin Islands and Puerto Rico, are divided into seven regions. Contained within these regions are 44 subordinate district offices or area offices under which there are approximately 240 ports of entry."

>**EMPLOYMENT INFORMATION -** The Customs Service recruits through the Treasury Enforcement Agent examination. Address employment inquiries to 2120 L. St., NW., 6th fl., Washington, DC 20037. There are approximately 14,000 Customs employees.

- **BUREAU OF ALCOHOL, TOBACCO, & FIREARMS**
  650 Massachusetts Avenue NW
  Washington, DC 20226
  (202)927-8500, www.ustreas.gov/jobs

"The Bureau is responsible for enforcing and administering firearms and explosives laws, as well as those covering the production, use, and distribution of alcohol and tobacco products." There are approximately 3,500 employees, most of which are Special Agents and Inspectors.

- **BUREAU OF ENGRAVING & PRINTING**
  Office of Industrial Relations
  14TH and C Streets, SW
  Washington, DC 20228
  (202) 847-3019

"The Bureau of Engraving & Printing designs, prints, and finishes a large variety of security products including Federal Reserve notes, U.S. postage stamps, Treasury securities, and certificates. The bureau is the largest printer of security documents in the world; over 40 billion documents are printed annually. The bureau's headquarters and most of its production operations are located in Washington, DC. A second currency plant is in Fort Worth, TX."

>**EMPLOYMENT INFORMATION -** Selections are highly competitive. Major occupations include Police Officer, Computer Specialist, Engineer, Contract Specialist, Engraver, Production Manager, Security Specialist, Accountant, Auditor, and Administrative and Clerical positions. Phone 202-874-3747 for information.

- **U.S. MINT**
  801 Ninth Street NW
  Washington, DC 20220
  (202) 354-7200

The U.S. Mint employs some 2,300 employees at six locations including Washington, DC. Field facilities are located in Philadelphia, PA, Denver, CO, San Francisco, CA, West Point, NY, and Fort Knox, KY. The U.S. Mint produces bullion and domestic and foreign coins, distributes gold and silver, and controls bullion.

- **BUREAU OF PUBLIC DEBT**
  999 E Street NW
  Washington, DC 20239-0001
  (202) 219-3360, http://www.publicdebt.treas.gov

"The bureau administers the public debt by borrowing money through the sale of United States Treasury securities. The sale, service, and processing of Treasury securities involves the

Federal Reserve Banks and their branches, which serve as fiscal agents of the Treasury." This bureau also manages the U.S. Savings Bond program.

EMPLOYMENT INFORMATION - The major occupations include Accountant, Operating Accountant, Computer Systems Analyst, Computer Programmer, Computer Analyst.

- **SECRET SERVICE**
Chief of Staffing
Suite 8400, 950 H Street NW
Washington, DC 20223
(202) 435-5708, **www.treas.gov/usss**

The Secret Service has over 4,000 employees operating from 65 field offices. Agents protect the President, Vice President, and government officials including the heads of foreign governments. They also enforce counterfeiting laws, and fraud and forgery of government checks.

EMPLOYMENT INFORMATION - Major occupations include Corrections, Criminology, Law Enforcement, and Special Agent.

DEPARTMENT OF VETERANS AFFAIRS

810 Vermont & Avenue NW
Washington, DC 20420
(202) 273-4900, http://www.va.gov
"The Department of Veterans Affairs employs 235,304 and operates programs to benefit veterans and members of their families. Benefits include compensation payments for disabilities or death related to military service; pensions; education and rehabilitation; home loan guaranty; burial; and a medical care program incorporating nursing homes, clinics, and medical centers."

EMPLOYMENT INFORMATION - The VA employs physicians, dentists, podiatrists, optometrists, nurses, nurse anesthetists, physician assistants, expanded function dental auxiliaries, registered respiratory therapists, certified respiratory therapists, licensed physical therapists, occupational therapists, pharmacists, and licensed practical or vocational nurses under the VA's excepted merit system. This does not require civil service eligibility.

Other major occupations include Accounting, all BS, BA Majors, Architecture, Business, Computer Science, Engineering, Law, Statistics, and numerous Administrative and Clerical positions. There are hundreds of national Veterans Affairs facilities within the United States. Consult your local telephone directory for the facility nearest you.

INDEPENDENT AGENCIES (Partial List)

CENTRAL INTELLIGENCE AGENCY
Office of Personnel
Washington, DC 20505
(703) 482-1100, www.cia.gov

COMMISSION OF CIVIL RIGHTS
624 Ninth St., NW
Washington, DC 20425
(202) 376-8177, www.usccr.gov

COMMODITY FUTURES TRADING COMMISSION
1155 21st St., NW
Washington, DC20581
202-418-5000, **www.cftc.gov**

CONSUMER PRODUCT SAFETY COMMISSION
Division of Personnel Management
East West Towers, 4330 East West Hwy
Bethesda, MD 20814
(301) 504-0580
http://www.cpsc.gov

DEFENSE NUCLEAR FACILITIES SAFETY BOARD
Suite 700, 625 Indiana Ave., NW
Washington, DC 20004
202-694-7000
http://www.dnfsb.gov/**jobs.htm**

ENVIRONMENTAL PROTECTION AGENCY
1200 Pennsylvania Avenue NW
Washington, DC 20460
888-372-8255, Employment 202-564-3300
http://www.epa.gov

EQUAL OPPORTUNITY COMMISSION
1801 L Street NW
Washington, DC 20507
202-663-4900, TTY, 202-663-4494
Employment, 202-663-4306
http://www.eeoc.gov

FARM CREDIT ADMINISTRATION
Human Resources Division
1501 Farm Credit Drive
McLean, VA 22102-5090
(703) 883-4000
http://www.fca.gov

FEDERAL COMMUNICATIONS COMMISSION
Human Resource Management
1919 M Street, NW
Washington, DC 20554
888-225-5322, Employment 202-418-0134
TTY,888-835-5322
http://www.fcc.gov

FEDERAL DEPOSIT INSURANCE CORPORATION
Director of Personnel
550 Seventeenth St., NW
Washington, DC 20429
(202) 393-8400
http://www.fdic.gov

FEDERAL EMERGENCY MANAGEMENT
Office of Personnel, Rm 816
Washington, DC 20429
(202) 646-4600, Employment, 202-646-4040
www.fema.gov

FEDERAL HOUSING FINANCE BOARD
1777 F. St., NW
Washington, DC 20006
202-408-2500
http://www.fhfb.gov

FEDERAL LABOR RELATIONS AUTHORITY
607 Fourteenth St., NW
Washington, DC 20424-0001
202-482-6560, Employment 202-482-6660
http://www.flra.gov

FEDERAL MARITIME COMMISSION
800 North Capital NW
Washington, DC 20573-0001
(202) 523-5707
http://www.fmc.gov

FEDERAL MINE SAFETY & HEALTH COMMISSION
1730 K St., NW
Washington, DC 20006-3867
202-653-5625
E-mail: info@fmshrc.gov, www.fmshrc.gov

FEDERAL RESERVE SYSTEM
Twentieth Street and Constitution Ave., NW
Washington, DC 20551
202-452-3000

FEDERAL TRADE COMMISSION
Director of Human Resources
Washington, DC 20580
(202) 326-2222, Employment 202-326-2021
http://www.ftc.gov

GOVERNMENT PRINTING OFFICE
Chief, Employment Branch
732 North Capital Street, NW
Washington, DC 20401
(202) 512-0000
http:wwwgpo.gov

MERIT SYSTEMS PROTECTION BOARD
Personnel Division
5th Floor, 1615 M Street NW
Washington, DC 20419
(202) 653-7200
http://www.mspb.gov

NASA
300 E. St. SW
NASA Headquarters
Washington, DC 20546
(202)358-0000, Employment 202-358-1543
www.nasa.gov

NATIONAL ARCHIVES AND RECORDS ADMIN.
8601 Adelphi Road
College Park, MD 20740-6001
301-713-6800
http://www.nara.gov

NATIONAL CREDIT UNION ADMINISTRATION
Personnel Management Specialist
1775 Duke St.
Alexandria, VA 22314-3428
(703)518-6300
http:www.ncua.gov

NATIONAL ENDOWMENT FOR THE HUMANITIES
1100 Pennsylvania Ave., NW
Washington, DC 20506
(202)606-8400
http:www.neh.gov

NATIONAL FOUNDATION OF THE ARTS
1100 Pennsylvania Ave., NW
Washington, DC 20506-0001
202-682-5400, www.arts.gov

NATIONAL LABOR RELATIONS BOARD
Personnel Operations
1099 Fourteenth St. NW
Washington, DC 20570
(202) 273-1000, TDD 202-273-4300
http://www.nlrb.gov

NATIONAL MEDIATION BOARD
Suite 250 East
1301 K Street NW
Washington, DC 20572
202-692-5000, www.nmb.gov

NATIONAL SCIENCE FOUNDATION
Division of Personnel Management
4201 Wilson Blvd.
Arlington, VA 22230
(703) 292-5111
http://www.nsf.gov

NATIONAL TRANSPORTATION SAFETY BOARD
490 L'Wnfant Plaza SW
Washington, DC 20594
202-314-6000
http://www.ntsb.gov

NUCLEAR REGULATORY COMMISSION
Washington, DC 20555
301-415-7000
http://www.nrc.gov

OFFICE OF GOVERNMENT ETHICS
Suite 500, 1201 New York Ave., NW
Washington, DC 20005-3917
202-208-8000
http://www.usoge.gov

OFFICE OF PERSONNEL MANAGEMENT (OPM)
Recruitment/Employment, Rm 1469
1900 E. Street, NW
Washington, DC 20415
(202) 606-5800, Employment 202-757-3000
http://www.opm.gov

PEACE CORP
1111 20th St., NW
Washington, DC 20526
202-692-2000, www.peacecorps.gov

POSTAL RATE COMMISSION
1333 H Street NW
Washington, DC 20268-0001
202-789-6800
http://www.prc.gov

SECURITY AND EXCHANGE COMMISSION
450 Fifth St., NW
Washington, DC 20549
202-942-4150, Employment 202-942-4070
http://www.sec.gov

SELECTIVE SERVICE SYSTEM
Arlington, VA 22209-2425
703-605-4000, www.sss.gov

SMALL BUSINESS ADMINISTRATION
409 Third St., SW
Washington, DC 20416
202-205-6600
http://www.sba.gov

SOCIAL SECURITY ADMINISTRATION
6401 Security Blvd.
Baltimore, MD 21235
410-965-1234
http://www.ssa.gov

Appendix D
Federal Occupation List

The government's classification system includes an occupational structure which groups similar jobs together. There are 22 occupational groups comprising 441 different white-collar occupations under the General Schedule; GS-000 through GS-2100. Each occupational group is further subdivided into specific numerical codes (for example: GS-856, Electronics Technician, GS-318, Secretary Series, etc.). The Wage Grade Trades and Labor Schedule offers an additional 36 occupational families; WG-2500 through WG-9000.

This Appendix presents a comprehensive listing of both GS and WG occupational groups, families and related series. First, locate the occupational group or groups in which you have specific knowledge, skill, and or training. Then, review each job series under the primary occupation group or family.[1]

More than a quarter (398,721 or 25.4%) of white-collar workers had an occupation in the General Administrative, Clerical and Office Services group. The other four large white-collar groups were: Medical, Hospital, Dental and Public Health (152,619 or 7.9 percent); Engineering and Architecture (145,824 or 9.3 percent); Accounting and Budget (142,598 or 9.1 percent); and Business and Industry (97,205 or 6.2 percent).

Certain white-collar occupations are concentrated in particular federal agencies. The Department of Agriculture employed 65.4 percent of Biological Science employees and 93 percent of Veterinary Medical Science workers. The Department of Health and Human Services was the major employer of the Social Science, Psychology and Welfare group (39.5 percent) and the Legal and Kindred group (39 percent). The Veterans Administration employed 73 percent of the Medical, Hospital, Dental and Public Health group. The Department of Commerce employed 85.6 percent of the Copyright, Patent and Trademark group. The Department of Transportation had 66.8 percent of the Transportation group employees. The Library of Congress and Department of Defense together employed 55.4 percent of the Library and Archives group. The Department of Treasury and Justice together employed 69.5 percent of the Investigative group. The Department of Defense was the major employer in all the other white collar occupational groups.

---

[1] References for the General Schedule Occupational Groups and Series are the Handbook of Occupational Groups & Series, September 1995 published by the U.S. Office of Personnel Management and Pamphlet PB97-170591.

GENERAL SCHEDULE (GS) OCCUPATIONAL GROUPS

GS-000: MISCELLANEOUS - This group includes all classes of positions, the duties of which are to administer, supervise, or perform work which cannot be included in other occupational groups either because the duties are unique, or because they are complex and come in part under various groups.

GS-100: SOCIAL SCIENCE, PSYCHOLOGY, AND WELFARE GROUP - This group includes all classes of positions, the duties of which are to advise on, administer, supervise, or perform research or other professional and scientific work, subordinate technical work, or related clerical work in one or more of the social sciences; in psychology; in social work; in recreational activities; or in the administration of public welfare and insurance programs.

GS-200: PERSONNEL MANAGEMENT AND INDUSTRIAL RELATIONS GROUP - This group includes all classes of positions, the duties of which are to advise on, administer, supervise, or perform work involved in the various phases of personnel management and industrial relations.

GS-300: GENERAL ADMINISTRATIVE, CLERICAL, & OFFICE SERVICES GROUP-This group includes all classes of positions the duties of which are to administer, supervise, or perform work involved in management analysis; stenography, typing, correspondence, and secretarial work; mail and file work; the operation of office appliances; the operation of communications equipment, use of codes and ciphers, and procurement of the most efficient communications services; the operation of microform equipment, peripheral equipment, duplicating equipment, mail processing equipment, and copier/duplicating equipment; and other work of a general clerical and administrative nature.

GS-400: BIOLOGICAL SCIENCE GROUP - This group includes all classes of positions, the duties of which are to advise on, administer, supervise, or perform research or other professional and scientific work or subordinate technical work in any of the fields of science concerned with living organisms, their distribution, characteristics, life processes, and adaptations and relations to the environment; the soil, its properties and distribution, and the living organisms growing in or on the soil; and the management, conservation, or utilization thereof for particular purposes or uses.

GS-500: ACCOUNTING AND BUDGET GROUP - This group includes all classes of positions, the duties of which are to advise on, administer, supervise, or perform professional, technical, or related clerical work of an accounting, budget administration, related financial management, or similar nature.

GS-600: MEDICAL, HOSPITAL, DENTAL, AND PUBLIC HEALTH GROUP - This group includes all classes of positions, the duties of which are to advise on, administer, supervise, or perform research or other professional and scientific work, subordinate technical work, or related clerical work in the several branches of medicine, surgery, and dentistry or in related patient care services such as dietetics, nursing, occupational therapy, physical therapy, pharmacy, and others.

GS-700: VETERINARY MEDICAL SCIENCE GROUP - This group includes all classes of positions, the duties of which are to advise and consult on, administer, manage, supervise, or perform research or other professional and scientific work in the various branches of veterinary medical science.

GS-800: ENGINEERING AND ARCHITECTURE - This group includes all classes of positions, the duties of which are to advise on, administer, supervise, or perform professional, scientific, or technical work concerned with engineering or architectural projects, facilities, structures, systems, processes, equipment, devices, material or methods. Positions in this group require knowledge of the science or art, or both, by which materials, natural resources, and power are made useful.

GS-900: LEGAL AND KINDRED GROUP - This group includes all classes of positions, the duties of which are to advise on, administer, supervise, or perform professional legal work in the preparation for trial and the trial and argument of cases, the presiding at formal hearings afforded by a commission, board, or other body having quasi-judicial powers, as part of its administrative procedure, the administration of law entrusted to an agency, the preparation or rendering of authoritative or advisory legal opinions or decisions to other federal agencies or to administrative officials of own agency, the preparation of various legal documents; and the performance of other work requiring training equivalent to that represented by graduation from a recognized law school and in some instances requiring admission to the bar; or quasi-legal work which requires knowledge of particular laws, or of regulations, precedents, or departmental practice based thereon, but which does not require such legal training or admission to the bar.

GS-1000: INFORMATION AND ARTS GROUP - This group includes positions which involve professional, artistic, technical, or clerical work in (1) the communication of information and ideas through verbal, visual, or pictorial means, (2) the collection, custody, presentation, display, and interpretation of art works, cultural objects, and other artifacts, or (3) a branch of fine or applied arts such as industrial design, interior design, or musical composition. Positions in this group require writing, editing, and language ability; artistic skill and ability; knowledge of foreign languages; the ability to evaluate and interpret informational and cultural materials; the practical application of technical or aesthetic principles combined with manual skill and dexterity; or related clerical skills.

GS-1100: BUSINESS AND INDUSTRY GROUP - This group includes all classes of positions, the duties of which are to advise on, administer, supervise, or perform work pertaining to and requiring a knowledge of business and trade practices, characteristics and use of equipment, products, or property, or industrial production methods and processes, including the conduct of investigations and studies; the collection, analysis, and dissemination of information; the establishment and maintenance of contracts with industry and commerce; the provision of advisory services; the examination and appraisement of merchandise or property; and the administration of regulatory provisions and controls.

GS-1200: COPYRIGHT, PATENT, AND TRADE-MARK GROUP - This group includes all classes of positions, the duties of which are to advise on, administer, supervise, or perform professional scientific, technical, and legal work involved in the cataloging and registration of copyright, in the classification and issuance of patents, in the registration of trade-marks, in the prosecution of applications for patents before the Patent Office, and in the giving of advice to government officials on patent matters.

GS-1300: PHYSICAL SCIENCE GROUP - This group includes all classes of positions, the duties of which are to advise on, administer, supervise, or perform research or other professional and scientific work or subordinate technical work in any of the fields of science concerned with matter, energy, physical space, time, nature of physical measurement, and fundamental structural particles; and the nature of the physical environment.

GS-1400: LIBRARY AND ARCHIVES GROUP - This group includes all classes of positions, the duties of which are to advise on, administer, supervise, or perform professional and scientific work or subordinate technical work in the various phases of library archival science.

GS-1500: MATHEMATICS AND STATISTICS GROUP - This group includes all classes of positions, the duties of which are to advise on, administer, supervise, or perform research or other professional and scientific work or related clerical work in basic mathematical principals, methods, procedures, or relationships, including the development and application of mathematical methods for the investigation and solution of problems; the development and application of statistical theory in the selection, collection, classification, adjustment, analysis, and interpretation of data; the development and application of mathematical, statistical, and financial principles to programs or problems involving life and property risks; and any other professional and scientific or related clerical work requiring primarily and mainly the understanding and use of mathematical theories, methods, and operations.

GS-1600: EQUIPMENT, FACILITIES, AND SERVICES GROUP - This group includes positions the duties of which are to advise on, manage, or provide instructions and information concerning the operation, maintenance, and use of equipment, shops, buildings, laundries, printing plants, power plants, cemeteries, or other government facilities, or other work involving services provided predominantly by persons in trades, crafts, or manual labor operations. Positions in this group require technical or managerial knowledge and ability, plus a practical knowledge of trades, crafts, or manual labor operations.

GS-1700: EDUCATION GROUP - This group includes positions which involve administering, managing, supervising, performing, or supporting education or training work when the paramount requirement of the position is knowledge of, or skill in, education, training, or instruction processes.

GS-1800: INVESTIGATION GROUP - This group includes all classes of positions, the duties of which are to advise on, administer, supervise, or perform investigation, inspection, or enforcement work primarily concerned with alleged or suspected offenses against the laws of the United States, or such work primarily concerned with determining compliance with laws and regulations.

GS-1900: QUALITY ASSURANCE, INSPECTION, AND GRADING GROUP - This group includes all classes of positions, the duties of which are to advise on, supervise, or perform administrative or technical work primarily concerned with the quality assurance or inspection of material, facilities, and processes; or with the grading of commodities under official standards.

GS-2000: SUPPLY GROUP - This group includes positions which involve work concerned with finishing all types of supplies, equipment, material, property (except real estate), and certain services to components of the federal government, industrial, or other concerns under contract to the government, or receiving supplies from the federal government. Included are positions concerned with one or more aspects of supply activities from initial planning, including requirements analysis and determination, through acquisition, cataloging, storage, distribution, utilization to ultimate issue for consumption or disposal. The work requires a knowledge of one or more elements or parts of a supply system, and/or supply methods, policies, or procedures.

GS-2100: TRANSPORTATION GROUP - This group includes all classes of positions, the duties of which are to advise on, administer, supervise, or perform work which involves two or more specialized transportation functions or other transportation work not specifically included in other series of this group.

GENERAL SCHEDULE GROUPS & RELATED SERIES
GS-000-Miscellaneous Occupations Group (Not Elsewhere Classified)

Correctional Institution Administration Series	GS-006	Chaplain Series	GS-060
Correctional Officer	GS-007	Clothing Design Series	GS-062
Bond Sales Promotion Series	GS-011	Fingerprint Identification Series	GS-072
Safety and Occupational Health Management Series	GS-018	Security Administration Series	GS-080
Safety Technician Series	GS-019	Fire Protection and Prevention Series	GS-081
Community Planning Series	GS-020	United States Marshall Series	GS-082
Community Planning Technician Series	GS-021	Police Series	GS-083
Outdoor Recreation Planning Series	GS-023	Nuclear Materials Courier Series	GS-084
Park Ranger Series	GS-025	Security Guard Series	GS-085
Environmental Protection Specialist Series	GS-028	Security Clerical Assistance Series	GS-086
Environmental Protection Assistant Series	GS-029	Guide Series	GS-090
Sports Specialist Series	GS-030	Foreign Law Specialist Series	GS-095
Funeral Directing Series	GS-050	General Student Trainee Series	GS-099

GS-100-SOCIAL SCIENCE, PSYCHOLOGY, AND WELFARE GROUP

Social Science Series	GS-101	Geography Series	
GS-150Social Science Aid and Technician Series	GS-102	Civil Rights Analysis Series	GS-160
Social Insurance Administration Series	GS-105	History Series	GS-170
Unemployment Insurance Series	GS-106	Psychology Series	GS-180
Economist Series	GS-110	Psychology Aide and Technician Series	GS-181
Economics Assistant Series	GS-119	Sociology Series	GS-184
Food Assistance Program Specialist Series	GS-120	Social Work Series	GS-185
Foreign Affairs Series	GS-130	Social Services Aide & Assistant Series	GS-186
International Relations Series	GS-131	Social Services Series	GS-187
Intelligence Series	GS-132	Recreation Specialist Series	GS-188
Intelligence Aide and Clerk Series	GS-134	Recreation Aide and Assistant Series	GS-189
Foreign Agricultural Affairs Series	GS-135	General Anthropology Series	GS-190
International Cooperation Series	GS-136	Archeology Series	GS-193
Manpower Research and Analysis Series	GS-140	Social Science Student Trainee Series	GS-199
Manpower Development Series	GS-142		

GS-200-PERSONNEL MANAGEMENT AND INDUSTRIAL RELATIONS GROUP

Personnel Management Series	GS-201	Employee Development Series	GS-235
Personnel Clerical and Assistance Series	GS-203	Mediation Series	GS-241

Military Personnel Clerical and Technician Series	GS-204
Military Personnel Management Series	GS-205
Personnel Staffing Series	GS-212
Position Classification Series	GS-221
Occupational Analysis Series	GS-222
Salary and Wage Administration Series	GS-223
Employee Relations Series	GS-230
Labor Relations Series	GS-233
Apprenticeship and Training Series	GS-243
Labor Management Relations Examining Series	GS-244
Contractor Industrial Relations Series	GS-246
Wage and Hour Compliance Series	GS-249
Equal Employment Opportunity Series	GS-260
Federal Retirement Benefits Series	GS-270
Personnel Management Student Trainee Series	GS-299

GS-300-GENERAL ADMINISTRATION, CLERICAL, AND OFFICE SERVICES GROUP

Miscellaneous Administration and Program Series	GS-301
Messenger Series	GS-302
Miscellaneous Clerk and Assistant Series	GS-303
Information Receptionist Series	GS-304
Mail and File Series	GS-305
Correspondence Clerk Series	GS-309
Clerk-Stenographer and Reporter Series	GS-312
Work Unit Supervising Series	GS-313
Secretary Series	GS-318
Closed Microphone Reporting Series	GS-319
Logistics Management Series	GS-346
Equipment Operator Series	GS-350
Printing Clerical Series	GS-351
Data Transcriber Series	GS-356
Coding Series	GS-357
Electric Accounting Machine Operation Series	GS-359
Equal Opportunity Compliance Series	GS-360
Equal Opportunity Assistance Series	GS-361
Clerk-Typist Series	GS-322
Office Automation Clerical and Assistance Series	GS-326
Computer Operation Series	GS-332
Computer Specialist Series	GS-334
Computer Clerk and Assistant Series	GS-335
Program Management Series	GS-340
Administrative Officer Series	GS-341
Support Services Administration Series	GS-342
Management and Program Analysis Series	GS-343
Management Clerical and Assistance Series	GS-344
Electric Account. Machine Project Planning Series	GS-362
Telephone Operating Series	GS-382
Telecommunications Processing Series	GS-390
Telecommunications Series	GS-391
General Communications Series	GS-392
Communications Clerical Series	GS-394
Admin. & Office Support Student Trainee Series	GS-399

GS-400-BIOLOGICAL SCIENCES GROUP

General Biological Science Series	GS-401
Microbiology Series	GS-403
Biological Science Technician Series	GS-404
Pharmacology Series	GS-405
Agricultural Extension Series	GS-406
Ecology Series	GS-408
Zoology Series	GS-410
Physiology Series	GS-413
Entomology Series	GS-414
Toxicology Series	GS-415
Plant Protection Technician Series	GS-421
Botany Series	GS-430
Plant Pathology Series	GS-434
Plant Physiology Series	GS-435
Plant Protection and Quarantine Series	GS-436
Horticulture Series	GS-437
Genetics Series	GS-440
Range Conservation Series	GS-454
Range Technician Series	GS-455
Soil Conservation Series	GS-457
Soil Conservation Technician Series	GS-458
Irrigation System Operation Series	GS-459
Forestry Series	GS-460
Forestry Technician Series	GS-462
Soil Science Series	GS-470
Agronomy Series	GS-471
Agricultural Management Series	GS-475
General Fish and Wildlife Administration Series	GS-480
Fishery Biology Series	GS-482
Wildlife Refuge Management Series	GS-485
Wildlife Biology Series	GS-486
Animal Science Series	GS-487
Home Economics Series	GS-493
Biological Science Student Trainee Series	GS-499

GS-500 ACCOUNTING AND BUDGET GROUP

Financial Administration and Program Series	GS-501
Financial Clerical and Assistance Series	GS-503
Financial Management Series	GS-505
Accounting Series	GS-510
Auditing Series	GS-511
Internal Revenue Agent Series	GS-512
Accounting Technician Series	GS-525
Tax Technician Series	GS-526
Cash Processing Series	GS-530
Voucher Examining Series	GS-540
Civilian Pay Series	GS-544
Military Pay Series	GS-545
Budget Analysis Series	GS-560
Budget Clerical and Assistance Series	GS-561
Financial Institution Examining Series	GS-570
Tax Examining Series	GS-592
Insurance Accounts Series	GS-593
Financial Management Student Trainee Series	GS-599

GS-600-MEDICAL, HOSPITAL, DENTAL, AND PUBLIC HEALTH GROUP

General Health Science Series	GS-601
Medical Officer Series	GS-602
Diagnostic Radiologic Technologist Series	GS-647
Therapeutic Radiologic Technologist Series	GS-648

Physician's Assistant Series	GS-603	Medical Instrument Technician Series	GS-649
Nurse Series	GS-610	Medical Technical Assistant Series	GS-650
Practical Nurse Series	GS-620	Respiratory Therapist Series	GS-651
Nursing Assistant Series	GS-621	Pharmacist Series	GS-660
Medical Supply Aide and Technician Series	GS-622	Pharmacy Technician Series	GS-661
Autopsy Assistant Series	GS-625	Optometrist Series	GS-662
Dietitian and Nutritionist Series	GS-630	Restoration Technician Series	GS-664
Occupational Therapist Series	GS-631	Speech Pathology and Audiology Series	GS-665
Physical Therapist Series	GS-633	Orthotist and Prosthetist Series	GS-667
Corrective Therapist Series	GS-635	Podiatrist Series	GS-668
Rehabilitation Therapy Assistant Series	GS-636	Medical Records Administration Series	GS-669
Manual Arts Therapist Series	GS-637	Health System Administration Series	GS-670
Recreation/Creative Arts Therapist Series	GS-638	Health System Specialist Series	GS-671
Educational Therapist Series	GS-639	Prosthetic Representative Series	GS-672
Health Aid and Technician Series	GS-640	Hospital Housekeeping Management Series	GS-673
Nuclear Medicine Technician Series	GS-642	Medical Records Technician Series	GS-675
Medical Technologist Series	GS-644	Medical Clerk Series	GS-679
Medical Technician Series	GS-645	Dental Officer Series	GS-680
Pathology Technician Series	GS-646	Dental Assistant Series	GS-681
Dental Hygiene Series	GS-682	Industrial Hygiene Series	GS-690
Dental Laboratory Aid and Technician Series	GS-683	Consumer Safety Series	GS-696
Public Health Program Specialist Series	GS-685	Environmental Health Technician Series	GS-698
Sanitarian Series	GS-688	Medical and Health Student Trainee Series	GS-699

GS-700-VETERINARY MEDICAL SCIENCE GROUP

Veterinary Medical Science Series	GS-701	Veterinary Student Trainee Series	GS-799
Animal Health Technician Series	GS-704		

GS-800-ENGINEERING AND ARCHITECTURE GROUP

General Engineering Series	GS-801	Computer Engineering Series	GS-854
Engineering Technician Series	GS-802	Electronics Engineering Series	GS-855
Safety Engineering Series	GS-803	Electronics Technician Series	GS-856
Fire Protection Engineering Series	GS-804	Biomedical Engineering Series	GS-858
Materials Engineering Series	GS-806	Aerospace Engineering Series	GS-861
Landscape Architecture Series	GS-807	Naval Architecture Series	GS-871
Architecture Series	GS-808	Ship Surveying Series	GS-873
Construction Control Series	GS-809	Mining Engineering Series	GS-880
Civil Engineering Series	GS-810	Petroleum Engineering Series	GS-881
Surveying Technician Series	GS-817	Agricultural Engineering Series	GS-890
Engineering Drafting Series	GS-818	Ceramic Engineering Series	GS-892
Environmental Engineering Series	GS-819	Chemical Engineering Series	GS-893
Construction Analyst Series	GS-828	Welding Engineering Series	GS-894
Mechanical Engineering Series	GS-830	Industrial Engineering Technician Series	GS-895
Nuclear Engineering Series	GS-840	Industrial Engineering Series	GS-896
Electrical Engineering Series	GS-850	Engineering/Architecture Student Series	GS-899

GS-900-LEGAL AND KINDRED GROUP

Law Clerk Series	GS-904	Legal Clerical and Assistance Series	GS-986
General Attorney Series	GS-905	Tax Law Specialist Series	GS-987
Estate Tax Examining Series	GS-920	General Claims Examining Series	GS-990
Hearings and Appeals Series	GS-930	Workers' Compensation Claims Examining Series	GS-991
Clerk of Court Series	GS-945	Loss and Damage Claims Examining Series	GS-992
Paralegal Specialist Series	GS-950	Social Insurance Claims Examining Series	GS-993
Pension Law Specialist Series	GS-958	Unemployment Compensation Examining Series	GS-994
Contact Representative Series	GS-962	Dependents and Estates Claims Examining Series	GS-995
Legal Instruments Examining Series	GS-963	Veterans Claims Examining Series	GS-996
Land Law Examining Series	GS-965	Claims Clerical Series	GS-998
Passport and Visa Examining Series	GS-967	Legal Occupations Student Trainee Series	GS-999

GS-1000-INFORMATION AND ARTS GROUP

General Arts and Information Series	GS-1001	Music Specialist Series	GS-1051
Interior Design Series	GS-1008	Theater Specialist Series	GS-1054

Exhibits Specialist Series	GS-1010	Art Specialist Series	GS-1056
Museum Curator Series	GS-1015	Photography Series	GS-1060
Museum Specialist and Technician Series	GS-1016	Audiovisual Production Series	GS-1071
Illustrating Series	GS-1020	Writing and Editing Series	GS-1082
Office Drafting Series	GS-1021	Technical Writing and Editing Series	GS-1083
Public Affairs Series	GS-1035	Visual Information Series	GS-1084
Language Specialist Series	GS-1040	Editorial Assistance Series	GS-1087
Language Clerical Series	GS-1046	Information and Arts Student Trainee Series	GS-1099

GS-1100-BUSINESS AND INDUSTRY GROUP

General Business and Industry Series	GS-1101	Property Disposal Series	GS-1104
Contracting Series	GS-1102	Purchasing Series	GS-1105
Industrial Property Management Series	GS-1103	Procurement Clerical and Technician Series	GS-1106
Property Disposal Clerical and Technician Series	GS-1107	Crop Insurance Administration Series	GS-1161
Public Utilities Specialist Series	GS-1130	Crop Insurance Underwriting Series	GS-1162
Trade Specialist Series	GS-1140	Insurance Examining Series	GS-1163
Commissary Store Management Series	GS-1144	Loan Specialist Series	GS-1165
Agricultural Program Specialist Series	GS-1145	Internal Revenue Officer Series	GS-1169
Agricultural Marketing Series	GS-1146	Realty Series	GS-1170
Agricultural Market Reporting Series	GS-1147	Appraising and Assessing Series	GS-1171
Industrial Specialist Series	GS-1150	Housing Management Series	GS-1173
Production Control Series	GS-1152	Building Management Series	GS-1176
Financial Analysis Series	GS-1160	Business/Industry Student Trainee Series	GS-1199

GS-1200-COPYRIGHT, PATENT, AND TRADE-MARK GROUP

Patent Technician Series	GS-1202	Patent Attorney Series	GS-1222
Copyright Series	GS-1210	Patent Classifying Series	GS-1223
Copyright Technician Series	GS-1211	Patent Examining Series	GS-1224
Patent Administration Series	GS-1220	Design Patent Examining Series	GS-1226
Patent Advisor Series	GS-1221	Copyright and Patent Student Trainee Series	GS-1299

GS-1300-PHYSICAL SCIENCES GROUP

General Physical Science Series	GS-1301	Oceanography Series	GS-1360
Health Physics Series	GS-1306	Navigational Information Series	GS-1361
Physics Series	GS-1310	Cartography Series	GS-1370
Physical Science Technician Series	GS-1311	Cartographic Technician Series	GS-1371
Geophysics Series	GS-1313	Geodesy Series	GS-1372
Hydrology Series	GS-1315	Land Surveying Series	GS-1373
Hydrologic Technician Series	GS-1316	Geodetic Technician Series	GS-1374
Chemistry Series	GS-1320	Forest Products Technology Series	GS-1380
Metallurgy Series	GS-1321	Food Technology Series	GS-1382
Astronomy and Space Science Series	GS-1330	Textile Technology Series	GS-1384
Meteorology Series	GS-1340	Photographic Technology Series	GS-1386
Meteorological Technician Series	GS-1341	Document Analysis Series	GS-1397
Geology Series	GS-1350	Physical Science Student Trainee Series	GS-1399

GS-1400-LIBRARY AND ARCHIVES GROUP

Librarian Series	GS-1410	Archivist Series	GS-1420
Library Technician Series	GS-1411	Archives Technician Series	GS-1421
Technical Information Services Series	GS-1412	Library and Archives Student Trainee	GS-1499

GS-1500-MATHEMATICS AND STATISTICS GROUP

Actuary Series	GS-1510	Statistical Assistant Series	GS-1531
Operations Research Series	GS-1515	Cryptography Series	GS-1540
Mathematics Series	GS-1520	Cryptanalysis Series	GS-1541
Mathematics Technician Series	GS-1521	Computer Science Series	GS-1550
Mathematical Statistician Series	GS-1529	Mathematics/Statistics Student Trainee Series	GS-1599
Statistician Series	GS-1530		

GS-1600-EQUIPMENT, FACILITIES, AND SERVICES GROUP

General Facilities and Equipment Series	GS-1601	Steward Series	GS-1667
Cemetery Administration Series	GS-1630	Equipment Specialist Series	GS-1670
Facility Management Series	GS-1640	Equipment/ Facilities Mgmt Student Series	GS-1699
Printing Management Series	GS-1654		
Laundry and Dry Cleaning Plant Mgmt.	GS-1658		

GS-1700-EDUCATION GROUP

General Education and Training Series	GS-1701	Training Instruction Series	GS-1712
Education and Training Technician Series	GS-1702	Vocational Rehabilitation Series	GS-1715
Educational and Vocational Training Series	GS-1710	Education Program Series	GS-1720
Public Health Educator Series	GS-1725	Instructional Systems Series	GS-1750
Education Research Series	GS-1730	Education Student Trainee Series	GS-1799
Education Services Series	GS-1740		

GS-1800-INVESTIGATION GROUP

General Insp. Investigation & Compliance Series	GS-1801	Consumer Safety Inspection Series	GS-1862
Compliance Inspection and Support Series	GS-1802	Food Inspection Series	GS-1863
General Investigating Series	GS-1810	Public Health Quarantine Inspection Series	GS-1864
Criminal Investigating Series	GS-1811	Customs Patrol Officer Series	GS-1884
Game Law Enforcement Series	GS-1812	Import Specialist Series	GS-1889
Air Safety Investigating Series	GS-1815	Customs Inspection Series	GS-1890
Immigration Inspection Series	GS-1816	Customs Entry and Liquidating Series	GS-1894
Mine Safety and Health Series	GS-1822	Customs Warehouse Officer Series	GS-1895
Aviation Safety Series	GS-1825	Border Patrol Agent Series	GS-1896
Securities Compliance Examining Series	GS-1831	Customs Aid Series	GS-1897
Agri. Commodity Warehouse Examining Series GS-1898	GS-1850	Admeasurement Series	
Alcohol, Tobacco and Firearms Inspection Series	GS-1854	Investigation Student Trainee Series	GS-1899

GS-QUALITY ASSURANCE, INSPECTION, AND GRADING GROUP

Quality Assurance Series	GS-1910	Agricultural Commodity Aid Series	GS-1981
Agricultural Commodity Grading Series	GS-1980	Quality Inspection Student Trainee Series	GS-1999

GS-2000-SUPPLY GROUP

General Supply Series	GS-2001	Packaging Series	GS-2032
Supply Program Management Series	GS-2003	Supply Cataloging Series	GS-2050
Supply Clerical and Technician Series	GS-2005	Sales Store Clerical Series	GS-2091
Inventory Management Series	GS-2010	Supply Student Trainee Series	GS-2099
Distribution Facilities / Storage Management Series	GS-2030		

GS-2100-TRANSPORTATION GROUP

Transportation Specialist Series	GS-2101	Transportation Loss and Damage Claims	
Transportation Clerk and Assistant Series	GS-2102	Examining Series	GS-2135
Transportation Industry Analysis Series	GS-2110	Cargo Scheduling Series	GS-2144
Transportation Rate and Tariff Examining Series	GS-2111	Transportation Operations Series	GS-2150
Railroad Safety Series	GS-2121	Dispatching Series	GS-2151
Motor Carrier Safety Series	GS-2123	Air Traffic Control Series	GS-2152
Highway Safety Series	GS-2125	Air Traffic Assistance Series	GS-2154
Traffic Management Series	GS-2130	Marine Cargo Series	GS-2161
Freight Rate Series	GS-2131	Aircraft Operation Series	GS-2181
Travel Series	GS-2132	Air Navigation Series	GS-2183
Passenger Rate Series	GS-2133	Aircrew Technician Series	GS-2185
Shipment Clerical and Assistance Series	GS-2134	Transportation Student Trainee Series	GS-2199

WAGE GRADE) TRADES & LABOR JOB FAMILIES & OCCUPATIONS

The Government's Personnel Classification System includes Wage Grade occupations grouped into families of like jobs. The 36 occupational families range from WG-2500 to WG-9000. Each occupational family has its own group number and title which makes it distinctive from every other family grouping. The following is a list of the Wage Grade families.[2]

Each occupational family has a three part identifier: the Pay System, Occupational Group Number and Title. In the example, WG-2500, Wire Communications Equipment Installation and Maintenance Family, WG means the job is in the Wage Grade Schedule (or blue collar) pay system; 2500 is the Occupational Family Number; and Wire Communications Equipment Installation and Maintenance is the Occupational Family Title. Each occupational family lists the individual jobs that comprise the family with their corresponding Job Series Numbers and Titles. A brief description is provided for each of the occupational Wage Grade families and the jobs within that family.

WG-2500 - Wire Communications Equipment Installation and Maintenance Family

This job family includes occupations involved in the construction, installation, maintenance, repair and testing of all types of wire communications systems and associated equipment which are predominantly electrical-mechanical. Work involved in the installation and repair of communications equipment which requires in-depth knowledge of operating electronic principles should be coded to electronic equipment installation and maintenance family, 2600.

| WG-2502 | Telephone Mechanic | WG-2508 | Communications Line Installing and Repairing |
| WG-2504 | Wire Communications Cable Splicing | WG-2511 | Wire Communications Equip. Install/Repair |

WG-2600 - Electronic Equipment Installation and Maintenance Family

This job family includes occupations involved in the installation, repair, overhaul, fabrication, tuning, alignment, modification, calibration, and testing of electronic equipment and related devices, such as radio, radar, loran, sonar, television, and other communications equipment; industrial controls; fire control, flight/landing control, bombing-navigation, and other integrated systems; and electronic computer systems and equipment.

WG-2602	Electronic Measurement Equipment Mechanic	WG-2698	Electronic Digital Computer Mechanic
WG-2604	Electronics Mechanic	WG-2610	Electronic Integrated Systems Mechanic
WG-2606	Electronic Industrial Controls Mechanic		

WG-2800 Electrical Installation & Maintenance Family

This job family includes occupations involved in the fabrication, installation, alteration, maintenance, repair, and testing of electrical systems, instruments, apparatus, and equipment.

| WG-2800 | Electrician | WG-2854 | Electrical Equipment Repairing |
| WG-2810 | Electrician (High Voltage) | WG-2892 | Aircraft Electrician |

WG-3100   Fabric & Leather Work Family

This job family includes occupations involving the fabrication, modification, and repair of clothing and equipment made of (a) woven textile fabrics of animal, vegetable, or synthetic origin; (b) plastic film and filaments; © natural and simulated leather; (d) natural and synthetic fabrics; and (e) paper. Work involves use of handtools and mechanical devices and machines to lay out, cut, sew, rivet, mold, fit, assemble, and attach bindings to articles such as uniforms, rain gear, hats, belts, shoes, brief cases, holsters, equipage articles, tents, gun covers, bags, parachutes, upholstery, mattresses, brushes, etc.

| WG-3103 | Shoe Repairing | WG-3106 | Upholstering |
| WG-3105 | Fabric Working | | |

---

[2]The Wage Grade listing is taken from the Government Printing Office publication TS-PB97-170591.

WG-3111 Sewing Machine Operating   WG-3119   Broom & Brush Making

WG-3300 Instrument Work Family

This job family includes occupations that involve fabricating, assembling, calibrating, testing, installing, repairing, modifying, and maintaining instruments and instrumentation systems for measuring, regulating, and computing physical quantities such as movement, force, acceleration, displacement, stress, strain, vibration or oscillation frequency, phase and amplitude, linear or angular velocity, voltage, current, power, impedance, etc. Examples of such instruments and equipment are: gyro, optical, photographic, timekeeping, electrical, metered, pressure, and geared instruments, test equipment, and navigation, flight control, and fuel totalizing systems. The work requires knowledge of electrical, electronic, mechanical, optical, pneumatic, and/or hydraulic principals. Work that primarily involves fabricating and repairing electronic instruments should be coded to the electronic equipment installation and maintenance family, 2600.

WG-3306 Optical Instrument Repairing   WG-3359   Instrument Mechanic
WG-3314 Instrument Making   WG-3364   Projection Equipment Repairing
WG-3341 Scale Building, Install/Repair

WG-3400 Machine Tool Work Family

This job family includes occupations that involve setting up and operating machine tools and using hand tools to make or repair (shape, fit, finish, assemble) metal parts, tools, gages, models, patterns, mechanisms, and machines; and machining explosives and synthetic materials.

WG-3414 Machining   WG-3422   Power Saw Operator
WG-3416 Toolmaking   WG-3428   Die Sinker
WG-3417 Tool Grinding   WG-3431   Machine Tool Operating

WG-3500 General Services & Support Work Family

This job family includes occupations not specifically covered by another family that require little or no specialized training or work experience to enter. These occupations usually involve work such as moving and handling material (e.g., loading, unloading, digging, hauling, hoisting, carrying, wrapping, mixing, pouring, spreading); washing and cleaning laboratory apparatus, cars, and trucks, etc.; cleaning and maintaining living quarters, hospital rooms and ward, office buildings, grounds, and other areas; and doing other general maintenance work, by hand or using common hand tools and power equipment. They may involve heavy or light physical work and various skill levels. Skills are generally learned through job experience and instruction from supervisors or, in some instances, formal training programs lasting a few days or weeks or longer.

WG-3502 Laboring   WG-3515   Laboratory Support Working
WG-3506 Summer Aid/Student Aid   WG-3543   Stevedoring
WG-3508 Pipeline Working   WG-3546   Railroad Repairing
WG-3511 Laboratory Working   WG-3566   Custodial Working
WG-3513 Coin/Currency Checking

WG-3600 Structural & Finishing Work Family

This job family includes occupations not specifically covered by another family that involve doing structural and finishing work in construction, maintenance, and repair of surfaces and structures, e.g., laying brick, block, and stone; setting tile; finishing cement and concrete; plastering; installing, maintaining, and repairing asphalt, tar, and gravel; roofing; insulating and glazing.

WG-3602 Cement Finishing   WG-3609   Floor Covering Installing
WG-3603 Masonry   WG-3610   Insulating
WG-3604 Tile Setting   WG-3611   Glazing
WG-3605 Plastering   WG-3653   Asphalt Working
WG-3604 Roofing

WG-3700 Metal Processing Family

This job family includes occupations which involve processing or treating metals to alter their properties or produce desirable qualities such as hardness or workability, using processes such as welding, plating, melting, alloying, annealing, heat treating, and refining.

WG-3702	Flame/Arc Cutting	WG-3720	Brazing & Soldering
WG-3703	Welding	WG-3722	Cold Working
WG-3705	Nondestructive Testing	WG-3725	Battery Repairing
WG-3707	Metalizing	WG-3727	Buffing & Polishing
WG-3708	Metal Process Working	WG-3735	Metal Phototransferring
WG-3711	Electroplating	WG-3736	Circuit Board Making
WG-3712	Heat Treating	WG-3741	Furnace Operating
WG-3716	Leadburning	WG-3769	Shot Preening Machine

WG-3800 Metal Working Family

This job family includes occupations involved in shaping and forming metal and making and repairing metal parts or equipment. Includes such work as the fabrication and assembly of sheet metal parts and equipment; forging and press operations; structural iron working, stamping, etc. Doesn't include machine tool work.

WG-3802	Metal Forging	WG-3818	Springmaking
WG-3804	Coppersmithing	WG-3819	Airframe Jig Fitting
WG-3806	Sheet Metal Mechanic	WG-3820	Shipfitting
WG-3807	Structural/Ornamental Iron Working	WG-3830	Blacksmithing
		WG-3832	Metal Making
WG-3808	Boilermaking	WG-3833	Transfer Engraving
WG-3809	Mobile Equip. Metal Mech.	WG-3858	Metal Tank & Radiator Repairing
WG-3815	Pneumatic Tool Operating	WG-3869	Metal Forming Mach. Operating
WG-3816	Engraving	WG-3872	Metal Tube Making & Installing

WG-3900 Motion Picture, Radio, Television, and Sound Equipment Operation Family

This job family includes occupations involved in setting up, testing, operating, and making minor repairs to equipment such as microphones, sound and radio controls, sound recording equipment, lighting and sound effect devices, television cameras, magnetic video tape recorders, motion picture projectors, and broadcast transmitters used in the production of motion pictures and radio and television programs. Also includes occupations that involve related work.

WG-3910	Motion Picture Projection	WG-3940	Broadcasting Equip. Operating
WG-3911	Sound Recording Equip. Operating	WG-3941	Public Address Equip. Operating
WG-3919	Television Equip. Operating		

WG-4000 Lens and Crystal Work Family

This job family includes occupations involved in making precision optical elements, crystal blanks or wafers, or other items of glass, polished metals, or similar materials, using such methods as cutting, polishing, etc.

WG-4005	Optical Element Working	WG-4015	Quartz Crystal Working
WG-4010	Prescription Eyeglass Making		

WG-4100 Painting & Paperhanging Family

This job family includes occupations which involve hand or spray painting and decorating interiors and exteriors of buildings, structures, aircraft, vessels, mobile equipment, fixtures, furnishings, machinery, and other surfaces; finishing hardwoods, furniture, and cabinetry; painting signs; covering interiors of rooms with strips of wallpaper or fabric, etc.

WG-4102	Painting	WG-4104	Sign Painting
WG-4103	Paperhanging	WG-4157	Instrument Dial Painting

WG-4200 Plumbing & Pipefitting Family

This job family includes occupations that involve the installation, maintenance, and repair of water, air, steam, gas, sewer, and other pipelines and systems, and related fixtures, apparatus, and accessories.

WG-4204	Pipefitting	WG-4255	Fuel Distribution Systems
WG-4206	Plumbing		Mechanic

WG-4300 Pliable Materials Work Family

This job family includes occupations involved in shaping, forming, and repairing items and parts from non-metallic moldable materials such as plastic, rubber, clay, wax, plaster, glass, sand, or other similar material.

WG-4351	Plastic Molding Equip. Operating	WG-4370	Glassblowing
WG-4352	Plastic Fabricating	WG-4371	Plaster Pattern Casting
WG-4360	Rubber Products Molding	WG-4373	Molding
WG-4361	Rubber Equipment Repairing	WG-4374	Core Making

WG-4400 Printing Family

This job family includes occupations involved in letterpress (relief), offset- lithographic, gravure (intaglio), or screen printing; including layout, hand composition, typesetting from hot metal type, platemaking, printing, and finishing operations.

WG-4402	Bindery Work	WG-4422	Dot Etching
WG-4403	Hand Composing	WG-4425	Photoengraving
WG-4405	Film Assembly-Stripping	WG-4441	Bookbinding
WG-4406	Letterpress Operating	WG-4445	Bank Note Designing
WG-4407	Linotype Machine Operating	WG-4446	Bank Note Engraving
WG-4413	Negative Engraving	WG-4447	Sculptural Engraving
WG-4414	Offset Photography	WG-4448	Sidergraphic Transferring
WG-4416	Platemaking	WG-4449	Electrolytic Intaglio Platemaking
WG-4417	Offset Press Operating	WG-4450	Intaglio Die & Plate Finishing
WG-4419	Silk Screen Making & Printing	WG-4454	Intaglio Press Operating

WG-4600 Wood Work Family

This occupation includes jobs involved in blocking, bracing, staying, and securing cargo for shipment by land, sea, or air. It requires skill in construction, placing, and installing wooden blocks, wedges, bracing, structures, and other staying devices, as well as skill in securing items using wires, ropes, chains, cables, plates, and other hardware.

WG-4602	Blocking & Bracing	WG-4618	Woodworking Mach. Operating
WG-4604	Wood Working	WG-4620	Shoe Lasting Repairing
WG-4605	Wood Crafting	WG-4639	Timber Working
WG-4607	Carpentry	WG-4654	Form Block Making
WG-4616	Patternmaking		

WG-4700 General Maintenance & Operations Work Family

This job family includes occupations which (1) consist of various combinations of work such as are involved in constructing, maintaining and repairing buildings, roads, grounds, and related facilities; manufacturing, modifying, and repairing items or apparatus made from a variety of materials or types of components; or repairing and operating equipment or utilities; and (2) require the application of a variety of trade practices associated with occupations in more than one job family (unless otherwise indicated), and the performance of the highest level of work in at least two of the trades involved.

WG-4714	Model Making	WG-4741	General Equipment Operating
WG-4715	Exhibits Making/Modeling	WG-4742	Utility Sys. Repairing-Operating
WG-4716	Railroad Car Repairing	WG-4745	Research Laboratory Mechanic
WG-4717	Boat Building and Repairing	WG-4749	Maintenance Mechanic
WG-4737	General Equipment Mechanic	WG-4754	Cemetery Caretaking

WG-4800 General Equipment Maintenance Family

This job family includes occupations involved in the maintenance or repair of equipment, machines, or instruments which are not coded to other job families because the equipment is not characteristically related to one of the established subject-matter areas such as electronics, electrical, industrial, transportation, instruments, engines, aircraft, ordinance, etc., or because the nature of the work calls for limited knowledge/skill in a variety of crafts or trades as they relate to the repair of such equipment, but not a predominate knowledge of any one trade or craft.

WG-4802	Musical Instrument Repairing	WG-4839	Film Processing Equip. Repairing
WG-4804	Locksmithing	WG-4840	Tool & Equipment Repairing
WG-4805	Medical Equipment Repairing	WG-4841	Window Shade Assembling, Repairing
WG-4806	Office Appliance Repairing		
WG-4807	Chemical Equipment Repairing	WG-4843	Navigation Aids Repairing
WG-4808	Custodial Equipment Servicing	WG-4844	Bicycle Repairing
WG-4812	Saw Reconditioning	WG-4845	Orthopedic Appliance Repairing
WG-4816	Protective/Safety Equip. Fabrication	WG-4848	Mechanical Parts Repairing
WG-4818	Aircraft Survival/Flight Equipment	WG-4850	Bearing Reconditioning
WG-4819	Bowling Equipment Repairing	WG-4851	Reclamation Working
WG-4820	Vending Machine Repairing	WG-4855	Domestic Appliance Repairing

WG-5000 Plant and Animal Work Family

This job family includes occupations involved in general or specialized farming operations; gardening, including the general care of grounds, roadways, nurseries, greenhouses, etc.; trimming and felling trees; and propagating, caring for, handling, and controlling animals and insects, including pest species.

WG-5002	Farming	WG-5034	Dairy Farming
WG-5003	Gardening	WG-5035	Livestock Ranching/Wrangling
WG-5026	Pest Controlling	WG-5042	Tree Trimming and Removing
WG-5031	Insects Production Working	WG-5048	Animal Caretaking

WG-5200 Miscellaneous Occupations Family

This job family includes occupations which are not covered by the definition of any other job family or which are of such a general or miscellaneous character as to preclude placing them within another job family.

WG-5205	Gas and Radiation Detecting	WG-5221	Lofting
WG-5210	Rigging	WG-5222	Diving
WG-5220	Shipwright	WG-5235	Test Range Tracking

WG-5300 Industrial Equipment Maintenance Family

This job family includes occupations involved in the general maintenance, installation, and repair of portable and stationary industrial machinery, tools, and equipment such as sewing machines, machine tools, woodworking and metal working machines, printing equipment, processing equipment, driving machinery, power generating equipment, air conditioning equipment, heating and boiler plant equipment, and other types of machines and equipment used in the production of goods and services.

WG-5306	Air Conditioning Equipment Mechanic	WG-5334	Marine Machinery Mechanic
WG-5309	Heating and Boiler Plant Mechanic	WG-5335	Wind Tunnel Mechanic
WG-5310	Kitchen/Bakery Equipment Repairing	WG-5341	Industrial Furnace Building & Repairing
WG-5312	Sewing Machine Repairing		
WG-5313	Elevator Mechanic	WG-5350	Production Machinery Mechanic
WG-5317	Laundry/Dry Cleaning Equip. Repairing	WG-5352	Industrial Equipment Mechanic
WG-5318	Lock & Dam Repairing	WG-5364	Door Systems Mechanic
WG-5323	Oiling & Greasing	WG-5365	Physiological Trainer Mechanic
WG-5324	Powerhouse Equipment Repairing	WG-5378	Powered Support Systems Mechanic
WG-5326	Drawbridge Repairing	WG-5384	Gas dynamic Facility Installing/ Repairing
WG-5330	Printing Equipment Repairing		

WG-5400 Industrial Equipment Operation Family

This job family includes occupations involved in the operation of portable and stationary industrial equipment, tools, and machines to generate and distribute utilities such as electricity, steam, and gas for heat or power; treat and distribute water; collect, treat, and dispose of waste; open and close bridges, locks and dams; lift and move workers, materials, and equipment; manufacture and process materials and products; etc.

WG-5402	Boiler Plant Operating	WG-5435	Carton/Bag Making Machine Operating
WG-5403	Incinerator Operating	WG-5438	Elevator Operating
WG-5406	Utility Systems Operating	WG-5439	Testing Equipment Operating
WG-5407	Electric Power Controlling	WG-5440	Packaging Machine Operating
WG-5408	Sewage Disposal Plant Operating	WG-5444	Food/Feed Processing Equip. Operating
WG-5409	Water Treatment Plant Operating	WG-5446	Textile Equipment Operating
WG-5413	Fuel Distribution System Operating	WG-5450	Conveyor Operating
WG-5414	Baling Machine Operating	WG-5454	Solvent Still Operating
WG-5415	Air Cond. Equip. Operating	WG-5455	Paper Pulping Machine Operating
WG-5419	Stationary-Engine Operating	WG-5473	Oil Reclamation Equipment Operating
WG-5423	Sandblasting	WG-5478	Portable Equipment Operating
WG-5424	Weighing Machine Operating	WG-5479	Dredging Equipment Operating
WG-5426	Lock and Dam Operating	WG-5484	Counting Machine Operating
WG-5427	Chemical Plant Operating	WG-5485	Aircraft Weight & Balance Operating
WG-5430	Drawbridge Operating	WG-5486	Swimming Pool Operating
WG-5433	Gas Generating Plant Operating		

WG-5700 Transportation/Mobile Equipment Operation Family

This job family includes occupations involved in the operation and operational maintenance of self-propelled transportation and other mobile equipment (except aircraft) used to move materials or passengers, including motor vehicles, engineering and construction equipment, tractors, etc. some of which may be equipped with power takeoff and controls to operate special purpose equipment; ocean-going and inland waterway vessels, harbor craft, and floating plants; and trains, locomotives, and train cars.

WG-5703	Motor Vehicle Operating	WG-5736	Braking-Switching & Conducting
WG-5704	Fork Lift Operating	WG-5737	Locomotive Engineering
WG-5705	Tractor Operating	WG-5738	Railroad Maint. Vehicle Oper.
WG-5706	Road Sweeper Oper.	WG-5767	Airfield Clearing Equip. Oper.
WG-5707	Tank Driver	WG-5782	Ship Operating
WG-5716	Engineering Equip. Oper.	WG-5784	Riverboat Operating
WG-5725	Crane Operating	WG-5786	Small Craft Operating
WG-5729	Drill Rig Operating	WG-5788	Deckhand
WG-5731	Mining/Tunneling Mach. Oper.		

WG-5800 Heavy Mobile Equipment Mechanic

This job family includes occupations involved in repairing, adjusting, and maintaining self-propelled transportation and other mobile equipment (except aircraft), including any special-purpose features with which they may be equipped.

WG-5803	Heavy Mobile Equip. Mech.	WG-5823	Automotive Mechanic
WG-5806	Mobile Equip. Servicing	WG-5876	Electromotive Equip. Mechanic

WG-6500 Ammunition, Explosives, & Toxic Materials Work Family

This job family includes occupations involved in the manufacturing, assembling, disassembling, renovating, loading, deactivating, modifying, destroying, testing, handling, placing, and discharging of ammunition, propellants, chemicals and toxic materials, and other conventional and special munitions and explosives.

WG-6502	Explosives Operating	WG-6511	Missile/Toxic Materials Handling
WG-6505	Munitions Destroying	WG-6517	Explosives Test Operating

WG-6600 Armament Work Family

This job family includes occupations involved in the installation, repair, rebuilding, adjusting, modification, and testing of small arms and artillery weapons and allied accessories. Artillery includes, but is not limited to, field artillery, antitank artillery, antiaircraft weapons, aircraft and shipboard weapons, recoilless rifles, rocket launchers, mortars, cannon, and allied accessories. Small arms includes, but is not limited to, rifles, carbines, pistols, revolvers, helmets, body armor, shoulder-type rocket launchers, machine guns, and automatic rifles.

WG-6605	Artillery Repairing	WG-6641	Ordnance Equipment Mechanic
WG-6606	Artillery Testing	WG-6652	Aircraft Ordnance Systems Mech.
WG-6610	Small Arms Repairing	WG-6656	Special Weapons Systems Mech.

WG-6900 Warehousing & Stock Handling Family

This family includes occupations involved in physically receiving, storing, handling, and issuing supplies, materials, and equipment; handling, marking, and displaying goods for customer selection; identifying and condition classifying materials and equipment; and routing and expediting movement of parts, supplies, and materials in production and repair facilities.

WG-6902	Lumber Handling	WG-6912	Materials Examining & Identifying
WG-6903	Coal Handling	WG-6915	Store Working
WG-6904	Tools and Parts Attending	WG-6941	Bulk Money Handling
WG-6907	Materials Handling	WG-6968	Aircraft Freight Loading
WG-6910	Materials Expediting		

WG-7000 Packing and Processing Family

This job family includes occupations involved in determining the measures required to protect items against damage during movement or storage; selecting proper method of packing, including type and size of container; cleaning, drying, and applying preservatives to materials, parts, or mechanical equipment; and packing, equipment, parts, and materials.

WG-7002	Packing	WG-7009	Equipment Cleaning
WG-7004	Preservation Packaging	WG-7010	Parachute Packing
WG-7006	Preservation Servicing		

WG-7300 Laundry, Dry Cleaning, & Pressing Family

This job family includes occupations involved in receiving, sorting, washing, drying, dry cleaning, dyeing, pressing, and preparing for delivery clothes, linens, and other articles requiring laundering, dry cleaning, or pressing.

WG-7304	Laundry Working	WG-7306	Pressing
WG-7305	Laundry Machine Operating	WG-7307	Dry Cleaning

WG-7400 Food Preparation & Servicing Family

This job family includes occupations involved in the preparation and serving of food.

WG-7402	Baking	WG-7407	Meatcutting
WG-7404	Cooking	WG-7408	Food Service Working
WG-7405	Bartending	WG-7420	Waiter

WG-7600 Personal Services Family

This job family includes occupations concerned with providing grooming, beauty, or other personal services to individuals, patrons, guests, passengers, entertainers, etc., or attending to their personal effects.

WG-7603	Barbering	WG-7641	Beautician
WG-7640	Bus Attending		

WG-8200 Fluid Systems Maintenance Family

Includes occupations involving repair, assembly, and testing of fluid systems and components of aircraft, aircraft engines, missiles, and mobile and support equipment. These fluid systems store, supply, distribute, and move gases or liquids to produce power, transmit force, and pressurize, cool, and condition cabins.

WG-8255	Pneudraulic Systems Mechanic	WG-8268	Aircraft Pneudraulic Systems Mechanic

WG-8600 Engine Overhaul Family

This job family includes occupations concerned primarily with the manufacture, repair, modification, and major overhaul of engines (except where covered by another job family) including the disassembly, reassembly, and test phases of engine overhaul programs.

WG-8602	Aircraft Engine Mechanic	WG-8675	Liquid Fuel Rocket Engine Mechanic
WG-8610	Small Engine Mechanic		

WG-8800 Aircraft Overhaul Family

This job family includes occupations concerned primarily with the overhaul of aircraft, including the disassembly, reassembly, and test phases of aircraft overhaul programs.

WG-8810	Aircraft Propeller Mechanic	WG-8862	Aircraft Attending
WG-8840	Aircraft Mech. Parts Repairing	WG-8863	Aircraft Tire Mounting
WG-8852	Aircraft Mechanic	WG-8882	Airframe Test Operating

WG-9000 Film Processing Family

This job family includes occupations that involve processing film, for example, operating motion picture developers and printers; cleaning, repairing, matching, cutting, splicing, and assembling films; and mixing developing solutions. Does not include processing work that requires specialized subject-matter knowledge or artistic ability.

WG-9003	Film Assembling and Repairing	WG-9055	Photographic Solution Mixing
WG-9004	Motion Picture Mach. Operating		

Appendix E
Agency Skills Index

Use this index to locate Federal agencies and departments that are seeking your skills, academic major, or related field of study for entry level jobs.

Individuals interested in government employment seldom know where to begin their job search. Larger agencies offer employment in a wide range of occupations and many smaller agencies use a diverse cross section of skills and trades.

This index captures 24 of the largest departments and agencies plus various independent government organizations. After locating the organizations that utilize your skills, education, and background review the earlier chapters for specific guidance and interviewing techniques.

Skills and occupations are listed alphabetically and agencies or departments that utilize these skills follow each listing. An asterisk precedes the agency that is the largest employer for a skill. The total number of federal employees within each occupation is identified in parentheses following each entry.

This list is not complete. A broad cross section of occupations is presented to steer you in the right direction. If a related occupation is identified it is highly probable that your skills will also be required by that agency. Agencies other than those identified for each skill or occupation may offer employment in small numbers for a specific occupation. Many agencies hire small numbers of employees within a series or group. These agencies are not on this list.

The purpose of this list is to steer you to the agencies that offer the greatest opportunities and chance of employment. However, don't overlook any agency in your job search, especially those within your commuting area. Call local agencies listed under "U.S. Government" in the Yellow Pages or the Blue Pages of the regular phone directory.

ABBREVIATIONS LIST

ALL - All on this list
ATC - Architect of the Capital
CIA - Central Intelligence Agency
DOA - Dept. of Agriculture
DOC - Dept. of Commerce
DOD - Dept. of Defense
DOE - Dept. of Energy
EDU - Dept. of Education
DOI - Dept. of the Interior
DOJ - Dept. of Justice
DOL - Dept. of Labor
DOS - Dept. of State
DOT - Dept. of Transportation
EPA - Environmental Protection Agency

FAA - Federal Aviation Administration
FBI - Federal Bureau of Investigation
FCC - Federal Communications Administration
GSA - General Services Administration
HHS - Health & Human Services
HUD - Health & Urban Development
NAS - NASA
OPM - Office of Personnel Management
SBA - Small Business Administration
SMI - Smithsonian Institute
TRE - Dept. of the Treasury
USI - U.S. Information Agency
VET - Veterans Administration

*   The Largest Employing Agency
( )   The number in parentheses represents the total number employed.

The total employment number may represent a WG Family or GS Group. For example; Family 5300 has 23 individual occupations listed in Appendix D. The total employment is distributed among all 23 occupations.[1]

SKILLS / OCCUPATIONS

ACCOUNTING / AUDITING
ACCOUNTING TECHNICIAN - GROUP GS-500 All (115,369)

ADMINISTRATIVE / CLERK TYPIST / CLERICAL / SECRETARY GROUP GS-300
ALL (363,953)

AGRICULTURAL GS-1145/46/47
*DOA (1,017)

ADVERTISING
DOL

AERONAUTICAL ENGINEERING SERIES GS-861
NASA, *DOD, DOT, DOC (7,585)

AIR CONDITIONING/HEATING REPAIR FAMILY WG-5300
TRE, *DOD, DOA, DOJ, DOI, DOC, HHS, DOT, ATC, GSA, SMI, VET (13,540)

AIR TRAFFIC CONTOLLERS GS-2152
*DOT-FAA, DOD (23,926)

AIRCRAFT OPERATIONS (PILOTS) GS-2181 INCLUDES COPILOTS
*DOD, DOT-FAA, TVA, DOJ, DOI, DOA, DOC, DOE, NASA (2,668)

AIRCRAFT OVERHAUL FAMILY WG-8800
*DOD, DOT-FAA, NASA, DOJ, DOI, DOC (14,741)

AMMUNITION, EXPLOSIVES WORK FAMILY WG-6600
*DOD, GSA, DOJ, DOT (4,031)

AMERICAN HISTORY
National Archives & Records Administration

ANIMAL SCIENCE GS-487/700
DOA (1,913)

---

[1]Excerpted from Occupations of Federal White-Color & Blue-Collar Workers.

ARCHEOLOGY GS-193
*DOA, DOA (1,049)

ARCHITECTURE ENGINEERING GS-808
*DOD, DOJ, DOI, DOA, HHS, HUD, DOT,
DOE, GSA, TVA, VET (1,685)

ART GS-1056
*DOD, DOI, DOJ (92)

**ASTRONOMY & SPACE SCIENCE
GS-1330** *NASA, DOD (482)

AUTOMOTIVE MECHANIC WG-5823
*DOD, ALL (7,269)

BAKING WG-7402
DOD (143)

BANKING
DOA, Farm Credit Administration
DOT, Office of the Comptroller

BEAUTICIAN WG-7641
*HHS, DOD (7)

BIOLOGICAL SCIENCES GS-400 GROUP
*DOA, DOI, DOD, HHS, DOC, EPA, NASA,
VET (58,779)

BORDER PATROL AGENT GS-1896
DOJ (3,635)

**BUDGET CLERICAL & ASSISTANCE
GS-561** *DOD, ALL (4223)

BUILDING MANAGEMENT GS-1176
*GSA, DOD, DOJ, DOC, HHS, DOL (957)

**BUSINESS & INDUSTRY GROUP
GS-1100** *DOD, ALL (97,205)

CARPENTRY WG-4607
*DOD, ALL BUT DOS & USI (3,360)

CEMENT FINISHING WG-3602
*DOD, DOE (144)

CEMETERY CARETAKING WG-4754
*VET, DOD (568)

CHEMICAL ENGINEERING GS-893

*DOD, DOI, DOJ, DOI, NASA (1,286)

CIVIL ENGINEERING GS-810
*DOD (13,361)

CLERK TYPIST GS-322
ALL (2,227)

**CLERK-STENOGRAPHER & REPORTER
GS-312** *DOD, ALL (72)

CLINICAL PSYCHOLOGY
DOJ - Bureau of Prisons

COMPUTER GROUP GS-332/4/5
ALL (64,8583)

CONTRACTING GS-1102
*DOD, ALL (27,021)

COOKING WG-7404
*DOD, DOJ, DOI, DOA, HHS, VET (4,184)

COPYRIGHT GROUP GS-1200
*DOC, DOD, DOJ, DOI, DOE, NASA (3,864)

CORRECTIONS OFFICER GS-007
*DOJ, DOD (13,097)

**CRIMINAL INVESTIGATION SERIES
GS-1811** *DOJ, ALL (35,840)

CRYPTANALYSIS SERIES GS-1541
DOJ (17)

CUSTOMS SERIES GS-1884/90/94
TRE (7,959)

CUSTODIAL WORKING WG-3566
*GSA, ALL (14,040)

DECKHAND WG-5788
*DOD, DOJ, DOC (306)

DENTAL SERIES GS 680/1/2/3
*DOD, HHS, VET (4,593)

DIETITIAN & NUTRITION GS-630
*VET, HHS, DOD (1,644)

DISPATCHING GS-2151
*DOD, DOI, GSA (443)

EARTH SCIENCE
DOD - Defense Intelligence Agency, Defense
Mapping Agency

ECOLOGY GS-408
*DOD, DOA, DOI, DOC, DOE, EPA (863)

ECONOMICS GS-110/119
*DOL, ALL BUT NASA & USI (5,004)

EDUCATION/TRAINING GS-1700
*DOD, ALL BUT SBA (32,632)

ELECTRICAL ENGINEERING GS-850
*DOD, ALL BUT HUD, OPM, USI & SBA
(4,228)

ELECTRICIAN WG-2805
*DOD, ALL BUT DOS & USI (7,224)

**ELECTRONIC EQUIPMENT INSTALLA-
TION & MAINTENANCE FAMILY WG-
2600** *DOD, ALL BUT USI & TVA (17,650)

ELECTRONICS TECHNICIAN GS-856
*DOD, DOT-FAA, DOS, DOT, DOJ, DOI,
DOA, DOC, HHS, DOE, EPA, GSA, USI,
NASA, VET (12,133)

ELEVATOR MECHANIC WG-5313
*Architect of the capital, DOD,
HHS, VET, DOS, DOT (201)

ENGINE OVERHAUL FAMILY WG-8600
*DOD, DOI, DOT (4,463)

ENGINEERING PSYCHOLOGY
Consumer Product Safety Commission

ENGLISH
Federal trade Commission
DOL, DOD, DOT, USI

ENTOMOLOGY GS-414
*DOA, DOD, HHS, EPA (707)

ENVIRONMENTAL ENGINEERING GS-819
*GSA, DOD, TVA, DOE, HHS, DOJ, DOA
(5,525)

EQUIPMENT OPERATOR GS-350
*DOD, ALL (1,866)

EXPLOSIVES OPERATING WG-6502
DOD (1,892)

FACILITY MANAGEMENT GS-1640
*DOD, TVA, DOJ, DOI, DOC, NASA, HHS
(1,442)

FINANCIAL ADMINISTRATION GS-501
*DOD, ALL (6,980)

FINGERPRINT IDENTIFICATION GS-072
*DOJ, DOD (1,450)

FIRE PROTECTION GS-081
*DOD, VET, DOE, NASA, GSA, HHS, DOE,
DOT (11,300)

FOOD INSPECTION GS-1863
*DOA, DOC (6,559)

FOOD TECHNOLOGY GS-1382
*DOA, DOC, DOD (240)

FOREIGN AFFAIRS GS-130
*USI, DOE, DOD, DOC (3,823)

FORK LIFT OPERATOR WG-5704
*DOD, DOC, HHS, GSA, VET (897)

FORESTRY GS-460
*DOA, DOD, TRE, TVA (6,212)

FUEL DISTRIBUTION WG-5413
*DOD, DOI, DOT (1,138)

**GENERAL ADMINISTRATION, CLERI-
CAL, & OFFICE SERVICES GS-300** ALL
(398,721)

GARDENING WG-5003
*DOD, DOJ, DOI, DOA, DOC, HHS, DOT,
GSA, VET (1,199)

**GENERAL MAINTENANCE &
OPERATION**
WG-4700 *DOD, ALL (19,312)

GENETICS GS-440
DOA, HHS, DOC (340)

GEOCHEMICAL ENGINEERING
Nuclear Regulatory Commission

GEODETIC TECHNICIAN GS-1374

*DOC, DOD (75)

GEOGRAPHY GS-150
*DOC, DOD, DOA, DOI (331)

GEOLOGY GS-1350
*DOI, DOD, DOT, DOA, EPA, DOE, DOL, TVA (2,128)

GUARD GS-085
*DOD, TRE, DOJ, DOI, DOC, HHS, DOT, DOE, TVA, VET, GSA, USI (6,275)

GUIDE GS-090
*DOJ, DOT, DOD, DOI, DOA (171)

HEALTH GROUP GS-600
*VET, HHS, DOT, DOJ, DOA, DOS, NASA, DOD (139,132)

HISTORY GS-107
DOJ, DOI, TRE

HOME ECONOMICS GS-493
*DOA, DOD, HHS (100)

HORTICULTURE GS-437
*DOA, DOI, VET (125)

HOUSING MANAGEMENT GS-1173
*DOD, DOI, HHS, HUD (2,876)

HYDROLOGY GS-1315
*DOI, DOD, EPA, DOA, DOC (2,494)

ILLUSTRATING GS-1020
*DOD, DOI, DOJ, DOA, DOC, VET, DOT, DOE (752)

IMPORT SPECIALIST GS-1889
DOT (1,188)

INDUSTRIAL EQUIPMENT MECHANIC WG-5352
*DOD, TRE, DOI, DOA, DOC, VET, HHS, DOT, GSA (1,625)

INDUSTRIAL HYGIENE GS-690
*DOL, DOD, DOI, DOA, HHS, DOE, EPA, GSA, TVA, VET (1,480)

INSTRUMENT MECHANIC WG-3359
*DOD, DOI, DOA, DOC, HHS, DOT, DOE, GSA, TVA, VET (1,649)

INSURANCE EXAMINING GS-1163
*DOD, DOT, HHS (78)

INTELLIGENCE GS-132
*DOD, DOS, TRE, DOJ, DOI, DOC, DOT, DOE (4,732)

INTERNAL REVENUE AGENT GS-512
TRE (16,100)

INTERNATIONAL RELATIONS GS-131
*DOE, DOT, DOD, DOS, DOA, DOC (111)

INVENTORY MANAGEMENT GS-2010
*DOD, ALL (6,394)

INVESTIGATION GROUP GS-1800
*DOJ, ALL EXCEPT TVA (75,488)

LABOR RELATIONS GS-233
*DOD, ALL (1,246)

LABORING WG-3502
*DOD, ALL (9,573)

LANDSCAPE ARCHITECTURE GS-807
*DOA, DOI, DOD, VET, TVA (706)

LAND SURVEYING GS-1373
*DOI, DOD, DOA, DOE (504)

LANGUAGE SPECIALIST GS-1040
*DOJ, DOD, DOC, DOS, TRV, HHS, USI, NASA (614)

LAUNDRY WORK WG-7300
*VET, DOD, DOJ, DOI, HHS (1,914)

LEGAL GS-900
*HHS, ALL (78,341)

LIBRARIAN GS-1410
*DOD, ALL (2,887)

LITERATURE
DOL

LOAN SPECIALIST GS-1165
*HUD, DOI, DOA, DOC, VET, SBA (3,348)

LOCK AND DAM REPAIR WG-5318
*DOD, DOI, DOT (510)

LOCKSMITHING WG-4804
*DOD, VET, DOA, DOI, DOC, DOJ (360)

LOGISTICS MANAGEMENT GS-346
*DOD, ALL BUT HUD, OPM, SBA, VET
(10,961)

MACHINE TOOL WORK FAMILY WG-3400
*DOD, ALL BUT USI & DOS (7,607)

MAIL & FILE GS-305
*DOD, ALL (16,058)

MAINTENANCE MECHANIC WG-4749
*DOI, ALL (11,938)

MANUAL ARTS THERAPIST GS-637
VET (183)

MARINE CARGO GS-2161
DOD (59)

MARKETING
DOC, DOD, TRE

MATERIALS ENGINEERING GS-806
*DOD, NASA, DOI, DOA, DOC, TRE, TVA,
GSA, DOE (1,296)

MASONRY WG-3603
*DOD, VET, NASA, GSA, DOT, HHS, DOE
(761)

MATERIALS HANDLING WG-6907
*DOD, ALL (23,100)

MATHEMATICS GROUP GS-1500
*DOD, ALL (13,837)

MEATCUTTING WG-7407
*DOD, DOA, VET, HHS, DOT (2,420)

MEDICAL GROUP GS-600
*VET, ALL (149,250)

MEDICAL EQUIPMENT REPAIR

WG-4805 *VET, HHS, DOT, DOD, DOJ (495)

MESSENGER GS-302

*DOD, TRE, DOI, DOA, DOC, DOL, HHS,
VET, TVA (223)

METAL PROCESSING FAMILY WG-3700
*DOD, ALL BUT USI & TVA (5,837)

METALLURGY GS-1321
*DOD, TRE, DOI, DOC, TVA, DOE (397)

MICROBIOLOGY GS-403
*HHS, VET, DOD, EPA, DOI, DOA, DOC DOJ
(2,136)

MINE SAFETY & HEALTH GS-1822
DOL (1,339)

MOBILE EQUIP. SERVICING WG-5806
*DOD, DOJ, DOI, DOA, GSA, VET, TVA,
DOE, HHS (318)

**MOTION PICTURE, RADIO, TV WORK
WG-3900** *USI, DOD, TRE, DOJ, DOI, DOC,
DOA, VET (267)

MOTOR VEHICLE OPERATING WG-5703
*DOD, ALL (8,213)

MUNITIONS WORK WG-6500
*DOD, DOJ (2,333)

MUSEUM CURATOR GS-1015
DOI, DOD, Smithsonian (377)

MUSEUM SPECIALIST GS-1016
DOI, DOD, TRE, DOS, DOC, DOE, HHS,
Smithsonian (984)

MUSIC SPECIALIST GS-1051
*DOD, DOI (21)

NAVAL ARCHITECTURE GS-871
*DOD, DOC, DOT (905)

NAVIGATION AIDS REPAIR WG-4843
*DOT, DOI (11)

NUCLEAR ENGINEERING GS-840
*DOD, TVA, DOE, DOC, DOI, DOT (3,809)

NUTRITION
DOA, VET

NURSE GS-610
*VET, HHS, DOD, TRE, DOS, DOJ, DOI, DOC, DOA, DOT, DOL, NASA (43,082)

OCCUPATIONAL THERAPIST GS-631
*VET, HHS, DOD (688)

OFFSET PHOTOGRAPHY WG-4414
*DOD, TRE, DOA, DOI, DOA, DOC (356)

OPTOMETRIST GS-662
*VET, DOD, DOT

OUTDOOR RECREATION PLANNING GS-023 *DOI, DOA, DOD (684)

PACKAGING GS-2032
*DOD, GSA, DOT (457)

PAINTING & PAPERHANGING GROUP WG-4100 *DOD, ALL BUT DOS & USI (5,366)

PACKING & PROCESSING GROUP WG-7000 *DOD, TRE, DOJ, DOC, DOT, HHS, GSA, VET (7,523)

PARALEGAL SPECIALIST GS-950
*DOJ, ALL (5,341)

PARK RANGER GS-025
*DOI, DOD (6,524)

PATENT ADMINISTRATION GS-1220
DOC

PATHOLOGY TECHNICIAN GS-646
*VET, HHS, DOD (499)

PERSONNEL MANAGEMENT GROUP GS-200 *DOD, ALL (46,298)

PEST CONTROL WG-5026
*DOD, TRE, DOA, DOI, DOJ, HHS, DOT, GSA (886)

PHOTOGRAPHY GS-1060
*DOD, ALL (1,439)

PHYSICAL SCIENCE GROUP GS-1300

*DOI, ALL BUT HHS, OPM & USI (40,781)

PLUMBING WG-4206
*DOD, ALL BUT USI & NASA (1,539)

POLICE GS-083
*DOD, VET, TRE, DOI, HHS, GSA (9,140)

PROCUREMENT GS-1106
*DOD, ALL (6,729)

PSYCHOLOGY AID & TECHNICIAN GS-181 *VET, DOD, HHS, DOT (850)

PSYCHOLOGY GS-180
*VET, ALL (3,841)

PUBLIC AFFAIRS GS-1035
*DOD, ALL (4,351)

PURCHASING GS-1105
*DOD, ALL (6,086)

QUALITY ASSURANCE, INSPECTION, & GRADING GROUP GS-1900
*DOD (13,062)

RAILROAD SAFETY GS-2121
DOT (415)

RAILROAD REPAIRING WG-3546
DOD (45)

RECREATION AIDE & ASSISTANT GS-189
*DOD, DOI, DOA, VET, HHS (1,990)

REHABILITATION THERAPY ASSISTANT GS-636 *VET, HHS, DOT (850)

RESPIRATORY THERAPIST GS-651
*VET, DOD, HHS (457)

ROOFING WG-3606
*DOD, TVA, GSA, VET (330)

SAFETY ENGINEERING GS-803
*DOD, DOI, VET, TVA, DOL, HHS, DOT, DOE, GSA, NASA (555)

SALES STORE CLERICAL GS-2091
*DOD, VET (2,007)

SECURITY GUARD GS-085
*DOD, MOST AGENCIES (4,707)

SEWAGE DISPOSAL PLANT OPERATION
*DOD, DOE, DOA, VET (655)

SHIPWRIGHT WG-5220
*DOD, DOT (877)

SIGN PAINTING WG-4104
*DOD, DOI, DOA, TVA, VET (207)

SMALL ARMS REPAIR WG-6610
*DOD, DOJ, GSA (387)

SMALL ENGINE MECHANIC WG-8610
*DOD, DOI, DOA (97)

SOCIAL SERVICES GS-187
*DOD, VET, DOI, HHS (772)

SOCIAL WORK GS-185
*VET, DOD, HHS, DOJ, DOI, DOT (4,686)

SOIL CONSERVATION GS-457
*DOA, DOD, DOI, DOE (5,250)

SPEECH PATHOLOGY & AUDIOLOGY GS-665 *VET, HHS, DOD, DOI (726)

SPORTS SPECIALIST GS-030
*DOD, DOJ, HHS, VET (561)

STATISTICIAN GS-1530
*DOC, ALL (3,500)

SUPPLY GROUP GS-2000
*DOD, ALL (50,571)

SURVEYING TECHNICIAN GS-817
*DOI, DOD, DOA, DOC (1,600)

TAX EXAMINING GS-592
TRE (20,723)

TECHNICAL WRITING & EDITING GS-1083 *DOD, ALL (2,600)

TELEPHONE MECHANIC WG-2502
*DOD, HHS (663)

TELEPHONE OPERATING GS-382
*DOD, DOJ, DOI, DOA, DOC, DOL, HHS, GSA (1,622)

TOOLMAKING WG-3416
*DOD, DOJ, DOI, NASA (634)

TRANSPORTATION GROUP GS-2100 *DOT, ALL (46,378)

TRANSPORTATION MOBILE EQUIP MENT MAINTENANCE FAMILY WG-5800
*DOD, ALL EXCEPT DOS & USI (17,880)

UNITED STATES MARSHALL GS-082
DOJ (91)

UTILITY SYSTEMS REPAIR WG-4742
*DOD, MOST AGENCIES (2,641)

VETERINARY SCIENCE GS-701
*DOA, HHS, EPA, VET (2,067)

VOCATIONAL REHABILITATION GS-1715
*VET, TVA, DOL, DOI, DOJ (554)

WILDLIFE MANAGEMENT GS-485
DOI (636)

WOOD WORK GROUP WG-4600
*DOD, ALL (7,378)

WRITING GS-1082
*DOD, ALL (2,097)

ZOOLOGY GS-410
*DOI, DOD, DOA, DOC, HHS (103)

Index

283

Career Resource Catalog

THE BOOK OF U.S. GOVERNMENT JOBS: *Where They Are, What's Available, and How to Get One*, 8th Edition, by Dennis Damp.
$21.95, June 2002, 288 pages, paperback , ISBN: 943641-21-7

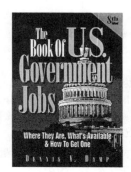

Damp guides readers through the federal employment system which has more employees than the top 10 Fortune 500 companies combined. You will discover what jobs are available, where they are, and how to get one. This **ALL NEW** *8th edition* covers the application process including KSAs and resumes, testing criteria, Internet resources, professional and entry level jobs, handicapped employment, veterans preference, student hiring, overseas opportunities, Postal jobs, law enforcement careers, interviewing techniques, and over 1,000 job resources. An easy-to-use Job Hunter's Checklist is provided in Appendix A to guide readers step-by-step through the federal employment system.

"An updated, comprehensive how-to-guide. Written in a clear, readable style, this book is Recommended."
— **LIBRARY JOURNAL**

"A year ago you gave me pointers on finding a federal job. Well it all worked out and I'm a paralegal specialist in Oklahoma. I just wanted to say thanks."
— **JG, Tulsa, OK**

POST OFFICE JOBS: *How To Get A Job With The U.S. Postal Service*
Dennis V. Damp $17.95, 224 pages, ISBN: 0-943641-19-5 *(Second Edition)*

A one-stop-resource for Postal Service employment. It presents what jobs are available, where they are, and how to get one. Includes a comprehensive 470 Battery Test study guide and features additional jobs in support occupations; from janitors and truck drivers to accountants, personnel specialists, technicians, and engineers. Many support jobs do not require written examinations. An applicant's background, work experience, and education is used to determine eligibility. Learn how to Identify job openings, Complete applications, match skills to jobs, Prepare for interviews, apply for jobs without written tests and score between 90% - 100% on tested occupations.

TAKE CHARGE OF YOUR FEDERAL CAREER: A Practical, Action-Oriented Career Management Workbook for Federal Employees, 202 pages, $17.95.

Do you dream of a better life, more pay, a challenging position with responsibility and one that takes full advantage of your background and experience? You can turn your dreams into reality and be one of the hundreds of thousands of federal employees each year who are promoted or obtain higher level jobs. This book is packed with proven tips and valuable assessment and evaluation tools, this unique workbook provides federal workers with the individualized know-how and guidance they need to identify, obtain, and successfully demonstrate the skills and experience required to qualify for new and better federal job

QUICK & EASY Version 6.1 FEDERAL JOBS KIT, Software (2002 Update)
WINDOWS 95, 98, 2000, NT, ME and XP COMPATIBLE.

$49.95   **(Personal Version)** Unlimited applications & resumes for 1 person
$59.95   **(Family Version)** Unlimited applications & resumes for 2 people
$129.95   **(Office Pack)** Unlimited applications & resumes for 8 people
$399.95   **(Professional Version)** Unlimited applications & resumes for 1 computer

Use DataTech's Quick & Easy Federal Jobs Kit to get the Federal job you want. The complete software package for getting a Federal job and completing your application. Contains everything you need including the SF 171, OF 612, OF-306, KSAOs, and eight Federal resume formats including RESUMIX. Also includes 7 new forms.

HEALTH CARE JOB EXPLOSION!: *High Growth Health Care Careers and Job Locator*, Third Edition, April 2001, by Dennis V. Damp. **$17.95, 288 pages**, ISBN: 0-943641-20-9

Explore high growth health occupations and use this book's 1,000 + resources to find job vacancies and networking contacts. This title presents detailed information for all major occupations. The Department of Labor projects that jobs in health care will grow by 31 percent **(OVER 3,100,000 NEW JOBS)** by 2005. This comprehensive **career guide** and **job finder** steers readers to where they can actually find job openings; periodicals with job ads, Internet sites, placement services, directories, associations, job fairs, and job hotlines. All major health care groups are explored including the nature of work for each occupation, describing typical working conditions, employment opportunities, training/advancement potential, necessary qualifications, Job outlook and earnings and related occupations.

"...this book will be a boon to those seeking jobs. Well rounded... Recommended for general collections; this book will be in demand."
— **LIBRARY JOURNAL**

ORDER FORM (Please Print)

❑ Send _____ copies of *The Book of U.S. Government Jobs* - 8th ed., 288 pages (8 ½" x 11") at $21.95 each.   _____
❑ Send _____ copies of *Post Office Jobs* - 2nd ed., 224 pages (8 ½" x 11") at $17.95 each.   _____
❑ Send _____ copies of *Health Care Job Explosion* - 3rd ed., 288 pg (6" x 9") at $17.95 each.   _____
❑ Send _____ copies of *Take Charge of Your Federal Career*, 202 pg (8 ½" x 11") at $17.95 each.   _____
❑ Send _____ *Quick & Easy*, **Personal** ❑ $49.95, **Family** ❑ $59.95, ❑ **Office** $129.95, ❑ **Pro** $399.95   _____
❑ Shipping , add $5.75 for the first book + $1.50 x _____ (# of additional books ordered) equals   _____
❑ Pennsylvania residents add 7% sales tax.

TOTAL: _____

Name:_____ Title: _____

Address:_____ Company Name:_____

City:_____ State:_____ ZIP:_____

Phone: _____ Ext:_____ Fax: _____

Make checks payable to: **Bookhaven Press LLC**
P.O. Box 1243, Moon Township, PA 15108. (Purchase Orders Accepted)
http://bookhaven.org - E-Mail: info@bookhaven.org
Credit card orders accepted toll free at **1-800-782-7424 (Orders Only)**

50 FAVORITE FURNISHINGS BY
FRANK LLOYD WRIGHT

50 FAVORITE FURNISHINGS BY
FRANK LLOYD WRIGHT

DIANE MADDEX

SMITHMARK

Compilation copyright © 1999 Archetype Press, Inc.

Text copyright © 1999 Diane Maddex

This edition published 1999 by SMITHMARK Publishers, a division of U.S. Media Holdings, Inc., 115 West 18th Street, New York, NY 10011.

SMITHMARK books are available for bulk purchase for sales promotion and premium use. For details write or call the manager of special sales, SMITHMARK Publishers, 115 West 18th Street, New York, NY 10011.

Produced by Archetype Press, Inc., Washington, D.C.
Diane Maddex, Project Director
Gretchen Smith Mui and John Hovanec, Editorial Assistants
Robert L. Wiser, Designer

This book was composed in Bernhard Gothic, designed by Lucian Bernhard in 1929 for American Type Founders. The display typography is Wade Sans, designed by Paul Hickson in 1990 for Esselte Letraset.

Printed in Singapore

10   9   8   7   6   5   4   3   2   1

Library of Congress Cataloging-in-Publication Data
Maddex, Diane.
50 favorite furnishings by Frank Lloyd Wright / Diane Maddex.
p.   cm.
Includes bibliographical references and index.
ISBN 0-7651-1670-7 (hardcover)
1. Wright, Frank Lloyd, 1867–1959—Criticism and interpretation. 2. Wright, Frank Lloyd, 1867–1959—Contributions in furniture design. 3. Architect-designed furniture—United States. I. Wright, Frank Lloyd, 1867–1959. II. Title. III. Title: Fifty favorite furnishings by Frank Lloyd Wright.
NK2439.W75M33 1999
749.213—dc21   99-29716
                                                                CIP

Endpapers and chapter dividers: Adaptation of Design No. 104, a fabric pattern created by Ling Po of Frank Lloyd Wright's office for production by F. Schumacher and Company in 1955. The interlocking spheres and ellipses were inspired by Wright's plans for houses for his sons David and Robert Llewellyn Wright. Drawing by Robert L. Wiser, Archetype Press

Page 2: Spindled chairs and other furnishings from Wright's early career and Prairie-style period on exhibition in a gallery devoted to his work.

INTRODUCTION

The chairs must have been the first thing guests noticed when they walked into Frederick and Lora Robie's dining room in Chicago—as righteous as church pews but so mysterious, their spindled backs screening the table yet inviting tantalizing glimpses of wonders beyond. Nary a Victorian curlicue forced onto the wood, no paint or high finish to hide the proud oak, not a trace of the past in these chairs. In this room, completed in 1910, Frank Lloyd Wright's genius for furnishing a harmonious space is clear. Enclosing the table, the chairs form a room of their own within the larger room. The dining surface is as long and broad as the chairs are tall, but its corner posts mimic the erect chair backs. The ensemble is repeated in miniature in a breakfast nook tucked into the room's projecting bay, where windows with geometric tracery create a screen of light subtly distinguishing inside from outside. A built-in sideboard is the only other furniture to be seen. Most of the decorative flourishes are similarly integrated: lamps atop the table corners with shades reflecting the window patterns; pointed table runners carrying the same diamond shape; wood bands gliding across the ceiling and down the walls to terminate in globes of light; a carpet whose small motif underscores the house's geometry. The Robies were allowed a few personal touches, among them china displayed like art objects on the sideboard's cantilevered ledge. A vase on the dining table holds dried flowers as simple messengers from nature. "If a man has twenty cents for the family meal," Wright said in 1894, "he had best invest three cents of that in a flower; for the glass in the middle of the table the family will be better fed in the long run."

1910 photograph of the Robie House dining room in Chicago

This was not his first perfect dining room—the one he designed in 1895 for his own home in Oak Park, Illinois, had led the way—but the Robies' space (completed with the help of George Mann Niedecken) presented one of Wright's most eloquent lessons of what a home should look like inside. Each house, he said then, should be a complete work of art. "It is quite impossible to consider the building one thing and its furnishings another," Wright explained in 1910. The chairs and tables, the windows, the lighting, the objects were "mere structural details" of a building's overall character. Like individual citizens in a democracy, each had its role to play in creating a harmonious union.

Wright (1867–1959) called houses of the day little more than notion stores, bazaars, and junk shops. He was pained when his own clients dragged in furnishings he thought did not belong in his progressive houses, items that were "the horrors of the old order." But at the start of the twentieth century, modern homeowners had few alternatives. So Wright added to his architectural repertoire everything inside a house, even preparing plans showing where furniture was to be placed. He began articulating Wright's rules of domestic order in 1894, restating them in sometimes identical language over the next sixty years:

Furnishings should be seen as parts of the whole composition, not aggregations, "a great thing instead of a collection of smaller ones." A single basic idea—a geometric motif, a plant form—should govern. "Every house worth considering as a

work of art," said Wright, "must have a grammar of its own." Ornament should be integral, arising from the materials and construction themselves. And those materials, chief among them wood, should be limited and natural to be "honest." Natural finishes bring out the nature of materials rather than cover it up as paint would. Natural colors come from the woods and fields—tones of the earth and autumn are "optimistic," in contrast to the "pessimistic" blues, purples, and cold greens "of the ribbon counter." Natural accessories such as simple flowers, dried or fresh, bring the outdoors in. Furniture, heating, lighting, and nearly everything else should be built in as far as possible to make them part of the building. Human scale must be observed. Geometry, with its straight lines conducive to machine manufacture, should prevail. And, said Wright, "above all, integrity," the end product of simplicity and unity.

Wright's principles had many ancestors. As a boy, he learned to revere nature from the Wisconsin landscape and the writings of Emerson and Thoreau. His Unitarian relatives taught him to sanctify unity. His mother introduced him to scale, proportion, and geometry with a set of Froebel kindergarten blocks. His father suggested to him that music was really "an edifice of sound." The twenty-year-old Wright carried these ideas with him when he arrived in Chicago in 1887, eager to build. From Louis Sullivan, his famous mentor and employer from 1888 to 1893, he learned how to mold surfaces as if they were plastic; this was a talent that would aid his furniture making. Once he ventured out on his own in 1893, Wright quickly transformed

Wright's photograph of a living area at Taliesin, rebuilt after a fire in 1914

himself into an organic architect, making buildings grow from nature just as the trees and flowers emerged from the prairie.

To fill his more than five hundred commissions that were built (as many more remained unrealized), Wright needed thousands of furnishings, from chairs and tables to music stands, from art glass to glass mosaics, from carpets to table linens. Many trusted associates served as the "fingers" on his hands, fleshing out an idea or designing items on their own. At his studio in the early days, for instance, he relied heavily on the architect Marion Mahony's exceptional skills to finish furniture and glass designs. During the Prairie years he also called on George Niedecken, an "interior architect" in Milwaukee, to execute furnishings that completed his architectural schemes. Artists such as Richard Bock and Alfonso Iannelli added sculptures and murals, and in Wright's later years his apprentices saw to it that each building was as well dressed inside as outside:

Furniture. Wright himself admitted that he was "black and blue in some spot, somewhere, almost all my life from too intimate contact with my own early furniture." But he kept striving, relying on machine technology to eliminate the fussy joinery and overwrought products of the day. Straight lines, natural markings, and unvarnished finishes became his hallmarks.

These were precepts that others such as the Japanese and Arts and Crafts designers on the Continent and in the United States espoused as well, and it is easy to point out similarities

between their work and Wright's. But Wright helped revolutionize interiors in the way he used his furniture as interior architecture to mark divisions of space. The number of pieces should be limited, he cautioned, with as many as possible built in—at one with the building. Then there was nothing to arrange, nothing to disturb the architect's vision.

Wright's furniture styles evolved from the stolid oak pieces of the Prairie years (1900–17) to the even simpler lines of his Usonian designs (1936–59), which were often of plywood and built by carpenters on site. As late as 1954, when he was eighty-seven, he confided that he thought perfect furniture could be made "someday."

Art Glass. Early on, Wright discovered that glass could be more than merely the "eyes" of a building—it could be the building itself. He used windows to make walls and sometimes ceilings disappear, ushering in light through movable casements, often grouped in expansive bands, or through innovative materials such as Pyrex tubing. Glass was his mirror, as lakes are nature's, and he molded it into screens of light.

The geometrically patterned windows, clerestories, and skylights that Wright designed in the first decade of the twentieth century are among the most beloved of all his furnishings. Infused with the natural colors of the earth, they turned his houses into "shimmering fabrics—woven of rich glass." Sunlight streamed in through them, he said, as if sifted

through tree leaves. As building economics changed, he gave them up entirely after the early 1920s. Instead, Wright found other imaginative ways to encase his buildings in crystal.

Decorative Arts. Wright contended that decoration was dangerous in the hands of those who did not understand it. (Everyone else's work was "inferior desecration" to him.) He urged clients to avoid a wagonload of items with no real use and concentrate on "one really fine thing." All ornament had to be integral, growing organically from the building itself.

Mellow walls tinted with autumnal hues took the place of most pictures. Built in even more surely than furniture, they were simply framed, almost like works of art, in wood given the sheen of a flower petal. Wallpaper would only cover a wall's true nature. Carpets on the floors became as much a part of the building as the plaster on the walls. Textiles such as a table scarf clothed a home with a "shimmering robe." Here and there a Japanese print, as an ode to simplicity, or a three-dimensional sculpture provided a key focal point. Such objects might rest on narrow wooden ledges, or decks, that surrounded a room and hid indirect lighting. Nearby, vases held fresh flowers, dried weeds, or tree branches, a sign of nature's lure.

Although all of the fifty furnishings singled out in the following pages are notable in and of themselves, Wright meant each one to be appreciated not in isolation but as an integral component of its own individual space—a part of the building itself.

Wright seated in one of his origami chairs at Taliesin West in 1957

FURN

When he began his practice of designing furniture about 1895, Wright adopted the credo of the Arts and Crafts movement: simplicity of design, natural materials treated naturally, and visible construction methods, preferably turned over to machines. These principles stayed with him even as the form of his buildings changed during his lifetime. No ornate carvings for

TURE

him, no twisted wood, no painted or strained finishes. Beginning with the spindled tall-back chairs that became his signature, he made his furniture honest, from assertive tables cantilevered like his houses to office desk sets striking in their efficiency. Wright excelled at built-in furniture: benches, sofas, sideboards, and tables that became an integral part of the architecture.

TALL-BACK CHAIR

Few pieces of furniture are as closely associated with Wright as his tall dining chairs with spindled backs. They epitomize his attempt to bring simplicity and rationality into American households, and they consequently have become icons of modern design. The first tall-back chairs appeared in Wright's own home in Oak Park, Illinois, built in 1889. By 1895, anxious to try out his ever-evolving ideas, the twenty-eight-year-old architect remodeled the family's kitchen into a new dining room and furnished it with a solid oak table, tall chairs with leather seats, built-in cabinets, recessed lighting, and windows of his own creation. The ensemble, clothed in the colors of a prairie autumn, was hailed by the new *House Beautiful* magazine in 1897 and again in 1899, when its furniture was singled out for being "in perfect harmony with the room." Wright himself began to assert that any freestanding furniture should possess the attributes of a house's built-ins and "should be seen as a minor part of the building itself." Originally the chair backs, which rise to playful round finials, were lined with rows of ball chains. Wright eventually changed these to squared spindles of oak and flared the rear legs. Encircling the table, the chairs screen out distractions, concentrating the diners' attention on the task at hand. Moving the spindles to the sides, the architect miniaturized his vision into a high chair for his son Llewellyn in 1902. For each family member, the chairs helped induce good posture if not the moral rectitude they seem to imply. Wright returned over and over to this chair design throughout his lifetime, extending the spindles down to the floor, up to the top rail, and along the sides and using different materials and bolder strokes. A vertical link to the earth, each one of them firmly anchored the sitter. Although one boy later recalled the "unequalled agony of sitting" in the Robie House dining chairs, this design became one of Wright's most dramatic signatures—mere board transformed into an abstract version of lace, light and dark, there and not there.

HUSSER DINING SET

Continuing to experiment with his tall-back dining chairs, Wright in 1899 designed a masterful oak dining set for Helen and Joseph Husser in Chicago. Wright found it maddening, from a design standpoint, that humans had to sit, but if they had to sit anywhere he preferred the dining room because its furniture was much more "easily managed in the architecture," he confessed in 1910. His dining table and chairs for the Hussers held center stage in an octagonal dining bay that projected out to frame a private view of Lake Michigan. Although the house was demolished in 1926, the dining room furniture has survived. The Hussers could choose from not one but three dining tables and twenty-four chairs designed to be combined for entertaining. To elongate the line of the chair backs, Wright dropped the spindles nearly to the floor, terminating them in a small band that wraps around the legs. A gentle curve begins at the terminals and wends its way down to the rear feet. The back still begins in a deep crest rail, like the chairs in Wright's own home, but he would soon eliminate this in favor of a simple line of spindles from top to bottom. The effect recalls Japanese screens and woodwork, motifs that also inspired English Arts and Crafts designers of the time. Carved with a woven-wood border, the table soars over its spindled base in a dramatic cantilever that hints at the Prairie houses and, later, the world-famous Fallingwater still to come from Wright's drafting board. Built-in lamps over flower holders originally lighted the four corners of the table, a device that Wright would use as well on tables in his houses for the Martins (1904) in Buffalo, New York, the Robies (1908) in Chicago, the Mays (1908) in Grand Rapids, Michigan, and the Boyntons (1908) in Rochester, New York. With chairs pulled up close to screen the diners and soft lights glowing at each corner, this dining ensemble was a smaller-scaled room within a room.

SLANT-BACK CHAIR

In 1901 Wright set himself clearly apart from English Arts and Crafts designers who extolled the satisfactions of handmade furnishings. Wright embraced their fondness for a simple life in harmony with nature, but for him the future lay in modern technology, not in medieval handicraft. In a speech entitled "The Art and Craft of the Machine," the young architect called machines the artist's "best friend." Their gift, he said, was to free wood to be wood and to allow "the poor as well as the rich [to] enjoy beautiful surface treatments of clean, strong forms...." Wright soon added to his repertoire a slant-back chair exemplifying these ideals. Paying homage to a machine's ability to produce perfect lines, a spare oak board slides past a simple leather seat down to the rear stretcher to support the sitter's back at just the right angle. It peeks provocatively above the stiles, which are cuffed with rectangular blocks top and bottom. The act of sitting is reduced to its most basic elements—creating almost "a machine to sit in," as Wright in 1931 described the first step in furniture design. The chair shown here dates from about 1904 and was in Wright's own home, which often became the repository for copies of client designs that he particularly liked. Similar examples appeared about the same time at his aunts' Hillside Home School (1887) in Spring Green, Wisconsin, without the bottom cuffs; at the Little House (1902) in Peoria, Illinois, with a rectangular back perforation and low, slanted stiles; at Unity Temple (1905) in Oak Park; and at the Robie House (1908) in Chicago. At the Larkin Administration Building (1903) in Buffalo, New York, some of these chairs offered an arm rest for stenographers, others had short, capped stiles for the dining room, and still others came with a truncated back. Apparently inspired by Wright, the Dutchman Gerrit Rietveld built his startling Red-Blue Chair in 1920, in which the seat and back planes are even more exaggerated to eliminate all need for applied ornament—achieving an almost fully reclining position, which Wright found to be the only "attractive posture of relaxation."

PRINT TABLE

After Commodore Matthew Perry helped open Japan to trade with the West in 1854, many Americans became infatuated with a culture that until then had been relatively unknown to them. As a young architect in Chicago in the 1890s, Wright was one of them. He was inspired by Japanese buildings, and he soon became a collector of Japanese woodblock prints, a hobby that intensified after his first trip to Japan in 1905. To him, these prints distilled the essence of modernity. In his *Autobiography* of 1932, he praised them as a democratic art form that eliminated "the insignificant, a process of simplification in art in which I was engaged...." Although he was frequently financially pressed into using his prints as barter and he often sold them outright for the income, Wright loved to display his *ukiyo-e* at home and urged his clients to show them as well. He thus designed an ingenious folding print table for this purpose. A poplar-and-pine version standing about four feet tall was made for the Oak Park house around 1895. Others were installed in Susan Lawrence Dana's 1902 house in Springfield, Illinois (opposite), and in the Little House of 1903 in Peoria, Illinois. To display prints, spindled sides were swung out to support a broad, hinged table top, one side of which could be tilted up. When not in use, the print table was folded up into a compact H-shaped unit, its two-sided top lowered between posts underneath. Wright also designed a narrow, spindled mahogany print stand and used it in 1908 to exhibit his Japanese print collection at the Art Institute of Chicago. Every furniture designer of the day, Wright believed, mistreated wood—except the Japanese. His print tables, with their evocation of Japanese screens, paid tribute both to that country's respect for natural materials and to its esteemed art. Toward the end of his life, Wright insisted that he looked to Japan more for its prints than for its architecture. When he died in 1959, his collection included this woodblock print (c. 1853) by Ando Hiroshige (left) among some six thousand others—probably less than half the number he had amassed.

20

LARKIN DESK SET

Always the innovator, Wright in 1903 designed a futuristic
office building for the Larkin Company in Buffalo, New York,
and filled it with equally forward-looking furniture. Here
Wright rejected architecture's "old order" and replaced it from
the walls in with a completely coordinated business environment. Workers in this mail-order company offering soap and
household products toiled in and around a wide-open, sun-
filled interior court. Little did customers know that as the
employees worked, they sat and tallied orders on some of the
earliest metal office furniture. It was the perfect choice for
the building Wright called "a great fire-proof vault." Everything
in it was designed for safety, efficiency, durability, cleanliness,
and comfort, down to the workspace of the most junior clerk.
One of Wright's most imaginative designs was a metal desk
with a swing-out chair: at night, the back folded down and
the unit could be tucked into the kneehole to allow mops
to glide underneath without obstruction. On top of the desk
was a layer of magnesite, a vinyl-like compound of wood
and concrete that was poured on to create an indestructible
surface (it was also used for flooring). Executives directed
the business from painted steel armchairs with leather seats.
The rectangular back tilted and provided ventilation through
a perforated pattern of squares. Under a swiveling seat, the
cruciform base sat on casters for easy movement. Elsewhere,
built-in metal file cabinets and wall-hung toilets proclaimed a
new age in office design. The Larkin Administration Building
lasted only until 1950, when it came down, but Wright's ideas
for open workplaces with custom furnishings have lived on.

MARTIN BARREL CHAIR

Turning from clean right angles to the curves that enchanted him into the 1950s, Wright produced one of his most successful and sophisticated chairs about 1904 for Isabel and Darwin Martin of Buffalo, New York. A few years earlier he had designed a low, octagonal barrel-style chair for the Bradley House in Kankakee, Illinois, an effort that was soon modified with spindled sides for Susan Lawrence Dana in Springfield and the Francis Littles in Peoria. But for the magnificent Martin House, home to the secretary of the Larkin Company, Wright found the perfect form to address the "unfortunate necessity" of sitting. A round, padded seat cantilevers out from a semi-circle of oak spindles, recalling his earliest chairs. At arm height, the screen turns into a solid back and majestically flares out and back, tapering toward the edges. On the sides the wood rises slightly to cradle the sitter's arms. Matthews Bros. Manufacturing Company of Milwaukee made and shipped about eight of these chairs for the living and dining rooms and the library, where they could work as architectural ensembles. In the living room, a pair flanked a high-back settle, offering a circular counterpoint to the otherwise rectilinear lines and matching ball sconces above. When Wright visited the house in 1936, he became so enamored of his own early work that he decided to refine the Martin barrel chair for his second home at Taliesin in Spring Green, Wisconsin. He also specified it for two of his new commissions: Fallingwater (1935) in Mill Run, Pennsylvania, and Wingspread (1937), outside Racine, Wisconsin. In those, the rotund seats extended beneath the wood frame to approximate a globe, bringing Wright's spherical play full circle.

ROBIE SOFA

In the midst of designing the Robie House in Chicago—one of his most assured Prairie-style homes—Wright abruptly left the country in the fall of 1909 to work on a German publication that would tell the world about his revolutionary work. He took with him his mistress, Mamah Borthwick Cheney, and did not return for a year. The task of completing the Robie furnishings fell to George Mann Niedecken, the "interior architect" from Milwaukee with whom Wright had worked first in 1904 and then more regularly after 1907. Niedecken filled the forty-four-foot-long living room with a geometrically patterned carpet and gave the Robies a unique red oak sofa with built-in elements, one of several unusual combination units to appear in Wright houses. Eliminating the need for side tables (which owners might move around to suit themselves), the architectonic sofa bears wide arms that spread outward like wings and connect with a narrower wood shelf, or console, at the back. A separate rear table was thus also made redundant. Wood strips along the edges and sides emphasize the cantilevered effect and mirror the horizontal layering of the house itself. Wright liked to use built-in furniture to organize and simplify a space—creating "complete harmony, nothing to arrange, nothing to disturb: room and furniture an 'entity.'" In reality built-ins let the architect control the look of a room by foreclosing homeowners' individual tastes, which from time to time conflicted with Wright's. The Robie furnishings, for which Niedecken billed them directly, included a small footstool, called a tabouret, that could double as a table; its feet flare outward in imitation of the sofa legs. A tall-back chair appears in yet another guise: with upholstery, rather than spindles, to comfort the sitter's back. It is not as dramatic as the house's dining chairs, whose spindles cascade from the crest rail to the floor (page 6), but its stiles are capped with blocks that could grace a throne. The space is pulled together with wood ceiling bands that stretch from side to side and art glass windows with stylized prairie flowers framing motifs representing the house's own geometry.

COONLEY DESK

As he did with a large handful of Wright's other complex Prairie houses, George Mann Niedecken took charge of seeing that the interiors of the Coonley House in Riverside, Illinois, were furnished to Wright's specifications. A small desk for the rear guest room obviously struck his fancy, for about 1910 he made a presentation drawing of it as poignant as a Japanese print. Not even four feet tall or wide, this charming nook that invites letter writing synthesizes the key design features of the house. Its white oak writing surface boldly cantilevers outward to recall Wright's Prairie houses. Rectangles within rectangles on the doors bring to mind the outswinging windows and the geometric tiles that enliven the facade. Door and drawer pulls underscore the square motif. Hipped metal-and-glass lamp shades resemble the roofs overhead. It is a gem of a piece, just one small item in a significant house once filled with furniture of all kinds, a mural by Niedecken, carpets, tableware, and monogrammed linens. Said Wright, "I put the best in me into the Coonley House." So did Niedecken, who completed the furnishings during Wright's year-long absence. The desk, which was manufactured by the Niedecken-Walbridge Company in Milwaukee, must have been one of the interior designer's own favorites: similar pieces have turned up in the Midwest, indicating that Niedecken adapted this sturdy design for some of his own later clients.

IRVING TABLE·COUCH

A desk of a different sort was made for the house of Edward and Florence Irving in Decatur, Illinois. One of the projects orphaned when Wright departed for Europe in 1909, it was left in the hands of Hermann von Holst, who in turn called on one of Wright's ablest employees to help him. Marion Mahony, an architect, had joined Wright's office in 1895 and spent the next fourteen years preparing exquisite presentation drawings and assisting Wright with designs for his furnishings. George Mann Niedecken joined her in executing the Irving furnishings. A skilled designer well versed in progressive interiors, European and American, Niedecken—like Mahony—could almost read Wright's mind when it came to fleshing out the furnishings. Mahony, however, asserted that the conception of the Irving furnishings rested with her. The unique table-couch-desk-lamp combination created for the living room fits perfectly into the Wrightian system of built-ins that mark interior architectural boundaries. Placed close to the fireplace, with its sumac and prairie-flower mural by Niedecken, the couch would have allowed one of the residents to lounge against pillows or sit beneath a large box of a lamp (now lost), while another could work at the oak fall-front desk secluded in the pier. On the dramatically cantilevered table sat a custom-designed lamp. Either separately or together, the Irvings would have been able to enjoy the fire, not to mention the satisfaction of using a piece of furniture so thoughtfully crafted. Planes intersect freely, and light meets dark, much like the fireplace and the exterior of the house, one of a trio bearing Mahony's mark in the small Millikin Place community.

31

GREENE SETTLE

Toward the end of his Prairie years, after he returned from his sojourn in Europe, Wright in 1912 designed a wood-trimmed cube of a house in Aurora, Illinois, and placed in it one of his most assertive freestanding sofas. Unlike his early high-back, high-sided settles in the Dana and Martin Houses and the Robie sofa, with its low back and roomy arms, this piece for the Greene family resurrects the spindles with which Wright launched his career in furnishings. A screen of oak surrounds the settle on three sides, while the leather seat pushes out past the arms in a subtle cantilever. One or more cushions probably filled the back, although the settle's good bones show well without adornment. Rails running atop the spindles and beneath the seat intersect with simple post legs, which stop at broad, square front feet that visually carry the settle's weight. Wright did not like to acknowledge many sources of inspiration, but the Greene settle bears at least a family resemblance to one promoted by Gustav Stickley in a 1901 issue of his *Craftsman* magazine. The great Arts and Crafts furniture maker's piece, however, was no match for the master's later creation. Wright called Mission furniture "crude," its plainness a far cry from the simplicity achieved in his own work. While Stickley's settle needed to rest on six legs, Wright's made do with four. Stickley raised his frame well off the ground, whereas Wright lowered his to within touching distance of the floor. And although Stickley had to add a vertical support at the back for his spindles, Wright created a wide, unbroken screen. Not a single line is out of place. Form and function are one, as Wright said they should be.

MIDWAY DINING SET

By 1913 Wright had essentially abandoned the ground-hugging Prairie houses that had sustained him for the past decade and began to write a new chapter in his practice. That year an opportunity came his way to design an indoor-outdoor entertainment complex in Chicago to rival the joyful beer gardens of Europe. At Midway Gardens, developed by the son of a former client on the midway of the 1893 World's Columbian Exposition, Wright was able to surround his architecture with music, and he played many variations on what was to become a lifelong theme of circles. Above doors in the tavern, colored bubbles floated across wall murals, bumping into each other in sheer delight. Clustered globes of light hung down or were hoisted by stylized statues. And to go with them Wright planned sprightly metal dining chairs with discs for the backs and seats. For these and other features at Midway, Wright turned to his "trusty T Square and aspiring triangle." Tapping out a counterpoint to the two linked circles on each chair, triangles step down the back and enlarge themselves below in steel to form the legs. They would not have looked out of place at a stylish neighborhood soda fountain. Neither these nor matching tables were ever built, however, because Midway Gardens never had the financial backing it needed. The popular center closed in 1916 and was torn down in 1929. Wright's metal dining set, with solid chair backs, was first made in the 1960s for use in the Fellowship dining room at Taliesin West, his home in Scottsdale, Arizona. As on the chairs, triangles support the base of the table, a reproduction of which is now manufactured with either the originally planned square top or a circular one that replays the chair's theme. Wright's designs for lamps, dishes, and even beer mugs were made in Midway's short life—all that was missing were the Wright tabletops on which to put them.

MORI CHAIR

Wright's affinity for Japan stood him in good stead when he was called on in 1914 to design an oriental art shop in Chicago for Shigehisa Mori, an art dealer. His shop was one of three commercial spaces Wright transformed in the Fine Arts Building, where Wright himself had a studio for a time in 1908 and 1910. The cubic chairs installed in the shop were as sparely drawn as one of the Japanese woodblock prints Wright so admired. A dozen years earlier he had exhibited at the Chicago Architectural Club another cube chair from his studio that was more daringly modern but certainly less Japanese. The Mori chairs, made of oak with drop-in seats covered in leather, seem as square as boxes, which is what the exhibited chairs were. Subtle touches, however, make this an illusion. The rear stiles are set in to meet the seat back, whereas the front stiles slide by at the sides. It is the top line—arms that meld into a back rail—that carries through the seat's square motif. The arms gracefully cantilever over the seat, which floats forward beyond the line of the front stiles and the bottom stretchers. The Mori shop was closed in 1922, and its other furnishings, including cabinets and tables, were dispersed. The chairs here are shown in front of the fireplace in Wright's Oak Park drafting room, where, not far from the earlier cube chairs, they help illustrate his genius at turning a few simple sticks of wood into an understated masterpiece.

IMPERIAL CHAIR

One of Wright's most important commissions, the Imperial Hotel in Tokyo, has now vanished except for some furniture and ruins of the lobby that have been reconstructed at an outdoor museum. The sprawling, three-story hotel, reached only by long train and boat trips from Wright's home, challenged all of his skills for eight years beginning in 1915. He responded with an ode to a country he greatly admired, filled with sculpted stone walls, murals, and an astonishing array of public and guest room furnishings, all infused with geometric legerdemain as only Wright could do it. On its opening day in 1923, the Imperial suffered—but survived—a massive earthquake that destroyed lesser buildings. It stood through World War II but fell to "progress" in 1968. A few oak chairs from the hotel's promenade, covered with more recent upholstery, made it to safety. With their hexagonal backs, they mimic the peaked rise of the ceiling in the "peacock alley" and the shape of its uppermost panels. Braces along the sides repeat the six-sided motif. Photographs show earlier chairs like these with caned seats, backs, and side panels. Both types fit neatly around octagonal tables. For Midway Gardens in Chicago, Wright had specified larger hexagonal-back chairs with short, angled "wings" in lieu of arms. Lack of money prevented their manufacture then, but an almost identical version shows up in a photograph of an Imperial bedroom, reinforcing the hexagonal theme introduced downstairs. Wright often found inventive ways of shuffling the deck he was dealt.

HOLLYHOCK SOFA

During their protracted effort to build her a house in
Hollywood, Aline Barnsdall begged Wright to "please do as
wonderful a thing with the inside of my house as … with the
outside." He did, despite being in Japan much of the time to
direct work on the Imperial Hotel. He left supervision of the
plans in the hands of his son Lloyd and the Austrian émigré
Rudolph M. Schindler. When Hollyhock House, as it was
nicknamed, was ready for Barnsdall in 1921, some extraordinary
fittings awaited her. Many rooms blossomed with hollyhocks,
her favorite flower—molded in art stone, stylized in art glass,
and carved in wood on chairs. In the living room she found
an imaginative group resembling built-in furniture (now
reconstructed) that was placed not along the walls but at the
heart of the space, encircling an octagonal hearth. An oak sofa
is combined with two tables plus a torchère on either side of
a narrow aisle, each section angled to surround the fireplace—
fulfilling the same idea behind the inglenooks in his early
houses. Spindled chairs, some with high backs and some with
low backs, pull up to desklike tables on four sides. Like leggy
hollyhocks, the lamps stretch seven feet toward the ceiling
and cast their light from upturned, etched pyramids. (Somewhat simpler torchères also appeared in the lobby and
bedrooms of Tokyo's Imperial Hotel, which Wright was then
building.) Water flowed in front of the fire over golden tiles,
a tone repeated in the walls and two built-in Japanese
screens. Hardly just a room within a room, the novel furniture
group was more an island in a world of Wright's making.

HOLLYHOCK DINING SET

The best dining room, suggested Wright, is a "bright, cozy, cheerful place you involuntarily enter with a smile." From the entry hall of Hollyhock House in Hollywood, the dining room beckons just four steps up. This serene area, as small as the living room is large, is set aside like a serving platter. Beaded panels of white mahogany wrap the walls, one of Wright's rare concessions to a client. Clerestories interrupt the wood to draw light down into the room; below them, asymmetrical pieces of purple glass in casement windows mediate between outside and inside. At the center of the room are more hollyhocks to please Aline Barnsdall. Along a trellis of stepping squares they climb the backs of a half dozen ingenious seats— a twist on Wright's classic tall chairs—and poke above the crest. Falling straight to the floor, the decorative back takes the place of rear legs . An unusual triangular pedestal on the table repeats the abstract pattern and holds aloft a hexagonal top; below is a rotated hexagonal base. Squares, triangles, hexagons—the geometry of the house came together supremely in its furniture. For Wright, arranging people around a dining table was much easier than accommodating their diverse activities in living rooms or elsewhere in the house. Dining, he said in 1931, "always was a great artistic opportunity."

FALLINGWATER BUILT-INS

As Wright suggested early in his career, as much furniture as possible should be built in as part of the architecture. The idea was not new, but he carried it out to perfection in order to unify the design, conserve space, reduce the number of furnishings, and, not insignificantly, control how his clients lived. Ample window seats, he said, did away with the need for chairs, which only cluttered up a room. By the mid-1930s, when Wright designed his world-famous Fallingwater, lifestyles were becoming more informal and servants were less frequently available to take care of housework. The weekend retreat planned for Edgar and Liliane Kaufmann in Mill Run, Pennsylvania, in 1935 had to be especially carefree. Built-ins abound, from bedrooms and guest rooms to the kitchen, dining area, and, most spectacularly, the forty-eight-foot-long living room, much of them made by the Gillen Woodwork Corporation of Milwaukee. Sofas designed as simple slashes cantilever out from the sandstone walls, their beige upholstery harmonizing with the stone itself. They cleverly hide indirect lighting and radiators. Bands veneered in black walnut run along the bottom and lead the eye toward tables, and then square footstools, in the same rich material. Tabletops with subtly rounded edges also cantilever over their bases just as Wright's masterpiece spreads its arms out to the rocky waterfall below. Stepping down from low to lower to nearly the floor, these small freestanding pieces of furniture mirror the architectural dynamism outside. Bright pillows on the window seats and cushions in the wood-framed footstools, like fallen leaves in an autumn forest, bring nature's colors into the house.

JOHNSON WAX DESK

The office revolution Wright launched with the Larkin Building at the turn of the century was won three decades later at the S. C. Johnson Administration Building in Racine, Wisconsin, begun in 1936. For this manufacturer of Johnson Wax, Wright produced a low, red brick building with sinuous curves that telegraphed the essence of modernity. In the Great Workroom, a refinement of the Larkin Building's innovative interior court, rows of tall, pale columns taper upward from slender feet to hold broad disks—they have been compared to lily pads, but the effect is much more akin to a forest shaded by leafy canopies. Rays from the skylights break through the "boughs" to dapple the workers below. As they have since the building was opened in 1939, employees sit at desks designed to harmonize with the architecture. Wright again turned to metal for efficiency, this time to tubular steel that was rounded like the building's own outline. Drawers as red as the brick outside swing forward, and a wastebasket hangs clear of the floor. Above them, parallel maple desktops seem to float in midair. Circles reappear in the chair, spiraling down from disks that form the pivoting back and the seat to rest on an offset half circle lined with red tubes. Not only do they match the desk's side supports, they also mimic the novel Pyrex tubing that lights much of the building. Wright allowed only three legs on the secretarial chairs, requiring the sitters to add their own two feet for balance. Executives were permitted to have four steady legs on their chairs, and other variations in the furniture were used to fit office duties and changing requirements over the years. With its cheerful color, streamlined shapes, and materials that the Bauhaus would have approved, the modular furniture in this early open-office environment was as important as any brick in the building.

TALIESIN DINING SET

Change and adaptation, adaptation and refinement—only by constant tinkering did Wright test his ideas and inch toward perfection. The dining area of his second home, Taliesin, in Spring Green, Wisconsin, served as one of his architectural laboratories. Spurred in part by necessity—calamitous fires in 1914 and 1925—he reworked the space and furnishings over nearly a half century. At first, after the limestone house was begun in 1911, severely rectilinear plank chairs not much taller than the dining table were paired with spare benches. After the 1914 fire, the chairs became more complex: square in shape with broad oak arms, a broad crest rail, an open back, intricate interlocking rear stiles, and padded seats. Replaced again after the 1925 fire, Wright's new chairs were more delicate but still spartan, featuring side panels and a deep, tilted crest rail, both in plywood to frame an open back and an upholstered seat; they were joined by several tall-back spindled chairs similar to the Robie dining chairs from two decades earlier, with the addition of arms, a slanted crest rail between clipped wings, and an oversize scale fit for a giant. In 1936 Wright reached further back into his store of early furniture designs when he rediscovered the barrel chair made about 1904 for Isabel and Darwin Martin of Buffalo, New York. He decided to make a new version for Wingspread, the house he began designing in 1937 for the Herbert Johnson family near Racine, Wisconsin. Made of plywood and chestnut, rather than oak as originally, the chair arms did not rise upward, the crest flared less, and the seat bottom was rounded to a semicircle. Wright placed a set of these modernized chairs around his table at Taliesin, the base of which is spindled like the chairs. What was once all angles is now full of curves, the barrel chairs forming a scalloped edge around a golden sea of rectangles.

CANTILEVERED DESK

Although so much of Wright's furniture changed—and improved—over the years, one item did not need much refinement. His tables remained basically as they started in his 1895 dining room in Oak Park, with just a few minor variations on his one great theme: the cantilever, which he regarded as "the most romantic, most free, of all principles of construction." Showing the daring that characterized his whole career, tabletops from the very beginning soared out over modest bases to provide unobstructed platforms for dining, writing, or temporarily resting coffee cups and magazines. The desk in his own bedroom-study at Taliesin in Wisconsin follows this functional form. A broad expanse of plywood rests on a simple wooden cube. The cantilever metaphor—bringing to mind the overhanging roofs of his Prairie houses and the outstretched terraces of Fallingwater—is amplified here with lower pieces that fit under the wings of the desktop. At the front is a square, two-level coffee table similar to others Wright designed in the 1930s, its four slat legs moved from the corners to the center of each side like the filling in a sandwich. A cantilevered credenza and a cruciform table tuck under the opposite edges. Between them rests a low, overstuffed ottoman. The dynamic planes jut forward and recede, rise up and settle down gently. And in the command chair, its rotund lines matched only by the glass vase, sat Wright.

TALIESIN WEST CHAIRS

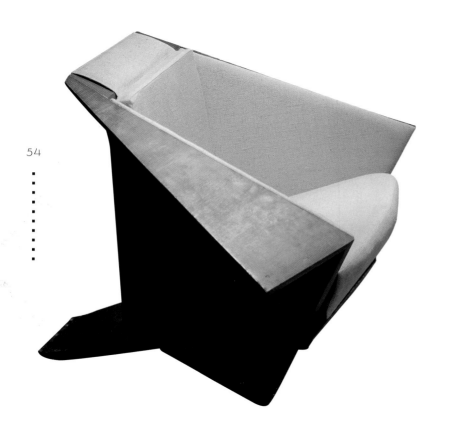

Wright liked to call concrete the "gutter rat" of building materials, and he reveled in raising it above its lowly origins. When it came to furniture, plywood occupied the same place in his bag of tricks. Contemporaries of Wright also took up plywood in the 1930s and 1940s, compressing it, molding it, and stretching it as far as new technologies would take it. But Wright was already expert at building furniture with plywood. Because it was inexpensive and could be assembled by the carpenters on site, it became part of the grammar of his Usonian houses. Conjuring up the image of a Japanese artist deftly folding paper into delicate origami, Wright in 1937 created one of his most famous chairs for use at Taliesin. Like a butterfly with wings poised for flight, the origami chair, said Wright, helped make sitters look graceful in spite of themselves. The arms of the Taliesin chairs had cutouts recalling his wood screens, but other versions such as those designed for Taliesin West after 1946 were solid and narrower (left). Today these folded butterflies brought down to earth fill the living room of Wright's winter home in Scottsdale, Arizona, begun in 1937. Just beyond, in a room called the cove (opposite), is a set of equally inventive plywood chairs placed around a hexagonal table identical to ones in the living room. Wrapped in a playful jumble of shapes, these seats seem almost anthropomorphic, like many of Wright's chairs.

USONIAN BUILT-INS

Wright turned to built-in furniture for his own 1889 home in Oak Park and continued to specify it throughout the rest of his life's work. It made the furnishings an extension of the architecture, helped coordinate materials and colors, and limited homeowners' sometimes inappropriate choices—built-ins were simplicity itself. As at Fallingwater, living room sofas were excellent candidates for this treatment. Pushed against a wall, they became background items, clearing the foreground for selected accent tables, side chairs, and footstools. Space and money were both at a premium in the Usonian houses that Wright designed beginning in the mid-1930s, so built-ins again became his solution. In the 1950 house of Mary and William Palmer of Ann Arbor, Michigan, a built-in sofa holds the prime spot next to the fireplace. Autumn gold cushions fill a frame of the same cypress that lines the walls and rises to the center point of the peaked ceiling. Behind are cantilevered shelves that serve as a divider, and below is a triangular table that snuggles up close to the sofa. The triangle, in fact, is the module, or plan, around which the house was conceived. More tables carry out the motif, and the waxed red floor underneath is inscribed to underscore the grand plan. Pale green footstools—triangles, of course—can be rearranged as needed not just for comfort and extra seating but also to extend the geometric possibilities of the space. Even the lighting was planned in advance and built in: hidden behind wood decks to bathe the room in a soft, diffused glow.

MUSIC STAND

Next to a built-in sofa, music was a necessity for Wright. Wherever he looked he found, or created, affinities between music and architecture. "The symphony, as my father first taught me, is an edifice of sound," the architect wrote in his 1932 *Autobiography*. Wright built buildings with visual rhythm and harmony and used mathematical systems not unlike those on which Beethoven based a piano sonata. Architecture was the superior art, he suggested, but noted that the "idiosyncrasy of the client does not exist for the great composer," nor does he have to worry about utilitarian needs and the laws of physics as do the great architects. Wright was happy to share his own love of Beethoven, Bach, and Mozart with his clients, even the idiosyncratic ones. In addition to theaters, churches, and other public venues for music, Wright designed a number of residential spaces for musical owners: a living room that doubled as a concert hall for one, a musicians' balcony for another. But for the compact Usonian house of Isadore and Lucille Zimmerman of Manchester, New Hampshire, he could fit in little more than a piano and a handsome music stand. The couple had admired the quartet stands he had devised in the mid-1940s for Taliesin's living room and its Hillside Playhouse, so when he designed their house in 1950 he gave them one of their own. A far cry from the typical, unstable metal stand, Wright's creation calls attention to the importance of music, not to mention his own ingenuity. Four broad ledges, joined with a triangular motif, amply support the musicians' scores in front of coordinated stools. Above the stand, a cap hipped like one of Wright's roofs hides indirect lights. Space was even allowed on top for plants—nature, music, and architecture all brought together in one perfect composition.

LOVNESS DINING SET

Wright's tall-back chairs took many forms during the seven decades of his career, but—with perhaps one exception—none were as exotic as the ones built by Donald and Virginia Lovness for their lakeside cottage in Stillwater, Minnesota. The chairs are especially unusual here in the northern woods because they were originally intended for the sunny hillside in Hollywood, California, on which Wright built Hollyhock House for Aline Barnsdall in 1921. Instead, another chair motif with stylized hollyhocks was used. The two designs are standouts in Wright's great panoply of dining chairs. Salvaged from potential oblivion, the set in the Lovness cottage was fabricated in 1972, almost two decades after the couple began their main house in 1955. Along the layered oak backs, three squares upended to form diamonds range along a background of half octagons on either side—allusions to the octagonal fireplace and the square patterns that energize Hollyhock House. Wrightian red cushions, made by Virginia Lovness, are attached with tasseled ties that cascade down the backs, a feature used on earlier Wright chairs. The table edges and the sides of the base pick up the chairs' geometric theme. Placed between a generous built-in sideboard and a hanging pole lamp of Wright's design, the set has taken on a woodsy, organic quality and made itself right at home here.

RAYWARD FURNITURE

Although Wright liked to view each house as a unique commission, he sometimes made his work easier by recycling some old favorites among his furniture designs—perhaps modifying them, perhaps not. In 1955, when he designed Tirranna for the John L. Rayward family of New Canaan, Connecticut, Wright was eighty-eight years old. Sixty years' worth of tables and chairs were behind him, and he brought some of them back to life here. Bright nesting tables used in the living room (below) were first tried out at Taliesin West about 1937. Crisply geometric, they feature a hexagonal top paired with its shadow; a bottom shelf is held in place by three slat legs that form a triangular base. Nearby were low plywood side chairs with gently rounded, spindled backs and flared arms—designs similar to chairs used in the 1930s and adapted in the 1950s . For the Raywards' oak dining table, Wright produced a set of similar side chairs whose angled plank legs are joined by a stretcher with triangular cutouts (pages 64–65). Compared to Wright's more traditional tall spindled dining chairs, these seats with low curved backs are conspicuously dainty. The house was later furnished with dining chairs from the first commercial line of Wright's furniture launched in 1955 by the Heritage-Henredon Furniture Company. Another variation on the Robie chair theme was also made for the Raywards. With solid panels beneath the seat, sculptural molding, and a deep crest rail, it looked satisfyingly substantial. In addition, at some point some of Wright's most unusual tall-back chairs were moved into the house (opposite), but it is unclear where these might have been used. A solid plank of oak rises from the floor and tapers toward the head. Five triangles march down in descending order, pointing on the back to a triangular buttress. It is no-nonsense seating but regal in its conception. This same chair design is known to have been placed in houses for the Davis family (1950) of Marion, Indiana, and the Ablins (1958) of Bakersfield, California. Beginning with his own dining room in 1895, the high-back chair remained a staple of Wright's furniture vocabulary for his entire lifetime.

ART

Glass was Wright's métier, and he used it boldly to furnish his buildings with light, pattern, and color. Not much else mattered as much in his early commissions—one might do without a chair or a table by Wright but not, especially in the Prairie years, without his windows. They broke down solid walls into "limpid surfaces" like water in the landscape, he said. As screens

GLASS

of glass, often grouped innovatively in broad bands, they coaxed the out-side in. Geometric motifs abstracted from nature reinforced that link and brought joy from morning to evening, as light changed the colored glass and swept floors and ceilings with patterns and shadows. Throughout his long life, Wright continued to experiment with glass—his favorite building material.

ROBERTS WINDOW

The art glass for which Wright is renowned today did not
rise up from his drafting board fully conceived. It took a few
years—not many, to be sure—for him to perfect the form
that homeowners coveted and other designers envied. For
his remodeled dining room of 1895 (page 14), Wright simply
adapted a lotus design from a pattern book to bathe the room
in the mystique of Egypt. The next year he produced a far
more elaborate window in the stair hall of a house he remodeled for the Charles Roberts family in Oak Park. Wright's
debt to his mentor, Louis Sullivan, seems clear. Under his *Lieber
Meister's* tutelage from 1888 to 1893, the young architect
absorbed Sullivan's fluid style of portraying nature. The Roberts
window is Sullivanesque ornament transferred to glass. Like
a floral bouquet, petals spread gracefully across the arch and
drift down into the center "stem." Segmented circles touch
and overlap—even forming lotus patterns here and there.
Smaller windows in the study and elsewhere repeat the main
theme. Some of the details may be transitional in style and
the whole may owe a debt to Sullivan, but Wright's growing
ability to control light and views is as clear as glass. Speaking
in 1928 about its magic, Wright said that "we can think of
uses to which it might be put as various and beautiful as the
frost designs upon the pane of glass itself." This early piece
of window wizardry must still have been fresh in his mind.

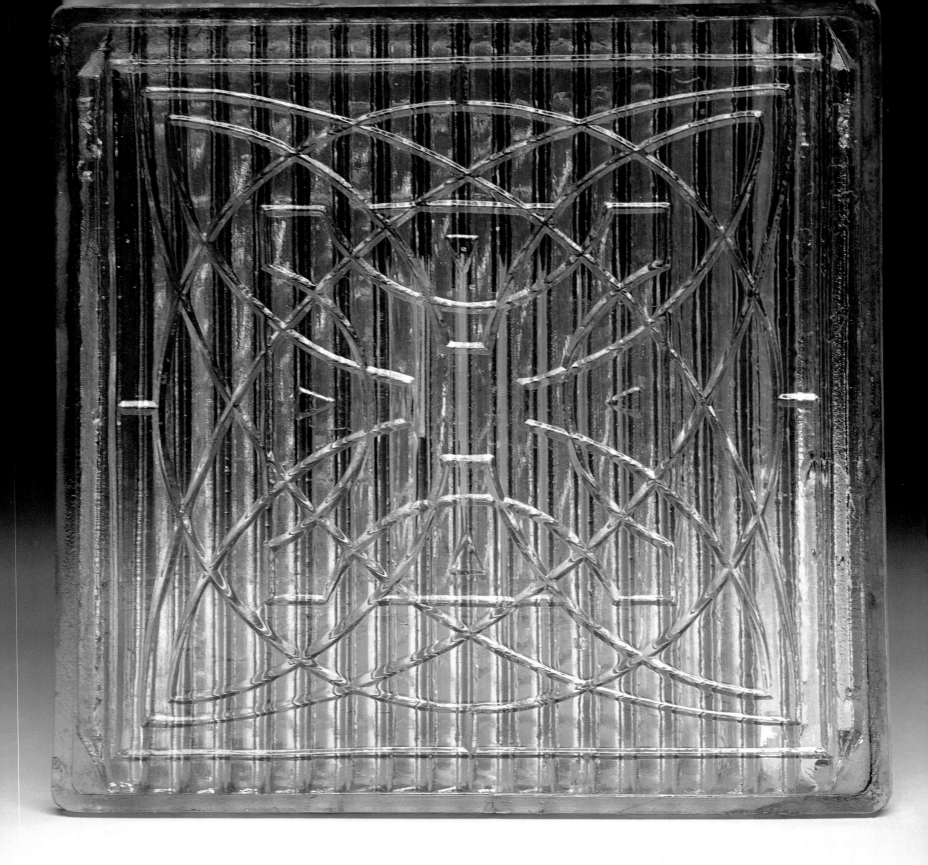

LUXFER PRISM GLASS

Wright was not done with his compass, although he was soon to put it aside in favor of a T-square for his glass designs. Circular forms reappeared in 1897 on an innovative glass block he designed—and patented, guaranteeing him enough income to add a studio to his Oak Park home. In the years before electricity, the far reaches of offices, stores, basements, ships, and similar spaces could be dark. For decades inventors had been seeking a way to bring in more light. Prismatic glass, inspired by the Fresnel lenses in lighthouses, became the answer. Ribs of triangular prisms on the backs of molded, four-inch glass blocks directed the light where it was needed, providing up to fifty times as much light as plate glass. Rows of blocks were placed in grids and electroglazed to make them watertight and fireproof. In an 1894 design competition Wright drew the entire facade of an office building using prismatic glass (never built), but the blocks were more typically installed in transoms or on sidewalks. The American Luxfer Prism Company, the industry leader that was owned by some Wright clients, lost little time in asking the up-and-coming architect to design blocks for the firm (whose name meant "to carry light" in Latin). Although Wright eventually created and patented about forty plate and prism designs, the one most frequently produced was this Sullivanesque pattern from 1897. A square-within-a-square motif frames the four-inch block and encloses a circle and a swirl of ellipses—flattened circles—that collide like atoms. Luxfer prisms were a great commercial success, but by the 1920s and 1930s they faded in importance as electricity became widespread. Wright is not known to have installed any of them in his own buildings.

STUDIO WINDOW

Using money earned from his Luxfer prism glass, Wright in 1898 built a complete studio adjacent to his home in Oak Park. To the left of the reception hall is a two-story drafting room, to the right an octagonal library in which he met clients. Secluded between was the architect's own private office. Natural light for the room comes in through a skylight and a window triptych that showers it with the colors of spring. Wright had finally found his language for glass. Rectilinear lines substituted for naturalistic shapes and told their own story. Realism in glass was anathema to Wright; in 1928 he decried anything that got "mixed up with the view outside" and ordered that a "window pattern should stay severely put." He had made a partnership with the machine. Squares, rectangles, and bars weave themselves into a frame surrounding plain plate glass. Privacy is protected without resorting to draperies lacking "rhyme or sanitary reason," while the view is clearly focused. Other Wright windows of the time used a similar frame motif, including ones later removed from the studio reception hall. Three years earlier Wright had lined his children's playroom upstairs with glass screens whose square motifs masqueraded as pale tulips, but here he took a step forward into bold color. The windows are a reminder that the delights of nature are never far away. Relatively simple glass fills the rest of the studio and the entire house—Wright may have saved some of the best glass for his own space.

THOMAS VESTIBULE

Mystery was at the heart of Wright's entrances. Visitors would often be required to snake along a circuitous path until finally the architect let them behold the door. To gain entry to the Thomas House in Oak Park, one travels under a ground-floor arch and up a flight of stairs, turns, ascends higher to the house's second floor—and steps into a glass-enclosed bower. Owners and visitors alike know that they have arrived. The extraordinary vestibule that Wright created here in 1901 reaches out to welcome like a clearing on the prairie. Recalling wispy prairie grass or plants, the doors and windows are dressed in squares and bars of opalescent glass and gold leaf topped by attenuated triangles. They screen the view, allowing light in but serving more subtly than any curtain to keep prying eyes out. Ceiling lights above elaborate on the feathery triangles; in the four corners mother-of-pearl applied to the glass heightens the golden effect. Tucked into the ell between the living and dining rooms, the entry is part of an almost unbroken band of glass, all fabricated by the glass designers Giannini and Hilgart, that makes the second-floor walls vanish. The roofs seem to float above. Wright had found a single tool with which to bring nature inside, naturally, and to break down solid walls. His great era of art glass had begun.

DANA WINDOWS

Susan Lawrence Dana's home in Springfield, Illinois, was a house of glass long before there were glass houses in America. Her wealth allowed Wright almost free rein in 1902 to create a wonderland where glass sparkled in hundreds of windows and doors, hanging lamps and standing lamps, sconces and skylights, as well as nooks and crannies in between. The glass display begins at the front door (right), where Wright took the old-fashioned idea of a fanlight and transformed it into a dancing brigade of butterflies *en pointe*. A pair of arches on either side of a glass vault reinforces the motif, which is unusual in the architect's more typical repertoire of stylized plant forms. Some say that the butterflies refer to an old fireplace left in the house, or to the house's roofline, or to the freedom of flight—or perhaps to Dana's role as a social butterfly. The greens, golds, and browns, in any case, bring inside the hues of a prairie autumn, when butterflies take wing. In the dining room and along the walkway to the gallery designed for entertaining, hanging lamps (pages 106-7) pick up the lepidopteran theme. Also in the dining room is an overscaled lunette presenting the house's signature sumac motif. A half-moon–shaped relative rises over the dramatic two-story gallery (pages 78-79), but it sings a different tune. The chevron shapes of sumac leaves and butterfly wings were forsaken in favor of rectilinear abstractions of plants. Side windows repeat its weave of squares and rectangles. Wright was said to be averse to unrelieved arches—perhaps they were too classical and symmetrical for him—so he bisected this lunette with horizontal and vertical wood trim. His associate Marion Mahony helped him design the acres of glass his office turned out during the Prairie years and no doubt assisted him with the Dana commission as she did for the Martin and Robie Houses and the Coonley Playhouse. Linden Glass Company of Chicago received the princely sum for the time of $15,000 to help turn Dana's house into an iridescent jewel.

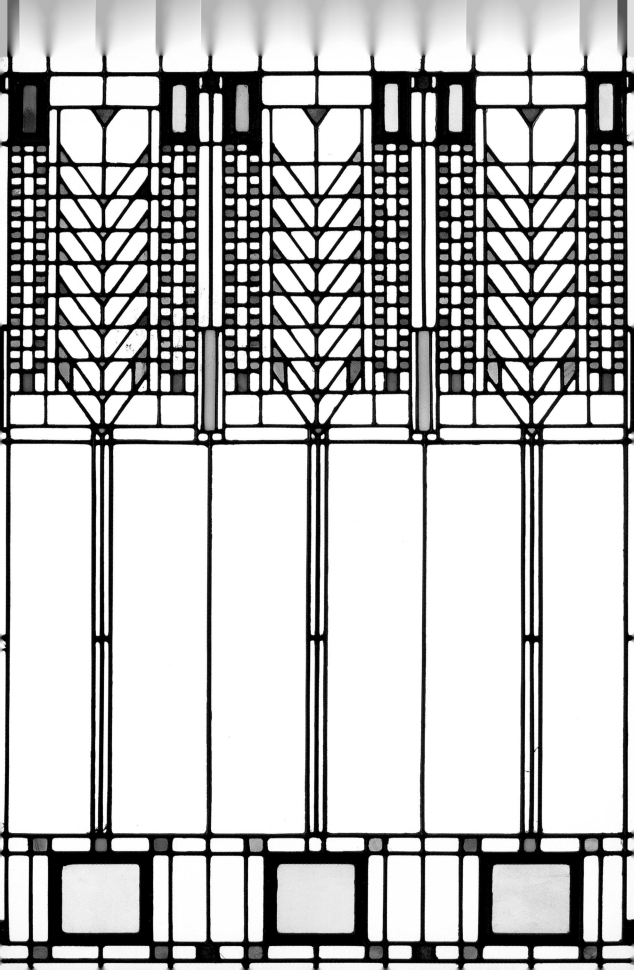

TREE OF LIFE WINDOW

Pattern, said Wright in 1928, "is made more cheaply and beautifully effective when introduced into the glass of the windows than in the use of any other medium that architecture has to offer." But he chose to use art glass not just for its patterns or even its colors. Thanks to a new electroglazing process designed to anchor the glass pieces, he was able to use metal tracery to add yet another layer of meaning to these screens of light. In few places is this concept as clear as in the windows of Darwin and Isabel Martin's house in Buffalo, New York, designed in 1904. Ringing the upper stories and lighting the reception hall, these windows have come to be known as the Tree of Life pattern because of their obvious debt to nature. Wright's desire to stylize plants and trees—inspiration without imitation—was entirely successful here. In this window, three geometric forms grow organically from square roots and branch out overhead in leaves formed from chevrons. The autumnal-colored glass, manufactured also by Linden Glass, sits in caming that etches the pattern in zinc and copper. As in many of Wright's windows, much of the glass is iridescent so that it takes on one hue in daylight and another at night. Clear glass fills the rest of each window for uninterrupted views. Used solo, in trios, and in quartets, the Tree of Life windows composed a sonata in glass for the Martins, a couple who enjoyed nature as much as Wright did.

MAY SKYLIGHT

For Wright, light did not stop at the ceiling. Early on in his career as an architect and a glass designer, he moved his windows up beyond the walls and turned them into skylights. This elevated source sends light gently down into a room, bathing it in a diffused glow. Wright created this effect both with skylights that used the sun and with ceiling lights—he called them "moonlight"—that relied on the new invention of electricity. From window to high clerestory to skylight, a room could be painted in well-balanced light. He combined all three techniques in a nearly seamless composition for Sophie and Meyer May's house in Grand Rapids, Michigan, completed in 1910. The living room faces south to coax in as much sunshine as possible, helped along by a wall of geometrically patterned art glass. Tall panels reach above the oak molding to a row of clerestories. The banded square in the center, framed by copper outside, repeats the square motif in the glass itself. Like the molten material it once was, the glass slides up and onto the ceiling, where coordinated skylights illuminate the night or day. A glass-shaded lamp continues the theme, which extends even to the feathery pattern on the embroidered table runner; both were the work of George Mann Niedecken. The wall has vanished and in its place is light. "Glass and light—two forms of the same thing!" Wright exclaimed in 1928

MAY WINDOWS

Using the lines of the living room windows as his thread,
Wright wove a tapestry of glass throughout the May House.
A wall of windows in the dining room picks up its warp and
woof, and elements are echoed in a glass-front sideboard
and light standards attached to the table. The upstairs was not
forgotten. Even in one of the children's bedrooms, art glass
brings nature right indoors. The rows of golden squares top and
bottom were seen downstairs, but the central motif has been
changed and strengthened to suspend a leafy plant nearly in
the center of each window. Repeated in openings all along
the wall, it acts like a valence to increase the sense of privacy.
The parents' bedroom, a morning room for reading, and
another child's room open to the neighborhood with the
identical glass, which in intense sunlight casts magical patterns
on floors and ceilings. Now displayed in the corner child's
bedroom (in a house museum open to the public) is a set
of the Froebel blocks that set the young Wright himself on
his journey into architecture. They serve as a tactile reminder
of the geometry that was at the heart of all his designs.

COONLEY TRIPTYCH

Wright wrote music into the windows for the Coonley Playhouse of 1912 in Riverside, Illinois. He called them his "Kinder Symphony"—and what could be more appropriate for a school than these exuberant shapes and colors? For inspiration Wright turned not to nature but to that great American institution, the parade. Balloons fly high in the air, tangling on occasion with square confetti. A flag waves in the breeze. Variations on this central triptych lined the side walls in bands of clerestories raised well above the heads of the young children. Compared to the subdued natural tones used in his earlier glass, the primary colors are almost shockingly daring. Wright thought that their "primitive color" caused less interference with a window's function and added "a higher architectural note to the effect of *light* itself." Some credit for his change in palette and form may go to Wright's stay in Europe during 1909 and 1910, when he was probably exposed to the newly emerging abstract art. If so, he transformed those ideas into a medium of which he was the master: glass was Wright's best canvas. He had long had a fascination with balloons, bringing them home to his children to float in their tall playroom with its bursting ceiling. "Human beings," observed Wright in 1932, "are really childlike, in the best sense, when directly appealed to by simple, strong forms and pure, bright color." These curvilinear forms never left him; he pulled them out again the next year at Midway Gardens and continued to roll them around in one material or another—think of the Guggenheim Museum of Art—until the end of his career.

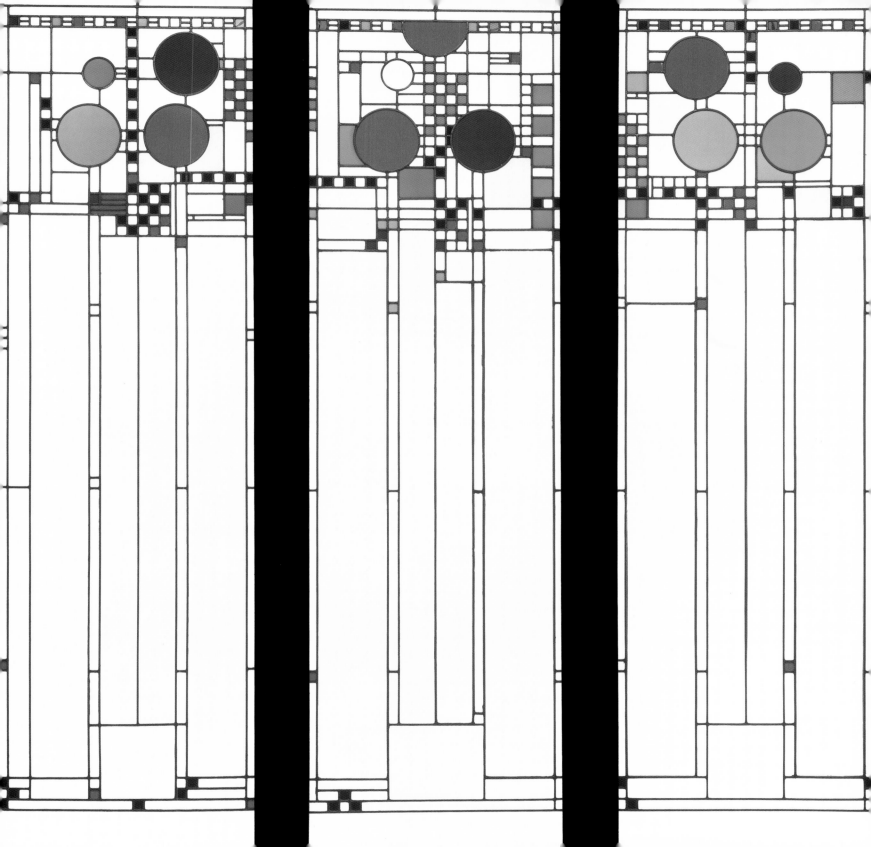

TALIESIN WINDOW

Wright thought of Taliesin, his home in Spring Green, Wisconsin, as "a broad shelter seeking fellowship with its surroundings." It was his "shining brow" (its meaning in Welsh), built not *on* the hill but *of* it. The architect spent boyhood summers in his family's gently rolling river landscape and returned in 1911 to fit a new home for himself into its beloved hills. It was to be a natural house in every sense, and Wright opened it to nature from nearly every room. Fires tragically destroyed the living quarters not just once, in 1914, but again in 1925. Taliesin rose a third time afterward—Wright's own phoenix, his work in progress over the three and a half decades remaining to him. The living room offers one of the most engaging views, focused through an art glass window from the Heath House of 1905 in Buffalo, New York. An architectural scavenger of sorts, Wright was adept at acquiring clients' castoffs or adapting previous designs for use in his own homes (the barrel chairs in the nearby dining alcove, for one). The Prairie-style window's feathery geometry of squares, diamonds, triangles, and parallelograms suits its new home, particularly when it mirrors the valley's fall colors. Glass meets the layered wall of limestone, a reminder of the riverbed below, without need of any distracting sash or frame. A sweeping "birdwalk," added in 1953, thrusts itself right into nature, where just like Wright's glass the lakes "catch ... the sky."

HOLLYHOCK WINDOWS

In 1917, as Aline Barnsdall and Wright were in the throes of "birth pangs," as Wright characterized their efforts to build her a theater and house in Hollywood, Barnsdall herself gave birth. The theatrical oil heiress was not married. Moving her little Sugar Top (Aline Elizabeth, later known as Betty) into a home became a priority. Any child, not to mention her mother, should have been delighted with the suite that Wright finally designed. Hollyhock House's child's quarters on the first floor numbered a bedroom, a dressing room, a bathroom, space for a nursemaid, and this playroom where art glass patterns danced in a magical kingdom for one. (Overhead was the room intended for Mother Barnsdall, who decided to sleep downstairs.) In this house built around open courtyards, well out of the California sun's glare, glass was a vital component. The playroom's side walls, each filled with four panels of glass, mysteriously slope inward five degrees. The ceiling is low, as Wright liked it, creating just the right childlike scale here. Bordered by sidelights mitered at the corners, the glassy door at the far end releases the tension and opens up the space. Triangles on the diagonal dart in from the sides and down from the tops of the panels, carrying out the glass theme introduced in the house's living spaces. More abstract even than most of Wright's earlier glass designs, the door is symmetrical while the sides explore abstraction's unlimited possibilities. The door pattern reaches toward the ceiling as hollyhocks push skyward. Purple, an unusual color in Wright's palette, may have been suggested by Sugar Top's mother, who pointed it out in some of her architect's Japanese prints. Judson Studio, a noted art glass maker in Los Angeles, fabricated the windows. The young émigré architect Rudolph M. Schindler helped supervise construction of the house and later explained its windows: "They are not wall holes but a dissolution of the building material into a grid—leaded glass—as the ground dissolves and becomes lost in the tree branches." His astute observation describes all of Wright's forays into art glass.

90

ENNIS WINDOW

The art glass in Hollyhock House had its roots in the architect's Prairie years, but three of the other four Los Angeles–area houses he designed in the early 1920s, all built of innovative concrete blocks, went without such windows. The textile patterns woven by the blocks themselves produced nearly all the ornament these progressive houses needed. That art glass reappeared in Wright's 1923 house for Mabel and Charles Ennis, the last of the textile-block houses, remains somewhat of a puzzle. It is certainly one of the last of Wright's houses to have art glass, and it may have been dictated by the owners, who made a number of changes at odds with the building's conception. Hardly anyone, however, could wish away the view of Los Angeles framed by the towering dining room window. Its three-part composition, almost classically Palladian, resonates with delicate tracery. The same diagonals used in the Hollyhock windows appear here, but the stark abstraction paints a flatness not seen in Wright's early work. Other glass in the house, such as the library doors, drips with lush hanging vines in complex combinations more reminiscent of his early midwestern commissions. If they are meant to be wisteria—portrayed more realistically in a glass fireplace mosaic in the loggia—fingers may point to Orlando Giannini. An artist responsible for murals in Wright's Oak Park home, Giannini had also executed similar wisteria overmantels for the houses of the Hussers (1899) in Chicago and the Darwin Martins (1904) in Buffalo, New York, both now lost. Some of the Ennis windows branch out into feather and arrow motifs—an interest in American Indians that Giannini shared with Wright.

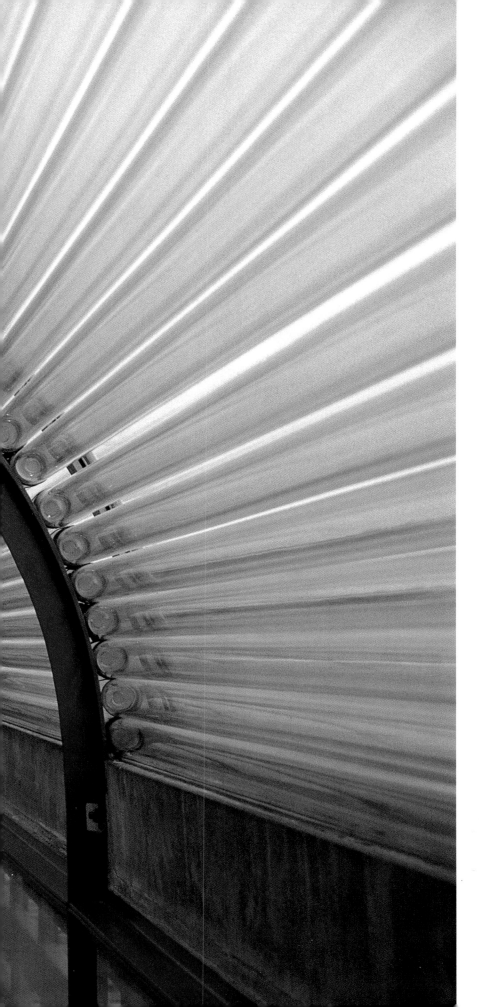

PYREX GLASS TUBING

By the time Wright came to design an office building for the maker of Johnson Wax in 1936, flat planes were giving way to curves in his work. In the Administration Building, the first of two workspaces built for the S. C. Johnson Company's headquarters in Racine, Wisconsin, the circle holds sway: in the tops of the dendriform columns in the Great Workroom, in the sinuous curves of the desks, in the narrow red piping around the chairs (pages 48–49). The glass followed suit. At first, to push light into the far reaches, Wright had in mind to use prism glass like his Luxfer designs of four decades earlier. Because the building turns away from its setting, drawing light inside was a major hurdle for the architect. He soon tossed out his nineteenth-century material and settled on a unique solution after envisioning the possibilities that lay in modern technology. When the Corning Glass Company said that it could make Pyrex glass tubes a mile long if he wanted, Wright was off and running with this new tool. The translucent tubing not only would bring in light without distraction, its sealed air was also its own insulation. He stretched it into a canopy of light, ringed the cornice line with it, snipped it into geometric patterns on walls, and molded a dome filled with encircling constellations. Rhythmic patterns arose from the necessary act of joining the tubes. More weatherproof adhesives since invented have replaced the originals. Today light still softly filters over the Johnson Wax employees from Wright's inspiration of long ago. When day turns to night, light bulbs take the sun's place in this universe of one man's creation.

DECORAT

Details mattered to Wright, and none were too small to escape his notice.

An urn to hold dried flowers from the prairie. A lamp for a library table.

China for all occasions. Carpets and upholstery fabrics to signify the mod-

ern age and classical sculpture to remember civilizations long past. Fireplace

accoutrements—and even the mortar in the wall itself. Each decorative

IVE ARTS

object chosen for a Wright house was carefully integrated into the overall scheme. Geometric designs in art glass were matched in the lamp shades. Patterns in a rug were echoed in embroidered table linens and runners. Wright's respect for Japanese simplicity is obvious in the design and placement of these items: each stroke is vital to his picture of domestic serenity.

WINGED VICTORY

Even Frank Lloyd Wright did not dare to claim that he
created the Winged Victory (*Nike of Samothrace*). But
plaster casts of this world-famous Hellenistic sculpture from
the second century B.C. found their way into the houses of
many of his early clients as well as his home in Oak Park.
Before he gained the confidence to design his own decorative objects, Wright liked to add a touch of antiquity as
"worthy entertainment" for the eye. Once he traveled to
Japan in 1905, he intensified his efforts to collect all things
Japanese: prints in particular but also pottery, sculpture,
screens, and other antiques. At Taliesin, his home in Wisconsin
after 1911, he gave them prized places, where they stood as
"messengers . . . from other civilizations." Historic objects were
spirits of peace and good will, traces of the human spirit "left
behind in the human procession as Time went on," Wright
wrote in his 1932 *Autobiography*. As "ancient comment on the
New," they heightened the stark contrast between the old
order and the new one he was inventing. For those who did
not have rare oriental objects, reproductions of the *Nike*
would do. His clients the Littles are known to have displayed
a copy in the living room of their second Wright home in
Wayzata, Minnesota (right), designed in 1912, and he placed
one over the doorway in his children's playroom in Oak Park
(page 100). Another guarded the atrium of the Larkin
Administration Building of 1903 in Buffalo, New York, and
still others were sketched into Wright's presentation drawings
for various clients. Ward and Cecilia Willits of Highland Park,
Illinois, accompanied Frank and Catherine Wright to Japan
in 1905, where they may have acquired some relics of their
own, but today it is the iconic Greek statue that guards the
top of the stair hall in their 1902 Wright house (page 101). In
Wright's day the Winged Victory was a powerful symbol of
flight—landed on the prow of a ship, the goddess embodied
motion itself. With her wings spread tautly behind her, she
still seems to be flying. Her wet garments both cling and swirl,
allowing for the play of light and dark. A votive figure, this
monument to victory originally graced a shrine, as perhaps
Wright may have visualized her in his own architecture.

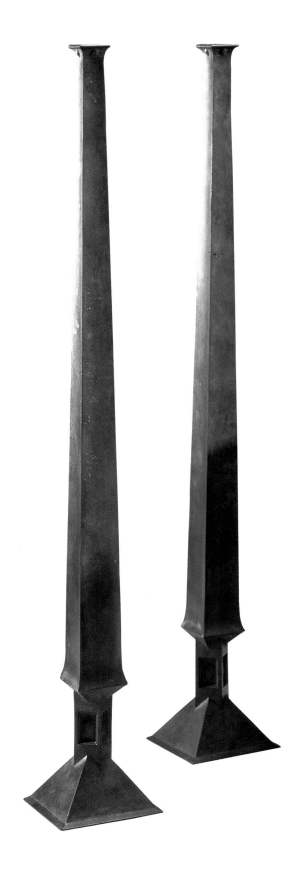

COPPER VASES

Wright was intrigued by relics from ancient civilizations, but it did not take him long to realize that his own creativity might be a match for the talents of the artists of Greece, China, and Japan. Conjuring up artistic objects for a home, he recalled in his 1932 *Autobiography,* was "the most fascinating phase of the work, involving the true poetry of conception." He began working with decorative arts at the apogee of the Arts and Crafts movement, whose practitioners were exploring new forms that expressed the harmony of nature. Like a number of these designers, Wright turned to metalwork and "fell in love with sheet copper as a building material." Two extraordinary vases—one a tall, attenuated weed holder, the other a squat, rotund urn—were made and parceled out to select clients beginning about 1895–98. The urn, shaped from répousée, not cast, copper, is a study in circles and squares (opposite). Rising from a crossed base, its four circular motifs mirror the object's own round form but are reined in by squares and intersecting geometric motifs. Standing on a pyramidal base, the weed holder, in contrast, is the essence of simplicity— proud testimony to the ability of the machine (left). Its sleek form seems to forecast the mile-high skyscraper Wright proposed for Chicago in 1954. Both vases were made by James A. Miller and Brother of Chicago, a firm Wright knew from his early days working for Adler and Sullivan. And both appear in drawings and photographs of the period: in Wright's Oak Park home and studio; at the Waller (1899), Dana (1902), and Coonley (1907) Houses in Illinois; at the long-gone Browne's Bookstore (1907) in Chicago; and at an architectural exhibit of the architect's favorite work in 1902. Wright wanted each urn and vase filled with summer blossoms, dried flowers, or even weeds—anything that would be a reminder of nature's fields and woods. Copper's autumnal tones made it the perfect vessel for these plants and Wright's houses. He later produced silver services for the Imperial Hotel (1915–23) in Tokyo, but it was copper that captured his true colors.

PEDESTAL LAMP

Electric lights had barely come on the scene—perfected during his boyhood in the 1880s—when Wright began his work as an architect. It was a novel toy for a designer who remained challenged by new technology all his life. As with everything else, he integrated it into the fabric of each site. "No longer an appliance nor even an appurtenance," said Wright in 1928 about his early lighting, "but really architecture ... made a part of the building." For Susan Lawrence Dana's 1902 home in Springfield, Illinois, he made the house itself shine like a glass prism. Thousands of facets reflected light from art glass windows and doors, skylights and sconces, and ingenious table lamps resembling Wright's buildings. His double-pedestal lamp for the Dana House is rightly famous. Hovering above

sturdy bronze-and-glass piers, the hipped shade calls to mind a sheltering Prairie-style roof. The leaded glass pattern repeats the stylized sumac refrain and prairie hues that turn the grand house into an autumn forest. Cube feet provide a solid foundation. Not to be outdone, a related single-pedestal lamp in the house fans out into a sixteen-sided glass shade—an umbrella of soft, colored light. Wright placed similar but less impressive lamps in other Prairie houses, such as the Heath House (1905) in Buffalo, New York, and the Robie House (1908) in Chicago. The spindled oak armchair, a variant of his tall-back dining chairs, appeared in different forms in other houses of the period. Paired with the double-pedestal lamp in the library, it created a cozy reading nook inviting one to linger.

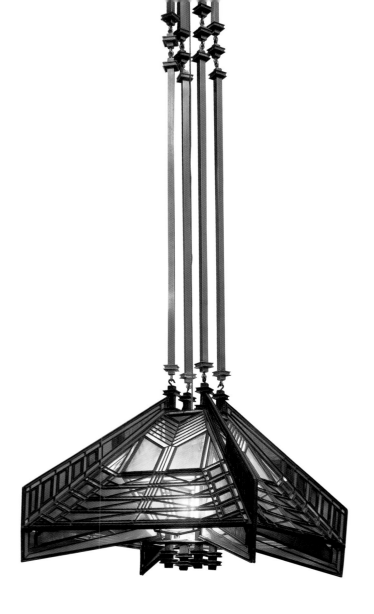

BUTTERFLY LAMP

In 1902, the year in which Wright began designing the Dana House in Springfield, Illinois, he announced that he considered "everything in the nature of a hanging fixture a weakness." What he had in mind in those early days of electricity was the bare bulb that jangled lonely from the ceiling at the tail end of a naked cord. His solution here was a delicate butterfly whose wings metamorphosed into shimmering glass. Four chandeliers in the dining room and another hanging lamp in the stair landing near the gallery are part of the same swarm that greets visitors in the glass transom over the front door (pages 76–77). In the dining room these lemony butterflies seem poised to feast on the goldenrod and purple aster in the mural ringing the walls. Fabricated by the Linden Glass Company of Chicago, the composition reinforces the sumac motif of the house's glass and lamps but is an unusually complex interweaving of planes. In the stair landing that serves as a platform to the gallery, the lamp's modernity is a foil for another of Wright's favorite antiquities, the Venus of Milo (*Aphrodite of Melos*). He may have liked the way the rough folds of her drapery set off her smooth skin, or how light plays against shadow—contrasts that appear in his own work. Sculpted in the late second century B.C. but not rediscovered until 1820, this Hellenistic ideal of beauty remained compelling to Wright in the early years of his independent practice. A nearly life-size version kept watch over the drafting tables in his Oak Park studio, no doubt offering inspiration, and he prescribed Venus for clients along with the Winged Victory (pages 98–101). Here in the Dana House, surrounded by Wright's new masterpieces, she stands as if preserved in a glass vitrine.

107

"FLOWER" SCULPTURE

A modern-day Venus awaits visitors as they enter Susan Lawrence Dana's house in Springfield, Illinois. At first sight this terra-cotta sculpture seems a world apart from the classic *Aphrodite* at the far end of the house. Realism has given way—in part—to abstraction; sensuous curves have yielded—in part—to geometric forms. But the arms and face of the *Flower in the Crannied Wall* retain the gentle classical beauty of her forebears. She is a provocative enigma. Wright conceived the idea for the sculpture, based on a Tennyson poem of the same name, but it was executed by Richard Bock in 1904 after a previous sculptor failed to translate Wright's vision into stone. The nude figure—nature? the architectural muse?—rises from the same block as a geometric, skyscraper-stepped pylon, nurturing a structure as organic as one of Wright's buildings. Inscribed on the back of the sculpture are Tennyson's lines, which Wright had liked enough to include in *The House Beautiful,* the book he designed in 1896:

> Flower in the crannied wall,
> I pluck you out of the crannies,
> I hold you here, root and all, in my hand,
> Little flower—but if I could understand
> What you are, root and all, and all in all,
> I should know what God and man is.

In the living hall directly behind, a fire screen and a tall, octagonal Teco vase repeat the statue's Wrightian motifs. But it took the architect another decade to relinquish the last vestiges of classicism in his sculpture. At Midway Gardens in Chicago in 1913, working this time with Alfonso Iannelli, he pared a host of sculpted concrete sprites to their geometric essence. The *Flower in the Crannied Wall,* however, remains the purest expression of the roots of Wright's own creativity.

GOLDEN MORTAR

Families gathered around the warming hearth—this was the picture of domestic tranquillity Wright liked to paint in his houses. From Chicago to South Carolina to southern California, each of his homes had a fireplace, if not several. The hearth was the dominant furnishing in every Wright house. Solidly built into the core of the structure itself, it was as integral as any ornament could be: arched with brick, framed by a slab lintel, or opening from a cave of stones. Of all his fireplace designs, one stands out for its ingenuity and audacity. For the May House in Grand Rapids, Michigan, completed in 1910, Wright faced the mortar with slices of iridescent glass. A brick and limestone fireplace in the living room fills the wall opposite a south-facing bank of windows. When the sun streams in, the glass turns to golden light, the mortar vanishes, and the bricks seem suspended weightlessly in air. Turned to mirrors, the glass reflects the autumnal colors of the house. It was a sleight of hand only a magician such as Wright could carry off impeccably. A smaller version of the fireplace illuminates the master bedroom upstairs. Just as Wright worked to destroy the confining walls of houses, here he dematerialized once-solid bricks and mortar. He suffused this home with light from an unexpected source and created a reminder of the very flat plane of the prairie outside.

IMPERIAL CHINA

The Imperial Hotel in Tokyo, built between 1915 and 1923, was Wright's *magnum opus*. Inside its solid stone walls was a symphonic blend of custom furniture, carpets, textiles, lamps, silver services for tea and coffee, and china to fill three different dining needs. Just a few years earlier, for Chicago's vibrant Midway Gardens, Wright had designed his first dinner-ware. For that he chose to ring oval white dishes with a pattern resembling square confetti—his son John Lloyd Wright called them "vermilion beauty spots." When Wright reached Tokyo, it seems that Midway was still on his mind. He picked up the circles that had enlivened several murals there, as well as the windows in the Coonley Playhouse (page 87), and scattered them on the dinner service for the hotel's cabaret dining room. The overlapping disks in red, yellow, green, and blue are poignant reminders of Wright's failed hopes for Midway, which was left unfinished and then went bankrupt in 1916, falling to the wreckers in 1929.

Festive circles float like champagne bubbles over the sides of some of the seven pieces and down into the porcelain bowls. One circle encloses the Imperial's "IH" monogram. Beginning about 1922, several versions of this design were created and used in the hotel. For its more formal dining room, Wright designed an elegant gold-ringed pattern of crosses built of squares; a short pendant motif recalled the building's architecture and was repeated on a third and simpler set of room-service china. Even before the hotel was demolished in 1968, reproductions of the lively cabaret china by Noritake allowed admirers to set their own dinner tables with it. At the Lovness House of 1955 in Stillwater, Minnesota, the dashing circles make perfect counterpoints for the square cushions covered in Wright's favorite red. The pattern actually seems more at home here—as it would have been at Midway—than in the exotic halls of the Imperial Hotel. It was an idea that may have come too late for Midway, but Wright was not yet done with it.

112

TALIESIN LAMP

Among the first lighting fixtures Wright designed was a
lacy fretwork screen of wood recessed into the ceiling above
his Oak Park dining table. The house had been electrified just
four years before Wright redesigned the dining space in 1895,
but he was quick to devise a novel way to install electric light
behind a thin membrane of rice paper. Filtered through this
screen of wood and paper, beams embraced the Wright family
"as sunlight sifts through leaves in the trees," he said. Even
larger panels lighted the children's playroom on the second
floor. Three decades later, in 1925, Wright reassembled
these early materials into a table lamp that has become one
of his most recognized furnishings. Used first at Taliesin, his
Wisconsin home, the lamp turns three squares into a source of
softly diffused light. At the top a small square opening makes
room for the socket and lets air circulate, while the shade
slopes downward into a larger square, which is itself mirrored
in a square wooden base. Hipped like Wright's Prairie-style
roofs, the shade hangs from a cantilevered arm to completely
shelter the bulb. Tapered ribs mark its sides. Envious clients
asked Wright for similar versions for their own homes, and
he complied at times with identical lamps and at others with
shades that substituted cloth for rice paper. Wright had
experimented ten years earlier with lamps cantilevered over
the dining tables of Midway Gardens in Chicago. As he
worked on the Imperial Hotel in Tokyo into the 1920s, the
idea no doubt benefited from the Japanese aesthetic. Back
home at Taliesin, he used the new lamp to keep a subtle
reminder of Japan with him as he read in his bedroom-study.

GLASS·LESS LIGHT

Always perfecting designs that he especially liked, Wright again returned to his past in 1932 for another lamp. In 1914 he had developed a standing light fixture for the Summer Garden terrace of Midway Gardens, his European-style entertainment center in Chicago. Placed alongside tall, geometric spires by Alfonso Iannelli, Wright's lamps stepped eleven cubes of light upward on either side of a pole—staggered lights that made a stairway to the stars. Nearly two decades later, when he needed hanging fixtures for the Hillside Playhouse at Taliesin, Wright plucked the Midway design from his repertoire but transformed it into wood. To light the space without glass, he placed bulbs into open wooden boxes angled in opposite directions around a wooden pole. Flat, rectangular reflectors softly directed the light downward from these "magically hanging pendants." This lamp also had great appeal to Wright clients, for whom he created various versions that stood on the floor or a table or were built into the wall (pages 51 and 113). In these, the light boxes were turned to 90- or 180-degree angles and the reflecting shades were above or below, depending on the light needed. Unlighted, the lamp is pure Wrightian sculpture. Lighted, it bathes a house in the mysteriousness that Wright worked so diligently to produce.

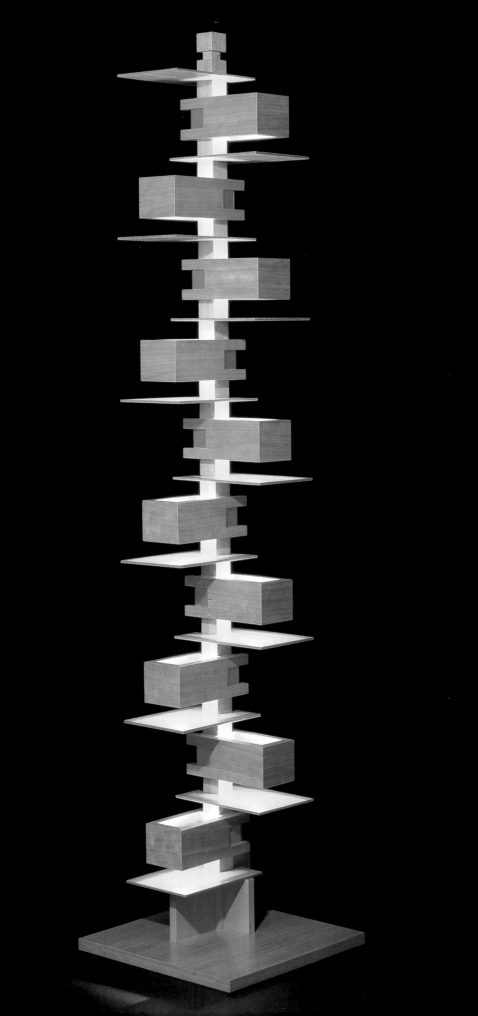

FIREPLACE KETTLE

Wright not only gave each house a fireplace, he often designed the equipment for it. Fire screens, andirons, and grates completed this composition at the heart of the home. Nestled into its rocky promontory above Bear Run in Pennsylvania, Fallingwater demanded a hearth as spectacular as its setting. In 1935 Wright shaped Edgar and Lilianne Kaufmann's fireplace out of local sandstone, situating it carefully behind a boulder found on the site and simply left in place. That was all he needed for a hearth. But Wright did not stop with an iron grate in the same red used for accent throughout the house. He devised a spherical kettle suspended from an arm holding an intricate system of hooks and supports. When not in use, the kettle was to be swung back into a specially carved niche in the wall. On cold evenings, when some hot mulled wine or cider was called for, it was meant to be shifted over the center of the fire. By his implements, Wright helped define the lifestyles of his clients. The kettle's circular shape—a red balloon from the Coonley Playhouse windows turned to metal—was one that the architect found increasingly fascinating in his later years. The kettle itself reappeared in other Wright commissions, first at Wingspread, the house he designed for the Johnson family near Racine, Wisconsin, in 1937. There, the three-story freestanding fireplace is itself rounded as if to accommodate the kettle. But in others—such as the Neils House (1949) in Minneapolis and the Usonian Exhibition House (1953) in New York—the round kettles, usually black, contrast strikingly with the rectilinear fireplaces, as if they were a punctuation mark left as part of Wright's signature.

119

WOOD SCREENS

Screens were among Wright's earliest devices for subtly
dividing spaces and diffusing light. At his Oak Park home he
placed them overhead in 1895 as sawn-wood light fixtures.
In his Prairie-style houses during the early 1900s he spindled
them to interrupt a view without closing it off, to reveal but
not conceal. And by the time he entered his Usonian phase in
the mid- to late 1930s, he had determined that screens could
replace most other ornament and stand alone as a house's
defining decorative feature. For these efficient homes of
modest cost, Wright created wood cutouts that screened
windows and clerestories as well as features in the open
interiors. The complex art glass of his earlier houses was too
expensive for these Usonians, but their owners could make
do just fine with geometric wood panels that channeled views
in much the same way. Some of the richest paneling of this
type can be found in the home that Sara and Melvyn Maxwell
Smith built over four years in Bloomfield Hills, Michigan,
beginning in 1946. A stepped motif cut from Tidewater
cypress faces doors to the terrace and, above the dining table,
draws "moonlight" into the compact space at the elbow of the
L-shaped plan. In a small sitting area, a folding screen sets apart
the inner sanctum. Like trees growing in a forest, the cutouts
bring nature indoors. Warm wood such as this, said Wright,
is lovely to the touch and "grateful to the eye." As ornament,
it is organically woven into the fabric of the house itself.

PATTERNED CARPET

What was underfoot was as important to Wright as the ceiling, the walls, and all the furnishings in between. Despite this, he was rarely allowed to finish his buildings with carpets that pulled together all their design elements. Of his outstanding examples—such as those for the Coonley (1907), Robie (1908), May (1908), and Bogk (1916) Houses during his Prairie years and the Imperial Hotel in the early 1920s—the carpet designed in 1951 for his son David Wright shows how active the architect's imagination remained even at the age of eighty-four. Built in the desert of Phoenix, Arizona, in the midst of a citrus orchard, the house (based on a plan called "How to Live in the Southwest") spirals up from a ground-floor garden court to a ring of living quarters on the upper level. It is a swirl of concrete block, and Wright gave his son and daughter-in-law, Gladys, a swirling confection of a carpet to reinforce its spherical shape. Balloons of many colors and sizes bounce off one another in a tightly controlled nod to whimsy. In 1926–27 Wright had designed a similar pattern as one of twelve monthly covers for *Liberty* magazine; they were rejected then as too exuberant, but, transferred to vibrant yarn, the March design at last found a good home. The *Liberty* designs, Wright once explained, were for "the Children, obvious arrangements of familiar objects or easy abstractions—intended to be 'not too difficult.'" His play with spheres can be traced back to the Coonley Playhouse windows of 1912 (page 87) and two murals executed for Midway Gardens in 1913. Whatever the medium, he clearly found delight in what his compass had to offer. The wide range of colors in this carpet found its counterpart four years later with the release of Wright's Taliesin Palette of paint colors for the Martin-Senour Company. And in 1957 Wright tried his hand at another carpet filled with interlocking circles but was rebuffed when his client Maximilian Hoffman said no to Wright's vision for his house in Rye, New York. In 1959, however, after the architect's death, the carpet maker V'Soske (manufacturer also of the David Wright carpet) loomed the Hoffman design and it was placed in the living-dining area at Taliesin in Wisconsin.

FABRIC NO. 105

Wright never had complete success with his carpets—even a commercial line planned for release by Karastan in 1956 never made it off the drafting boards. Better luck came with mass-produced fabrics and wallpapers offered by F. Schumacher and Company beginning in 1955. For sixty years before this, Wright had insisted that each of his designs was unique: a response individually fitted to the needs at hand. And wallpaper had been a tool of "inferior desecrators," not of Wright. But in the 1950s he was persuaded, in large part by Elizabeth Gordon, the editor of *House Beautiful,* to lend his name to furniture, paint, textiles, and wall coverings that middle-class buyers could purchase for their own homes. If they could not come to Wright directly for a house, he could come to them in care-fully conceived patterns and colors designed to harmonize with a range of living places. Schumacher and Wright worked together to create some designs that were adapted by the company from Wright's work and others that the Taliesin Fellowship designed based on items such as architectural plans (see the book's endpapers). Design No. 105, offered as both linen and wallpaper, was inspired by a carpet in Wright's Coonley House of 1907 in Riverside, Illinois, one of his great Prairie houses. In its translation to a different time and use., the strongly rectilinear design showed its longevity and its universality. Wright himself proved his flexibility, his ability to change with the times. Over the years Schumacher has introduced other lines of Wright furnishings, even rugs, underscoring the staying power of Wright's vision and his concern that not one single item—not the furniture, not the windows, not the small objects that bring joy to daily life— should be overlooked in furnishing a house to make it a home.

124

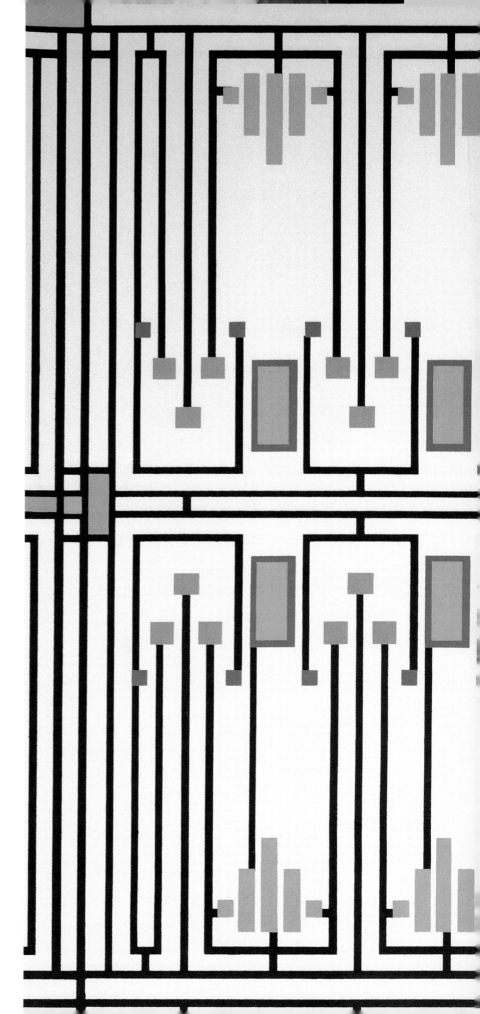

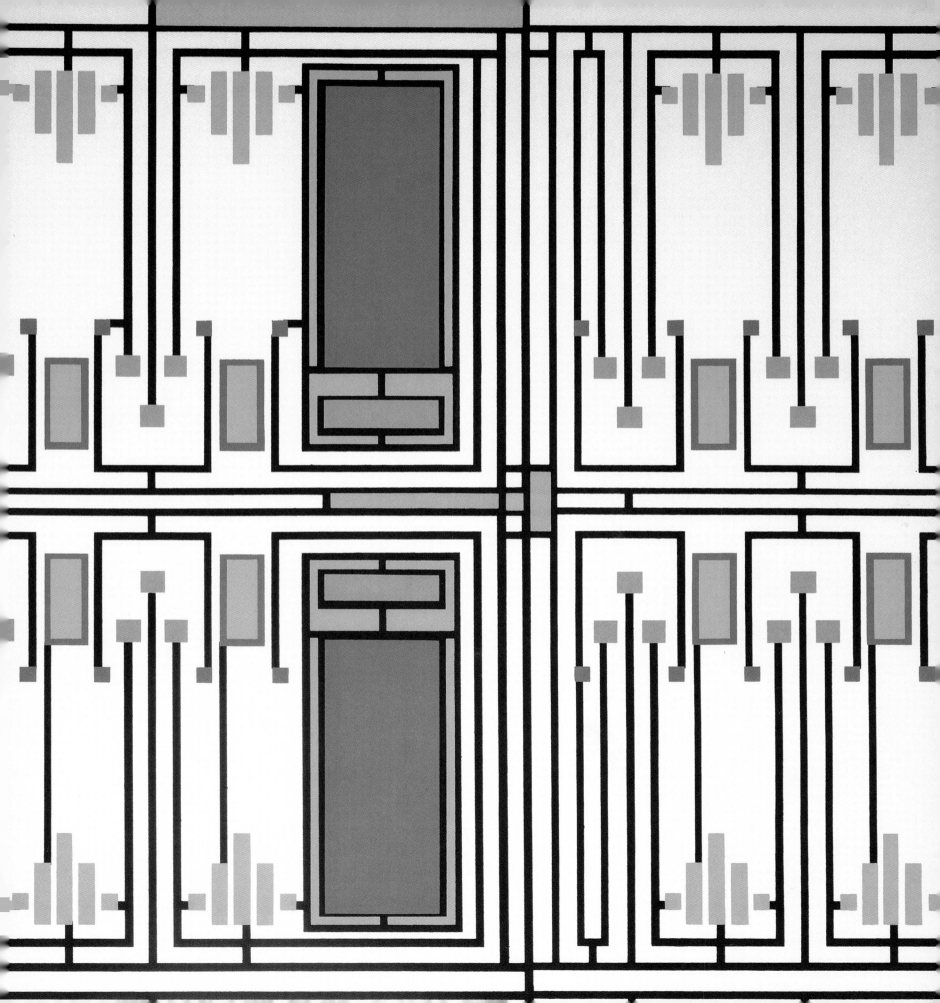

SELECTED BIBLIOGRAPHY

Fowler, Penny. "Please Be Crated." In *Frank Lloyd Wright:
    The Seat of Genius. Chairs: 1895–1955.* West Palm Beach, Fla.:
    Eaton Fine Art, 1997.

Frank Lloyd Wright Quarterly, 1990–99.

Hanks, David A. *The Decorative Designs of Frank Lloyd Wright.*
    New York: Dutton, 1979.

————. *Frank Lloyd Wright: Preserving an Architectural Heritage.
    Decorative Designs from The Domino's Pizza Collection.* New York:
    Dutton, 1989.

Harrington, Elaine. *Frank Lloyd Wright Home and Studio, Oak Park.*
    Stuttgart: Edition Axel Menges, 1996.

Heinz, Thomas A. *Frank Lloyd Wright: Glass Art.* London:
    Academy Editions, 1994.

————. *Frank Lloyd Wright: Interiors and Furniture.* London:
    Academy Editions, 1994.

Hoffmann, Donald. *Frank Lloyd Wright's Dana House.* New York:
    Dover, 1996.

————. *Frank Lloyd Wright's Hollyhock House.* New York: Dover, 1992.

Kaufmann, Edgar, Jr. *Frank Lloyd Wright at the Metropolitan Museum
    of Art.* New York: Metropolitan Museum of Art, 1985.

Lind, Carla. *Lost Wright: Frank Lloyd Wright's Vanished Masterpieces.*
    New York: Simon and Schuster, 1996.

————. *Wright at a Glance Series.* 12 vols. San Francisco: Pomegranate,
    1994–96.

————. *The Wright Style.* New York: Simon and Schuster, 1992.

Pfeiffer, Bruce Brooks. *Frank Lloyd Wright: The Masterworks.* New York:
    Rizzoli, 1993.

Robertson, Cheryl. *Frank Lloyd Wright and George Mann Niedecken:
    Prairie School Collaborators.* Lexington, Mass.: Milwaukee Art Museum
    and Museum of Our National Heritage, 1999.

Secrest, Meryle. *Frank Lloyd Wright.* New York: Knopf, 1992.

Sittenfeld, Michael, ed. *The Prairie School: Design Vision for the Midwest.*
    The Art Institute of Chicago Museum Studies, vol. 21, no. 2, 1995.

Storrer, William Allin. *The Frank Lloyd Wright Companion.* Chicago:
    University of Chicago Press, 1993.

Wright, Frank Lloyd. *Frank Lloyd Wright: Collected Writings.* 5 vols.
    Edited by Bruce Brooks Pfeiffer. New York: Rizzoli, 1992–95.

126

PHOTOGRAPH CREDITS

INDEX